INK ON PAPER **2**

INK ON PAPER 2

A Handbook of the Graphic Arts

Edmund C. Arnold

HARPER & ROW, PUBLISHERS
NEW YORK, EVANSTON, SAN FRANCISCO, LONDON

INK ON PAPER 2: A HANDBOOK OF THE GRAPHIC ARTS. Copyright © 1972 by Edmund C. Arnold. All rights reserved. Printed in the United States of America. No part of this book may be used or reproduced in any manner whatsoever without written permission except in the case of brief quotations embodied in critical articles and reviews. For information address Harper & Row, Publishers, Inc., 49 East 33rd Street, New York, N.Y. 10016. Published simultaneously in Canada by Fitzhenry & Whiteside Limited, Toronto.

STANDARD BOOK NUMBER: 06-010131-8
LIBRARY OF CONGRESS CATALOG CARD NUMBER: 70-156503

To Francis R. VanAllen and Mattie Gay Crump,

who first exposed me to printer's ink—

from which, fortunately, I never recovered

Contents

When man first walked on the moon, he left as the official memento of that awesome event a plaque that had been made by a graphic arts process. This is not surprising; the graphic arts have been recording the great events of mankind—and the most trivial—for the past half-millennium.

"The art preservative of all arts" is the description commonly given to the art and craft of printing. By extension it describes the graphic arts, for they are all siblings of the printing press.

Beyond that, it is difficult to define the graphic arts, for it is a field so vast and so overlapping of other activities that its outer boundaries have yet to be sharply defined. And it is expanding at such a pace that it requires the immediacy of a daily newspaper rather than the permanence of a book to keep abreast of new developments.

Graphic arts is all the skills, talents, and experience required to make permanent and multiple copies of written communication.

Man made a tremendous stride when he developed a spoken language. Although gestures could convey much information and emotion—warnings, defiance, directions, and commendation—manual conversation ended at darkness or when communicators were out of sight.

Spoken language extended communication and made it more precise. Still, perpetuation of knowledge depended on memory; dissemination was confined to earshot. Besides, words change meanings; spoken language can become gibberish in a few generations.

Man needed a way to store communication with unchanging fidelity and to transport it across small or vast chasms of time and space. Written language was the only solution to these problems, and man began writing in many ways. Twigs broken to form pointers were "writing." So were blazes on tree trunks. Cavemen painted pictures on the walls of their shelters to communicate as much as to decorate. Warriors decorated shields to record history as well as to intimidate opponents.

But twigs and trunks became humus; men fol-

1

The Graphic Arts

The Art Preservative

GUTENBERG BIBLE, first product of movable type, is a benchmark in human history.

It was printed in 10 sections; as soon as one was complete, the type was distributed, ready for setting the next. At first, pages had 40 lines of type, but Gutenberg filed down the body so the next section had 41 per page. Still anxious to conserve paper, he further decreased the space between lines, and the rest of the book is in 42-line pages, from which the Bible gets its familiar name.

About 150 copies of the Bible were printed on paper and about 35 on vellum. Of these, only 35 on paper and a dozen on vellum still exist. Nine are in their original binding.

Ornamentation was painted by hand, to simulate as closely as possible illuminated manuscripts. Genuine gold leaf added a luster that remains undimmed today.

Apparently it took five years to complete the first printing project. It was finished no later than August 15, 1456, the date written by hand in a copy that belonged to Vicar Henry Cremer.

Absolutely priceless, the last copy of the 42-Line Bible that was sold brought a price of $1.5 million even in the very depth of the Great Depression. That copy is in the Library of Congress.

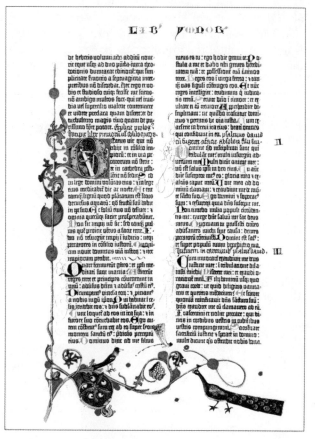

lowed their herds away from caves; shields were hacked or captured. The writing was not permanent enough. Worse, it was less precise than spoken words; only broad ideas could be thus recorded. Such "writing" was far more *mnemonic*—a crutch for memory—than definitive.

When man finally found precision and permanence for his language, he recognized a man-made miracle. *Devanagari*—the name of the Sanskrit alphabet—means "pertaining to the city of the gods." That most permanent of Egyptian writing—*hieroglyphics*—was "sacred stone writing." Cultures from Mayan to Assyrian called their writing a gift of the gods.

Men tried many tools and materials for writing.

A sharp stick and a smooth beach could hold a message until the next tide or tempest; a sharp stick and a tablet of wax lasted far longer. A broad tropical leaf held a scratched message for days; a clay brick, "written" on with impressing wedges, has lasted for six thousand years.

Man wrote on birchbark, shells, hides, and papyrus. He wrote with juices of berries, trees, sea creatures, and even himself, his blood. But no writing was easier—or much more permanent— than that of ink on paper.

Printing is a form of writing that lubricates all the wheels of modern living. Plenitude of printing is the hallmark of advanced civilization; it is one of the major ways in which such civilization came about.

Development of a written language brought demands for extra copies; "scribes" are mentioned in the earliest written records, and much of their work was copying. When a pharaoh promulgated a decree, instead of circulating a single letter through the provinces, he had duplicates made for simultaneous distribution. The man who had written down axioms of a religious leader wanted a copy for each of his sons. Missionaries wanted to pass sacred words quickly to many peoples and regions.

When time and labor were cheap, a platoon of scribes could be assigned to making copies. Religious men devoted their lives to copying and re-copying the Bible and theological works. But even with that low overhead, books were priced only within the range of the rich.

The hunger for permanence of knowledge that spurred the development of written language prodded the search for easy, inexpensive methods to make stored knowledge and new discoveries available to many men at once. The Renaissance was a natural corollary of the invention of printing as we know it today.

Printing had its origins in the Orient. As early as A.D. 770, Empress Shotoku of Japan, a devout Buddhist, had a million prayer-charms printed from wood blocks. This useful art migrated to Europe,

OLDEST EXISTING PRINTING is believed to be this fragment of a *sutra,* a Buddhist scripture. It was printed between 700 and 750 A.D. and was recently found in an ancient Kyongju pagoda in Korea.

The sutra is a 20-foot-long scroll made of 13 sections of *tak* paper, of mulberry-tree fibers, glued together.

Twelve wooden blocks were used to print the scroll. The language is Chinese together with some transliterations of Sanskrit. Previous sutras had been printed from intaglio plates cut in stone.

The scroll, along with vessels, images, incense, and other charms, had been sealed into the walls of the Pulguk-sa pagoda, much as we place memorabilia in the cornerstones of buildings. The artifacts that accompanied the scroll supposedly confirm the date of the printing. Also found in the sutra were live worms which had eaten parts of it. It is presumed that the worms are "of more modern origin."

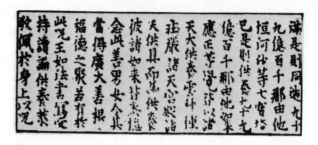

probably via the ubiquitous Marco Polo. At least wood-block printing was known on the Continent shortly after his return from the East.

But it awaited Johann Gensfleisch zum Gutenberg of Mainz to launch the modern craft of printing with his invention of movable type, about A.D. 1450. Then began "graphic arts" as we define it today. Although no one had enough sense of history to keep precise records of this milestone, even the ignorant peasantry sensed that here was an awesome power. The public believed that printers had acquired their profound power from Satanic sources. Even the ink-stained apprentice boy was called *the printer's devil.*

If printing was not black magic, it certainly spread like it. In less than a generation the new craft had blanketed Europe—recorded dates for printing include: Germany, no later than 1454; Italy, 1465; Switzerland, 1468; France, two years later; Holland, 1473; Austria-Hungary, that same year; Spain, 1474; England, 1476; Denmark, 1482; Sweden, a year later, and Portugal, 1487. The first printing press in North America was operated by Spaniards in Mexico City, almost a century before the Pilgrims disembarked at Plymouth Rock.

There is evidence suggesting that a Dutchman named Coster printed from movable type before Gutenberg did. No matter, Gutenberg deserves the title of "father of modern printing" because he was the first to replace the manuscript with the printed book. Whether or not he drew upon earlier experiments really does not matter; his invention is the one we still use today with surprisingly little improvement or change.

To mark again the close tie between printing and religion, the first products of Gutenberg's press were for the Church. Either a hymnal, the *Mainz Psalter*, or the famous 42-Line Gutenberg Bible was the first "modern printing"; the Bible remains the most-often printed work.

Men of the cloth used printing as a most effective tool to propagate Christianity. As they spread the Gospel, they dispelled illiteracy. Men who read become educated, and educated men seek freedom. So the printing press has always been a weapon for liberty; our own Colonial forebears rallied the land by means of pamphlets and debated its new Constitution through printed pages.

Typesetters and pressmen are among the oldest race of craftsmen; probably only carpenters can trace their vocational ancestry back as far.

At hundreds of jobs "people with ink on their fingers" make up that vast complex of activity we call "the graphic arts."

Because the graphic arts make permanent and multiple written communication, the stonecarver who "wrote" panegyrics to the Ptolemies was not a graphic artsman; he made only one "copy." The lad who indites his affection for a young female may repeat the same phrase on my sidewalk as he did on the side of your garage. But he fails to qualify; his message, like his emotion, is not permanent.

But there are thousands upon thousands who can claim ink on their fingers, for graphic arts is a most important segment of a developed economy.

Even in this age of astronomical figures—literally in space flights, figuratively even in family budgets—the statistics relating to the graphic arts are impressive. Graphic arts people, by nature, don't particularly like numbers or statistics, so they will be kept brief.

In the decade of the 1960's:

The annual sales volume of printing rose 60 per cent to $24 billion, making it the seventh largest industry in the nation and, by some standards, the fifth.

Approximately 180,000 employees were added, to reach a total of 1,191,000. This was a 20 per cent

PRINTING PRESS, from a seventeenth-century engraving, might have been that used by Peter Schoeffer in Mainz, for it appears to be his colophon on the press at the right.

By 1450, the date arbitrarily ascribed for the invention of movable type, Gutenberg had borrowed 800 florins from a group of goldsmiths. Johannes Fust was the broker who eventually raised for Gutenberg the equivalent of $60,000 in today's purchasing power.

In 1455, Fust foreclosed the mortgage and took over Gutenberg's printing plant. With his son-in-law Schoeffer, Fust produced some incunabula of highest quality.

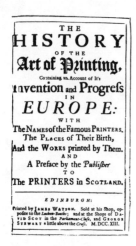

HISTORY OF PRINTING, pub-
lished in 1713, is one of many
such records. Printers have unusually high respect for their
craft and its traditions and produce many books on the subject.
A notable work was written by
Joseph Moxon, who around 1679
published *Mechanick Exercises,*
or *The Doctrine of Handy-Works,*
which is the basic repository of
all the technical aspects of printing for its first 200 years. It also
was the first book to suggest the
wide range of industries that are
offshoots of the graphic arts.

increase, and comparison to the 60 per cent growth
in dollar volume indicates that there was a substantial real increase in productivity beyond the expansion of monetary inflation.

Capital expenditures, which made such productivity possible, rose from $420 million in 1960 to
$950 million ten years later, an increase of 126 per
cent.

Employment of women increased 39 per cent to
348,000. The percentage of female employees increased during the same period from 28 to 32 per
cent. Many observers believe that the increase in
the number of women in executive and other responsible positions is even greater than that of the
distaff side in the whole employment rolls.

We can only guess at the number of graphic arts
establishments. There are currently some 50,000
"graphic arts companies." But this does not accurately report the grand total of the graphic arts.
Many small, often one-man, businesses are not
included, and countless people whose work is
totally or in part in the graphic arts are listed under
other Census Bureau categories; so is their product.

Many employees of supplying firms, such as
papermakers, machinery manufacturers, and ink
makers—not to mention the huge photography industry—must be considered as graphic arts personnel.

Bound so loosely, many members of the clan do
not even recognize their kinship. Men who make
paper, mix ink, edit books, design business forms,
draw cartoons, remelt stereotype plates, shoot pictures, or type mimeograph stencils are all profes-
sionals in the graphic arts.

Even a simple listing of job titles in the graphic
arts would—literally—take several pages of this
book. For the sake of blessed brevity, we consider
seven major areas:

TYPE, requiring a variety of artists from type
designers to calligraphers to typesetters.

ILLUSTRATIONS, with an even wider spectrum of
artists and craftsmen. They range from the cutter of
linoleum blocks to the oil painter to the photog-

rapher and then to the photoengraver and the maker of plates for offset lithography and rotogravure—and what an over-abbreviation this is!

COMPOSITION, the arrangement of typographic elements into strong nonverbal as well as verbal communications. This includes people who plan such arrangements as well as those who combine metal or film elements that actually print the job.

PAPER, the *sine qua non* of printing. The ranger who plants fir seedlings, the research chemist, the papermaker, and the delivery boy who carries in a thousand letterheads are all involved here.

INK, the lifeblood of the industry, requires the skills of chemists, chromotographers, and even—'tis true—perfumers.

PRESSES, the keystone of the graphic arts. From the engineer who designs the machinery to the computer programmer who often guides it, from the electronic engineer to the man who pushes the START button on a block-long machine, from the man who prints by "smoke" or electric ions to the one who uses the humble but ubiquitous Mimeograph or Ditto machines, the list of people in this department is lengthy.

BINDERY, where printed words are packaged. From craftsmen who fold and cut, emboss or stamp, die-cut and paste, to artists who design jackets or handtool leather bookbindings, this is a conglomeration of picturesquely differing skills and talents.

These major divisions of the graphic arts don't even include the constantly growing graphic arts in the film and television industries. The ability to add motion to printed letterforms gives not only excitement and interest but a whole new area of career opportunities based on sound knowledge of static written communication.

Three-dimensional printing requires whole platoons of supporting services as well as the people actually producing this striking new form of communication. The constantly growing field of packaging uses all the graphic arts, of course, for everything from perfume bottles to toothpaste

GUTENBERG, who was born Genzfleisch, is shown in this Hungarian stamp of 1962 commemorating the centennial of the Hungarian printers' and papermakers' union. It was a custom in sixteenth-century Germany for a woman whose family name was about to die out because she had no brothers to give the name to one of her sons. Thus the inventor took the maternal name. Here he holds a type punch, in a pose in which he is often shown.

tubes to sacks for flour, nails, or pantyhose is a product of the printing press. That 1,191,000 count a few paragraphs back may well prove to be a low estimate!

The United States Department of Labor predicts that the printing and publishing industry—and hence its suppliers, too—will enjoy continued growth "as a result of population growth and the expansion of the American economy as well as the tendency toward relatively greater use of printed material for information, advertising and various industrial and commercial purposes."

Amateurs are even more numerous: housewives who are tapped to produce the membership roster for their Ladies Aid Society; men who order printing of company letterheads or tickets for their lodge's annual dinner dance; farmers who write copy for auction sale handbills; families who design or color or fold or even print their Christmas greetings; hobbyists who operate a basement hand press; Sunday artists who make etchings or dry points.

This book is written for everyone who works for—or is served by—printing presses. No single book can cover this vast field in depth. Daniel B. Updike, for instance, wrote two volumes, containing 611 pages, on printing types alone—and there has been a whole generation of type designers since them.

This book might be subtitled "Printing for Non-Printers." Yet "printers" might find something interesting—and even useful—in these pages. The pressman might learn to advantage from the problems of the engraver. The compositor may delight in the affinity of his craft to that of the glamour photographer.

Primarily, this book is directed to those removed, even if only by a thin partition, from the actual mechanics of printing: executives who plan and purchase printing for business; newspapermen who dummy editions for the composing room; artists who prepare copy for the engraver—slapstick cartoons, technical diagrams, or oils for magazine covers. It is for the amateur: book collectors, Cub

DEATH OF GUTENBERG in 1468 is commemorated by this stamp from Dahomey. It shows the inventor at his press in Mainz. Little is known of Gutenberg's death—or of his life. A victim of a bloody war between contenders for a political bishopric, he was apparently blind and destitute before the winner, Archbishop Adolf of Nassau, made him a pensioner. Gutenberg is buried in St. Francis Church in Mainz.

Scout publicity chairmen, or vestrymen who plan a scroll for their pastor's testimonial dinner.

Most of all, it is for the young people from whom graphic arts must replenish and expand talents and skills. In an economy that lives on paper and ink, such expansion is almost without limit. Graphic arts can offer careers with monetary attraction, but they also provide other satisfactions far more rewarding.

The graphic artsman knows the thrill of creation. Here is a career that electric brains and vacuum tubes can never threaten; creativity is still man's monopoly.

The graphic artsman knows the deep satisfaction of discipline. Part of this is inherent in the rigidity of the metal with which he eventually works. "Type isn't made of rubber" is an early lesson, but he feels no more constriction from type that can be neither stretched nor squeezed than the poet does from the inflexible fourteen lines of a sonnet.

The graphic craftsman learns the value of time. Deadlines are stern taskmasters; they are judicially constant.

The final satisfaction is the realization that the graphic artsman is making a substantial and permanent contribution to this society. Granted that our press gives forum to demagogues, it also preserves our freedom by alerting the citizens to encroachments and educating them so that grave decisions can be made from knowledge instead of prejudice. And the graphic arts, today as from their inception, are the evangelists for all our religions.

The art preservative will shelter all the arts, be they the fading "Last Supper" of Leonardo da Vinci, the oratory of Churchill, the Beatitudes, or $E = mc^2$. The recipe for Texas chili, the philosophy of Niebuhr, and even the choreography of Nijinsky —every art and every knowledge of mankind—will be preserved by the printer and the graphic crafts.

The world of graphic arts is an exciting one, a world which has earned the genuine affection of those who labor in it. Many supplementary readings are suggested in these pages, which serve to

EARLY AMERICAN BOOK, printed in Mexico City in 1544, is saluted by this Mexican commemorative stamp which bears a woodcut from the title page, the first printing plate made in the Western Hemisphere.

flesh out the broad strokes of this single volume and enable detailed study of any aspect that most concerns the reader. In each of these suggested books there is one common characteristic: the author truly loves his work.

Poor Richard, 1737.

A N

Almanack

For the Year of Chrift

1 7 3 7,

Being the Firft after LEAP YEAR.

And makes fince the Creation	Years
By the Account of the Eaftern *Greeks*	7245
By the Latin Church, when ☉ ent. ♈	6936
By the Computation of *W. W.*	5746
By the *Roman* Chronology	5686
By the *Jewifh* Rabbies	5498

Wherein is contained,

The Lunations, Eclipfes, Judgment of the Weather, Spring Tides, Planets Motions & mutual Afpects, Sun and Moon's Rifing and Setting, Length of Days, Time of High Water, Fairs, Courts, and obfervable Days.

Fitted to the Latitude of Forty Degrees, and a Meridian of Five Hours Weft from *London*, but may without fenfible Error, ferve all the adjacent Places, even from *Newfoundland* to *South-Carolina.*

By *RICHARD SAUNDERS*, Philom.

PHILADELPHIA:
Printed and fold by *B. FRANKLIN*, at the New Printing-Office near the Market.

POOR RICHARD ALMANACK, spelled with an extra *k*, but no *apostrophe s*, was the most famous of American books for decades. Benjamin Franklin, its author and publisher, is known as the patron saint of American printers. He furnished money and younger partners furnished the "sweat equity" for establishing new print shops from the Bahamas to the Canadian coast. When he wrote his own epitaph, Franklin, the great statesman, described himself: "Here lies B. Franklin, printer. . . ."

SUGGESTED READINGS

Chappell, Warren. *A Short History of the Printed Word.* New York: Alfred A. Knopf, 1970.

Eckman, James. *The Heritage of the Printer.* Philadelphia: North American Publishing Co., 1966.

Lawson, Alexander S. *A Printer's Almanac.* Philadelphia: North American Publishing Co., 1965.

Printing and Publishing Quarterly. Washington, D.C.: United States Department of Commerce.

Spencer, Herbert (ed.). *The Penrose Annual.* London: Hastings House, 1895—

If printing began in China at least 800 years before it came to Europe and if the Koreans cast bronze type as early as A.D. 1403, why did Western civilization forge ahead of these nations whose culture was well developed when our Anglo-Saxon ancestors were still adorning themselves with blue paint?

The answer is: the Latin alphabet.

Requisites for a good written language are permanence and convenience. China's and Korea's, though permanent as those of the West, are nowhere near as convenient. Even a hasty survey illustrates the flexibility and convenience of our alphabet over that of Oriental *ideograms*.

Man's oldest known existing "visual communication" was done by the Reindeer Men, between 35,000 and 15,000 B.C., in pictures they drew on the walls of deep caves in France and Spain. These could be classified as simple declarative sentences: "This is a mammoth." Then pictures became more explanatory—tribesmen stalking the quarry, making the kill, feasting on the trophy. For people familiar with the subject matter, such picture stories were quite complete communications, just as a series of sketches might narrate a baseball game to a knowledgeable fan.

Later the writer found that he need not draw a complete picture; he could simplify an object into *symbol* writing that was just as recognizable to the "reader."

But language must include abstract as well as concrete concepts. It is easy to picture *Man kills caribou;* how do we write *Man loves freedom?*

At first, man wrote abstract terms by combining existing symbols for the concrete. The symbol of a tangible *sun* with seven little marks under it became the intangible *week*. A charming symbol was made by combining the sign for *woman* with that for *son* to designate *love*.

Writing progressed to a device familiar to our children, the *rebus*.

When man discovered this method, he made a huge leap toward the ideal written language. He was learning that if there is a method of writing

2
The Latin Alphabet

Our Most Valuable Tool

STYLIZATION of pictures to pictograms is shown in this example of Spanish drawings, which trace the female from the quite realistic to the absolutely abstract.

SYMBOLIZATION reduces the realistic form of a man to a figure that is much simpler to draw. The stick figure was one of the earliest forms of "writing."

sounds, it is possible to combine sound-pictures into words just as spoken sounds are combined. The *can* and *ewe* of a rebus can combine into *canoe*.

The step now was to convert the rebus pictures into sound-symbols; it is easier to write *I* than to draw a picture of an eye. Logical as this step is, it took centuries for man to accomplish it.

There is no definite time to which we can point and say, "Here our alphabet came into being." Most of its history is deductive and thus open to rebuttal. But to find the origin of the alphabet becomes a fascinating detective story.

We know our alphabet was developed along the shores of the Mediterranean and is an amalgam of many systems that developed simultaneously and probably quite independently.

The Egyptians had gone through all the steps. In that process, a realistic picture of a leaf was simplified into a symbol of a strikingly modern air-foil form and became the sign for the *l* sound. But the Egyptians never completed a sufficiently workable alphabet, though they made substantial contributions to our system of writing.

picture   *symbol (hieroglyphic)*   *transition (hieratic)*

The closest we can come to the actual beginning of our alphabet is a tiny country, Phoenicia, now part of Syria. Phoenicians were traders too busy at commerce to produce literature or art. But they did produce an alphabet, purely as a business tool. They needed a system for keeping ledgers and writing business messages with a minimum of fuss or bother. Phoenicians stripped sound pictures of everything extraneous so that they could write rapidly.

Undoubtedly, the Phoenicians started with pictures. It seems reasonable to assume that the butcher drew a picture of an ox in his ledger, like this:

Later, because business men are always pressed for time, he simplified that drawing into:

Eventually this symbol came to represent not an ox but a sound. We still use the same symbol (although turned around 180 degrees) for the very same sound. The Phoenician word for ox was *aleph*. This was later translated into the Greek *alpha* and remains in our language as two-thirds of *alphabet*. The other third is from a picture of a house, *beth*, simplified into our *B*. All the characters in this early alphabet were simplified drawings of common objects.

The Phoenicians developed 19 such letters. Many came from Egypt, some undoubtedly from farther east, where the Assyrians, Babylonians, and Hittites were developing their *cuneiform* writing about the same time, pressing small wedges into clay tablets. Although they never advanced beyond the ideogram stage, they probably showed the Phoenicians how to simplify symbols to the bone.

It is interesting to note that two Phoenician alphabets developed at the same time—and only 20 miles apart. Tyre and Sidon, cities of Biblical fame, each created its own collection of symbols, although both clearly sprang from a common origin and shared many individual letters.

Between Tyre, the greatest commercial city of its

PICTURE WRITING of early men in widely separated areas of the earth shows delightful similarity despite the obvious fact that there was no physical connection between the various cultures. Could the figure at the right in the Swedish drawings be the precursor of skiers?

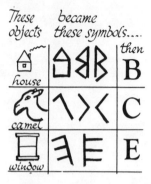

These objects *became these symbols....*

		then
house		B
camel		C
window		E

LETTERS in the Latin alphabet have all developed from pictures of familiar objects although there are differences of opinion on what those were. *Gamel* is a camel, but experts differ on whether the symbol is derived from the long neck of the beast or from the simpler camel goad.

BOUSTROPHEDONIC WRITING results in two letterforms for each asymmetrical character. This is confusing to archaeologists who attempt to decipher early writing, especially because in many written forms there were no divisions of letters into words. Nor was there punctuation—a nicety invented by printers rather than scribes—or paragraphing.

THIS IS WAY
UTXO ƎHT
RNS WHEN
SWO⅃ꟼ ƎH

era, and Mycenae and Tiryns, brightest cities in the splendid peninsula of Greece, trade was lively. The Greeks, aflame with intellectual curiosity, saw in the Phoenician alphabet a useful tool for preserving the knowledge they sought so eagerly and respected so highly. By the ninth century B.C. the Greeks had taken the Phoenician alphabet, then about 300 years old, and transformed it into their own.

Total transformation took hundreds of years. By 403 B.C. the Greek alphabet had been finely polished and was officially adopted by Athens. Letters had crystallized into definite, unchanging forms. This was a major contribution of the Greeks. Until that time, there was as much variation in letter forms as there is in individual handwriting today—even more variation, for you and I, no matter how scrawling our handwriting, have a common, accepted form upon which to base our script.

Contributing to the rugged individualism of early letter forms was the casual way in which the early scribes wrote. Some wrote left-to-right, as we do now; others wrote right-to-left; some wrote up and down. Still others wrote both ways, changing direction at the start of each new line.

This system was called *boustrophedon*—"ox-turning," the way an ox turns as it plows a field. About 600 B.C. the ox no longer turned; by common agreement Greek writing was now done left-to-right.

Greeks also contributed vowels. Like present-day Hebrew and Arabic, the Phoenician alphabet consisted only of consonants. (We still write like that with abbreviations such as *bldg.* and *St.*) In a simple language the reader could easily decide which vowel was needed; as vocabulary grew, confusion was compounded. Fr. could mean *for, four,* or *far.* Many scholars believe that major discrepancies in the Bible may have sprung from the freedom permitted the translator from ancient Hebrew when he was forced to insert vowels. *Written in our alphabet, this is a simple sentence.* Without vowels, it would be: *Wrttn n r lphbt, ths s smpl sntnc.* If not dangerously confusing, it is hardly conducive to unmistakable and rapid reading.

The Greeks took several Phoenician consonants for which they had no need and converted them into vowels, then added several of their own. Eventually many characters were dropped as unnecessary and the Greek alphabet solidified at 24 letters, all capitals.

ALLTHESEAIDSTOSWIFTANDEASY
READINGWEREYETTOBEDEVELOPED
ANDFORMOSTOFTHEMWEAREIN-
DEBTEDTOTHEROMANS.

The Romans and the Greeks were developing our modern alphabet simultaneously. The first kings of Rome were Etruscans. Their country, Etruria, north of Rome, had borrowed the Greek alphabet only about a century after the Greeks had helped themselves to Phoenicia's.

Long before the wolf boys founded Rome, Greece had built magnificent colony-cities on the toe of the Italian boot. So by the time Rome grew into a state, it was surrounded by users of the Greek alphabet. Romans never wasted much time creating anything they could take; now they simply took the Greek alphabet and subjected it to the same refining and expansion given to the Phoenician alphabet by Athens.

Half our present Latin alphabet moved unchanged from Greek: A, B, E, Z, H, I, K, M, N, O, T, X, and Y. Eight letters were revised: C, G, L, S, P, R, D, and V. The Greek *gamma*, for instance, looks like a *T* with the left part of the crosspiece missing; it came from a picture of an ox goad. The Romans rounded off the right angle, curved the bottom, and made it into a semicircle, a *C*. Later, to distinguish between the crisp sound of *C* and a more guttural variation, they put a distinguishing mark on the letter and used it to denote the sound of *G*.

The Greeks had created the *F* and *Q*, then abandoned them. Romans rescued these letters from the junk pile and put them back into use. Now they had the 23 letters that they needed to write Latin.

All this had happened by about 2,700 years ago, a very brief interval in the time of the world. But the alphabet as we know it is even newer. We

added the last letter as recently as 500 years ago
and abandoned a form of one within the lifetime of
our nation.

The Romans used *V* as a vowel and a consonant.
But, about a thousand years ago, the vowel *V* was
rounded off to become *U*—number 24—and two
V's, *VV*, with a special sound all their own, were
tied together into *W*—number 25.

Our newest letter, only about five centuries old,
is *J*. This was derived from *I*, which had been used
as both vowel and consonant. Though its most
important use was as the initial in the name of the
Saviour, there is no *J* in the Authorized Version of
the Bible, printed in 1611. It was not until the nineteenth century that *J* was firmly in our alphabet.

The last deletion from our Latin alphabet was
the long *s*, which looked like an Italic *f* without the
crosspiece.

So today our Latin alphabet consists of 26 letters,
from *A* to *Z*. (Although commonly known as the
Roman alphabet, its designation is more properly
Latin. This avoids confusion between the alphabet
itself and the Roman letterform, which we shall
soon consider.)

As Christianity spread, its sacred writings came
into constantly greater demand. These were copied
by hand by scribes who devoted their whole lives to
this labor. As they became intimately familiar with
the forms of letters, they learned to make them with
the least effort.

If you were to write and rewrite many times a
simple sentence in all capitals, you too would
modify the letter forms. Instead of using three
separate strokes to make an *A*, you would soon
make the left stroke and crossbar without lifting
your pen. Then you would round off the top corner,
in the interest of speed, and the result would be
very much like the lowercase *a*. Soon you would tie
letters together to avoid wasting time by lifting the
pen; and eventually you would have a new letterform—*handwriting*.

That is just what happened. Over the centuries
the original capital letters were retained to start

Ancient Seiritic 1850 B.C.	
Phoenician 1200 B.C.	
Greek VI Century B.C.	
Early Latin B.C.	
Square Capitals I Century B.C. to XX Century A.D Book Script from IV Century	
Rustic Capitals I to XII Century	
Early & Later Latin Cursive I to VII Century	
Uncials III to XII Century	
Half Uncials V to XII Century	
Caroline Minuscules VIII to XII Century	
Blackletter XIII to XVI Century (Gutenberg)	
Batarde XIII to XVI Century (Caxton)	
Rotunda XIII to XVI Century	Conjoined to A
Secretary Writing XIII to XIX Century	
Humanist Bookhand & Early Roman Types XV Century	
Humanist Cursive & Early Italic Types XV to XVI Century	
English Roundhand XVIII to XX Century	
Sans-serif & Grotesk XIX & XX Century	
Egyptians, Clarendons, Slab Serif XIX & XX Century	
American Business Hands XIX & XX Century	
Initial Teaching Alphabet England & U.S.A., 1962	

LATIN LETTERFORM went through many variations before it became the one familiar to us today. Many of these were ethnic styles designed by the early type-founders as well as by the scribes who developed "national hands."

(The Book of Kells is the most famous example of an ethnic art form in writing. Done in the ninth century by a group of anonymous monks in Ireland, it is considered the most beautiful of all illuminated manuscripts.)

This family tree of M was one of a series done for Scott Paper Company by Arnold Bank, one of America's noted typographers and calligraphers. It is reproduced by courtesy of the paper company.

CONCEIVED BY ARNOLD BANK

sentences or proper names; these were called *majuscules,* "a little larger." The newer and smaller letters were formalized and named *minuscules;* we call them *lowercase* because of their position in old type cases.

The first true minuscules were developed at Tours, France, by Alcuin, a famed scholar from England. He designed the *Carolingian* alphabet, named for his patron Charlemagne, under whose direction Alcuin reedited and rewrote the classical Greek and Roman literature that had been lost or poorly copied in the Dark Ages. All this was done somewhere between A.D. 781 and 810, the most definitive dates in the history of our alphabet.

By that time the practice was well established that words should be separated. A slash/was/used/by/some/scribes; others.used.a.period.or a-dash-as-separation; finally the words were separated only by white space.

Punctuation, like Topsy, just growed. Sometimes it was almost part of the words themselves; punctuation marks were placed where there happened to be room for them, in the bowl of an *a* or the vertex of a *v* or *w* or over or under any letter. Not until printing was invented did punctuation become regular and specific.

Our alphabet was crystallized with the advent of metal type. Attempts to change it have been desultory and ignored. The printing presses that have

LONG S, a form similar to our lowercase f, was used within a word, sometimes at the start, but never properly at the end. The form continues in use in the German *Fraktur* alphabet today.

It had become rare in this country by the time of Andrew Jackson's administration. The fragment shown here is from the *New-England Courant,* published by Benjamin Franklin in 1723.

His MAJESTY's moſt Gracious SPEECH to both Houſes of Parliament, on Thurſday *October* 11. 1722.

My Lords and Gentlemen,

I Am ſorry to find my ſelf obliged, at the Opening of this Parliament, to acquaint you, That a dangerous Conſpiracy has been for ſome time formed, and is ſtill carrying on againſt my Perſon and Government, in Favour of a Popiſh Pretender.

The Diſcoveries I have made here, the Informations I have received from my Miniſters abroad, and the Intelligences I have had from the Powers in Alliance with me, and indeed from moſt parts of Europe, have given me moſt ample and current Proofs of this wicked Deſign.

The Conſpirators have, by their Emiſſaries, made the ſtrongeſt Inſtances for Aſſiſtance from Foreign Powers, but were diſſappointed in their Expectations:

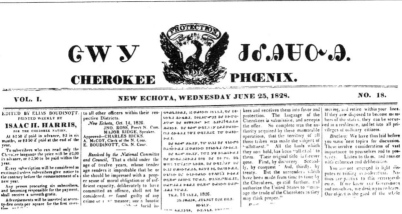

perpetuated the alphabet have also disseminated it so widely that it is virtually impossible to make any changes in it. Such changes can be made only when an alphabet is plastic and without a formal standard as common reference, when it is being changed at least a little by every person who writes it. Once committed to unyielding metal, the alphabet is as permanent as anything man has created.

New alphabets are still being created. Many a spoken language is today being transformed into written language. A comparatively new and most interesting written language is that of the Cherokee Indians. Their chief, Sequoyah, developed a *syllabary,* which uses a sign for an entire syllable. But most new alphabets are based on the Latin and are being created by men who have total knowledge of all the earth's alphabets and thus can by scientific methods achieve in a short time what our ancestors labored over so long by trial-and-error.

CHEROKEE SYLLABARY was invented by Sequoyah, the American Indian genius. Within a dozen years he did what had taken centuries for other cultures, and in 1828 he began publishing a daily newspaper, *The Phoenix,* in New Echota, Georgia. Half the paper was in Cherokee, the rest in English. Type cast by Sequoyah himself has recently been found in archaeological diggings. As the nameplate shows, the syllabary used modified Latin forms.

SUGGESTED READINGS

Anderson, Donald M. *The Art of Written Forms.* New York: Holt, Rinehart and Winston, 1969.

Denman, Frank. *The Shaping of Our Alphabet.* New York: Alfred A. Knopf, 1955.

Laird, Charlton. *The Miracle of Language.* Cleveland: The World Publishing Co., 1953.

Nesbitt, Alexander. *Lettering: The History and Technique of Lettering as Design.* Englewood Cliffs, N.J.: Prentice-Hall, Inc., 1957.

Ogg, Oscar. *The 26 Letters.* New York: Thomas Y. Crowell, 1948.

Pei, Mario. *The Story of Language.* Philadelphia: J. B. Lippincott Co., 1949.

Each of us has a name, and it's a good thing we do. For it would be a virtually impossible task to keep track of friends, acquaintances, neighbors, and even relatives if we had to describe each individual instead of referring to him by name. So it is with type. There aren't as many typefaces as there are human beings, of course, but there are several thousand types, and graphic arts workers, from designers to compositors, must have simple and accurate terms with which to refer to a specific one.

Like humans, type is first classified by *race*, then *ethnic group*, and finally *family*. The racial classification demonstrates convincingly the subtitle of this chapter: form follows the tool.

Our alphabet took its classical, permanent form from the tools used to create it. Although we usually think of these beautiful characters as being created by the stonecutter's chisel across splendid Roman arches and facades, it was the painter's brush that determined their basic shapes.

Before the carver began to incise his ineradicable lines, he wanted to make sure that all the letters would fit in the given space. It would be more than embarrassing if he carved a 50-foot panegyric to Caesar across some vaulting arch and then found out there wasn't quite enough room for the last *R* in the emperor's name. So first he placed the letters onto the stone in a form that could be easily changed before cutting began.

It was the paintbrush that created the distinguishing shape of the classical *Roman* letters. That brush was broad and thin, similar to the ones we use today to paint a house. When you painted a vertical stroke, such as the two on an *H*, the broad side of the brush made a wide line. When you painted the horizontal crossbar on the *H*, the brush drew a narrow line, only as wide as the thickness of the brush. When a brush like this draws an *O*, it paints with its thin edge at the very top; on the curve the line thickens to the full width of the brush; then the line thins to its narrowest at the bottom, swells to another maximum, and finally thins down to its starting width.

3

Printing Type

Form Follows the Tool

PIN
emotion
FINE FA
for use in b
WIDELY
lower case

ROMAN OLD STYLE has some of
the most elegant of all letter-
forms. Specimens shown here in-
clude (from the top, in pairs)
Goudy Old Style and Kennerley
Old Style, both designed by
F. W. Goudy, and Garamond
Bold.

The last is based on the types
of the Imprimerie Nationale of
France, known as *Caractères de
l'Université*. It is named for
Claude Garamond of Paris, who
died in 1561. He was the first to
make type design and production
an enterprise separate from
printing. Goudy, who lived from
1865 to 1947, was perhaps the
most notable of all American
type designers. An outspoken
man, he once threatened to design a font without a *k* "so
those @#$%¢&* won't be able
to misspell my first name,"
Frederic.

Another Roman tool for the same purpose was
one you can readily duplicate for an interesting
demonstration. Take a rectangular eraser and, with
a rubber band, fasten a pencil at each side. Now
draw familiar letterforms, the *R* is a good one. The
two pencils will meet and depart to create the same
swells and thinnings as the paintbrush. The
Romans tied charcoal sticks to a board that was the
proper width of the broad vertical stroke.

This thinning and swelling of curved strokes is
the primary distinguishing mark of the Roman race.
Equally important are the *serifs*, the form created
by another tool, the stonecarver's.

After the carver had incised a straight stroke—
again let's look at the *H*—he had to finish off the
ends. This he would do, naturally, by cutting across
the main stroke. It is difficult to start such a horizontal stroke at the exact corner of the vertical one.
Rather than risk a slip of the chisel that could spoil
the whole letter, the carver started a little outside
the main stroke and let it go across and a little
beyond on the other side. To avoid a fragile point,
he then rounded—*bracketed*—the serif, that little
finishing stroke, into the main stroke.

This solution satisfied not only the needs of the
stonecutter, but the artistic eye of the beholder. It
became an integral part of the classic alphabet and
today the serif is the second distinguishing feature
of the Roman letterform.

The letters carved into the great Trajan Column,
erected in Rome about A.D. 113, are the finest
example of Roman. Although scholars and artists
have, almost ever since, attempted to reduce these
characters to mathematical formulas, none has succeeded in bettering the work of the original
craftsmen.

As Roman legions spread across Europe, their
alphabet went with them. In Germany and the Low
Countries, scribes' tools also influenced letterforms.
They used quill pens that lacked the flexibility of
the brush to sweep in graceful curves. They could
write straight lines smoothly; on curves the two
points of the nib overlapped and the pen spluttered

and splashed. The solution was to abandon curved lines and replace circles or arcs with a series of straight lines.

The result is the letterform and race called *Text* (because it was used primarily for the text of holy writings), or *Black Letter* (for obvious reasons).

Note that type race names, like the humans' Oriental, Occidental, Negro, etc., are capitalized.

Two common misnomers should be noted . . . and zealously avoided. *Old English* is the name of a family in the Text race; it may not be used for the basic classification. Nor is Text properly referred to as *Gothic;* that is another family name from an altogether different race and has no connection with the Black Letter except that the latter's form suggests to some people the steeply pitched roofs of Gothic architecture.

It is ironic that the offspring, Text, should have been used as movable type for a long time before its Roman parent. But Gutenberg was a Teuton, of course, and he sought to make his printed books look just like the Germanic handlettered ones which were done in Black Letter. It wasn't until 1464 in Strasbourg that the first Roman letterform was committed to type metal and 1470 that the first classical Roman was cast, by Nicholas Jenson, a French printer who had migrated to Venice along with the new craft. Considering the rapid spread of printing, those are long intervals indeed.

Text has no ethnic classifications; though there are subdivisions of that race, they are not major enough to warrant consideration in an overview such as this. The Roman race, though, has two ethnic groups: *Old Style* and *Modern*. Some classifiers add a third group, *Transitional*. Again, for our purposes we need not subdivide that finely.

When the ancient Roman painted letters on the walls of the Forum—or anywhere else—he held the brush at about a 45 degree angle. The thinnest portion of the stroke was at about 11 and 5 on a clock face and the widest at 2 and 8 o'clock. The difference between thicks and thins was not drastic. The serif was bracketed, connected to the main

Charlemagne ord church books rewr a lower-case alpha

Frankenmuth

abrdeîmn

TEXT, or BLACK LETTER, was the first letterform made permanent in metal form; the last line shows the original letters Gutenberg designed for his 42-Line Bible. The top word is in Engravers' Old English, the block in Cloister Black, and the next line in Goudy Text Handtooled, the most distinguished of all American Black Letters. Old English is a family name, but the term is commonly and erroneously applied to the whole Text race.

RATED
for legibility
COP
yle
condense
THE EARLY

ROMAN MODERN all began with Bodoni, the Bold version of which makes up the two top lines. The next two are Ultra Bodoni, or Poster Bodoni, and the next, Onyx. The last is Corvinus Light, designed by the Hungarian artist Imre Reiner in 1929.

stroke by a curve. Later, when the serif was designed by a type-punch cutter, that finishing stroke became thicker and coarser. All these characteristics are found in the Old Style Roman ethnic group.

While the letter itself stands perpendicular, the bowls of fully circular letters such as o and a tilt to the left. In the oldest typefaces an occasional character will look as if it didn't belong to the others of the alphabet; they will seem to be smaller or wider or have different serifs and curves.

A contemporary of Benjamin Franklin, patron saint of American printers, created one of the ethnic subdivisions. Giambatista Bodoni, a Parmesan printer, drew his Roman letters with thin and sharp unbracketed serifs, showing the influence of the engraving tools of the punch cutter. He made his O and other bowls on a perpendicular axis with the thinnest portions at 12 and 6 o'clock and the widest at 3 and 9. The difference between thick and thin strokes is marked. People gave the new type the accolade of each generation: "It's modern!" To this day Bodoni s type is not only a Modern Roman but *the* Modern Roman.

Romans that combine characteristics of Modern and Old Style are called Transitional. Remember that the date of the design of a face does not necessarily indicate its category; Bodoni cut his Modern in 1788 and Goudy his Old Style in the 1930's.

The auxiliary to the alphabet, the Arabic numerals, also have Old Style and Modern versions. *Modern numbers* align on the base line; in Old Style, the 3, 4, 5, 7, and 9 drop below the baseline. In this illustration

1234567890   1234567890

the numbers on the left are Old Style, those at the right, Modern. Old Style or Transitional Romans have both versions in a standard font.

The third race is *Monotonal*. Its ethnic groups are *Gothic* and *Sans Serifs*.

Europeans today call the Gothics *Grotesk*, and that name was once highly descriptive. The term Gothic, as applied to letterforms, refers to the war-painted savages who were to Caesarian legions what the Sioux were to General Custer. Some un-

head AND printer

HOLIDAY In Ribbon NEUL

known lexicographer thought that the ugliness of a letterform was compatible to the Goth tribesmen's lack of beauty.

The Gothic letterform was originally a block letter similar to those children cut out of construction paper in grade school. The bowls were rectangles or octagonal forms, and all the strokes were of the same weight. Eventually the angles were replaced by curves, but they were tight and graceless.

The Sans Serifs came much later. As always, type reflects the culture of the era and the area. In the Victorian or Gay Nineties era, type was as over-decorated as houses and clothes. Bustles, ruffles, and whalebone disguised the female form almost beyond recognition; flowers, cherubs, animals, and ribbons gussied up the alphabet nearly to illegibility.

When, after World War I, creative people rebelled against all reminders of that gaudy era, they began stripping gingerbread off furniture and architecture. "Functional" became the watchword. At the famed Bauhaus, where this revolt began, the Latin alphabet came up for disapproving scrutiny, too. Just as they had stripped buildings and their contents of all ornamentation, Bauhaus designers tore the furbelows off the ABC's, not only the tasteless gaudies but the beautiful serifs as well, and reduced the pleasantly swelling and thinning strokes to a uniform, monotonal stroke. To this new letterform they gave the French title *Sans Serifs*, "without serifs."

Between the original square-letter Gothics and

GOTHIC, oldest ethnic group in the Monotonals, is well-known in the form shown in the words *head* and *and*, Franklin Gothic Condensed. This is highly popular for newspaper banners. Note how the bowls of the *h, a,* and *d,* are pinched and how the bar of the *e* is lightened. There is a thinning of the verticals in the *N* and the bar of the *A,* too.

The words *holiday* and *ribbon* appear in Lydian Bold, which shows the influence of the broad-nibbed pen, especially in the *O. Printer* is set in Venus Bold extended, a contemporary face of many series, and the last face is Neuland, designed by the famed Rudolf Koch in 1923.

President

Children

WhiteHou

Measles

printer

SANS SERIFS are demonstrated by a group of Spartans, the most widely used Sans in the United States.

The top line is in Spartan Bold, the only face ever designed specifically for newspaper headlines. The next line is the Bold Oblique; then, Bold Condensed. *Measles* is in Spartan Extra Black, an excellent accent face. Note its lowercase a; this is the so-called *Greek a*. This form is prevalent in the Monotonals, although the Roman version is available as an alternate character in many fonts. There are seven weights of Spartan, each with its Oblique, and five of them are also in Condensed.

The last line is in Tempo Light.

the Sans Serifs there was once a marked difference. But the Gothics have been so refined that now the distinguishing features are often almost imperceptible. The only concrete difference is that the Gothics are not always entirely monotonal. Sometimes there is a difference in the weight of Gothic strokes; especially where the bowl meets the stem, the curved stroke may be *pinched*. If there is a difference in the weight of any strokes, the letter is a Gothic.

This difference sometimes creates an anomaly. Lydian, a handsome face, and the even handsomer and more recent Optima must be considered Gothics. But Lydian shows strongly the influence of the broad-nibbed pen and, especially in its so-called Italic form, is strongly calligraphic in flavor. Optima is actually a Roman with the serifs removed; its thicks and thins are as Roman as Brutus' dagger. But any classification must, apparently, have some square peg that just won't fit into the neat, round, logical holes.

The Square Serifs race is a bridge between the Romans and the Monotones. The letterstrokes are all of equal weight, but the serifs are not the unobtrusive ones of Jenson or Bodoni; as their name indicates, the Squares' serifs are at least as heavy as the main strokes.

Printer's lore says that these Squares were used by Napoleon for communication during his military campaign in Egypt. Messages were written in Square Serifs on large boards, held high atop a sand dune, and read from a distance by telescope. There the messages were rewritten and held up for reading by the next relay station.

Whether for that reason or because anything pertaining to Egypt was most fashionable in the Napoleonic age, this style of letter was known as *Egyptian*. (Some authorities, with logic, believe the name came from the resemblance of the slab serifs to the strong horizontal lines of Egyptian architecture.) It is interesting to note that the trade names for the best-known Square Serifs in the United States bow to the legend; they are called *Memphis*,

HIT

A JOB COMPOSING
room in which choice
in method is made on
a machine 1234567890

GOOD

use in

lan

EGYPTIAN SQUARE SERIFS are typified by the Stymie family. The word *hit* is its light version, and *good* and *use in* are its Bold Oblique. The rest of the specimen is in Memphis Bold.

The Egyptians have a pleasant texture in body-type sizes, as the small block here demonstrates. Its readability is fairly high, too.

Cairo, and *Karnak.* A famous French-designed Square is *Ramses,* and in England there is *Scarab.*

The term Egyptian is now used for an ethnic classification of the Squares. The other ethnic is *American.*

Serifs on the American Squares are always heavier than the main strokes themselves. This style is associated in the American mind with P. T. Barnum, Wild West shows, and old opera-house posters. In fact, the most popular American Squares are called *P. T. Barnum* and *Playbill.* In Europe the Egyptian Square is called *Antique,* the name by which the first Square Serif was shown in a specimen book by Vincent Figgins in 1815.

The fifth race is the *Written.*

Just as Gutenberg and Manutius used written hands as the bases for their type, so later designers turned to handwriting when they created *Script* or *Cursive* faces. The names—*scriptum* is Latin for "writing," *cursus* means "running"—describe the flowing manner in which handwriting runs from one letter to the other. The only slight difference between the two: Script letters are tied together, the Cursives are separated, although sometimes so narrowly that it is not easily apparent.

Script and Cursive are the ethnic divisions of the Written race, and some typographers are tempted to create a third ethnic classification and assign it to *calligraphy.* Literally translated "beautiful writing," calligraphy is really not type. It is handwritten, then converted into a printing plate. It may be in

Layout and
for over three
farms it still, ho
THE YEOMAN
Layout

AMERICAN SQUARE SERIFS are redolent of greasepaint and circus peanuts. P. T. Barnum is immortalized in the name of the top line, Barnum Bold Condensed, and the next three, Barnum Medium Condensed.

The last line continues the tradition; it's Showboat.

Barnum's initials are or are not used in the type name without any apparent pattern, even by the typefounders themselves.

Annual

May First to

in the social p

Thespian
Art

Puppet Show

Glacier

SCRIPT has a spectrum that ranges from Signal Black, the rugged face in the top line, to the formal elegance of Typo Script in the next two. Commercial Script, which also shows influences of Spencerian handwriting, set *Thespian Art*. The last two lines are Kaufman Bold and Kaufman Script.

script or cursive form, depending on whether the calligrapher chooses to connect his letters or let them stand unjoined.

Handlettering is an extension of calligraphy. Here also letterforms are produced by an artist and made into a printing plate. "Lettering" characters are "drawn" with formal care and often cannot be distinguished from regular type. In both calligraphy and lettering, the artist can accentuate the unique combinations of letters in a specific word, headline, or paragraph. He can, for instance, create his own *ligatures,* tying letters together. He can tuck a lowercase *o* under the arm of a cap *T;* he can let a cap *F* share its top serif with an *l* or let an *f* and *i* use the same dot. *Cartoon* letterforms are swiftly, casually done and are a cross between calligraphy and handlettering.

The last race is *Ornamented;* the last syllable should be noted—it is not *tal.* Its ethnic groups are *Shaded, Shadowed,* and *Novelty.*

Ornamentation fills a basic human need, and our alphabets are still often decorated although rarely as ornately as in the days before World War I. If such decoration is applied to the face of a letterform, the letter is Shaded. The most common forms of shading are an *Inline* letter, where a white line runs down the center of the black stroke, and the *Shading Line,* a white line running close to one side of the black strokes. Sometimes letters are grayed by a *cross-hatching* of fine parallel or intersecting lines, and this alteration to the face itself makes it Shaded. An *Outline* letter is technically a Shaded letter, for something has been done to the face—it's been eliminated!

Any decoration added to the outside of the letterform makes it Shadowed. This is commonly a broad stroke placed like the shadow cast by a three-dimensional letter. A thinner line may run all around the perimeter of the letters.

Sometimes both kinds of ornamentation are applied to the letters. Beton, for instance, is an Outline (thus Shaded) face to which a shadow has been added to make it both Shaded and Shadowed.

SAPHIR

FRE

ONE OF

used type

DELPHIAN

NTOUR

Bodoni Open

Comst

COMST

OMB

AB

GOLD

ORNAMENTED RACE includes Shaded as an ethnic group, and these specimens hint at the many, many varieties.

Saphir, the only typeface designed by a woman, is the creation of Gudrun Zapf, the wife of Hermann Zapf, the greatest living type designer. It is elegant and feminine. The second line is Flash, from France. Next is Goudy Handtooled, substantial and credible, not at all prettified by the shading line. Delphian is most elegant. Contour, which has lost part of its cognomen here, is an outline letter; it's in the Shaded ethnic group because something was done to its face— it was removed. Bodoni Open, shown here in Roman and Italic, is an interesting design in which all right-hand strokes are heavier than those on the left. This is not a Shadowed letter because the heavier strokes are part of the letterform and are not added to the face.

SHADOWED LETTERS take many forms. The ornate Balle A is technically Shadowed because something has been added to its face, the leafy tendril.

Comstock and Comstock Condensed are simply Shadowed in comparison with the Ombrees, a three-dimensional form dearly beloved of the French Empire.

Gills Sans Floreated (in the second to last line) is one of those borderline examples so difficult to classify. It may be Shadowed, if we consider the vegetation as an outline of a simple Written letter, or Shaded, if we think of this as an Outline letter with a serated right edge, or it may even be a Novelty.

The final specimen, fortunately, is a clear-cut Shadowed; it is Gold Rush, which gives the effect of a three-dimensional letter.

NOVELTY FACES are great fun and offer a handy catch-all for faces that don't fit neatly into other classifications. Rustic and Astur, with their wood forms, unhewn and sawed, certainly are drastically different from conventional letters.

Futura Black was actually designed by Paul Renner during the Bauhaus period as a series of the popular Futura Sans Serifs. This is incredible, for there isn't even a vague family resemblance to the genuine Sans Futuras.

Broadway uses the same point of departure, an exaggerated Roman from which the serifs have been lopped. Broadway was widely used in the early 1930's and epitomizes the Art Deco of that period.

Flex is made of ribbon and comes from Amsterdam. Just below it is Romantique No. 4. (There were five Romantiques, each trying to outdo the other in floridity.)

Prisma is really Rudolph Koch's Kabel (or Cable, both pronounced the same way) with three inlines. So it might go into the Shaded ethnic.

Caslon Antique has been "distressed" to make it look as if it came from the case of a Colonial printer. The original copies of the Declaration of Independence were printed in Caslon, and a psychologist has declared that all Americans therefore have an atavistic affection for Caslon, especially for the Antique version.

RUSTIC   Flex

Astur   BCDE

Futura   PRISMA

BROADWA   Caslon Antique

Antique Italic

CALLIGRAPHY has sales appeal in the contemporary world despite its ancient roots. Ability to create ligatures at will unifies this design.

No. 2 in a Series

Rosa Zagnoni Marinoni

VILLA ROSA / FAYETTEVILLE ▸ ARKANSAS

CALLIGRAPHY is well named "beautiful writing." The letterhead at the left and the one above were done by Raymond DaBoll, one of the great American calligraphers, who recently calligraphed an entire book of memoirs by his wife, a well-known singer on the old Chautauqua circuit.

The thistle of the letterhead is repeated in tiny form on the envelope to designate the proper place to write the address. J. L. Frazier is himself an outstanding practitioner of and writer on typography.

J. L. Frazier
1862 Sherman Avenue · Evanston · Illinois

There aren't enough examples, though, to warrant establishing a whole new ethnic grouping for them.

If the letterform is drastically changed, it becomes a Novelty. This last ethnic gives what every filing system needs, a *Miscellaneous* drawer. Any letterform that won't fit into some other pigeonhole will inevitably be so markedly revised in shape that it is by definition a Novelty.

It should be noted that when any kind of ornamentation is added to a letter, it immediately becomes part of the Ornamented race.

Not all historical developments of type design create a separate race. One that failed to do so is the *Italic* designed by Aldus Manutius in Venice in 1500. Like Gutenberg, Manutius based his type design on the letters most familiar to him. These were not the classical Trajan letters but the written hand of Italy. Its marked characteristic was its slant to the northeast that right-handed people naturally impart to *roundhand* or cursive writing.

Aldus used his new type to set inexpensive books which were as popular as their twentieth-century counterparts, the ubiquitous pocketbook sold in every drugstore and bus depot today. His type zoomed into popularity. Called *Aldine* in his own country, the type was known as Italic to the rest of Europe and to us today.

CURSIVE has a wide range in style, weight, and flavor.

Trafton, top line, is an elegant face designed by an Englishman and cast in Germany. Note its e, indistinguishable from an Old Style Italic. Park Avenue, the next line, is a popular American Cursive. Its lowercase, especially, shows the influence of the broad pen.

Legenda—for *The Sheik*—has a strong Oriental or Arabic flavor, although it, too, is a German design. *Fashion* is set in Lydian Cursive. Note that the original Lydian is a Gothic, while this Cursive, commonly listed as a series of the original family, is by definition a member of an entirely different race.

The last line is in Grayda, an American face.

SHADED AND SHADOWED LETTERS may be as simple as Umbra or as ornate as Ombre Initial in Line 2.

Umbra is considered by many as the prototype of the Shadowed letter. It does cast a shadow, obviously, but then the face itself is eliminated, making it a Shaded face. Something has also been added—making it Shadowed—and, in combination, Shaded and Shadowed.

Ombre Initials are just about as far as an Ornamented letterform can be taken without losing all legibility . . . and many would even argue that!

Beton Outline is just what its name indicates—plus the shadow; in England it's known as Beton Open. Thorne Shaded is another face whose official name is technically incorrect; it should be Thorne Shaded—because it's Outline—and Shadowed. Designed in 1820, it is one of the earliest three-dimensional letters and is still, a century and a half later, a handsome face.

The last line of Initiales Florides looks Napoleonic in its Empire style, but it goes back only to 1937. Imre Reiner designed this one.

SHADED LETTERS have three subdivisions. Egmont shows the Inline form, where a thin line runs down the center of the letterstrokes. The next is Punch, strongly reminiscent of Neuland. This has a shading line that runs down one side of the letterstroke. (This face, incidentally, is confusingly misnamed Punch Inline.) The last line is in Normandia, an Outline letterform. It is an Italian design.

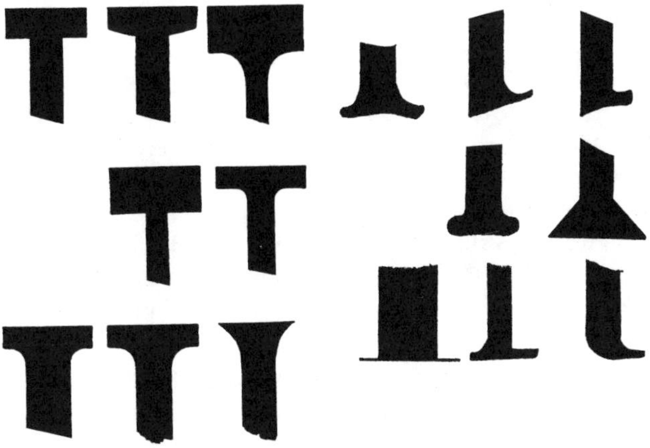

SERIFS differ widely among faces, and often they are the major characteristics of national and Transitional styles. At the top left is an Egyptian and the third one in the top row is an American, Square Serifs. The first foot serif is typical of the curves of an Old Style, and the third one from the right in the bottom row is a Modern.

In some systems Italic was considered a separate race. It does have some unique characteristics, but these do not disguise the strong similarity to Roman, especially its most obvious tie: it swells and diminishes and has serifs. So today we place it in the Roman race and use the term to designate the right-slanting form of both Old Style and Modern Romans.

All the races except Text and Written have letter-forms that slant to the right. In common usage these are all erroneously referred to as Italics. For the specific needs of typographic observers, the distinction must be made: "Italic" refers only to the slanted forms of the Roman race; for all other races the correct designation is *Oblique.*

"Roman" is also commonly misused to refer to

*A B C D E F G H I J
K L M N O P Q R S
T U V W X Y Z & ! ?
a b c d e f g h i j k l m
n o p q r s t u v w x y z
. , - : ; ' ' fi ff fl ffi ffl $
1 2 3 4 5 6 7 8 9 0*

FONT OF TYPE is basically the collection of letters shown here plus spacing materials. Note that both these fonts—Bodoni Bold Italics above and Twentieth Century Extrabold Condensed—have f ligatures.

**A B C D E F G H I J
K L M N O P Q R
S T U V W X Y Z
a b c d e f g h i j k l m
n o p q r s t u v w x y z
& fi ff fl . , - : ; ' ' ' ( ) ! ?
$ 1 2 3 4 5 6 7 8 9 0**

IME and money

MARIGOLD   **WALLOP!**

CARTOON LETTERS are a cross between writing and lettering. The top line is in Flash, the lower two in Balloon Light and Balloon Extrabold.

A CAREFUL

a practical face

E FULL

table 90

ality

ITALICS are in both Old Style and Modern. The top specimen here is Garamond Bold. Notice how the *i* and *a*, especially, look like those characters in Cursive, thus demonstrating the Written bases on which Aldus designed his variation.

The middle specimen is Ultra Bodoni and the lowest one, Bodoni Bold. Note how, in the latter, the *i* has a straight Modern serif at the top but a finial at the foot and how the top of the *t* is slightly concave.

letters that stand up straight. But the correct term is *Perpendicular* when referring to races other than Roman. To avoid confusion, it is often wise to ask whether a correspondent's use of "Italics" refers to the Aldine form or to the angle of the letter.

We must note another variation of angle, *Back-slant*. As the name suggests, this letterform slants backward, to the left. It is awkward and, because it leans against the grain of normal eye movement, often actually discomforts the reader. Fortunately this aberration is rare.

Type races or ethnic groups are divided into families. Like people, they have family names. Some —like Swensson—are named for their fathers, their designers: Bodoni and Goudy are only two of the more famous of these. Others, human and type are named for geographical origins: Karnak, Caledonia, Ionic. Others—like the surnames Smith and Miller —are named for their jobs: Playbill, Copperplate, and Poster. Others have just names: Techno, Stymie, Aurora.

Each family includes varying numbers of *series*. A series bears the family name, either alone or, usually, with one or more adjectives that describe the basic variations of a type face. These include *slant*—perpendicular or oblique, Roman or Italic; *weight—Heavy, Book, Extra Bold*, etc.; *width—* normal or *fullface, Condensed*, and *Extended*.

The term "normal," in weight or width, and "Roman" or "Perpendicular" are usually omitted unless the distinction must be stressed. Thus "Univers" means "Univers Perpendicular, neither Condensed nor Extended."

Typical series names are *Fairfield, Spartan Bold, Garamond Italic, Venus Bold Extended*.

The smallest subdivision is the *font*. This is designated by the series name and a size, for a font consists of all the characters and spacing material necessary to set normal composition in one size. A typical font name, then, would be *8-point Caledonia Bold Italic*. There will be several to many fonts in a series; Spartan Medium, for example, has 11 fonts, from 6-point through 36-point.

The font is divided into capitals and small letters. Sometimes the font will also have *small caps*, letters in the form of regular caps but in size only a little, if any, larger than the small letters. The lowercase letters consist of *primaries, ascenders,* and *descenders*. These are explained in the next chapter. The font also has punctuation marks and special characters such as $, ¢, *, etc.

This book is set in Caledonia 10-point. All the Roman characters and supplemental material such as &, *, #, $, !, etc., make one font. Italics used here come from another font. Both fonts of typefaces are produced from a single font of linotype matrices, though, as we shall see later.

One of the most widely used families was Cheltenham, the first one cut for both mechanical and hand setting. By race, Cheltenham is a Roman; by subdivision, a Transitional. Its series are many: Cheltenham (the original fullface version), Cheltenham Wide, Condensed, and Extra Condensed (variations in width), and Medium and Bold weights. Often there are combinations of more than one variation, so that series names include Cheltenham Medium Condensed and Extra Condensed Italic.

The number of different characters in a font varies with the face and its use. A California job case has 89 spaces. These contain capital and lowercase alphabets, eight punctuation marks, five *f* and the *æ* and *œ* ligatures, 10 numbers, dollar and pound signs, and ampersand. The other receptacles contain spacing from em quads to 5-em spaces. The standard Linotype has 90 channels for characters and spacing other than the spacebands.

There are many special characters to augment a given font, symbols for scientific composition, footnote marks, or commercial signs, such as *lb.* and @.

The number of pieces of type or matrices in a font also varies. In America or for setting English, the *e* is the most frequent character, and its receptacle is the largest in the job case, so the compositor has an adequate supply. In a standard font of Linotype matrices, there are 20 *e* matrices. Because

STYMIE

is an ope

THE SER

is mediu

OBLIQUE LETTERS are those that slant to the right in Square Serifs —as the Stymie Bold above—and the Monotonals—as the Twentieth Century Medium, below. These forms are commonly but incorrectly known as Italics.

A comparison of the Perpendicular and Oblique versions illustrated here shows that there is no appreciable difference in the letterforms themselves, as there often are between Roman and Italics of the same family.

TYPE SE

should a

STORIES

comes g

BCƆ

abcðefghíjkl

UNCIALS are named for the Latin *uncia*, an inch. In that size, always in caps, they were used to decorate manuscripts. Half-uncials were the transition from majuscules to minuscules. This specimen is American Uncial and is so freely translated from the original that it has both upper and lower cases. Uncials combine well with Text, especially as decorative initials.

AUGUSTEA

AUGUSTEA

TWO RACES may claim a single letter design, as these two versions, Augustea and Augustea Inline, well demonstrate. The original is obviously a classical Transitional Roman. But when it is converted into a form apparently incised into stone, it immediately—and without right of appeal—is consigned to the Ornamented race.

Examination of specimens of Shaded and Shadowed letters on previous pages emphasizes how many of them retain characteristics of their origins in other races.

of less frequent use, there are only five *z* matrices in a linecaster font and only a small space is left for *z* in the job case.

Foundry-type fonts are designated by the number of lowercase *a*'s they contain. The standard for 36-point Caslon Oldstyle is a 7-*a* font—seven *a*'s, five *A*'s, and all other characters in proper ratio. In 6-point Caslon the standard is a 65-*a* font. Thus a font will vary from as many as 200 pieces of type to 1,500, plus necessary quads and spaces.

Decorative faces, such as those used only for initials, may be fonted with as few as three *A*'s.

We classify type for the same reason the botanist classifies plants, to make it easier to study and discuss them. A tomato is a tomato whether it is called a fruit or a vegetable. A type is good or poor, useful or not, whether it is a Modern, Old Style, or Transitional. Classifications are most useful if accepted as a tool and not as a straitjacket.

The system suggested here—or any other—underlines the great number and variety in the world of type. There are so many forms of our alphabet that a person could spend his whole life in studying and classifying them.

Whether a person wants to immerse himself in the subject or learn only basic facts, the study of type is fascinating. The typophile finds as much pleasure in browsing through a specimen book as the artist does in visiting the Louvre.

SUGGESTED READINGS

Haab, Armin (ed.). *The Lettera Books*. New York: Hastings House, 1960.

Lindegren, Erik. *ABC of Lettering and Printing Types*. Askim, Sweden: Lindegren Grafisk, 1965.

Massin. *Letter and Image*. New York: Van Nostrand Reinhold, 1970.

Steinberg, S. H. *Five Hundred Years of Printing*. Edinburgh: Penguin Books, 1955.

Updike, D. B. *Printing Types*. 2 vols. Cambridge, Mass.: Harvard University Press, 1951.

Zapf, Hermann. *Manuale Typographicum*. New York: Museum Books, 1959.

Early printers were obsessed with secrecy about their craft. From Gutenberg on, printers hoped to maintain their monopoly, and woe to him who divulged trade secrets. Fortress cities even passed laws which forbade printers to leave their jobs or their cities, lest they give a potential competitor the information he needed about the new business. Employees met in secrecy to organize their medieval craft unions.

As in any such group, a jargon was developed that would allow communication only among the initiated and exclude the dangerous public. For more than 500 years that language has been expanding, and even the glossary at the end of this book, sizable as it is, does not include all the phrases familiar to the printer. (Some are too salty for inclusion.) Terms will be explained as they crop up in discussion. Many of them are used so infrequently that there is no need to dwell on them. This chapter will discuss the more common ones.

Today secrecy is no longer required. The public knows, just as the boss does, that when the printers are going to *chapel,* their activity concerns their union rather than religious rites. And most people are well aware that the *hellbox* is not a Satanic receptacle where the *printer's devil* incarcerates unwary passersby. But if the public is confused by a great part of the printer's jargon . . . well, so is the printer himself.

The problem is the ambiguity of many terms and a tendency to use the same one for several incompatible meanings. The public finds the very term "graphic arts" confusing because fine artists use those words to describe a subdivision of their art, *printmaking*, while the printer's definition is the one given in the first chapter of this book.

There are sporadic attempts to give the great field of communicative graphic arts the name of *graphics*. But popular usage changes with no more alacrity than that of a glacier. We can probably canonize Coster as the patron saint of printers or Marlowe as the author of *Hamlet* long before "graphics" becomes universally accepted.

4

Printers' Terms

The Jargon of the Craft

There is no single word that refers to all practitioners of the graphic arts. *Graphic artist* is inappropriate as a name for the many *craftsmen* in the field; *graphic artsman* has a contrived sound. So, in this book, the specific name of the performer of a specific task will be used.

In many instances one person will perform a whole series of assignments, sometimes two or more simultaneously. A man may be a *designer* and a *type specifier* at the same time. An advertising manager·may function in the role of the "author" even as he is a proofreader.

But until an acceptable substitute for graphic artist/artsman is coined, the reader must be content with names of the parts, rather than the whole, of the industry's personnel.

Printer, itself, is a name claimed by many craftsmen: the *compositor* sets type; the *make-up man* (or *stoneman*) combines typographic elements into larger units, an advertisement, a page, or a *signature* (a group of pages). They work in a *composing room*. In a newspaper plant, it is divided into the *ad alley* and the *news line*. In a *job shop*, which does commercial composition or printing, the basic division is between machine and hand composition.

The hand compositor works before a shallow tray, a *California job case*. Each case contains one font and is subdivided into small rectangles, each containing one character. In older days, he used two cases; one held capitals, beneath it was one of small letters. Today we still refer to *uppercase* or *lowercase* for majuscules or minuscules.

Type is set by hand in a *composing stick* (a shallow, three-sided tray) and is later placed in a

CALIFORNIA JOB CASE came onto the printing scene in the mid-nineteenth century in that state. One James Dearing is sometimes identified as the inventor. It succeeded the *Yankee* and *New York job cases,* each of which combined the upper and lower cases.

The California case is about 32 inches wide, 16 inches long, and an inch deep. A good typesetter, accustomed to the case, could set as many as 1,500 characters an hour. Such a compositor was called a *swift,* and many demonstrated their skills by setting type blindfolded.

similar but longer tray, a *galley*, and stored on the *bank*.

The make-up man's work surface is the *stone*. Formerly it was actually a slab of smooth stone; today it is a metal surface. Here the type and any headlines, illustrations, or rules needed are assembled into a *form*. Later the form is placed in a metal frame, a *chase*, which holds it firmly, while printing, by means of iron wedges, *quoins*.

A single piece of type contributes many entries to the printer's lexicon. The main mass is called the *body*; it stands on *feet*, separated by the *groove*. The top plane of the body is the *shoulder* from which projects the printing surface, the *face*. The side of this projection is the *beard*. The depressed area between the raised lines of the face is a *counter*. *Nicks* are grooves in one side of the body, varying in number and placement to identify it as from an individual font.

Some faces, notably classical Italics, project over the side of the body. The projecting elements are called *kerns* and are supported by the shoulder of adjacent characters. *Kerned letters* are apt to break off during handling or printing and therefore are not popular with frugal printers.

COMPOSING STICK, now a finely tooled metal instrument, was originally of wood. Even today printers in Ethiopia use an actual wood stick, hollowed out to accommodate only a line or two. The left side of this shallow box is movable and is adjusted to the measure being set. Type in a stick reads left to right, just as the printed image will, but it is upside down to the printer and, of course, in mirror form. (Courtesy American Type Founders)

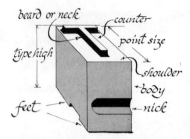

beard or neck — counter — point size

type high

shoulder

body

feet — nick

NOMENCLATURE OF TYPE illustrates many points that often confuse the tyro. The type-high dimension is the same for all type, its longest top dimension changes with point size and its width with the character involved.

This is a 60-point character; in text sizes the body is considerably taller (type-high) than either dimension of its printing face and thus is very unstable, making pi-ing—mixing up the pieces—a constant hazard.

The nicks vary to identify the font and also to show when the letter is right-side up, thus helping avoid confusion between *b* and *d* and *p* and *q*.

Spacing, at the start of a paragraph, between words or at the end of a short *widow* line, is created by *quads.* The *em,* or *mutton, quad* is a square of the point size. Thus, in a 14-point font the em will be 14 points high (as are all the characters) and 14 points wide.

The *en,* or *nut, quad* is half as wide; in a 14-point font the en is 14 points high and 7 points wide. Smaller spacing material are the one-third, one-fourth, and one-fifth of an em. By shortening their names to *em spaces,* the printer saves breath but creates confusion. A 3-em quad, in 14-point, is 14 points high and 42 points (3 × 14) wide, but a 3-*em space* is 14 points high and only one-third of 14 points—4⅔ points—wide.

Thin spaces of brass or copper, in ½- and 1-point, are used in more meticulous composition, and in some instances the compositor even uses tissue paper for exactly right spacing.

Horizontal spacing—between lines or other printing elements—is created by *ledds,* metal strips 2 points tall, or *slugs,* which are 6 points tall. (To prevent confusion, this book uses the phonetic form "*ledd*" instead of the common *lead.*) *Reglets,* of wood or metal, are 12 points. Larger spacing material is called *furniture.*

There are also 1- and 3-point ledds and slugs from 4- through 12-point. Unless otherwise designated, a ledd is 2 points, a slug is 6.

The printer scorns inches; he has his own linear

KERNS are portions of type that overhang its own body and are supported by the shoulders of adjacent characters in the form. Kerning is done primarily with Italic letters, although in photocomposition it is also done to bring characters closer together; the o in *To* is tucked under the arm of the *T* by *negative spacing.* In the finest handsetting the compositor will sometimes mortise out the individual letters for a more pleasing fit.

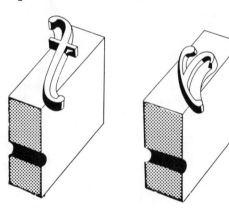

measurement, the *American point system*. This he might well cherish; it had a long, hard birth.

When metal type was first cast for sale, each foundry used its own measurements; a customer would thus be committed to a single source of supply to avoid the nuisance of making disparate type fit into a smooth line or form.

It was not until 1737—after almost 200 years of measurement anarchy—that a French printer, Pierre-Simon Fournier, devised a standard for type measurement. His smallest unit was the point. Sensible as it was, the system was resisted, and it took a royal decree by King Louis XV, who was intensely interested in printing, to make founders conform.

Later another famous French printing family, the Didots, modified Fournier's point to make it conform to the French inch, and that system is still in use in Europe. A Didot point is .0148 inches; 12 Didot points equal a *cicero*.

English printers adopted the point system; it came to America and, in 1886, was standardized here as the American point system. This brought a uniformity that made it possible for printers to use type and spacing material from any source.

The American *point* is .01384 inches, close enough to ½2 for all practical purposes. Twelve points equal a *pica*, the common unit of horizontal measurement. Thus, 6 picas (72 points) equal one inch.

Printers almost invariably—and very incorrectly —use em and pica interchangeably. A 12-point em, of course, is 1 pica wide and 1 pica tall. But it must be remembered that an em is a unit of area, a pica is a lineal measurement.

The em is commonly used as a measure for composition. Obviously, a compositor who sets a 30-pica line of 36-point type would have to handle only about 26 pieces of type; to set the same length line in agate (5½ point), he would need more than a hundred characters. Ems give a measurement that eliminates such discrepancies. In a 30-pica line (360 points) there are only 10 36-point ems (360 ÷

1 point
1½ point
2 point
3 point
4 point
5 point
6 point
8 point
10 point
12 point
18 point
24 point
30 point
36 point

POINTS AND PICAS are the printer's units of measurement. The American point was standardized in 1886 when several small type foundries, each of which had used its own system, were combined into the still-existing American Type Founders. Then they had to establish a common system, if only for internal compatibility.

Today printers are resisting suggestions that they adopt the metric system, and even phototype is designated by the points shown here. Twelve points make a pica.

36). In the same length of line there are 65.4 agate
(5½-point) ems.

*To determine the amount of composition, convert
line length into points and divide by the point-size
of the type used. This gives ems per line. Multiply
by the number of lines for total production.* This is
the equivalent of *key-strokes* used to measure the
productivity of typists or operators of typesetting
keyboards.

The same anarchy that eventually demanded the
point system also applied to the height of a piece of
type, from the plane· on which it stood to the
printing surface. This was more annoying than
differences in other measurements, for type not
high enough to meet the paper at exactly the same
point as its neighbors just did not print at all; one
only a trifle taller than the rest of the form would
punch into the paper.

This vital measurement was finally standardized
at .918 inches. This is the *height-to-paper* or *type-
high* that is used in the United States, Canada,
England, and most of Latin America.

Until the point system came into use, type sizes
were indicated by name. *Agate* (5½ point) is the
only size still designated by name. Its primary use
is in classified ads, so should such ads be set in 6-
point, the printer—never a linguistic purist—
blithely calls that agate, too!

Smallest size was *diamond* (4½-point). *Minion*
(7-point) and *brevier* (8-point) were popular sizes.
Pica (12-point) gave its name to our measuring
system. *Long primer* was 10-point, *great primer*, 18-
point. *Canon* (48-point) was the largest.

In many ways this nomenclature was as good as
our point system for designating type size, for it has
only a vague reference to the typographical size. It
refers only to the measurement of the rectangular
body upon which the printing face rests.

Before we can explore this paradox, let us look at
the nomenclature of the type character itself. *Primary letters* are those such as *a, o, m,* and *x.* Theirs
is the *x-height* of that particular font. Those that
have projections upward are called *ascenders—d, f,
h, k, l,* and *t*—as are the "necks" themselves. *De-*

TYPE-DESIGN NOMENCLATURE varies a little from that of the metal type itself. The "counter" of a piece of type is the surface of the three-dimensional body from which the relief element protrudes. In type *design* the counter is that area enclosed by a bowl.

It gets its name from a technique of the early type punch-cutter. The face of the character was cut out of the end of a rod of soft iron which was later hardened by annealing. This was the *punch* which was then driven into a softer metal such as brass to make the *mold* or *matrix* from which the type itself was cast.

The punch-cutter could file away the outer perimeter of the letters but, of course, would have an impossible task to scoop out voids such as the inner portion of the O or any other bowl. So he made a *counter-punch*, a relief element in the shape of the area within the bowl. This counter-punch was driven into the punch itself to create the void. The method gives the name to the "counter" of the letterform.

"Leg" applies to the lower extension of the *K*, *k*, and *R* of all variations of the letterform, not only the Italic and Oblique shown here.

scenders refer not only to the downward projections but to the letters that own them—*j, p, q*.

Vertical strokes are *stems;* curved ones make *bowls.* Bottom alignment of primary letters is the *baseline;* at their top is the *mean line* or *x-line.*

Thin lines of Roman letters are *hairlines,* even if they are far thicker than the term commonly connotes.

Diagonal strokes meet at the *apex* of such letters as *A* and at the *vertex* of *V.* So *M* and *W* have both vertex and apex.

When outside strokes of the *M* are not vertical but spread outward, they form a *splayed* letter.

Although the *g,* as a letter, is a descender, its lower loop is called the *tail* (*Q* and *y* also have tails). From the upper loop projects the *claw* (the

ABCDE

ABCDE

FGH

FFGH H

IJKL

JKK LL

MNOPQ

MN OPQ

RSTUV

R STU

WXYZ &

WY gy ε h k

v w z & ct

SWASH LETTERS get their name from "swashbuckling." With the bravado of the Three Musketeers flinging their capes about them, the letterforms sweep out a finishing stroke with a swagger.

In capitals swash strokes to the right must be kerned. Those to the left may either be kerned and thus supported by the quad that precedes a word or be combined with the type.

Here is a typical Old Style Italic. Although this font has only a few swashed lowercase letters, in many fonts the minuscule swashes are almost as many as the caps. Swashed lowercase must always be the terminal letter in a word.

r also has a claw), and connecting the loops of the *g* is the *link* or *neck*. *Loops* are owned by the *e* and some forms of *k*.

Arms are the short strokes, horizontal or upward, from the stem of *Y*, *K*, and *T*. The *cross* of the *t*, *A*, and *H* and the bottom of the loop of *e* are the *bar*. But on *t* and *f*, the short line is the *cross-stroke*.

Serifs on arms are descriptively called *beaks*. The serif-like projection from the short stem on some forms of *G* is the *spur* and *G*'s cross-stroke is sometimes called the *beard* (not to be confused with the same term that is synonymous with the neck of a piece of type).

In most Italics and some Romans, instead of a serif, a hook or sharp curve finishes a stroke in a *finial*. When a letter contains a sweeping, decorative stroke, such as a flourishing tail on *R* or *Q*, both the letter and the stroke are a *swash*.

Those strokes which do not carry a serif or finial are *terminals*. These can be sliced into *acute* or *grave* terminals or they may end in a *ball* such as on certain *c*'s or *a*'s.

By their individual form, certain combinations of letters tend to tie themselves together. These are *ligatures*, the most common of which are those with combinations of *f* such as fi, fl, ff, ffi, and ffl. These are cast on a single body or from a single linecaster matrix.

Logotypes carry more than one letter—often a trademark—on a single body. Logoed letters are not tied together; the *Qu* combination is a logo.

In the process of standardizing height-to-paper and the point system, a standard *lining system* was also adopted, to great relief of printers. Until that time, the baseline of a type face came only where the whim of the designer placed it. If it came 3 points from the lower edge of the body, the printing face would not align with one whose baseline ran, say, 4 points from the bottom. This meant that the printer who had to go to another font to set a word in Greek—in a textbook, for instance—found that word sat higher or lower than the words in Latin letters.

In *standard lining*, all type of one point size will align at the baseline with all other characters of that size, no matter what their design or source.

Some letterforms, usually cursive or swash, have unusually long descenders and thus require more shoulder at the bottom to accommodate these elongated "tails." These are designed for *art lining*. Here the baseline is higher than in standard lining. Art-lining characters will align with all other art lining of the same point size and can be made to align with the standard by using only regular spacing materials.

An alphabet with only capitals needs no room for descenders; its baseline can come close to the edge of the body, *title lining*.

Now, finally, it can be understood why "point size" only vaguely defines the actual size of a face.

The designer, assigned to do an 18-point face, must first set a vertical dimension of 18 points for the body of the type. Then he must establish the baseline. From here on, he is as free as a bird. He may have tall or short primary letters to accommodate long or short ascenders and descenders. If he decides to have long ascenders and descenders, he must make the bowls—and primary letters—smaller; for the length of the projections is limited by the over-all 18-point dimensions of the body. Conversely, if projections are kept short, the bowls and primaries can be taller. So, instead of using the indefinite point size, typographers tend to size a type by its x-height and also by whether its round letters are nearly circular or more oval.

It is difficult to determine the size of type by measuring a printed character. We must remember to measure from the top of the ascenders to the bottom of the descenders and then add the shoulder. In the case of *display type*, from 14-point up, this is easy. But the difference in *body type,* through 12-point, can be slight. It takes a keen eye to differentiate between 5½- and 6-point type, for instance.

Most type used today is of metal. *Foundry type* is cast by type founders, each character, except

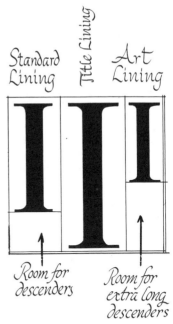

LINING SYSTEMS have been standardized so that all typefaces of the same point-size will have a uniform baseline.

Fonts in *title lining* have only caps. The name comes from the very early practice of setting book titles in all-caps. Fonts in art lining have elongated descenders in lowercase and often Swash capitals to take advantage of the extra space below the baseline.

An interesting face is the popular Caledonia, which, in effect, has both standard and art lining. In text sizes each font is available with short or long descenders. To accommodate the long ones, this Linotype face must then be cast on a slug 1 point deeper than normal. So the 10-point Caledonia in which this book is set would have to be cast on an 11-point slug if long descenders were used, which they are not in this instance.

xylxyl

POINT SIZES are only an approximate designation of size. These two faces are of the same point size—the distance from the top of the *l* to the bottom of the *y*, plus a slight shoulder at the bottom. But the true "size" of the letters is their *x-height*, the height of the x and all other primary letters. In this case the letter at the right has only 75 per cent the x-height of the one at the left.

ligatures, on a separate body. Type *slugs* are manufactured in the composing room; they are complete lines of type. *Monotype type* is cast by the machine that gives it its name, one character at a time but automatically assembled into lines.

Metal type goes as high as 144-point although 96-point is the largest in common use. Beyond that size *wood type* is generally used. Milled from hardwood, it is as smooth and practically as hard as lead and, of course, weighs much less.

All metal printing elements are known collectively as *hot metal,* in contrast to *cold type,* which is produced photographically.

Because cold type is two-dimensional, there is no rigid body to establish its point size. So attempts are being made to use the metric system or the ordinary inch for measurements, at least for cold type. The campaign is not successful. Photoengravers tried for almost a century to persuade printers to specify dimensions in inches; the printers haven't yet capitulated. An educated—and prejudiced—guess would be that points and picas will be around for a long, long time.

But be it hot or cold, the terminology of type and of the men who use it is a language comparatively easy to learn. And, as with all foreign languages, its mastery enables you to work better in the area where it is used.

SUGGESTED READINGS

Hymes, David G. *Production in Advertising.* New York: Henry Holt & Co., Inc., 1958.

Jahn, Hugo. *The Dictionary of Graphic Arts Terms.* Boston: United Typothetae of America, 1932.

Pasko, W. W. (ed.). *American Dictionary of Printing and Bookmaking.* Detroit: Gale Research Co., 1968.

Stevenson, George A. *Graphic Arts Handbook and Production Manual.* Torrance, Calif.: Pen & Pencil, 1961.

In 1470 scribes in Paris went on strike against Gutenberg's invention. In 1887 printers in Baltimore rioted against an infernal new machine that set type mechanically. In the 1960's typesetters struck against Teletypesetting; today in many newspaper plants bitter contractual bargaining goes on as craftsmen seek to keep wire-transmitted tape out of their composing rooms.

In each instance the craftsman fears that he will be displaced by a machine. In each instance he is wrong. Scribes—we call them calligraphers today—are still doing nicely, thank you. In the decade after the invention of the Linotype, production increase of the graphic arts was five times greater than in gross national product. Men set type by hand today, just as Caxton did in England in 1476. New processes seldom replace the old; they merely create new markets big enough for both the modern and ancient crafts.

Many people, especially younger students, are dubious about the need for or desirability of setting type by old methods. They may be assured, though, that this is no waste of time. Just as a pianist must master the simple scales before he can play Moog or Mozart, so the graphic arts practitioner must master the principles of setting hot metal, by hand or machine, if he is to understand the use of cold type for effective communication.

The modern printer still *sticks* or *pegs* type the same way Gutenberg set his first book. On his stick—once actually a wooden receptacle, now a finely tooled metal one—he sets the movable right side to the width of his line, the *measure*. Into it he places a slug of the same length. Then he picks each character from the job case with his right hand. He need not look for the proper compartment any more than a typist must search for the proper key. As he grasps the type and his skilled fingers detect the nick, he turns it to the proper position. In the stick the thumb of the left hand, which holds the stick, keeps the type standing properly. Letter by letter, the type is sticked. Quads or spaces create white space where required.

5

Hot Metal

Setting Type by Man and Machine

When the line is filled, or almost filled, the compositor reads it for errors.

Now he must *justify* it—bring the right-hand margin even with the side of the stick and with all succeeding lines—by adding more space between words or another word or syllable in the line. Justification not only takes time but requires great skill.

The *comp* then places a ledd under the first line and sets the second. When a *stickful* of type has been set, an inch or two, it is dumped into a galley.

One of the greatest calamities that can befall a compositor is to *pi the type*. Pi (pronounced "pie"), as a verb, means to mix up the type by allowing it to fall, either off its feet or out of the stick or galley. As a noun, pi is the mess that results from such a misfortune or clumsiness.

Although a skilled compositor, a *swift,* can set type at a surprising speed, it is still a most inefficient operation, for he works one-handed; the left hand just holds the stick and keeps the type standing.

Probably not long after Gutenberg's day ways were sought to speed the process; one comp hung his stick from his neck so he could peg type with both hands. But it was the Industrial Revolution and the mechanization of many tasks, from sewing to cleaning cotton bolls, that brought the greatest demand for mechanizing typesetting.

Think of the newspaper you read today. If it is an average one, it has over 250,000 individual characters and spaces. To set all of these by hand would require a crew of compositors far too large to house in an efficiently sized room. The increasing number of newspaper pages and the need for a fast method for composition spurred the search by inventors throughout the civilized world.

By 1880 over 40 such machines had been patented. The earliest ones stored each type character in a receptacle from which one piece was released by touching a corresponding key. But once the line was filled, justification still had to be done by hand. This machine was just an extension of an earlier system whereby several compositors set type, then sent their lines to one man who justified the product of several comps.

Neither of these systems solved a vexing concomitant to hand composition, namely, *distribution.* After a handset job is printed, each piece of type and each quad, space, ledd, or slug must be returned to its proper receptacle so that it can be used again. While this distribution takes far less time than setting, it is totally unproductive labor.

One of the first notable typesetting machines was the *Paige Compositor.* Its fame came not from its performance, which was disappointing, but from its major financial backer, Mark Twain. It now reposes in the Mark Twain Museum in Hartford, Conn. Before it was written off as a failure, it had consumed most of the author's considerable fortune and had forced him to spend his declining years, not in the leisure he deserved, but on the arduous lecture circuit to pay off his debts.

Solving the typesetting problem wrote a new name into the annals of the graphic arts: Ottmar Mergenthaler. A German like Gutenberg, he also shares a distinguished rank in history; his invention has been called one of the 10 greatest of all time.

He came to America as a young man and soon after his arrival met a court reporter, James O. Clephane, who sought a quick method of converting shorthand into multiple written copies. After several disheartening failures, which saw feasible laboratory devices fail in practice, Mergenthaler advanced on his own, backed by a group of newspaper publishers.

His typesetting machine was first demonstrated on July 3, 1886, in the composing room of the *New York Tribune,* which Horace Greeley had brought to fame and which was then edited by Whitelaw Reid, a giant in American journalism and organizer of the syndicate which financed the inventor.

The key to Mergenthaler's success was the *circulating matrix.* Basically, the operation of that 1886 machine was the same as that of today's refined and speeded-up machines.

CIRCULATING MATRICES, the key to the success of the Linotype, follow the path marked on this ghosted machine.

Action on the keyboard (A) releases matrices from the magazine (B). Tiny trapdoors at the bottom of the magazine open swiftly to allow the matrices to drop by gravity to where a belt (C) carries them to the assembling area (D).

Matrices are gathered in a vise, set to the measure being set. The line justified by expanding spacebands is moved up to the left and down again to E. In the circle behind E are four tiny boxlike molds to which the line of type makes the bottom. From the pot (invisible behind E) is forced molten type metal to fill the little box and make a Linotype slug.

After casting, the line of type drops into the galley (H). The matrices are lifted straight upward, and the spacebands are removed and returned to their storage area, directly above D. Like a mechanical hand and arm, a lever picks up the matrices and lifts them in an arc (F) to the distributing bar (G), from which they hang until sorted out and returned to their proper channel in the magazine.

This whole cycle takes place from eight to a score of times a minute. Cycles overlap; matrices are constantly being distributed. Others are being assembled at C and D while the casting operation goes on for the previous line. The operator who has assembled a line of matrices before the previous line has been cast is said to *hang the elevator*.

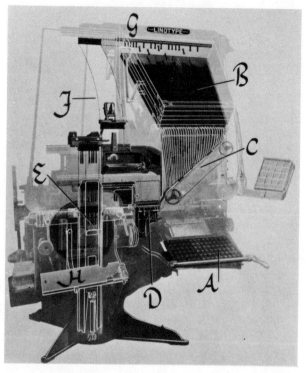

A shallow rhomboid-shaped container is divided into 90 vertical *channels*, each containing *matrices* for one character. This *matrix* is a piece of brass, bearing in one side the mold for the given character. When the operator presses a key, the corresponding matrix is released and drops onto a belt that carries it into an assembling area. Successively, each proper matrix is released until enough are assembled to fill a line. Justification is achieved by *spacebands* between words. These bands are an ingenious combination of two wedges. When they are pushed upward, they expand so that the line is exactly filled.

Now the line is moved over in front of a *pot* containing molten metal. A metal frame forms four sides of a box, the matrices the fifth, and the mouthpiece of the pot, the sixth. When the molten metal is forced into the "box," the result is a rectangular piece of metal bearing on one side the line of relief characters cast from the matrices. This is the "line of type" that gives the machine its name. The *type metal* is an alloy of lead, tin, and antimony. It is eutectic; it has the unusual characteristic of expanding when it cools. This assures that metal will be forced into the smallest cavities of the matrix and will cast a perfect mirror image of the matrix.

When the line has been cast, it drops into a shallow tray, the galley. The machine can cast up to 22 newspaper-column lines per minute.

After casting, matrices are lifted to the top of the machine and pushed back over the magazine. They are supported on a triangular, grooved *distributor bar* and hang from the teeth that are arranged in a characteristic triangular pattern at the top of the matrix. Grooves in the bar are keyed to the tooth combination just as a key matches notches in a lock. When the matrix is directly above its proper channel, it is released and drops for immediate reuse.

The number of matrices per channel depends on the frequency with which that letter appears in

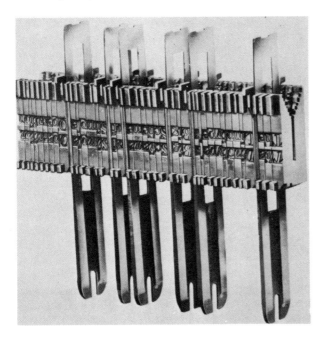

LINOTYPE MATRICES and spacebands are gathered in a line, ready for casting. The spaceband is a pair of wedges. When they are pushed from below, the two triangles of the wedges form a small rectangle which makes the space between words. If this space is not completely filled, an embarrassing *front squirt* occurs. The molten type metal is forced through the opening and may easily burn the operator as well as create the problem of removing the quickly hardening metal from other parts of the machine.

The side showing in this picture makes the bottom of the box in which the line of type is cast. On the other side of the matrices the operator can see small *reference characters* which tell him whether he has the proper characters in the proper order before he casts the line.

A simple safety device can prevent this calamity in most instances, fortunately.

LINOTYPE SLUGS, not to be confused with *spacing slugs,* are in the familiar upside-down position and in mirror form in the galley, the storage tray on the machine. From here the galley is taken to the *dump* or *bank,* where it is stored until ready to be locked into a form.

English sentences. The operator never has to wait for matrices; he sets one line while the preceding one is being cast.

The advantages of the *Linotype* are obvious. Each line of type is brand-new with perfect printing surfaces. There is no distribution problem; after the type has been used, it is simply remelted, and fresh type is cast from it. Keyboarding is much faster than sticking type by hand; justification is automatic. Slugs are much easier to handle than individual pieces of type, and danger of pi-ing is minimized.

The Linotype was so popular that within 10 years it had gone into use as far away as Hawaii, as well as in Europe. It gave an impetus that boomed the graphic arts industry; efficient typesetting lowered costs and increased demand.

When Mergenthaler's basic patents expired, a new machine, the *Intertype,* was put on the market. Basically, there is no difference between these two machines; both are *keyboarded linecasters.* Similar machines were made in Europe; all are given the generic label of "linotype" with a small *l.* In 1971 the

Mergenthaler Company considered manufacture of Linotypes in one of its European plants. Manufacture of matrices and replacement parts could continue profitably in the United States, but phototypesetting was displacing hot-metal in the new-machine market.

This does not suggest that the Linotype—with a cap or small *l*—will soon become obsolete. These machines seem never to wear out, and when they are replaced in a composing room, they don't go to the scrap heap but to a smaller shop while its machine goes down to the next-sized shop. Thus more and more printers can own their own typesetting machines, can lower the price of composition, and can make printing a competitive alternative to Mimeographing. The broadening of the economic base of linotype ownership will assure the existence of the machine for many more decades. And the keyboarded linecaster is still the most efficient means of producing the *straight matter*, the news content, of a metropolitan daily newspaper. We need not weep prematurely over the departure of an old friend.

For it even played a part in the moon flights and landings!

The constantly increasing electrical wiring required on airplanes and the even more complex systems in spacecraft long had made it impractical to designate various circuits by insulation of various colors. So Linotype slugs were developed in a concave form that would print identifying names right on the round surface of electric wires.

The melding of two crafts and two eras— Mergenthaler's and Werner von Braun's—is another of the pleasant incongruities so often found in the graphic arts.

Most Linotype and Intertype matrices through 24-point are *duplexed;* they have two individual molds on each piece of brass. The most common duplex is Roman with Italic, or *fullface*—the normal weight —with boldface. In a few instances two entirely different faces or sizes are duplexed. Twenty-four-point Spartan Black Condensed is duplexed with 18-

MAN AND MACHINE are compared in size in this diagram of an average man—5 feet, 10 inches—against a typical Intertype. Height of the machine remains constant although it may carry from one to eight magazines of matrices.

point Spartan Heavy, for instance. Standard machines cast a maximum 30-pica line, although there are some 42-pica machines for specialized composition.

Another American linecaster is the *Ludlow*. It does not have a keyboard; matrices are assembled by hand.

Although Ludlow casts type from 8- through 144-point, its major use is for larger sizes. Ludlow matrices are kept in a case roughly similar to the California case but with only a few matrices of each character. They are shaped so that the operator can easily gather several in his hand before placing them in a special stick. Spacing is created by blank matrices; justification and centering are performed automatically by the stick. The assembled line is placed into the casting device where the rest of the process is automatic. Matrices are distributed by hand after each line is cast.

Operation is far speedier than setting foundry type. Italic matrices are slanted so that the letters fit tightly, without kerning. Ludlow slugs are T-shaped. The body forms the stem; the type, the cross bar. Low slugs, *underpinning*, support the overhanging portion of the face. Although the maximum line cast by the Ludlow is 22½ picas, lines can be butted with no apparent break.

A companion to the Ludlow is the *Elrod Caster*, which produces *strip material:* ledds, slugs, rules, underpinning for Ludlow slugs, and bases for engravings and stereotypes.

The Elrod produces a continuous strip of material from 1- through 36-point thickness. Molten metal is constantly fed into the mold, where it is cast, solidified under pressure, and ejected at one end, while molding continues at the other. The machine can also be set to cut off the strips at any given length.

A year after Mergenthaler brought out his first Linotype, another inventor, Tolbert Lanston, received a patent for the *Monotype*. Instead of setting a whole line of type as a slug, the Monotype casts individual characters and assembles them in a justified line up to 60 picas wide.

Two separate machines make up the Monotype system. The operator works at a keyboard similar to, but larger than, that on a typewriter. This produces a roll of paper into which has been punched coded holes; it looks very much like the rolls for player pianos.

This *controller paper* actuates the second unit, the casting machine. Actual casting is done from matrices in a small *matrix case,* about the size of a man's hand. In body sizes, there are 225 matrices in the case, about two-and-a-half times more characters than are available in a Linotype magazine.

The matrix case is positioned over the casting mold. Holes in the controller paper direct a complex of springs that move the case so that the proper matrix is directly over the mold. Metal is forced into the matrix to form the character. The cast is cooled immediately by water and pushed into a galley until a whole line has then been assembled.

Justification is automatic. All characters in a Monotype font are designed in increments of one-eighteenth of an em. Quads necessary to justify the line are also made in such increments. As the operator punches keys, a gauge shows him how much space is left in the line. When the line is wide enough to justify, the operator is told by the gauge how wide the quads must be, and he presses the proper key to encode that information into the paper.

Advantages of Monotype composition are obvious. The operator has many characters available to him; this is especially useful in setting a textbook, for example, where words in non-Latin alphabets must be interpolated or where many scientific symbols are used. The casting machine is fast—150 casts per minute; thus, the output of several keyboard operators may be fed into the caster.

Corrections are easy. Instead of having to recast a whole line to correct one wrong letter, as with the Linotype, a Monotype error can be corrected by simply changing that single letter.

The ability to change a single character is especially valuable in the case of tabulated figures, a

stock market table, or a tariff schedule, which
change frequently but only partially. Figures can
be changed without resetting the entire line. Because such *tabular setting* is a time-consuming process, Monotype's flexibility is especially desirable.

The Monotype can also be used to produce strip
material.

Like the linecasters, Monotype produces material
for *nondistribution* use. This means that after the
type has been printed, it is not distributed but
remelted. In a newspaper plant, for instance, after
the edition has been printed, only a few elements
are saved from a page form, the nameplate on the
front page or an ad on an inside page which will be
rerun later. Then the whole page is pushed off the
edge of the stone into a wheeled container and
hauled to the remelt pot.

The Monotype *Giant Caster* and the *Monotype
Thompson Caster* produce individual type characters, which are stored in California job cases and
are set just like foundry type, by hand. Both are, in
effect, small type foundries and give the advantages
of new type for every job as well as those of nondistribution of used material.

The same needs of newspapers that encouraged
the invention of the Linotype later brought the
invention of the *Teletypesetter, TTS.* Although the
first commercially successful TTS was introduced in
1928, the device really came into its own only in the
period immediately after World War II, and its
use is still growing.

The TTS is an attachment to the Linotype or
Intertype. It is a tape-operated machine that translates coded information. It uses perforated tape,
similar to that of the Monotype but only about a
quarter as wide. This tape may be punched locally
on a unit very similar to an electric typewriter, or
may be transmitted by wire from distant points.

News services had long used *Teletypewriters* to
transmit copy. An operator types the story at a
central news bureau. Each key action is translated
into a series of electrical impulses, which are carried by telegraph or telephone wires, or even radio

TELETYPESETTER TAPE is shown
in the actual size in which it
emerges from wire-service machines or from local perforators.
This is a 6-level tape. The tiny
holes in the center are not part
of the code; they are engaged
by a cogwheel to move the tape.

waves, to a distant newspaper office. There the impulses actuate a typewriter, which simultaneously reproduces the original typing. These same impulses perforate tape in the news office even as they produce typescript.

The coded tape is fed into the TTS operating unit on the linecaster where its information is translated into mechanical movements which, in effect, duplicate the action of an operator's fingers on the keyboard to set type.

Advantages are many, in addition to those of tape already discussed for the Monotype. A single operator in New York City, let us say, can punch tape that is simultaneously reperforated in newspapers throughout the country. There, typesetting is virtually automatic. One man, the *monitor,* can service up to four or five linecasters. He feeds tape, removes filled galleys of type, keeps the metal pots filled, and corrects any minor mechanical difficulties. The substantial savings of TTS have enabled many a small newspaper to remain operative since World War II. Not only does this method save that time, which is never plentiful in news operations, it has also enabled many a publisher to overcome the pressing lack of Linotype operators which seems to be chronic in America.

Electro-Typesetting, ETS, is a newer variation of tape-operation. Although it uses electronic, rather than mechanical, power and bypasses the conventional keyboard to operate directly upon the matrix-release mechanism, its similarity to TTS is far greater than its disparity.

Tape operation has been expanded in several ways. Extra instructions can be coded into the tape so that matrices may be drawn out of more than one magazine within a single line. As this style is much used in foodstore advertising—name and price set in 36-point, separated by two lines of descriptive matter in 18-point, for instance—its mechanization saves crucial time.

Instead of being punched in rolls of paper, the coded holes may be placed in computer cards, which can be used to actuate the linecaster. Such

MIXED COMPOSITION such as these typical food-advertising elements are done on a special *mixer* Linotype. Matrices are drawn from two separate magazines and properly distributed after casting.

The *Silver Dust* item shows how the 2, the price, and the small word *large* are set in a single U-shaped slug (*a*). Then *pkgs.* is set on a separate recessed slug (*b*) that fits into the opening of the one above.

This work, so common in advertising today, formerly had to be done by hand with the operator cutting and assembling the slugs involved. Today the mixer does it automatically.

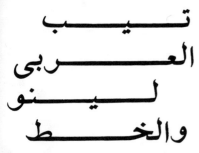

NASTALIQ, a form of Arabic Script, is set on the Linotype in a most ingenious technique.

A style of Arabic developed in Persia at the end of the four-teenth century, Nastaliq is much used for Urdu, one of the main languages of Pakistan. A lovely face, it reads right to left and is set in the conventional left-to-right manner by turning the matrices upside down.

An unusual characteristic of Nastaliq is that the same char-acter must be written with dif-ferent "base lines," depending on the letters adjacent to them. This requires a font of as many as 200 different characters and variations of them. This is some three times more matrices than a Linotype can store,. and con-sequently Urdu newspapers have been written by hand and printed lithographically.

Simplifying the Script to a single alignment now makes it possible to set Nastaliq me-chanically.

There is often great resistance to any modification of an alpha-bet, though. For years the hierarchy of the Coptic Church in Ethiopia prevented the altera-tions to Amharic which would allow machine setting. Theirs is a syllabary in which the vowel-sound character remains con-

cards may readily be sorted out, and any or all of the information coded into it may be used for specific composition needs. For a city directory all the material on the card can be typeset; the same card can be used to set only name, address, and number for a telephone directory. Adding and de-leting such cards is simple.

Tape or cards are easy to transport and store and eliminate two major problems affecting hot metal type itself.

Composition by tape is most frequently used by newspapers, but it is becoming increasingly popular for books and commercial typesetting. Union re-strictions have prevented its maximum utilization but leaders in the craft believe that, like the original mechanization of typesetting by the Linotype, wider use of automatic tape composition will prove to be a stimulus to the already important growth of the industry.

Almost a thousand different languages and dia-lects can be set in the Linotype. These include the beautiful Eastern Scripts as well as the right-to-left-reading Semitic languages. Only the ideographic languages cannot be keyboarded (and this because of the lack of storage for the many matrices re-quired). But Korean has been simplified and will be on the Lino too, it appears.

Although hot metal is certainly past its heyday, it remains and will remain the foundation upon which all good typography is built. Even today, a substantial number of the *Fifty Books of the Year* selected annually by the American Institute of Graphic Arts are set by hand. The most elegant advertising composition is entrusted only to the handsetter. The least expensive way of producing a small letterhead or a few calling cards is still by setting them in a stick.

The study of hand composition will long remain an elementary—and rewarding—one for everyone in the graphic arts.

SUGGESTED READINGS

Elements of Composition. Unit I of the ITU Lessons in Printing. Indianapolis, Ind.: International Typographic Union, 1950.

Jackson, Hartley E. *Printing: A Practical Introduction to the Graphic Arts.* New York: McGraw-Hill Book Co., Inc., 1957.

Mengel, Willi. *Ottmar Mergenthaler and the Printing Revolution.* Brooklyn: Mergenthaler Linotype Co., 1954.

Orcutt, William Dana, and Bartlett, Edward E. *Manual of Linotype Composition.* New York: Mergenthaler Linotype Co., 1923.

stant, with appendages to designate the consonant of the syllable.

To carry these on separate matrices meant that the strokes could not overlap a vertical division line. It was simple to swing the consonantal extension into its own area without destroying either its legibility or beauty.

But political opponents charged heresy; to change the form in which their Scriptures were written was altering the True Word, charged the defenders of the status quo. It was not until after World War II, when Emperor Haile Selassie personally sought a use for Linotypes captured from Mussolini's Fascist forces, that the necessary modifications of Amharic were made, so that today it can be set on the line-caster.

یہ اردو کے الفاظ جو کہ آپ پڑھ رہے ہیں ١
مشہور و معروف لائنوٹائپ مشین پر کمپوز
کئے گئے ہیں - یہ اردو تاریخ میں پہلی
دفعہ نستعلیق رسم خط مکانئی طریقہ کار سے
اپنایا گیا ہے - توقع ہے کہ نیا لائنوٹائپ ڈیزائن
اردو بولنے والوں میں کافی مقبول ہوگا اور
اس سے لوگوں کو اشاعت تعلیم میں فائدہ

The specimen above shows the interesting texture of Nastaliq even in this greatly reduced form. Below is an example of the written form showing the several alignments for three different characters, each indicated by the dotted lines, and the new single-alignment type.

6

The Electronic Era

Type by Camera and Computer

The graphic arts industry came into the electronic age legitimately. During World War II all civilian industries were converted to military needs, and manufacturers of graphic arts machinery helped build the arsenals for the Allies. Because of their skill in producing machines "as sturdy as a locomotive with the precision of a Swiss watch"—a description often applied to the Linotype and the rotary press—many graphic craftsmen became involved in the new field of electronics as well as the older one of optics. A marriage of the two produced phototypesetting.

Letterpress needs three-dimensional type to deposit ink on paper, but planography and intaglio need only a picture of the type from which to prepare plates. Ever since the latter processes came into practical use, men have sought ways to compose type photographically. They knew that manipulation of light photographic film or paper would effect substantial savings of time, energy, and money over the more laborious assembling of weighty metal.

As early as the 1880's patents had been granted for phototypesetting machines, but it was not until after World War II, when the whole graphic arts industry was in a ferment of research, that photocomposition became practical.

Photocomposition is called *cold type,* a logical differentiation from the *hot metal* of linecasters.

The first of such machines was Intertype's *Fotosetter.* This was a conventional Intertype with a camera device replacing the casting mechanism. It used the principle of circulating matrices. Through the wide side of the mat a hole is bored, and into it is inserted a piece of black plastic with the negative image of the character in reverse. This takes the place of the mold in the conventional matrix.

A line of matrices was assembled and justified, just as in hot-metal casting. But now each matrix was lifted so that a beam of light could project through the film and produce a picture of the character on photographic film or paper. After photography, the matrices are distributed, the film is moved up, and the second line is photographed.

By exposing the character negative through different lenses, it was possible to produce from 4- through 36-point type from only two fonts of matrices.

The Fotosetter and Mergenthaler's *Linofilm* were both shown for the first time at a great Chicago graphic arts show in 1950. The first one since the great war, it created tremendous excitement in the industry. But none of the fascinating displays drew greater crowds or generated more discussion and interest than these two phototypesetters.

Both these first-generation phototypesetters used the circulating matrix principle of the linecaster. But they also had all the handicaps of the linecaster —moving metal parts and a built-in speed limitation. Harnessing photography to metal-casting procedures was as inefficient as putting a jet airplane engine into the canvas fuselage of Snoopy's Sopwith Camel.

But Fotosetters went into production and commercial use immediately. For a few years they were alone in the field; today they are obsolete. That sentence indicates the speed with which major advances and radical new concepts have swept the typesetting field. These have been so many that even periodicals are hard-pressed to stay abreast of developments. This book will present categories rather than specifically named machines; the use or ignoring of trade names has definitely no implication of value judgment.

While the Fotosetters were being built and sold, the Linofilm went back to the drawing board and reemerged, along with the *Photon,* as a totally photographic-electronic machine. The Fotosetter served the industry well during the transitional period of the early 50's and later was replaced by the current *Fototronic.*

Of the second generation of phototypesetters, there are two major classes. The Photon—and today the Fototronic—carry their negatives on a *spinning disk* revolving up to 80 times a second. The latest model has 240 characters available on each of five interchangeable disks. When the selected negative is in the proper position, a stroboscopic light bulb emits a beam for .000004 seconds. This freezes the motion of the disk just as similar light stops the action of an athlete for the news camera.

A variation is the *revolving disk,* of which the *AIF Typesetter* was an early and typical version. Here negatives are on a glass disk that moves the desired character into position, stops long enough for the exposure to be made, then revolves to the next position.

The other major kind of machine is the Linofilm, which uses a stationary optical system.

The original Linofilm carries its negatives on a *grid* of one alphabet. It remains stationary behind a group of *lenslets,* one for each character and each covered with a tiny shutter. Each lenslet is focused on the identical spot; were they all to be exposed at one time, images would pile up on each other. But the shutters remain closed until the tape signals a specific character; its shutter opens, allowing a strobe beam to shine through the negative and onto the photo film or paper. A moving mirror directs each image to the proper position on the film.

The *Monophoto,* the photographic equivalent of the Monotype, uses the same principle as the hot-metal version, except that the matrix case now holds negatives and is called the *master negative case.* Just as the hot-metal case shifts to bring the Monotype matrix over the casting box, so the negative case shifts to bring the proper character into alignment between light, lens, and photo paper.

The Monophoto produces type on photographic film; the other three machines on film or paper. As the original image in all machines is a negative, the machines' products are right-reading positives. But a simple chemical reaction converts them into right-reading negatives. Thus the proper copy for letterpress, offset, and gravure platemaking may be produced without the intermediate step of photographing pasteups to obtain negatives.

The most sophisticated method in current use is the *cathode-ray tube* system, *CRT.* Because it takes many pages of a book this size to describe an

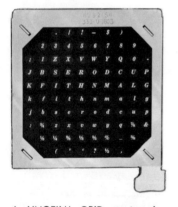

A LINOFILM GRID carries the equivalent of several fonts of foundry type because the image on the negative can be enlarged or reduced by lenses. The grid is 4 inches square.

operation that takes only a millisecond, the following explanation will be oversimplified. It will not necessarily describe specific features of any given machine but will show only the principles involved in sufficient detail to satisfy the needs of the generalist graphic artsman.

In simplest of terms, CRT composition creates pictures of the various characters on a television tube. This "video" picture is projected onto photographic paper. There are two ways of producing the "TV picture," *projection* and *digitizing*.

The first method is used by the *Linotron,* called at the Government Printing Office "the fastest, largest, and most expensive photocomposing machine in the business." As the first two syllables of its name indicate, this is a product of the Mergenthaler Linotype Company, which developed the $2-million machine after four years of collaboration with the CBS Laboratories. The photographic negatives of the more conventional Linofilm grid are projected upon the light-sensitive cathode of the tube, which converts the light-ray image into a cathode-ray image.

The *Videocomp* 822, built by the Radio Corporation of America, uses the digitized character method. Those initials—RCA and CBS—so familiar to audiences of broadcast and recording media, indicate only a hint of the many giants of other industries that have recently entered the graphic arts. International Business Machine is another.

The 822 is directed by a computer; its *computer composition* process is known as *ComCom*. A binary computer, which can make only a simple yes-or-no, on-or-off instruction, sends such advice to an electronic impulse racing across horizontal rows of phosphorescent spots.

In the Videocomp, 36,000 such spots are scanned each second. By lighting selected spots and allowing the others to remain dark, the desired character is formed. Each character must be fed into the machine in a series of off-on instructions.

A basic font consists of 80 characters, but this is only the beginning. Additional characters such as accented letters, small caps, Old Style figures, inferior and superior characters, and several others add another 120 characters. Then—and here is where the numbers get formidable—each digitized character can be displayed on the TV screen in over 100 configurations including Perpendicular and Oblique, Extended and Condensed, Extended, inferiors with normal prime characters, etc., etc., *and* etc.!

Speed of these machines is almost supersonic. The *Fototronic CRT* (the lineal descendant of the original Fotosetter) generates digitized images of 7-point type at a rate of 10 to 15 thousand a second.

The Linotron generates a thousand characters per second. But it is a *page* or *area printer*. Such machines produce a whole page at a time; the Linotron can do an 8 x 10½-inch page in 5 or 6 seconds. To reduce these figures to understandable terms: the Linotron could set the Bible in type in 77 minutes! This job, incidentally, took Gutenberg much the better part of five years.

It became apparent very early that the only efficient way to operate phototypesetters was by tape. Because the operator has no physical matrices and spacebands to readjust, as he often must in hot-metal setting, it is necessary to compute spacing specifications *after* characters have been assembled but before they can be photographed on the output material. This paradox can be resolved only by allowing the machine to read the spacing code first—although it is the last element in a line of instructions. That requires a memory unit within the machine or the much simpler and inexpensive tape.

Use of paper tape—or its equivalent of magnetic tape or wire—makes the typesetting machines—hot or cold—compatible with the ubiquitous computer. The electronic brain was already in the outer reaches of the graphic arts, for its output was in the form of printing, the *printout*. It was logical and inevitable that matrimony was in the offing. Today the computer is a familiar sight in many a compos-

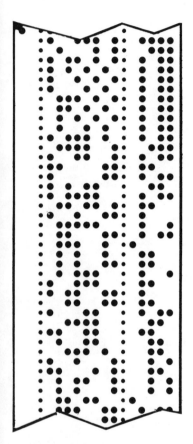

SOPHISTICATED TAPE used for most advanced phototypesetting machines as well as for computers carries 13 levels which allow the great number of codes required for complex composition. Note that this tape, shown in actual size, has two rows of holes for its propulsion system.

SHIFT / UNSHIFT	Tape Feed	T / t	Return	O / o	Space Band	N / n	H / h	M / m	Elevate	I / i	R / r	C / c	L / l	P / p	G / g	V / v	E / e	A / a	S / s	U / u	D / d	J / j	F / f	K / k	Z / z	W / w.	Y / y	Q / q	B / b	Shift
0																	•	•	•	•	•	•	•	•	•	•	•	•	•	•
1						•	•	•	•	•	•	•	•		•		•		•		•		•		•		•		•	•
2						•	•	•	•	•	•	•	•		•		•		•		•		•		•		•		•	•
TAPE FEED	∘	∘	∘	∘	∘	∘	∘	∘	∘	∘	∘	∘	∘	∘	∘	∘	∘	∘	∘	∘	∘	∘	∘	∘	∘	∘	∘	∘	∘	∘
3				•	•	•	•	•		•		•		•		•	•				•	•		•	•			•	•	
4		•	•		•		•		•		•	•					•	•	•	•							•	•	
5	•		•			•	•			•	•		•	•							•	•	•	•	•	•	•		

x / x	Unshift	Thin Space	⅜ 3	2 P.F. or Mag.	! £	add Thin/Mag. 4	Em Space	— 8	⅞ 7	‡	½ Hyphen	3 4 Bell or Mag.	Comma	Quad Left	En Space	1 Q.R. or Mag.	⅜ 5	( )	V. Rule Em Sp	¼ 2	¾ Em Leader	? 6	& En Leader	: 9	; Upper Rail	Lower Rail	Period 1	⅛ Quad Center	Rub Out
		•	•	•	•	•	•	•	•	•	•	•	•	•	•	•	•	•	•	•	•	•	•	•	•	•	•	•	•
•	•		•		•		•		•		•		•		•		•		•		•		•		•		•		•
	•			•	•		•	•			•	•			•	•			•	•			•	•			•	•	
∘	∘	∘	∘	∘	∘	∘	∘	∘	∘	∘	∘	∘	∘	∘	∘	∘	∘	∘	∘	∘	∘	∘	∘	∘	∘	∘	∘	∘	∘
∘	∘				•	•	•	•				•	•	•	•					•	•	•	•				•	•	•
•	•					•	•	•	•	•	•								•	•	•	•	•	•	•	•		
•	•										•	•	•	•	•	•	•	•	•	•	•	•	•	•				

ing room even though its function is unfamiliar to many printers.

The major use of computers in typesetting today is to solve the problems of justifying lines. It can do that with its simple binary, yes-or-no decision-making.

When a human typesetter approaches the end of a line of metal type, he must determine whether he can get in one more word or syllable. If the latter, he must determine whether the next word can be hyphenated and where. When he has gathered all the possible characters, he must determine how much more, or less, space is needed to justify the lines and where it can be placed, between words conventionally or as letterspacing within words. This end-of-line decision takes the time that sharply limits his productivity.

That same decision must be made by the tape-puncher, even though he doesn't have to do the physical manipulation of justification. But now the computer takes over. The operator punches the tape without any regard to the finished line of type. He merely indicates the regular paragraph indent and where that graf ends. Without making end-of-

VISUAL CODE in 6-level tape enables an editor to "read" it as he would ordinary typewritten copy. As tape comes off Teletype, it is rolled into a small loop, labeled, and then stored on a peg board until the time for setting. Often tape of different colors is used to designate local tape or that for future use, such as for a Sunday edition of a newspaper.

line decisions, he can increase his speed markedly. Now all that is needed is ordinary typist's skills, not those of a compositor.

His product is called *raw tape* or—out of his hearing—*idiot tape*. It is fed into a computer, which converts it into another tape that will ultimately produce justified lines of type, hot or cold. And this is all the computer does!

But this task is performed in degrees of finesse. If letterspacing is required to justify the line, a sophisticated computer will not place it in the first word or in a very short word but rather in a longer one and within the line where it will be less obtrusive. The simplest computer will justify lines without hyphenation of any kind; the more capable will syllabify as handily as a human being. Unfortunately, the computer must proceed according to the logic or set of rules stored in its memory. Equally unfortunately, in our polyglot English spelling there are many, many exceptions. So we have the computer breaking such unbreakable words as *thro/ugh* or *sho/es* or making a syllable of the silent *-ed* of *stopped, rowed,* etc. Each exception must be fed into the electronic memory so the computer can search that list before hyphenating. Names of prominent men—Khrushchev was a notable example—can be listed that way. But when a little-known name comes up, the poor computer is stumped.

When newspapers started using computers, they found it an easy alibi for slovenly craftsmanship. Lines of type garbled in a news story were blamed on the poor computer. Even poor presswork was sloughed off because, the reader was told, "We're using a computer now and this is a breaking-in period!" Don't you believe it.

One interesting machine, the *Linasec,* uses a human teammate. At the rate of 60 newspaper lines per minute, this computer justifies raw tape. But when it needs to hyphenate, it merely displays the word on a TV screen. By pushing an appropriate button between a pair of letters, the human suggests the point where a hyphen would be correct. If that word-break solves the problem, the machine continues. If not, the human tries again. The typical 11-pica newspaper setting creates a hyphenation once every five lines.

Working with the Linasec, the monitor can, in 25 minutes, handle an hour's output of five operators producing raw tape. A similar technique is used by the IBM *MTSC* (Magnetic Tape Selectric Composer), a sophisticated typewriter which types out the too-long word but allows a human typist to make the necessary and proper break by retyping the word or syllable.

Of course, the computer can do only what some human programmer instructs it to. So specifications for typesetting styles must be given in typewritable codes. To set the following typical entries in a phone directory requires the following typewritten instructions:

```
Mason M. W, 122 City rd EC1 ............SHO 7121
Mason N, 407 Green lanes NW3 ..........FIN 3120
Mason P. & K. Ltd, Nwsagt, Fig ct W4 ....ACT 4525
```

smuason sm. w, u122 scuity rd secul............rssho u7121R

smuason sn, u407 sgureen lanes snwu3 ....rsfin u3120R

smuason sp. & k. lutd, snuwsagt, sfuig ct swu4.....rsact u4525R

The boldface signals mean:

r, rail shift (giving boldface in this case, or Italic);

s, shift for upper case;

u, unshift from upper case;

R, return, and

E, elevate (send matrices over for casting).

To speed up the original typing, a keyboard shorthand has been developed by Mergenthaler for the Linasec. Highly repetitive words such as *the, and, of,* etc., can be keyboarded by a single stroke. Time savings for these common but unobtrusive words is substantial because of their frequency.

The word *the* normally requires five strokes—spaceband, *t, h, e,* and spaceband. A single stroke reduces this by 80 per cent, and the overall saving of time and effort typically is 14 per cent.

There are other fascinating alliances between

OPTICAL SCANNING NEWSLETTER

OPTICAL RECOGNITION CHARACTERS are designed for maximum distinction among letterforms so machines can read them. Note the marked difference between the C and O and the heavy serifs on the I.

computer and typesetter. The Navy translated Russian scientific articles into English with a machine that "read" printed pages and printed out the translation. Of course, the text was awkwardly phrased, but it was adequate to determine which article was important enough to warrant a smoother translation. The officers who read the computer output, though, were quickly fatigued by the poor readability of the printout, and their efficiency was limited. When the translating machine was connected to a Linofilm with its good typography, man-machine efficiency zoomed so rapidly that the investment was quickly repaid.

This ability of a machine to "read" type was dramatically illustrated by a "first" by the Linotron in 1970. A United States publisher wanted to bring out an American edition of a popular British novel, *Death's Bright Dart*, in an entirely new format and type face. The actual printed pages of the book, with no further markings, were fed one by one into an *OCR* (*optical character recognition*) machine. This produced digital electronic impulses—a form of idiot tape—which then went into a computer where the book was reformatted into a completely new typographic style with—*mirabile dictu!*—Americanized spelling and punctuation! Labour became labor; theatre, theater; cheque, check; etc. And all without human intervention. Setting was by Linotron.

At this writing an even more amazing machine is being readied for delivery to the Air Force. Verbal input to an advanced-model Linotron will be stored on magnetic tape while pictures—both line and halftone—will be stored on video tape. These two elements will be combined into complete pages by cathode-ray tube!

When we hear prophets predict that we will be "setting type" merely by speaking into a microphone, it takes a courageous skeptic to demur very loudly. For another conversion, from type to sensory tactile impulse, is already here. Called *Optacon*, it is designed for the blind. The "reader" passes a photoelectric sensor, fitted into a lipstick-sized case, over the printed page. His other hand rests on a signal-reading surface through which he feels the shape of the letters read by the sensor. Some blind persons have learned in only months of training to read as many as 60 words a minute, and those facile in Braille can read much faster than that. (*Braille*, incidentally, is produced on a printing press. Ingenious fitting makes it possible to emboss the raised dots of the code on both sides of the paper to reduce the·bulk of a book by a half.)

Some machines read printing only for their own purpose. The odd characters at the bottom of your checks are examples. These are read by a machine that directs fiscal information to the proper account, yours and your bank's. These odd characters are printed in *magnetic ink* around which are designed optically recognizable characters for the rare instances when a human eye must read it. Other systems use *optical scanning;* the machine recognizes the visual form of the letters. Here the characters must be changed markedly from their common form. No commercial machine scanner can as yet distinguish between an *e* and an *o*, for instance, although that OCR that "translated" the British novel can recognize even handwritten characters. It is, however, still only an experimental prototype.

Letterforms designed for mechanical reading are ugly to our eyes, but they are eminently functional for the electronic reader. Because the human eye need not cope with these forms very often, it can forgive the lack of aesthetic appeal.

It is possible to do drafting by phototypesetting. Architectural symbols can be combined from negatives and made into a "blueprint" much more quickly and uniformly than they can be drawn by a draftsman. And electrical circuits can not only be "drawn" quickly in the same manner, they can immediately be converted into *printed circuitry.* This technique, in which an electrically conductive ink is printed on a plate or where circuits are etched into metal similarly to a photoengraving, has played a major role in miniaturization that, among other things, makes space rocketry possible.

MAGNETIC-INK CHARACTERS are read by electric-sensitive scanners. Then a visually recognizable, if awkward, design is formed around the code.

PHOTOGRAPHIC MANIPULA-
TION of the letterform is shown
by this setting on the Linofilm
Composer. The *5* and *th* were
enlarged to an arbitrary size
with no regard to any point increments.

Experiments are proceeding favorably in the combining of elements in a newspaper ad by computer instruction, and some newspapers arrange classified ads into proper categories and in alphabetical order by computer, then set them into type photographically. This technique has been perfected by dictionary compositors. The alphabetizing of words is not too difficult. But when a word has more than one meaning, each supplied by a different editor, or when it can be different parts of speech or when its declensions or comparatives are not regular, the task becomes complicated. The need to use several different type fonts—often including foreign ones—adds up to a complexity that made strong editors and printers weep. The computer has eliminated most of this pain.

The output of all the phototypesetting machines discussed here is a *right-reading positive*—normal characters, in black—on photopaper or film. By a simple *chemical reversal,* black characters on film can be converted to the familiar camera-negative form and go directly to platemaking.

The computer-phototypesetter machines—the *hardware*—must be built by humans. The *software* —the programming which instructs the computer— is prepared by human beings. And always, human input is required for all these machines. Sometimes it is obvious: the punched tape of the simple TTS. Sometimes it is a step or two removed: the original typesetting of the Russian scientific article and the British novel that were "translated" by machine. The input may be tape, the simplest 6-level or the 15-level that affords many, many more coding possibilities. It may be cards, magnetic tape—7-track half-inch to 10-track three-quarter inch—or video tape. It may be produced on-site, or far away and transmitted physically, by wire, or even by wireless. But always the original input must be done by a human—whose race will never be replaced by a computer.

Conventional keyboards are similar to those of electric typewriters with a few extra keys added for specialized typesetting uses. *Keypunching* machines are very simple; the keyboards of many computers look like those of business computing machines. The giant Linotron at the Government Printing Office is compatible with and connectable, by phone, to 4,200 computers throughout the federal establishment.

The phototypesetting machines we have looked at will set type in various ranges of size. The *Justotext,* manufactured by the Friden Division of Singer and designed for simple text setting, *straight-matter,* handles 5- to 12-point. The standard Fototronic and Linofilm go up to 72-point. But, just as hot-metal composition demands the Ludlow to set large and/or infrequently used faces, so it is desirable to have comparable *photolettering* machines. These are simpler in construction and operation than the phototextsetters, as human hands and fingers, instead of gears, cogs, and electronic components, do many chores.

The least expensive hand machine is the *Fotorex.* In another simple machine, the *ProType,* the operator slides a strip of negative into place by hand. A grooved track provides horizontal alignment; a guideline on the film indicates proper letter placement. It uses film or paper sensitive only to fluorescent light, permitting the operator to work under natural or incandescent light. The *Strip-Printer* is a similar simple, and therefore inexpensive, machine. The *Foto-Riter* uses individual negatives of characters stored in loose-leaf envelopes, and the *Fototype* offers stepless sizes from 10- to 96-point.

More advanced—and more expensive—is the *Headliner,* made by the VariTyper company. The makers of *Alphatype,* a fine quality textsetter, manufacture the *Filmotype,* which goes up to 144-point production. Friden's *Typro* also goes up to 144, while the *Staromat* creates up to a giant 300-point type, more than half as tall as this page.

Keyboarded machines, capable of greater speed, include the *Morisawa* and the *Photo Typositor,* ATF's *KD-84,* and the *Compugraphic 7200.* The *Hadego* is popular among smaller newspapers. A

a CAMERA modifications

b CAMERA modifications

c CAMERA modifications

d CAMERA modifications

e CAMERA modifications

CAMERA MODIFICATIONS are made by using various distortion lenses with a single negative of the original character. These specimens by Lettering, Inc. (through whose courtesy they are used here) show:

a. Normal letterform;
b. Letters kept at same width and heightened by 30 per cent to create Condensed form;
c. Letters kept at same width and reduced 30 per cent in height to create Extended form;
d. Regular letterform slanted 20 degrees to the right to create unusually marked Oblique form;
e. Letterform angled to 340 degrees to form the Backslant, unpleasant to the typical reader.

2-3. Determine the poles

a) $\dfrac{0.167s^2 + 0.833s +}{s^2 + 8s + 116}$

b) $\dfrac{(s+5)(s+40)}{s^2 + 43s + 120}$

c) $\dfrac{(s^2 + 7s + 6)}{(s+2)(s+1)(s+}$

$$\text{Re } p_{11}(\omega^*) = -\frac{8f^2}{3\omega^*} +$$

$$\text{Re } p_{13}(\omega^*) = \text{Re } p_{31}(\omega^*)$$

$$F_1 = \frac{-\mu r_e^4 \sigma_4}{8a^5}\left[\left(3 - 15\eta_0^2 + \right.\right.$$

$$F_{1m} \equiv (2\pi)^{-1} \int_0^{2\pi} F_1 dl =$$

FORMULAE so complicated they seem to be *tours de force* by the typesetter are actual samples from textbooks. Phototypesetting makes such composition relatively simple.

European import, the *Diatype,* and the American *Photo Typositor* have a treasurehouse of typographic materials and controls to effect the most minute niceties demanded for quality composition.

Advantages of phototypesetting are obvious and already alluded to: added convenience and lower costs of tape, lightweight products, high speeds, typographic quality, ability to provide new typographic material at prices far lower than are possible in hot metal, where punch-cutting, matrix and inventory costs are almost unbelievable.

Typographic quality in photocomp is excellent. Most of the classic faces as well as newly designed ones are available. In many machines, notably the Photo Typositor, the operator actually sees where the photo image appears in relation to previously created letters and so can place the character with infinite precision.

Kerning is no problem whatsoever. Widths of type body or matrices have no bearing on where a photographic image can be placed. So spacing can be manipulated in ways utterly impossible with hot metal. Scripts can join without any break. Kerning is easy even on higher-speed machines. The Alphatype, for instance, lists common kerning for many letter combinations:

b, e, o, and *p* preceding *v, w, y,* period, and comma

V, W, and *Y* preceding *c, d, e, g, o, s,* period, and comma

r, v, w, y, period, and comma preceding a word space

the numeral 1 preceding any letter or any letter preceding that numeral

T, V, W, and *Y* preceding any lowercase letter or punctuation mark

F, T, V, W, and *Y* preceding *A*

A or *L* preceding *T, V, W,* and *Y*

the last character in any line

The typical keyboard that feeds the comp-photo machines also produces *hard copy*—a conventional typewritten script—simultaneously with paper or magnetic tape. If the operator sees an error on the hard copy, he can, on most machines, immediately erase it and put in the correction. Or the hard copy may be read in lieu of a proof. Corrections are punched into paper tape, which is physically inserted into the original. People doing this work soon learn to read the coded paper as easily as they do type.

In the case of the Linotron-class machines, type is actually produced, but at five times the normal speed. The quality of the product is not as good as the regular production speed provides, of course, but it is at least as good as typewriter quality. This is read just as any proof would be. Corrections are then interpolated into the tape, and the whole job is reset in perfect form.

Electronics are used for the earliest "correction" process, the *editing* or *copyreading* of copy in the editorial or advertising departments of a publishing or printing firm. *The Harris 1100 Editing Terminal* is being field-tested at this writing in some newspaper newsrooms. The operation is typically this:

The editor sits at a console which has a conventional electric typewriter keyboard flanked by an additional bank of keys at either side and a row of switches immediately above the board. From this rises an 8½ × 11-inch video screen.

Stories in the form of idiot tape produced locally or wire-service justified tape are stored on magnetic tape within a computer. The editor calls up the story he wants to copyread. Immediately the TV screen displays the first 2,000 characters of the story. This is in approximately the form of double-spaced pica typewriter type, in blue-green on a black background. The screen accommodates 25 lines in either of two measures, a single column of 80 characters or two legs of 40 each.

The *cursor,* a tiny blip of light about the size of a 12-point en, may be moved to any spot on the screen by UP, DOWN, RIGHT, or LEFT keys. It is moved to the position where editing is to be done. The editor strikes the INSERT CHARACTER key and types out the additional matter. Or he may position the cursor and strike a DELETE key to remove an

unwanted character. For larger deletions there are
DELETE LINE, PARAGRAPH, or BLOCK keys which remove larger sections.

Instructions for paragraphing or other formatting
are given in the same way. The editor's changes are
incorporated into the magnetic tape and are immediately shown on the screen.

When he has completed his work, the machine
will either produce 6-level paper tape or relay its
information directly to a computer. The machine
operates so rapidly that the editor need not wait for
it. A HOME key sends the cursor to the lower left
corner of the screen, or a NEXT LINE key sends it to
the start of the following line to increase speed.

The machine may also be used to read proof—
right on tape, as it were—in the same way.

There are disadvantages, of course, but many of
them appear to be psychological ones among the
would-be users. It now takes longer to edit than by
the familiar soft black pencil, but all that time, and
a little more, is saved in the actual typesetting and
proofreading. Models now in use don't give hard
copy, and the editor often has to rely too heavily on
his memory to recall what he has edited in the portions that are not displayed on the screen.

Computer memory is used more advantageously
by magazine editors who have many regional editions that require the complete remaking of pages
and sections. When the editor has a certain *hole* to
fill around newly placed ads, he tells the computer
the specifications, and the electronic brain scans its
memory of articles in type and suggests the proper
one. It stores information about illustrations, too,
and can tell the editor which pictures are vital to
verbal copy and which can be dispensed with to fit
the given space.

Used properly, computers can free the editor's
mind from details and be a valuable tool toward
the more creative aspects of editing.

Strikeon Composition

By strict definition, cold type is that produced
photographically. But several other kinds of non-

metallic composition are commonly grouped under the frigid label. The largest of these is growing so rapidly that its title—*strikeon composition*—is coming into more frequent and correct use.

It is obvious that the simplest way to "set type" for the platemaker is on an ordinary typewriter. Justification can also be achieved. The typist draws the right-hand margin and types the copy as close to that length as possible. If the line is short, he fills it up with periods or asterisks. If long, he types the number of excess spaces in the right margin. Then the copy is retyped. Should it be, say, four spaces short, these are inserted between words in addition to the normal word spacing. If the line is long, the necessary amount of word spacing is reduced from a full to a half space. Even regular typewriters allow this manipulation; those with space and backspace in half-unit increments make it easier.

Several makes of electric typewriters have this feature plus that of *proportional spacing*. In a standard typewriter, each character, be it an *i* or an *M*, gets exactly as much space as any other. The effect is that the *i* or *l* looks like a utility pole in the middle of a hayfield while the wide letters are cramped. Proportional-spacing machines provide usually four different spaces. This is an improvement even though it cannot match the spacing of a Linofilm, for instance, which provides increments in eighteenths of an em, or of hot metal where each character gets exactly its proper width with no relation to restriction of increments.

In some systems the operator types a line, sets the spacing at an increment indicated on a gauge, moves the paper over and retypes the line—now properly justified—at the right of the paper. This double typing is not very efficient, but the value of justification makes it worthwhile. But to avoid it, machines such as the *Justowriter* and *Flexowriter* produce paper tape from the human-operated keyboard which, in turn, actuates the second, *slave* typewriter which produces justified typing. Even more sophisticated is the IBM MTSC.

"190 TONS DROPPED ON OUR DODGES EVERY DAY!!

Our trucks work is equal to three on the road. We checked one of them at 150,000 miles. Not one part was worn enough to be replaced!" Stark Ceramics, Inc., Canton, Ohio

LETTERFORM DISTORTIONS should be used sparingly because they always reduce legibility. In this case, though, the letterforms add a nonverbal reinforcement to the written copy. The truck is able to bear the "weight" of the headline although it is so great that it bows the "platform" of body type on which the truck stands. (Courtesy Dodge Trucks)

The *Varityper* and a new *IBM Selectric* type-writer add versatility. They place their type, not on the end of permanent key bars, but in an individual element that can be changed in a matter of seconds. Thus a large selection of type faces is available for every keyboard.

Obviously, such machines cost considerably more than the inexpensive portable typewriters so common today. But the system is still a little less expensive than hot metal and therefore many smaller newspapers—daily and weekly—use strikeon composition. The wire services are using Teletype-like machines that typewrite justified lines in adequate quality on good paper ready for pasting-up and the camera. But advanced phototypesetting machines are being offered at prices highly competitive to strikeon, and many observers think that the high-water mark of strikeon has perhaps been passed.

Although quality of strikeon composition has improved steadily, it doesn't match the typographic excellence of hot or true cold type and the dyed-in-the-printer's-ink typographer detests strikeon as fervently as the pressman anathematizes the stencil duplicating machine.

Proofing of strikeon poses some difficulties. The original may be read—but must be handled carefully lest it be marred for camera use—or a photocopy may be made by *Bruning, Ozalid, Diazo* or similar machines. The same names are used for the photocopies themselves.

The error word or *error line* is retyped and pasted right over the original. This usually requires opaquing as we shall see later.

Errors in film are harder to correct; for now the error line must be removed before replacement. Correction lines are cut to the same dimensions, inserted into proper position while held in a vacuum box and then affixed by transparent tape.

On-Paper Type

Obviously not hot metal nor cold type, we might whimsically classify as "cool type" the various *on-*

paper typographic elements that are in common use today.

There are two kinds of *paste-on* type. One is printed on clear, self-adhesive plastic. Desired letters are cut out with a *stylus,* a needle placed in a pencil-size handle. They are arranged properly on the paper which shall become camera copy, and *burnished,* rubbed down so smoothly that they seem to be part of the original paper. Available in black or white, such type—*Artype* and *Craftype* are common trade names—can be used not only on white or black paper but also directly on photographs. Other trade names are *Chart-Pak, Transtik,* and *Micotype.* These are available in all sizes, but they are customarily used to produce only a small quantity of copy, a word or a line or two. The process is too slow to be economical for a large amount of composition.

Other paste-on letters are printed on paper and padded like a calendar. They are pasted right onto the copy paper or first arranged in a slotted wooden stick and then pasted down as a group with a plastic adhesive tape.

Reproduction proofs (*repros*) of any kind of hot metal may also be assembled and pasted.

Transfer letters are printed (again in black or white) on the reverse of a clear plastic sheet. Placed in the proper position on the paper or photograph, the face of the plastic is then rubbed and the letter transfers smoothly to the lower surface. It looks exactly as if it had been printed or handlettered to the copy paper.

Paste-on material can be lifted off and repositioned but transfer matter cannot. Therefore it requires much more painstaking care. Either method is faster by far—and affords more uniformity—than handlettering. A vast variety of styles, formal to casual, are available. American Typefounders has introduced *Spectype*—a transfer—which is an exact match for its foundry type. Other trade names are *Prestype, Cello-Tak,* and *Instatype.*

The cost of cold-type display machines is rela-

FLOATING FORMS are produced by the Statmaster (and used here by courtesy of the Statmaster Corporation). Normal letterforms are reflected off curved surfaces and then rephotographed for highly unusual effects.

tively low and of on-paper materials insignificant. So their use is widespread. Art agencies, advertising departments, and publications can use them to advantage. But there is a convenient and inexpensive source for photographic display type in the *photolettering* services. These commercial houses sell such type by the word and the buyer has the resources of extensive type libraries with no investment on his part.

By using various lenses, photoletters can distort type into almost countless variations of the original.

Temptation to utilize extreme potentials of photolettering is acute. The designer must constantly keep in mind that legibility should never be sacrificed to the design value of type. Fads sweep through the graphic arts like weevils through a cotton field. Most fads, fortunately, have a high mortality rate. This is fortunate because many are poor typography.

Newspapers are major users of the phototypesetters discussed, although magazines, book compositors, business-form manufacturers, and map makers also use cold type advantageously.

Most larger daily newspaper use is for advertising or for Sunday magazines, where deadlines are not too pressing and where type is handled as simple blocks. For the time being at least, news columns are best made up by manipulating linecaster slugs.

Newspapers make up ads by pasting up, for photoengraved plates; by placement of original photographic material on the Linofilm composer or by utilizing a *make-up guide* on the Photon; or by *metal paste-up*. In the latter method, all elements in several ads are engraved on a single flat. They are sawed into individual blocks and positioned and pasted onto a metal base. Although, on the face of it, metal paste-up may not seem to be advantageous, newspapers using the method report excellent results.

The "Suggested Readings" note below indicates the problems of attempting to put in book form subjects as fast-moving as those considered here.

MAPS require type in various styles and sizes as well as at angles or even in arcs. These are two same-size fragments of a negative produced on the Linofilm Composer. Other negatives carried the physical lines of the map itself as well as tints for various areas.

Note the difference in the sizes of type. The name of the Rio Grande River (in the portion above) is curved like the river

But it is in the area of cold type that the greatest strides will undoubtedly be made in the next decade or two. The potential market is vast, and free industry needs no greater incentive than that to achieve new and economically sound equipment, methods, and techniques.

itself, while that for the Sabine (below) bends at a sharper angle.

Geographers have an elaborate stylebook specifying the proper type to use for various cartographic elements. Political subdivisions are easily recognizable by the use of different races of type; varying point-sizes designate the size of cities. Man-made objects must be shown in a different form from those made by nature, etc. Photocomposition simplifies this complex setting.

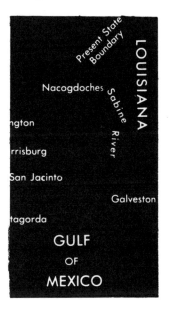

SUGGESTED READINGS

Wide commercial use of photocomposition is so comparatively recent that no definitive work on the subject has yet been published. The best available information is in materials prepared by the manufacturers of such equipment.

A wealth of information on almost every phase of the graphic arts is contained in the eight annual *Production Yearbooks* (New York: Colton) and in the *Penrose Annuals* (New York: Hastings House, Publishers, Inc.). Information on developments in typography and production are well reported in the following magazines: *Inland Printer/American Lithographer* (Chicago), *Western Printer & Lithographer* (Los Angeles), *Canadian Printer & Publisher* (Toronto), *Printing Production* (Cleveland, Ohio), *Advertising & Sales Promotion,* formerly *Advertising Requirements* (Chicago), *Graphic Arts Buyer* (Philadelphia), *Print* (New York), *Printers' Ink* (New York), *Productionwise* (New York), and *Printing Magazine* (Oradell, N.J.).

7

Use of Type

Channels of Communication

Whether it is hot, cold, or lukewarm, type is meant to be read. It is not a decorative element even though handsome abstract patterns can be achieved by using type nonverbally. Its primary function is to convey information, and that is the first consideration of the typographer.

We might make a distinction here between the "graphics designer" and the "typographer." The "designer"—in this rather pejorative sense—is interested in making a pleasing pattern on a page. He might be creating the design for a shower curtain or kitchen linoleum. The "typographer" is concerned primarily with communicating. He, too, seeks a pleasing page because he knows that printing that delights the eye puts the reader into a mood more receptive to the verbal message. He does not eschew beauty but only insists it be mated with utility. There are well-defined principles that assure maximum functionalism.

Two characteristics of type are often misunderstood because the terms are used interchangeably—and incorrectly. *Readability* is that characteristic which makes it easy and pleasant to read large masses of type. The pages of a book or columns of newspapers must be set in readable type. *Legibility* is that characteristic which brings a few words off the page and into the comprehension of the reader as rapidly and unmistakably as possible. The word STOP on a highway sign is an excellent example of legibility, but graphic artsmen are most concerned with this quality in headlines, title pages, chapter headings, and so on. Roman types have the highest readability; Sans Serifs, the highest legibility.

Sometimes it is easy to confuse the function of type in a specific use. In telephone directories, stock market quotations, and classified advertising pages we see Sans Serifs used well. Here are large masses of type, and the immediate conclusion of some people is that here we must use a face of high readability. Yet, despite the many lines of type, the reader is interested in only a few: a single name and phone number, two or three stocks, those want ads under a single heading.

The typographer has three choices that make for readability: the face itself, the line length, the spacing within and between lines. The selection of a type face is not always easy; there are literally thousands of fonts to choose from. What, then, are the characteristics the specifier should seek in a face?

Readable type is *big on the slug*. This is another way of saying that it should have a large x-height, the largest possible for a given point size.

A good type face should be *invisible*. The reader should easily grasp entire words and phrases without being aware of the individual letter forms. That precludes obtrusive letter designs; eccentric curves or serifs call so much attention to themselves that the reader is distracted.

The type must have a *pleasant texture*. As the letters are woven into a fabric of words, the over-all tonal value must be dark enough so the eye need not strain, yet not so heavy that it irritates. The only way to determine the texture is to scrutinize type, not by individual letters or a line or two, but in large blocks, as most type specimen books show.

Type should have *proper proportions*. The printer says: "You can see a pumpkin better than a goose egg." He means that a full, round *O* is easier to read than one that has been squeezed into an oval. Faces always lose readability in condensation. So, although there are times when small amounts of Condensed type can be used effectively, if choice is possible, a fullface type should be selected.

Other proportions contribute to the basic design of the letters that effect texture and invisibility. Whether a face is "beautiful" or not varies with the eye and taste of the beholder, whether that face belongs to type or a human being. In the final analysis, every type specifier must rely on his own judgment. It may be of help, though, to note the selection of body type for the Fifty Books of the Year, the annual selection by the American Institute of Graphic Arts of the best books produced in the United States. In the first 34 years of the show, Baskerville set 152 winners; Janson, 115; Granjon,

112; Caledonia, 94, and Caslon Old Face, 87. It should be noted that Caledonia achieved its success in only the last 18 of those years—it wasn't cut before then.

The type face must be *appropriate*. There is a definite, if hard to define, flavor to even the most unobtrusive type design. So the appropriately named Primer or Schoolbook has a natural affinity to textbook composition. Many faces have strong feminine or masculine connotations. Type must be appropriate to the paper on which, and to the process by which, it will be printed. Rough papers love Old Style Romans and other rugged faces; high-finish papers treat Modern Romans and lighter faces in a most kindly fashion. Newspaper ads should be set in faces that have been designed to withstand the distortions of stereotyping; for gravure, faces must have sturdy bodies lest their hairlines disappear in screening.

Copy set in all capitals is difficult to read. This is because we "read" only the top portion of letters in normally rapid reading. The top silhouette of lowercase letters is distinctive and easy to distinguish; that of all-caps is basically a rectangle with few variations to make word recognition easy. Capitals can be used for titles and very short headlines but all-cap matter should be kept at a minimum.

One of the few flat statements that can be made about type is this: Text, Script, Cursive, and ornamental initials can never be used in all-capitals. In most cases the result is not a pleasing design element. In all cases, it is the nadir of illegibility.

Most Italics are too light for effective readability in masses, but this lightness may be useful when a typographic accent is sought.

When William Addison Dwiggins designed Electra, he recognized that in many books, and other composition, there is a need to set large quantities of copy in an accent face. So he made Electra Italic as an Oblique Roman that retained the readability of the perpendicular letterform. Later he added Electra Cursive, which is a true

Italic; another example of the rugged independence of typographic nomenclature!

Typographic harmony must be sought whenever type is mixed. Rarely is it necessary to mix body types; the Perpendicular, Oblique and boldface readily available are almost always adequate to achieve the necessary differences. Sometimes a different font must be selected, of course, if words in a foreign language or mathematical or scientific symbols must be interspersed into the copy. In this case, the main factor is one of texture and color.

The choice of display type used with text sizes is important. If the body type is 10-point or smaller, any headletter will blend reasonably well. Thus we find newspapers using Roman or Sans headlines with equal effectiveness. A *headline schedule,* the complete assortment of all headline forms used by a newspaper, is most effective if it is entirely within one race and preferably within one family. To have to shift mental gears between Bodoni and Metro slows down reading as much as gear-shifting slows down driving.

This same harmony should be sought in all printing, advertising, books, letterheads, etc. Keep all display lines in one family.

Occasionally an *accent face* is desired. In the case of newspapers, the accent is used for *kicker heads,* small ones that ride above a main head as here, where *Once in Swiss Tower* is the kicker:

Once in Swiss Tower

Ancient Church Carillon
To Find Home in Museum

This accent is best when it is an exaggerated form of the basic headletter. In our example, Ultra Bodoni (or Poster Bodoni—they are the same Extra Heavy version—or Campanile or Onyx, the Condensed) is an excellent accent for a Bodoni schedule.

In other printing, the accent face may also be from the same family or from an entirely different

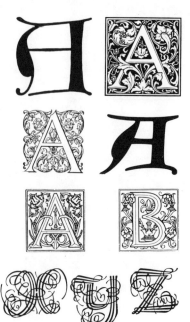

race. Whatever the accent, it should be used sparingly. The speaker who accents every word communicates as poorly as he who mumbles in a monotone.

Initials, although they help form text words, must be considered as display. They must match exactly or vary greatly. Initials are useful to add typographic color to large masses of body type which might otherwise be as gray and unappetizing as a big bowl of cold oatmeal. Many fonts of initials are available. Their size is indicated by points or by the number of lines of text type they occupy: thus, a 3-line initial.

The *inset initial* occupies a space cut out of the top left corner of a paragraph. Ideally it should align at the top with the x-line of the text and at the bottom with the baseline of the smaller letters. This is often difficult to achieve without spacing the adjacent text lines at a distance that is not desirable for succeeding lines. Inset initials pose problems in mechanical typesetting; under pressure of stereotyping, they frequently break.

Rising initials align with the baseline of, and rise above, accompanying text type. This is easy to achieve and, mechanically, the best way to use initials. The white space that they "build in" above the first line of text is useful in adding "fresh air" to the page.

Initials align at the left with body type. But those such as *T, A, V,* and *W* often have to be moved farther to the left so the alignment is on the mass of the letter, the stem of the *T,* for instance, rather than on the left edge of the lighter cross stroke.

The length of a line—or *measure*—of type has major bearing on its readability. Oldtime printers established a formula which modern researchers have validated: *the optimum line length is 1.5 times the lowercase alphabet length.*

We cannot always set type at the optimum measure. But we should never set it less than 25 per cent narrower or more than 50 per cent wider than the optimum. These, then, are the formulas:

DECORATIVE INITIALS are among the oldest—yet most contemporary—ways of ornamenting a printed page or of breaking up large masses of body type into more attractive portions.

From the top row (left to right) the styles are: Missal, Cloister; Tory (there are no X or Z in this font, so don't use it for a Zoo brochure); Caxton, named for the first English printer; Della Robia, named for an Italian painter, contemporary with Gutenberg, whose Madonnas set a new style, and Raffia (the last three characters). Always the word "Initials" is added to each name.

$$O = lca \times 1.5$$
$$Mn = O - 25\%$$
$$Mx = O + 50\%$$

Mn and Mx mark the outer limits of the readability range. To drop below or exceed them is to sacrifice readability.

A less exact formula is adequate in many instances: *the optimum line length is twice the point size of the type,* with the answer in picas. Thus, an 8-point type would have a 16-pica optimum, 12 picas as minimum and 24 picas as maximum measures.

Body type set on keyboarded linecasters should not be set wider than 30 picas to avoid butted slugs, lines set in two pieces.

Headlines should have a maximum of 32 characters and spaces per line. A greater number reduces legibility.

Display type is customarily read line by line and should be written so that each line is reasonably self-contained. Breaking closely knit phrases breaks the normal rhythm or stride of reading. Headlines such as these:

NEW BONNETS FOR LITTLE
GIRLS' EASTER PARADE
or
ASTRONAUTS' TRIP TO
MARS EXPECTED SOON

demonstrably result in a jarring disruption of reading as the eye reads the first line, embarks upon the second, realizes that a phrase has been split, then goes back to the first line to pick up the adjective or preposition and carries it down to the next line where it makes sense.

The loss in time is not significant. But the break in *reading rhythm* is. As long as the eye can move along at a normal stride and pace, reading is easy. But anything that breaks the rhythm irritates the eye. *Eye fatigue* is often the determining factor in how much of a printed message the reader will consume. When the eye gets tired—even though its

DECORATIVE INITIALS come in many styles. Note the great variety here. Specimens from top down (left to right) are: Caprice; Fry's Ornamented, which were cut in 1796; Burford (three characters); Balle; Bauer Text and Dutch, practically illegible until woven into a word. "Initials" should be added to each name to make it complete.

unaided, or rathe

*E*ventual
been sati
esthetic
and a si
render a
powerful, versatil
product.

INSET INITIALS are used effectively in these same-size fragments. Note how the left-side
alignment is on the mass of the
initial rather than its physical
edge, and how the body type is
set to accentuate the silhouette
of the large letter. The *E* is in
brown; the *O* in black, as are
both body blocks.

*O*ne concess
lowed, ai
tional reas
of the art
banknotes i
got a differe
set of border oi
counterfeiting. In mo
ornaments are enscrit

owner is not specifically aware of it—he will quit
reading. While the delay or annoyance of a single
misuse is almost too slight to measure, the cumu-
lative effect is considerable and serious.

Spacing, as much as any single factor, influences
reading rhythm. Interlineal spacing, ledding, must
be designated for all composition. Inadequate ledding makes it difficult for the eye to read a line of
type without distraction from those above and below. Too much ledding makes type "fall apart"; the
eye must search for the start of each line instead of
moving flowingly to that point from the end of the
preceding one.

Descenders help determine adequate interlineal
spacing. Where descenders are long, they create
more white space between lines of primary letters
than when short descenders are used. Up to 8-point
type, a half point of ledding is usually preferred.
From 8- through 12-point a whole point of ledding
is usually the best. It is wise to accumulate samples
of type with various ledding so that you can see the
effect of interlineal spacing on masses of the body
type. Ledding is a major determinant of texture.

Display type, too, must be kept close enough so
that the eye moves smoothly from line to line. For
headlines, type shoulders usually afford optimum
spacing. If any spacing other than this is required,
it is usually indicated on the dummy and supplied
by the make-up man.

Justification of columns by *ledding out* is almost
always done by the make-up man without consulta-
tion with the typographer. But this should not be
taken for granted; unobtrusive as it is, ledding
contributes greatly to the harmony of a page.

Extra ledding should be done from the top of a
page or column. If type must be stretched out to an
extreme, extra space—usually a slug—may be
dropped above the start of each paragraph. But if
the column is just two or three lines short, 2-point
ledds should be dropped between lines of the first
paragraph. Should ledding have to be done in more
than one paragraph, it is wise to drop, not 2, but 4
points of space between the first two grafs.

Under no circumstances may ledding be done from the bottom. This is an abominable practice in many newspapers. It saves the make-up man a few seconds, but the result is horrible. After the reader has read many lines spaced normally and then comes upon the last five or six lines with extra ledding, the effect is that of a bagpipe that is slowly expiring with disquieting grunts and groans.

The spacing between words is equally important to readability. Word spacing should never be wider than the division necessary to separate words. For machine composition, the typesetter should be instructed to use *narrow spacebands;* there are five different band widths. In hand setting, a quarter-em space is best. Word spacing will vary, of course, to justify the line. But in all cases, extreme word spacing that causes "rivers" of white to run down the column should be avoided.

It was customary to drop an em quad after a period on the theory that the pause between sentences is longer than between words and must be so indicated spatially. But the signal is the punctuation mark, not the space. So modern practice is to use normal word spacing after a period. Copy set all-caps usually requires an en quad between words.

Except in extreme cases, *letterspacing* should be avoided in body type unless justification is absolutely impossible by any other means. Often all-cap words must be letterspaced to create the optical effect of equal spacing, especially in display sizes. In the following example, the top word is spaced normally. Yet the *I* and *N* look much closer together than the *T* and *Y*. So, in the second line,

LINOTYPE

LINOTYPE

extra spacing has been added to make all letters look in proper relation to adjacent ones. Because this technique is used to create an optical effect, it

becomes over-ridin

The next decision
name dc
restrict
facet of
knows the
so do its customers
fits our economical

whereas the latter must car
or perish.

ou must also bear i
less of what designe
and functionalism, the
of fashion in design, an
that eventually weaken;
compose today what is i
fashionable design, chances
tative when the herd catches

of the delivery trucks.

The Jeffries embl

ecognition has be
effort in de
arts circle
pieces be
were displ
Angeles Art
More were accepted for the !

DECORATIVE INITIALS, shown here in two-thirds the linear measurement of the originals, are basically "sunken" although they also give the effect of stick-up usage. The *T* is in chocolate brown, *Y* and *R* in cyan; all body type is black. Note how the Old Style Bookman initials contrast vividly with the stark Sans Serifs text.

is also called *optical spacing*. When letterspacing is used, word spacing must increase proportionately.

Condensed letters should never be letterspaced. Their capitals are so designed that they will fit properly with normal spacing. It negates the only excuse for Condensed letters when they are stretched out to occupy more space. Never letter-space lowercase.

Paragraph indention is usually one em. Sometimes no indent is used at all, a blank line above the start of the paragraph serving as the indicator. This is effective but does carry the danger that this space will inadvertently be omitted. The result is confusion, which might adversely affect readership.

Some designers like to use *paragraph starters.* Instead of the normal indent, the paragraph begins with a paragraph mark, one of the standard symbols in many fonts, such as these:

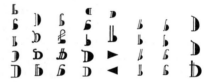

or a *bullet* (a large period), arrow, triangle, or some decorative element may be used. This technique is especially effective for listing a number of items, either alone or with explanatory text.

The end of a paragraph often creates a *widow line*. Some designers consider any line not completely filled as a widow. Others keep the term only for those less than a quarter filled.

Widows are particularly annoying to book designers. Pages that begin or end with a widow have a ragged look as opposed to the neat rectangle formed by full lines. In good books, type is manipulated to avoid placing widows at the top or bottom of pages.

Widows can be remedied by deleting or adding a word or two of copy. In some cases this is justifiable. But it is presumptuous of the designer to ask an author to change his copy just to make it fit into an arbitrary shape. Well-written copy suffers when it is edited by the mathematics of copyfitting rather than by its sense or style. Contemporary designers accept this and are far less concerned with widows than the past generation was.

But there are times when widows should be eliminated, even by drastic means. If the eye must travel a long distance from the end of Column 1 to the start of Column 2, it justifiably feels imposed upon if, having made the long trek, it finds only a word, or even a syllable, at the head of the succeeding column. Some designers, usually older ones, get quite exercised if more than two successive lines end in hyphens or punctuation marks. Surely it is annoying to the eye if many hyphens or points pile up on each other, or if too many successive lines begin with a capital. The effect is one of tabulation and does hamper reading rhythm. Whether a designer should set an arbitrary number of lines which can begin or end repetitively is a matter of argument; it is probably better to solve each problem as it arises than to attempt a formula to cover all situations.

Runarounds should be avoided. This is the practice of narrowing a group of lines to create an opening into which is dropped a picture, head, or subhead, etc. The change in line-length tends to break reading rhythm. If such matter must be inserted, space surrounding it is important. The opening in the type column should definitely be more or less than half the measure of body type; never should the column be divided evenly. Space above, below, and at the side of such inserts should be equal, and it should be appreciably greater than word spacing. If the insert is of irregular shape, such spacing must give the effect of being equal all around even though, mathematically, this is impossible. If the outline is very intricate, it is best to leave a rectangle of white upon which to place the insert, usually a picture.

Tabulations follow specific rules which need not be dwelled on here; every good typesetter is well aware of them. We might note, however, that in

Here in America we about our tradition of the press and jea tect it against enci A free press is one of the b democracy. Yet I often wc many Americans actually t what the reverse of a free pr

PLACEMENT OF INITIALS properly is shown in these specimens. Above, the sunken initial aligns top and bottom with adjacent body type. Note how the left-hand serifs project into the margin.

The rising initial (below) aligns at its baseline with that of the body type. Alignment at the left is on its lower serif, but its arm extends into the margin to give the effect that the mass is aligned.

THE First Amendme Constitution ordained American newspaper be ly owned and managed icated to the task of s the people with the infc

STAGGER

STAGGER

STAGGERED TYPE can be effective on rare occasions (as shown in the Dodge Truck ad a few pages back). But usually its loss of legibility is too great price to pay for an effect. This style, also called *bounced type*, was done photographically.

most fonts, numbers are all of equal width so that vertical columns are automatically achieved whether the numbers be a narrow 1 or a wide 5.

One form of tabulation which is entirely in the hands of the typographic designer is the coupon—an excellent device—which is used so much in advertising. Coupons defeat their own purpose if adequate space has not been left, both vertically and horizontally, for the respondent to write his name and address with ease. At least a pica of white space, and preferably 14 points, should be the minimum height of such blanks. The typical city needs at least 5 picas; a state, 2, and a street address, 8, to allow comfortable space for writing.

Another tabulation specification that the designer must make concerns the *leaders*. These are the line of dots or dashes that connect a tabulated item at the start of a line with other data:

Automobile registrations 8,796

Few designers realize that there is any difference in leaders. Yet the Linotype specimen book lists over 20 styles. They are either periods or hyphens, varying from two to six characters per em. Two-unit patterns are entirely adequate to lead the eye across the page, and they assure sharp, clean printing.

Whenever type is placed in a layout or on a page, it must have room to do its job. We would not expect an orator to convey an effective message in a telephone booth; we cannot expect type to carry a message unless it has elbow room.

If you make it your constant motto that *Type Was Made To Be Read,* you need not memorize formal axioms. Common sense will tell you when type is being forced to work under conditions that will make its job impossible.

Typographic fads come and go with the annoying regularity of locust infestations. Most of them are fatal to readability. The list of admonitions is long; only the most flagrant are singled out here:

Don't distort letterforms (as in the so-called psychedelic styles) so that their legibility is destroyed.

Don't set type diagonally, sideways, upside-down, or vertically.

Don't set type in wavy lines or in circles.

Don't set type *piggy-back* or *stacked* (this is placing one line of type directly atop the next).

Don't set type in *bounce* or *stagger* style (when it doesn't align horizontally).

Don't interlock type.

Don't overlap type so that the descenders of a top line come down lower than the top of the ascenders in the next line.

Don't screen type (the serrated edges caused by the dots of the Ben Day pattern that tone down the type give it an unpleasant mushy effect).

All these hideous things are comparatively easy to do by phototypesetting or by manipulating cold type in pasting-up, and so these sins are all too prevalent.

PIGGYBACK TYPE—also called stacked—is extremely difficult to read and occasions for effective use are very rare.

So a good rule of thumb is: *Anything that is difficult to set on a Linotype is difficult to read.* Take line length, for instance. The Linotype sets lines up to 30 picas. To set longer lines requires setting two *butted lines* that adjoin to make one longer line. This is difficult to do; as he comes to the end of each metal line, the operator must remember whether this is truly the end of the first or second half of the complete line. If it is the former, the line ends anywhere within a word, without, of course, a hyphen or space. If the latter, the line must end as a conventional one does, at the end of a word or syllable. There is a danger, moreover, that such lines will not butt tightly or that they will not align precisely. For these reasons, as well as the fact that it takes more time to set a line in two portions, it is wise to avoid butted lines.

When a line is extremely narrow, or when there are not enough spacebands to expand far enough to make the line tight, the operator must insert blank spacing by hand between the letters of a word. This not only takes valuable time, it makes reading difficult.

In both these instances the lines would violate our formula for the readability range.

SHAPED TYPE BLOCKS are usually not as effective as this one, used by Economy Lithography Co., of Los Angeles. The shape is that of a shrew, a very nervous, irascible animal. The moral: this shop is never nervous nor need its customers be.

For such setting, the silhouette is drawn onto a block of type of the same size and ledding; then the length of each individual line is measured and specified. All in all . . . it ain't worth the trouble!

Type is best read in equal, justified lines.

UNLIKE
THE SHORT-
TAILED SHREW*

*Smaller than a mouse, this ● is the most nervous and irascible of all mammals. Some are so high-strung that a sudden sound will cause them to leap into the air, fall in a dead faint, or even drop dead! They also shriek when enraged, which is very often. Unlike the Short-Tailed Shrew, Economy Lithograph is a monument of calm. If the pressures become unbearable, a few wives may be beaten with an old matrice, but there is never an intemperate word to a customer. Some customers claim that by dealing with Economy they save enough in Miltowns alone to pay for a small printing job each year. If you think this is just advertising chatter, start keeping track of your tranquillizer consumption. Then switch to Economy and marvel at the difference. ECONOMY LITHOGRAPH CO., 101 So. La Brea, Los Angeles WE-8-2511.

Overlapping, stacking, etc., just cannot be done in hot type. The rigidity of type metal imposes a discipline that the typographer can't readily ignore.

But even if the type is not set in metal, the admonition is valid. If it would be difficult to set in hot metal, it shouldn't be set that way in cold type either.

Type is most easily read in neat rectangles. It should not be set into diamonds and circles or to create the shape of vases or Christmas trees or crosses. The design created may be pleasant, but if the readability of type has been diminished even slightly, the typographer is as guilty—or foolish—as the man who uses a finely tempered straight-edge razor to cut linoleum or digs a fence-post hole with a soup spoon instead of a shovel.

Anyone who embarks on the task of communicating has voluntarily assumed an obligation to communicate clearly. The typographic designer must make communication his primary objective. Only by knowing his tools and using them with skill, respect, and honesty can he hope to achieve this difficult task.

SUGGESTED READINGS

Biggs, John R. Basic Typography. New York: Watson-Guptill, 1968.

Dair, Carl. Design with Type. Toronto: University of Toronto Press, 1967.

Lawson, Alexander (ed.). Typographer's Digest (quarterly). Philadelphia.

Lewis, John. Typography—Basic Principles. New York: Reinhold, 1963.

Wrolstad, Merald E. Journal of Typographic Research (quarterly). Cleveland.

"How much space will the President's Message take in the annual report?"

"I've got this much room for captions in this picture layout. How many words will it take to fill it exactly?"

"What is the biggest size type in which I can set this booklet and keep it in 16 pages?"

Problems like these are common and constant. Their solution is simple. For *copyfitting*—establishing area ratios between typescript and type—is not the bugbear it is commonly considered. This calumny springs from the cumbersome systems that are being slowly discarded; they will not even be mentioned here. Why should they be, when a simple and highly accurate one is available? It's the *character-per-pica system*. Copyfitting is sometimes called *casting off a manuscript*. Just as a type compositor in effect discards a page of a manuscript when he is finished with it, so the estimator determines how much of the manuscript will make a galley of type and figuratively "casts it away." He casts off such portions until the whole manuscript has been used up.

The most accurate and easy system—the one we shall consider here—parallels and anticipates the compositor's job and thus can foretell the results before the physical work is done. For all copyfitting problems, these steps must be taken in this order:

1. *Determine the characters in the manuscript, c/ms.*
2. *Determine the characters per average line of type, c/alt (cpp × no. picas per line).*
3. *Determine the number of lines of type, #lt.*
4. *Determine the number of lines per page, l/pg.*
5. *Determine the number of pages, #pgs.*

Let's analyze the procedure step by step.

1. *Determine the number of characters in the manuscript (c/ms):*

The first—and essential—thing a typesetter needs before he can start work is the manuscript. It makes

8

Copyfitting

Equalizing Type and Space

CONVERSION CHART used to determine characters per pica when the lowercase alphabet is known. Either or both of these data must be known for any typeface with which the copyfitter works.

Characters by Picas

Alphabet

Lengths

↓ ↓

73	4.35	91	3.55
75	4.25	93	3.5
76	4.20	94	3.45
77	4.15	96	3.4
79	4.05	98	3.35
80	4.	100	3.3
81	3.95	102	3.25
82	3.9	104	3.2
83	3.85	106	3.15
84	3.8	108	3.1
86	3.75	110	3.05
87	3.7	112	3.
88	3.65	114	2.95
90	3.6	116	2.9

a great difference if he has to set a single sheet of copy or if he is handed the manuscript of *Gone with the Wind*. So the first step is to evaluate the manuscript (*ms*).

The typesetter is concerned with the total number of *characters in the ms* rather than the number of words, even if the latter is the most popular editorial measurement. Five hundred words of *Look, Tom, look. The dog is here!* in a children's book would occupy far less space than 500 multisyllabic jawbreakers of a scientist writing about parthenogenesis or nuclear physics.

First, determine the length of the average typescript line, either by actually counting the characters or measuring it. *Pica* type, the larger of the two common typewriter faces, measures 10 characters per horizontal inch. *Elite*, the smaller face, measures 12 characters per inch.

Then determine the number of lines per average page. This too, can be done by counting; the usual page has about 30 lines so this is not a formidable task. Or you can measure: double-space (on which most editors insist) runs 3 lines per vertical inch. Single space has 6 lines and triple-space (rarely used), 2 lines per inch.

Multiplying the number of lines by the characters per line gives *characters per ms page*. This, multiplied by the number of pages, gives the total *characters in the manuscript*: (29 lines × 62 characters × 217 pages = 390,166). This is the first required information.

If a more accurate count is required, draw a faint pencil line within the right margin of the typewritten page. Then count the characters by which each line falls short or exceeds this mark, noting them as + or − in the margin. Multiplying the number of lines by the number of characters to the penciled limit, then adding the pluses and minuses, gives the precise number of characters.

Note that the first line in a paragraph is counted to include the blank spaces of the indention at the left. On average copy, count the short lines that end a paragraph as a complete manuscript line; this will average out with similar short lines in the typeset.

Counting manuscript characters is predicated on the fact that each typewritten character receives the same space horizontally. While this is true on standard typewriters, it does not apply to newer models which use proportionate spacing. So it is wise to have manuscripts typed on standard machines.

Undoubtedly there is a formula which will compensate for variations in typewritten characters just as it does for those in type metal. It will take time to derive such a formula, for it must be proved by applying it to a great many specimens of typescript, just as did the experts from Mergenthaler Linotype Company who devised the *cpp formula* for type.

Now the copyfitter follows the next steps that the typesetter must perform.

2. *Determine the number of characters in an average line of type (c/alt).*

To do this, we need the same information the compositor needs before he actually starts setting type: "What face do I set this in?" and "What is the measure—the line length?"

When he has this information, he can determine the number of characters in an average line of type.

Obviously the face and size have important bearing on the characters per line. In a 14-pica column there will be more letters of a Condensed face than of an Extended one. There will be more 6-point characters in that measure than there would be 36-point ones. And it is obvious that, all other things being equal, there will be more characters in a 42-pica line than in one of 15-pica measure. But our method gives us far more precise predictions. It is based on the exact knowledge of how many characters of a specific font will fit into one linear pica.

Ultimately the determining factor is the width of the individual character. A face with fat, round *o*'s and *a*'s and widespread *M*'s and *W*'s will fill more space than a face of the same point-size whose *o*'s are goose eggs and whose *M*'s are squeezed-together columns.

118	2.85	**200**	1.75
120	2.8	**206**	1.7
122	2.75	**212**	1.65
124	2.7	**218**	1.6
127	2.65	**225**	1.55
129	2.6	**233**	1.5
132	2.55	**241**	1.45
135	2.5	**250**	1.4
138	2.45	**260**	1.35
142	2.4	**270**	1.3
146	2.35	**260**	1.35
150	2.3	**270**	1.3
154	2.25	**280**	1.25
158	2.2	**295**	1.2
162	2.15	**310**	1.15
166	2.1	**325**	1.1
170	2.05	**340**	1.05
175	2.	**360**	1.
180	1.95	**380**	.95
185	1.9	**400**	.9
190	1.85	**425**	.85
195	1.8	**450**	.8
		475	.75
		500	.7

This *set-width* factor determines the number of *characters per pica* that any given face will fill. This information is usually given in the type specimen book with which the estimator works. As this factor, *cpp,* is a function of the *lowercase alphabet length, lca,* it may be determined by a simple conversion chart. Any face with an lca of 104 points, for instance, has 3.2 characters per pica.

It must be kept in mind that the estimator needs the cpp for the specific face with which he works. Linotype Baskerville 6-point, as an example, has 3.8 characters per pica, while the same face as cut by American Type Founders counts 4.96. This is a spread of some 30 per cent, and even in a short novel would make a sizable difference in the number of pages of type.

The lca is given in most type specimen books, and both Linotype and Intertype offer booklets with listings for their own cuttings. If the lca of the desired face is not shown on the conversion chart, go to the next larger lca that does appear. *Do not interpolate!*

Assume that the face specified for a job is 10-point Caledonia set in a 25-pica line. Its lca is 130 points and its cpp is 2.55. Multiplying characters per pica by the number of picas of the line length—2.55 × 25—gives 63.75 characters per average line of type (c/alt).

We stress "average" as a reminder that here—and only here—the fraction must be held. For only in an "average" line could there be fractions of a character. Obviously we couldn't have .75 characters physically dangling at the end of each line, but there will be some lines that run heavily to *l*'s and *i*'s, narrow characters, and perhaps have a total of 65, or even more. Others may contain only 60 or 61, should they have more *m*'s and *W*'s than usual. This average has been determined for the Latin alphabet used in the English language.

3. *Determine the number of lines of type the manuscript will make* (#*lt*).

Now the Linotype operator begins touching the

keys. Each time he has hit 63.75 of them, he has produced a line of type. He does that until all the manuscript is used up. We anticipate that process by "using up" 63.75 characters and counting up a line of type each time. This is actually simple division, c/alt into c/ms.

Note what happens in this step if the answer is a fraction. Assume that we have 390,166 characters in a manuscript. That number divided by the 63.75 c/alt tells us that there will be 6,120 and a fraction of lines of type.

Visualize that "fraction of a line." It is the customary widow at the end of any paragraph. The first part of the line is filled with characters. But the rest of the line is filled with quads, spacing material, so that "partial line" takes up exactly as much space as a full one. Thus, in step 3 any fractional lines are counted as whole lines.

4. *Determine the number of lines per page (l/pg).*

The typesetter couldn't care less where his type is used. He works the same if he is setting a news story for the *New York Times* or a novel or article for *Good Housekeeping* magazine. He stores the type in galleys, each holding only approximately the same number of lines as the others. It is when the printer breaks down the galleys into columns or pages that exact length becomes important. Incidentally, the word "page" means the space available into which the type must be placed. It may be a regular page of a book or magazine. It may be a portion of a column in a newspaper; it may be the space left for the type in an ad layout.

Two factors determine how many l/pg. The first is the depth of the given area, the "page." The other is the depth of the line of type, the type itself plus its ledding. The vertical dimension of the "page" will usually be given in picas, only occasionally in inches. This should be converted into points, for the thickness of a line of type is always designated by points. This dimension is given by the phrase that instructs the typesetter: "eight-on-nine" or "8/9."

a nia, Nevada, Wyoming, Montana, Alaska, Hawaii, Utah, Arizona, Oregon, Washington, Idaho, and the British Columbia and Alberta provinces of Canada. ▓▓▓▓▓
The 5,000-square-foot facility consists of service, sales, and administrative offices, and demonstration and parts storage
b areas.

FRACTIONAL LINE is counted as a complete line in determining the number of lines of type a manuscript will make. In the line marked a the black rectangle shows how the line must be completed with quads that take up all the remaining space.

The line marked b is only about one-tenth full—by mathematics—but occupies as much space as the full line just above it.

This means simply that 8-point type is ledded one point, therefore it is set on a 9-point slug. The second number, then, is the thickness of the "line" of type.

Assume that the area left for type is 36 picas deep. That converts to a page of 432 points. Divide 11 points (the thickness of one line) into the depth of the page. Answer: $39\%_{11}$ lines.

Visualize the situation now. After 39 lines have been placed in the page we have used up 429 points. All that is left is a sliver—3 points—at the bottom. Obviously we can't squeeze an 11-point line in there, can we? So we will fill that tiny hole with spacing material and carry the 40th line to the next page.

We must distinguish clearly between this "fraction of a line" which is actually only room available for a fractional line and that "fraction" which often results in determining c/alt. Therefore when a fraction turns up as an answer to step 4, we always drop it.

The measure (width) of the line must be considered in this step, too. If the line measure is 22 picas and the width of the "page" is 45 picas, we would assume that there will be two columns or *legs* of type in the area and the number of lines per page must reflect that. On a newspaper page we will commonly have eight columns.

5. *Determine the number of pages the type will fill* (#pgs).

Only after all the type has been taken from the galleys and locked up into page forms must the printer answer this question. For he must know how much paper to provide before he starts actual printing.

This is the easiest question for the copyfitter to answer. If a page will contain, let's say, 39 lines, and we have 390 lines of type, there will be 10 pages. But assume that there are 6,121 lines of type. Dividing l/pg into #lt, we find that our type will fill 156.9 pages.

Now visualize this fraction. Here is a page, like one in this book, of which only nine-tenths is filled

---

The Invisibl
late-movie f:
some of the
in the world
really put yc
    Some l
designers ha
fear concerr
fiber letterh
terrified of a
difference b
sulphite she
If they both
they'd see tl
almost invis

22 PICAS

LINES PER PAGE, as determined in copyfitting, show how many full lines can fit into a given area.

Here the "page" is 22 picas deep and the type is 18 point. So there are "14⅔ lines per page." The fraction is the thin horizontal slice marked by the arrow. So the fraction is dropped; only 14 lines will actually fit into the area.

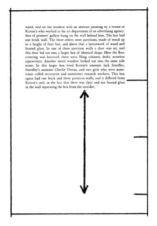

stand, and on the window wall an abstract painting by a friend of Kirton's who worked in the art department of an advertising agency. Sets of printers' galleys hung on the wall behind him. The box had one brick wall. The three others were partitions, made of wood up to a height of four feet, and above that a latticework of wood and frosted glass. In one of these partition walls a door was set, and this door led out into a larger box of identical shape. Here the floor covering was haircord, there were filing cabinets, desks, noiseless typewriters. Another metal window looked out into the same side street. In this larger box lived Kirton's assistant Jack Smedley, Smedley's assistant Charlie Owens, and two girls who were sometimes called secretaries and sometimes research workers. This box again had one brick and three partition walls, and it differed from Kirton's only in the fact that there was clear and not frosted glass in the wall separating the box from the corridor.

FRACTION OF A PAGE, as determined by the mathematics of the final step in copyfitting, is counted as a full page.

This page, by arithmetic, is only "15/39 of a page." Yet it occupies a full leaf of the book.

with type. The rest of the page is blank like those at the end of several chapters in this book.

But when the printer was cutting paper, he didn't use a smaller sheet for this fractional page; all the leaves of a book are of the same dimension. So this fractional page requires as much paper as a completely filled one would, and here again we count a fraction of a page as a full one.

When the final answer is given, it is always phrased as: "This type will make 157 pages, but the last page will have only 27 lines." It is important to add this codicil.

Suppose a book of 192 pages has been proposed. The designer—by subtracting the 156 pages and 27 lines—knows that he has 35 pages and 12 lines to devote to charts, illustrations, maps, headlines, and so on. Or, if the last page has only one or two—or a very few—lines, the designer may be able to gain enough space elsewhere in the book to avoid using this leaf of paper or even a whole "signature," as shall be discussed in Chapter 18.

Thus, by anticipating everything that will happen as a result of a process in the printshop, we may be able to make necessary changes very simply in the manuscript or in the planning steps rather than by the far costlier means of working with expensively set type or cut paper.

Let's work out a typical problem, remembering always to take each of the five steps in order.

PROBLEM: A 34-page manuscript is typewritten in elite type in lines 6½ inches long. There are 33 pages, 29 lines deep, and the 34th page is 23 lines long. Set in Fairfield 9-on-10, 24-pica measure, how many pages will it make if the type page is 5½ inches deep?

STEP 1: c/ms

	6.5	(length of ms line in inches)
×	12	(no. characters per linear pica in elite typewriter)
	78	(characters per typewritten line)
×	29	(lines per typewritten page)
	2,262	(characters per typewritten page of ms)
×	34	(no. ms pages)
	76,908	(c/ms if each page full)
−	468	(characters in 6 lines short)
	76,440	(CHARACTERS IN MANUSCRIPT)

This problem could be worked a little differently for the last steps:

	2,262	(characters per page of ms)
×	33	(no. complete ms pages)
	74,646	(characters in 33 full pages ms)
+	1,794	(characters in 23 lines of last ms page)
	76,440	(CHARACTERS IN MANUSCRIPT)

STEP 2: c/alt

Fairfield 9-point has a lowercase alphabet length of 114 points. The conversion chart shows that this lca gives 2.95 characters per linear pica.

	2.95	(characters per pica)
×	24	(length of type line in picas)
	70.8	(CHARACTERS PER AVERAGE LINE OF TYPE)

NOTE: Hold fraction here and do not confuse with typewritten characters in a typewritten ms line.

STEP 3: #*lt*

76,440	(characters in manuscript)
÷ 70.8	(c/alt)
1,079.6	NOTE: This fraction denotes a partially filled line of type, but it occupies space for a full line. So fraction is rounded upward to
1,080	(LINES OF TYPE)

STEP 4: l/*pg*

5.5	(depth of page in inches)
× 72	(points per inch)
396	(depth of page in points)
÷ 10	(depth of line of type)
39.6	NOTE: This fraction denotes portion of line that cannot fit into designated area. So fraction is dropped to
39	(LINES PER PAGE)

STEP 5: #*pgs*

1,080	(no. lines of type)
÷ 39	(no. lines per page)
27 27/39	NOTE: Fraction designates 27 lines of type that occupy whole paper page. So it is rounded upward to
28	(NO. OF PAGES)

The answer is given, though, as: "Twenty-eight pages, but last one is 12 lines short" or "Twenty-eight pages, but last one has only 27 lines."

Another constantly recurring problem is: "I have room in this ad for a block of copy 2½ inches wide and 3 inches deep. If we set it in 8-point Bodoni, set solid, how many words do I have to write to fill it exactly?"

Taking the five steps of copyfitting, we note that Step 1, c/ms, is really the answer we seek. So we designate that as X, the unknown in any problem, and proceed to Step 2, finding c/alt.

The lca for our 8-point Bodoni is 117 points. This is not on our chart so we go to the next higher lca that is listed: 118. This indicates a cpp of 2.85.

The measure of 2½ inches converts to 15 picas

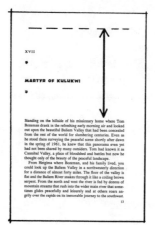

SINKAGE is that area of a page left open for the display at the beginning of a chapter in a book. It is indicated here by the arrow. Sinkage, in lines, is added to the number of lines of type the manuscript has made because sinkage "occupies space" just as type does.

and 15×2.85 gives us 42.75 characters per line of type. That's Step 2 answered.

For Step 3—finding 1/pg—we convert the 3-inch depth of the "page," the copy block, into 216 points: 3 inches $\times$ 72 points (per inch). The type is set solid, so each line is 8 points deep. Eight into 216 gives us 27 even, 27 lines per page.

If each line contains 42.75 characters and we have 27 lines to fill, we multiply the two figures and come up with 1,154.25 characters. As we can't write .25 characters, we drop that fraction.

But the question was, "How many words?" As has already been noted, "words" is a poor unit of measurement. But because many copywriters insist on this answer, a "word" has arbitrarily been defined as five characters. In this problem the answer would be given both as 230 words—dropping the last four characters because a fraction of a word is not possible—and as 1,154 characters, for a more accurate measurement.

Suppose the type will be set with 1 point of ledding. Then each line is 9 points deep. Dividing 216 points by 9 points gives 24 lines; now you need 24×42.75, or 1,026 characters, to fill.

If type is ledded 2 points, each line will be 10 points thick. Ten divided into 216 points is 21.6 lines. In this case, drop the fraction, as there cannot be just the top .6 of a line in print. Nor can the other .4 of a line extend beyond the specified copy block; there just isn't room for it.

All problems of copyfitting body type are variations of the two worked out here.

The important thing to remember, in copyfitting, is to visualize the actual steps that are taken in the composing room. Do not consider this as an abstract mathematical problem. When you visualize Linotype slugs fitting into a chase, common sense will save you from making common errors, such as moving a decimal and deciding there will be 422 characters in a line. You recognize at once that a line of that many characters will not fit on the page of any book ever seen.

Unusually short lines—less than 20 characters—will often require letterspacing or extra word spacing; so the number of printing characters may be fewer than cpp × line length will show. Unusually long lines may contain more characters than the formula determines. Such extremes in length reduce readability and should be avoided. When this is not possible, it is wise to have the compositor set about a third of a galley so you can determine the degree of accuracy of your estimate before the job proceeds to a point where any necessary revision in plans becomes too costly.

The problem of fitting display type into a given area (or determining the maximum characters that will fit into a layout) is much simpler. You are working with smaller numbers and can actually measure the space of a word.

Assume that you have the headline for an ad: *It's Paint-Up Time!* The layout indicates that 28 picas is the maximum line length that can be used.

You want to set this in the largest Caslon that will fit, so turn to the type specimen page showing this face (Example 1). Specimen books commonly repeat the same phrase for each showing. Now type the *key phrase* and, immediately under it, the headline:

Have The Chronicle-Telegram, The
It's Paint-Up Time

You know that your head will occupy approximately as much space as *Have The Chronicle.*

Measure the length of that phrase in 24-point; it occupies 20 picas. In 30-point, it is 24 picas long; in 36, it is 30 picas. To keep it within the 28-pica maximum, you have to use 30-point.

In the specimen book illustrated—and in many others—pica increments are underprinted in green. If there is no grid, we simply measure with a pica rule.

This method assumes that all letters, numbers, and punctuation points are exactly the same width and that all capitals are exactly twice as wide as any lowercase letter. Although this is not so, for most purposes wide and narrow letters will average out in almost any given line; if there are many wide letters, allow more space for them.

The same approximation may be used for body type, when accuracy within a line or two is adequate. Find a block of type set in the face and size you desire. Measure it off at the line length you need. Type three or four consecutive lines. Determine the average characters per line and set your typewriter right-hand margin at that number. Then, keeping always under that maximum, type the number of lines needed to fill your space.

When a more accurate fit is required for display type, the newspaper headline writer's *unit count systems* should be used. He gives a value to each character. Most lowercase letters, numbers, and spaces count 1; *m* and *w* count 1½; punctuation, *i*, and *l* count ½; *M* and W, 2½; *I*, 1; all other capitals, 2.

So our headline counts;

$$\frac{1\ 1\tfrac{1}{2}\ 1\ 1\ 2\ 1\tfrac{1}{2}\ 1\ 1\ 1\ 2\ 1\ 1\ 2\ \tfrac{1}{2}\ 1\tfrac{1}{2}\ 1\tfrac{1}{2}}{\text{I\ t\ ' s\quad P\ a\ i\ n\ t\ -\ U\ p\quad T\ i\ m\ e\ !}} = 20\tfrac{1}{2}\ \text{units}$$

Using the same system, count out 20½ units on the sample line in the key phrase; the head will occupy 24 picas in 30-point Caslon Bold.

In this case there is an ample margin—4 picas—for variation in letter widths. But in any case, and using any method, it is always best to write headlines a little short. It is simple to distribute extra

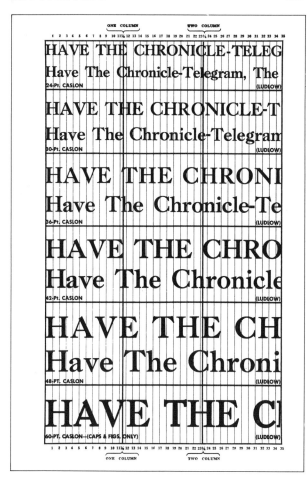

Example 1. TYPE-SPECIMEN PAGE from the book issued by the *Chronicle-Telegram* of Elyria, Ohio, for use of its advertisers. In the original, the vertical lines are printed in green, 1 pica apart.

spacing to fill out a line; often it is impossible to decrease spacing enough to squeeze type into a tight fit, or, at least, without damaging readability seriously. The practice of eliminating word spacing entirely to make a line fit—a practice of slovenly newspapers or advertisers—can never be condoned.

If these two methods indicate that the head will just fit, with no margin at all, the infallible check is to tick off the width of each letter on a strip of paper and determine the length of the whole head. This requires a specimen which has *ABC* in addition to, or instead of, a key phrase.

Accurate copyfitting is essential in all phases of

converting words into type. It is easy to delete a few words in the manuscript to fit available space; once copy is in type, it may mean resetting many lines in order to make a proper fit. This is costly in cash and time, and the results often show the pressure of deadlines under which such condensation is done.

Arithmetic must be precise. A minor error in addition may cause an unforeseen additional press run or result in wasted, blank pages. Prove every arithmetical answer.

It will pay handsome dividends to any designer to master copyfitting; he will use it as often as he uses multiplication tables.

SUGGESTED READINGS

Auble, J. Woodard. *Arithmetic for Printers*. Peoria, Ill.: Chas. A. Bennett Co., Inc., 1955.

Dalgin, Ben. *Advertising Production*. New York: McGraw-Hill Book Co., Inc., 1946.

De Lopatecki, Eugene. *Typographers Desk Manual*. New York: Ronald Press, 1949.

Melcher, Daniel, and Larrick, Nancy. *Printing and Promotion Handbook*. New York: McGraw-Hill Book Co., Inc., 1956.

Typesetters are instructed to "follow the copy . . . out the window."

The *proofreader* insists that copy be followed implicitly. It is his job to make sure that the printed word reproduces exactly the words of the manuscript. Should it have to be followed out the window, he will question the author about the accuracy of a statement or the use of a word. But basically the proofreader leaves to the author all responsibility other than that of cleansing the printed work of any compositor's errors.

This is a ceaseless task; to err is human and compositors are human. Add certain characteristics of typesetting machines and the opportunity for error is staggering.

Checking for accuracy begins long before the typesetter sees the manuscript. The author himself and several skilled readers examine the manuscript meticulously, to correct or query errors of fact, of grammar and construction, and of typewriting. (This is *copyreading*, which we shall not discuss in this volume, but which has been explained in many good books, including those listed in the bibliography at the end of this chapter.)

The typesetter makes the first *proofreading* check. Each time he sets a line of type, whether by hand or machine, he looks at the type, matrices, or hard copy to correct any mechanical errors which he or the machine may have made. We shall examine procedure with hot-metal machines although cold type follows the same general steps.

When a galley of type has been set it is *proved*— or *proofed*—by printing from it on a simple hand press. The proof is pulled on long narrow sheets of paper whose size and shape roughly duplicate that of the galley, which gives the name *galley proofs*.

This proof is read and corrections ordered. After they are made, a revised proof is pulled. This *first revise* is read as carefully as the first proof; special care is given to the corrections, lest new errors be introduced while original ones are remedied. There may be second or third revises, and on some jobs the revises may run to two numbers, not to correct

9

Proofreading

To Err
Is Human

errors but to achieve close to perfect spacing and word division.

After a form has been made up, it may be proofed on the same press used for galley proofs. If the form is too large to fit into this small press, a *stone* or *beaten* proof may be taken. The form, resting on the composing stone, is inked with a hand *brayer*. A piece of paper, sometimes dampened, is placed over the form. A *planer,* a flat block of wood with a large, flat handle, is placed on the paper and pounded with a mallet. The planer is moved so that all the type is thus impressed upon the paper. The resulting proof is crude but adequate.

Even after the form has been locked into the regular press, the first impressions, *page proofs*, are read once more. Although corrections are expensive at this stage, they still are made if necessary.

Proofreading is best done by two-man teams. When reading galleys, the *proofreader* works with the proof; the *copyholder* has the original manuscript. As they take turns reading from the material in front of them, the proofreader marks corrections on the proof.

Sometimes in the composing room, and most frequently by the printing customer, proofs are read by one man who concentrates on the proof and only occasionally compares it to the manuscript. This is called *horsing*.

Corrections are made by two methods, the *guideline system* and the *book system*. In the first, the error is corrected by circling it and running a line from the error to the margin where the correction is written. This method is invitation for confusion. Especially with a *dirty proof,* one containing many errors or changes, the guidelines may cross each other or may obliterate other errors.

In the book system, two marks are used for each error. One, at the scene of the crime, points out the error. The other, on exactly the same horizontal line but out in the margin, instructs the typesetter how to correct the fault. The book system is the most efficient one and the only one to be discussed in detail here. (The guideline system is best used only

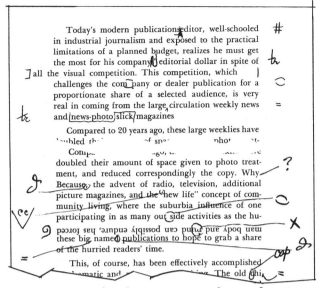

GUIDELINE SYSTEM of proofreading, shown in the lower portion of this fragment, can become confusing, especially with a dirty proof.

No matter how many errors are to be corrected, the book method, shown in the upper portion, is easy to follow accurately.

on page proofs when errors are few and margins are often far from type.)

Proofreading has many things in common—function and symbols—with copyreading. Both seek to correct errors, and the methods they use are similar enough to cause confusion. The copyreader makes his corrections within the copy. If he wants to change a word, he strikes it out and writes the replacement above it. He changes a lowercase *b* to a capital simply by writing a second bowl above the first. And so on. This would be impossible for the proofreader. There isn't enough room between lines of type, and attempts to make corrections within the type instead of marginally will simply confuse the printer and perpetrate even more errors.

Because the same person often performs the same jobs, copyreading and proofreading, he must remind himself which hat he is wearing at the moment and use the proper tools for that particular task. Proofreaders have a kind of shorthand, symbols that can be written quickly in a form impossible to misunderstand.

Each composing room seems to have its own variations on the basic proofreading system. But mastery of the elementary method will enable any proofreader to be unmistakably understood by any printer and to accommodate himself to any minor variations he may meet.

Let us consider the proofreader's symbols.

The simplest are those within the type, those that single out the error. There are basically three kinds of errors: something must be taken out; something must be added; something must be changed.

When a letter is to be deleted, it is marked out of the type by a single vertical stroke. (Make sure it is perpendicular to avoid confusion with almost similar notation for lowercasing.)

When several characters must be taken out, they are crossed out with a single horizontal stroke. When a whole paragraph is to be deleted, the top and bottom lines are crossed out with a horizontal stroke and these lines are connected with large X's.

When something is to be added to the type, a *caret*—like a tiny upside-down V—is placed within the type at the proper point. If the element to be added is a *superior character*—apostrophe, single or double quotes, or a numeral denoting the squaring of a number in a mathematical formula—the caret is inverted and inserted at the top of the line of type.

The regular caret indicates where spacing must be added and where it should be removed within a line of type.

If interlineal spacing—ledding—is to be added or removed, a caret lying on its side points to the place where the spacing is to go or come out.

Potential changes are many, and so are the proper intratype signals.

If a capital is to be changed to lowercase, the offending majuscule is slashed with a diagonal stroke, northeast to southwest. It may seem picayune to stress such minor details but, after all, there is not much difference between bell and boll—except that one form is incorrect!

When several adjacent letters—a whole word or more—are incorrectly capped, they are circled.

A lowercase character to be capitalized is underscored by three parallel horizontal strokes. If only two parallel lines are used, they indicate the element should be changed to small caps. A single underscore calls for Italics, a wavy underscore means boldface, a combination of both indicates bold Italics. A letter or word in bf or Itlx is circled.

When a letter must be replaced, because it is the wrong one, is in the wrong font, or is broken, it is circled. A whole word to be changed is also circled.

A common error in Linotype composition is a transposition of letters. Suppose a letter is taken from a channel at the far right of the Lino magazine. As it moves to the left for assembling, the second letter which is drawn from the left of the magazine may drop in front of the first one. A skilled operator anticipates this difficulty and pauses before hitting the second key of such combination. But despite this, transpositions are rather frequent. Intratype indication is a "lazy S," the character lying on its side and holding the two elements in its curves.

Transposed words are indicated the same way, simply by elongating the S.

Whole lines often become transposed as Linotype slugs are shuffled. To transpose two lines, the top line is enclosed at the left with a bracket and from it an arrow half-circles down under the next line. At the right margin, a bracket holds the second line and the arrow goes up above Line 1.

If several lines are misplaced, their correct order is marked, 1, 2, 3, etc., in the left margin.

Spacing material in hand-set composition has a habit of being forced up far enough to capture ink and print a smear. Such a blemish is circled.

When a character is deleted and the ones on either side are to be brought together, they are joined by a pair of parentheses ( ) lying on their side. This *closeup* sign may be used alone or bracketing a strikeout mark as well.

These marks are deliberately simple so they will not totally hide the characters on the proof. The marginal notations are more distinctive. They must be precise, of course, because an intratype symbol may be the same for several errors. They must be

PROOFREADER'S SYMBOLS go back into history almost to the first days of printing.

Early proofreaders were always scholars, men so learned that they were their own reference libraries.

Proofreaders were held responsible to a rather drastic extent. A notorious English edition of the Scriptures was called *The Thieves' Bible* because it left out the "not" on the commandment about stealing. The proofreader never repeated his error . . . he was executed before he had a chance.

Now is the time for all good men to come to the aid of the party.

⌐ HEADLINE

Now is the time for all good men to come

⌐ HEADLINE ⌐

Now is the time for all good men to come

| HEADLINE ⌐

Now is the time for all good men to come

HEADLINE

—— Now is the time for all good men to come to the aid

HEADLINE ——

Now is the time for all good men to come to the aid of the

Now is the time for all good men to come to the aid of the party. So the clarion call goes forth throughout the nation.

Now is the time for all good men *tr*

Now the time is for all good men *tr*

1 3 4 5 6 8 7 2 *tr*
Now the time for all men good is

Now is the time for all good men *tr* #

Now is the time for all good men to come to the aid of the party. So the clarion call goes forth today

to all the reaches of this glorious land

Now is the time for all good men to come to the aid of the party. So the clarion call goes forth today to all the reaches

Now is the time for all good men to come to the aid of the party. So the clarion call goes forth today to all the reaches

Now is the ti me for all good men　　⌣

Now is the the time for all good　　✓✓✓

Now is the time for all good men　　#

¶　Now is the time for all
good men to come to the

Now is the time for all
good men to come to the aid　　en quad

☐　Now is the time for all
good men to come to the aid

Now is the time for all good men　　wf

Now is the time for all good men　　lc

Now is the time FOR all good men　　lc

now is the time for all good men　　cap

now is the time for all good men　　cap

Now is the time
for all good men　　u + lc

Now is the time for all good men　　bf

Now is the time for all good men　　Italic

Now is the time for all good men　　bf Ital

Now is the time for all good men　　cap + s.c.

Now is the time for all good men　　cap + s.c.

Now is the time for all good men　　small cap

H O is water　　/2\

H O is water　　/2\

Is energy truly mc2?

Is energy truly mc?

Now its the time for all good men

Now, I say is the time for all good men

to come to the aid of the party

Now is the time, let all good men come

Now is the time, let all good men come

Now (or very soon is the time for all

Now (or very soon [so he said, very soon) is the time

"Now, he said, "is the time to come."

"Now, he said, "is the time to come."

The question is Is now the time for all good men?

He said, "Patriots have said 'Now is the time but
so have knaves."

He said, "Patriots have said 'Now is the time but
so have knaves."

Is this the time to come to the aid of the party

What is the proper time? Now! Now

This is the half time whistle blowing.

Now is the time—if ever it shall be for all good men

Now is the time—if ever there shall be for all good men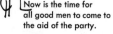

Now is the time for
all good men to come to
the aid of the party.

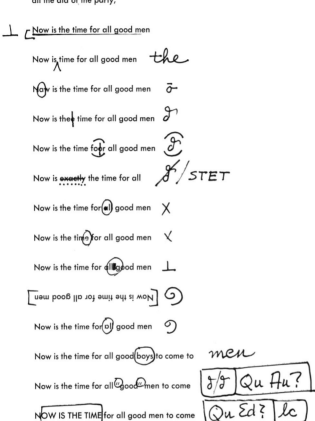

no ¶   ⌐Now is the time for
all good men to come to the
aid of the party.

Now is the time for⌃
all the aid of the party,

⊥ ⌐Now is the time for all good men

Now is̲ time for all good men   *the*
          ⌃

N⊙w is the time for all good men   ō

Now is thee̶ time for all good men   𝒥

Now is the time fo⊙r all good men   𝒥

Now is exactly the time for all   𝒥 / STET

Now is the time for⟨al⟩l good men   X

Now is the tim⟨e⟩ for all good men   X

Now is the time for all good men   ⊥

⌐Now is the time for all good men⌐   ◯ (reversed)

Now is the time for⟨al⟩l good men   ◯ (reversed)

Now is the time for all good⟨boys⟩to come to   *men*

Now is the time for all good men to come   𝒥/𝒥 Qu Au?

⟨NOW IS THE TIME⟩for all good men to come   Qu Ed? lc

unmistakable; the printer is working at high speed at the point of making corrections, especially if he is on a newspaper, and usually is working with unfamiliar copy. These symbols have been developed over the centuries by pragmatists and are used today for the simple reason: They work.

The most distinctive mark is the *delete* sign. This is an ancient version of the lowercase *d,* its final stroke looping off to the right of the ascender. Because this symbol is written rapidly, it varies as much as any handwritten character does. Care should be taken to write it the same way each time. The delete, as the name expresses, is used to take out unwanted letters, words, phrases, or whole sections of type.

Another frequently used sign is that indicating a *transposition.* The mark *tr* in the margin tells the printer to reverse the order of letters or words so marked. *Tr lines* tells him to manipulate whole lines that are in improper order.

The symbol *wf* means *wrong font.* This indicates that a matrix or piece of type of the wrong size or style has been used inadvertently.

A mark like an upside-down *T* represents a finger pushing down a slug or spacing material that has worked up high enough to print. A symbol like a square-bottomed *U* depicts a fist pushing type into proper position—left, right, up or down—depending upon the direction of the *U.* The sign that calls for inserting space is the old tick-tack-toe.

The same closeup sign, parens on their sides, that is used within the type is also used in the margin. When the closeup brackets the delete mark in the margin, it calls for bringing together letters separated when the deletion was made. If the extra *e* in *leetter* has been deleted, the *le* is moved up tight to the *t* by these instructions.

A small open square calls for an em quad. If more quads are needed, a square is drawn for each one or, in a single square, the required number is written.

A hyphen is indicated by two short, parallel lines like the equal sign. A dash is a longer line, with a serif at each end. Its length is indicated by writing a number above the dash and *en* or *em* under it. A paragraph is marked either with an L-shaped mark or with a mark like a reverse P with two vertical strokes.

If a line or a character is upside down, the mark is like a loose 9, as a finger would make didactic by describing clockwise motion.

Most of the other marks are self-explanatory. A few are exaggerated to avoid misunderstanding. A period, for instance, is circled so it is not over-looked. A comma is indicated by a heavy dot with a tail, something like a 9 with the bowl blacked in.

When the author has made what appears to be an obvious error—calling Lincoln our first President, for instance—the proofreader will ask the author about it by writing a circled *Qu?*, for *query*.

Comma symbols are usually tented with a caret. This distinguishes them from the same symbol used for apostrophes or quotation marks, which are written between the arms of a normal V.

The check mark that calls for *equalize spacing* is often confusing. If the compositor has put too much or too little space between two words, the proof-reader inserts the check mark between those words and repeats a single check in the margin. But if the space is irregular throughout the entire line, he places a check at each word space and puts three check marks in the margin. This tells the typesetter that spacing is incorrect between all, or at least most, of the words and that the whole line needs reworking.

Marginal notations may be written in either the left or right margin as long as they are level with the line of type. They must always be written in the order in which the errors appear. If there is more than one correction in a line, the notations are separated by a diagonal slash /. Each error must have a marginal correction even if it is repeated. Thus, if a line appeared as:

Naow is tha timme for all good men

marginal notations would be: *d/ e/ d* (the lowercase *d* represents the delete sign). The first *d* would remove the *a* in *Naow;* the second would take out the extra *m* in *timme.* Both also require the closeup sign. The *e* changes *tha* to *the.*

A single delete sign will take out a whole word or those adjacent letters struck out in the type by a single horizontal stroke. So the line

Now is the the time for all good men

would be corrected by a single marginal delete sign for the whole word *the.*

It must be emphasized that every error requires two marks, one at the point of the error and one in the margin. Every time one of the marks discussed in the previous grafs is used intratype, a proper symbol must appear in the margin.

Busy as they are in catching other people's errors, proofreaders make their own, too. When a "correction" turns out to be unnecessary, the proofreader writes *stet* in the margin. That means: *Stetare! Let it stand*—just forget it! Then he underscores, with a dotted line, those letters or words that were correct in their original form.

Sometimes the typesetter may follow copy faithfully and thus repeat an error in the manuscript. Suppose the phrase *bays and girls* appears in the galley proof. The proofreader checks the manuscript; it is the same way there. He thinks that this should be *boys* instead of *bays* but he, too, must follow copy. So he makes the obvious correction but at the same time queries the author and ties the two symbols together in a large circle. If the author agrees to the correction, he crosses out the query sign and lets the correction symbol stand. Or, if he were attempting a pun and really wanted the word to be *bays,* he crosses out both symbols, puts a dotted line under the word and commands, Stet!

All the signs and procedures discussed thus far are concerned with correcting typographical errors, those of the typesetter and so-called *office corrections.* The cost of making these corrections is absorbed by the printer as a normal expense.

But authors, too, are human; they change their minds or have second thoughts. These corrections and alterations must also be made to maintain accuracy. These are called *author's alterations*—AA's—and are charged back to the customer.

Suppose you are producing a catalogue for Amalgamated Widget Company. On page 7 of the manuscript, your typist hit the wrong key and the Super-Giant Widget is identified as C-105, not, correctly, as C-106.

If the job is set in foundry type or in Monotype, it is comparatively easy to remove the 5 and replace it with a 6. But if the error is in a Linotype slug, the whole line must be reset. This takes more time and costs more money. If the face used in this job is not on the machine at the moment, the operator must find the proper magazine and put it on, after taking off one in current use and storing it properly. This takes even more time, and the customer must pay for it.

People who buy large quantities of composition estimate that it costs $1 for every line that must be reset. This figure varies, of course, but it is indisputable that the cost is not inconsiderable.

This points up the necessity for close reading of the copy before it gets to the typesetter. Correcting the steno's bobble in the manuscript would have entailed two seconds for crossing out the 5 and writing a 6 above it. Professional copyreading will eliminate almost all such errors.

Now suppose that just before the catalogue goes to press, the sales department finds out that the Colossal Widget Corporation, your deadliest competitor, is selling their comparable model $3 under your price. "We've got to be competitive!" is the anguished cry. "Change the price from $159.95 to $153.88!"

The process of making this *author's alteration* is identical with that of correcting an error. This, too, is paid for by the customer. He is perfectly willing to assume the added expense that business exigencies have forced upon him.

But the author's alteration that can be costliest to make is an editing process that is done in type instead of at the typewriter. The cost may be not only in money but in time. Most printing is done under compelling deadlines and often the time involved becomes a major factor.

Let us suppose that the Super-Giant Widget has been described as a device that brings its own absolute contentment as the red sun slowly sinks in the west. The typesetter has dutifully converted this deathless prose into metal. The proof is delivered to the author. He has decided he doesn't like that word *red;* it lacks the fine feeling necessary to motivate the reader to rush out and buy a widget. He searches his memory, dictionary, and thesaurus and decides that this word should be *crimson.* He crosses out *red* and writes *crimson* in the margin and away goes the proof to the printer.

Now the typesetter resets the line in which *red* appears, putting *crimson* in its place. Alas! The new word has four more letters than the original. What does he do with them? He just breaks that long word at the end of the line and hyphenates it down to the next line. That means resetting Line 2, of course. But still he has those four extra letters. So he carries them, either in the form of hyphenation or as a smaller word, down to the third line, and then the fourth and so on. He may have to reset every line until the end of the paragraph before those excess letters find a permanent home.

So this alteration has cost, not the minimum $1 for resetting a single line, but several more dollars to reset many lines.

There may be some legitimate occasion for making revisions at this late stage. But if the need for change of content has not become apparent in the various editing stages, it is probably not necessary after the type has been set. All editing should be done with pencil on copy paper, not with type on a galley.

The author, or printing buyer, usually sees the first revised proof. (The printer's proofreader has corrected the typographical errors—*typos*—on the original galley proof.) The second or third revise is also sent to the author so he can determine whether his corrections or alterations were properly made.

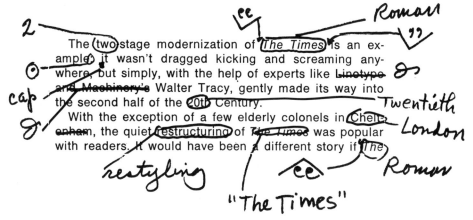

Great care should be given to reading the whole correction line, or lines, not just the single error that was originally marked. Correction lines usually have a higher incidence of additional errors than the original galley had.

When the typesetter has to set several lines in the process of making a correction or alteration, these lines will usually be indicated by blue brackets. They must be read even more carefully than on the first proofs, for they are brand-new composition and subject to as many mistakes as the original setting.

In reading galley proofs, determine first that the face, size, and ledding are correct. If the face has long or short descenders, check that the proper ones are used here. If Old Style or Modern figures are available, make sure that the proper ones—and only these—have been used. The compositor should use ligatures throughout or not at all; mixing confuses the reader. The buyer of printing is ultimately responsible for both editorial and mechanical accuracy. So first read the proofs for content, punctuation, and capitalization.

Read it a second time for typographical errors. Even when the composition is lengthy, two separate readings will usually save time in the aggregate and will also insure greater accuracy.

Reading with a copyholder is the best method, but often not available to the typical printing

AUTHOR'S ALTERATIONS add unnecessarily to the cost of typesetting. Here only one "correction" is actually required for accuracy; all others are editorial changes that should have been made in the manuscript. None makes obvious improvements on the literary quality of the typeset matter.

buyer. Reading alone demands painstaking attention to detail and should be done in an area free from distraction.

A sharp, clear proof is essential and should be demanded.

In the second reading, ignore words and phrases, concentrate on individual letters. For single errors, make the correction in the left margin. If there are more than two or three errors in a line (an uncommon occurrence), succeeding notations should be made in the right margin.

Once an error is found, be sure to give unusual attention to the balance of that line. Often the proofreader feels overconfident and just skims on after making the initial correction.

This is especially true if a whole line is upside-down. The reader corrects this obvious mistake, then neglects to turn the proof around to read the topsy-turvy line. Errors in transposed lines are also very easy to overlook.

A few usages are automatic danger signals; when you see them, beware. If the copy mentions a series, such as: *The first five states in automobile production are*—make sure that five states, not four or six, are listed. When names are repeated, make sure they are identical in each use. The *New Yorker* magazine delights in catching a character in a novel who turns from Anne in Chapter I to Ann in Chapter XXI, and perhaps to Constance somewhere en route. (And all too often her hair changes from red to black because author and copyreader dozed simultaneously.)

Remember that quotes, parentheses, braces, ellipses, and dashes are a pair of hands, holding phrases in apposition; one hand alone cannot enclose such set-apart material. Every time you see one of such a pair, look for the other. In some instances, the period may take the place of one of these separators. But never take that for granted. Nothing will disconcert a reader more than to wade through page after page of improbable conversation before he finds out that someone merely forgot to close a quote.

Whenever a date appears, it should be checked. Was December 22, 1959, really on Thursday? Is Sioux Falls in Iowa or South Dakota? Is Charles Smith's middle initial really *T*?

Hyphenated words require extra care. Have they been broken at proper syllables? Is it Eng-land or En-gland? Know-ledge or knowl-edge?

Combinations of *l* with *t* or *f* are inherently dangerous. For *tl* can easily be confused with *tt* at a casual glance.

But the most insidious errors are those in which a single wrong letter creates a common—even if incorrect—word. The eye instantly recognizes *pxrt* as an error. But if it is *part* instead of *port,* there is a tendency to overlook it. So you cannot completely shut off reading for sense even though you should concentrate on reading letters the second time.

Reading page proofs of magazines, newspapers, and advertising requires attention to several new points. First, determine that the layout is correct. If any elements are out of position, indicate their proper place. Do not make tiny changes, though. Often the form is not locked as tightly as it will be on the press, and the elements may well shift several points to the proper position in the lock-up process.

Then check art work. Are the proper pictures used? Especially in commercial printing—the hypothetical widget catalogue, for example—there is often little difference between the 2 × 3-inch picture of an economy model widget on page 3 and a 2 × 3 of the deluxe model on page 12. Especially those cuts of identical size must be closely scrutinized.

Then check picture captions. Those four men identified around a conference table may easily be the four men at a sales meeting shown three pages later.

Count faces and names in each picture and accompanying caption. Here particularly (although this holds true wherever several names are listed), make sure that each name is complete. If John H. Jones's name appears sixth in a group of 24 names —and especially if it breaks from one line to the next—it is easy to overlook the fact that only *John H.* appears at the end of Line 5 and that Line 6 starts with *Sylvester Q. Trumble.*

If prices are set in a different, usually larger, face, make sure that they are correct. They have been set separately and it is easy to mix them up when the contents of several galleys are combined in the form.

In advertising, the buyer usually sees his first proof as a made-up form. Type is scattered into several' separate groupings, not all together in a block the way it was in galleys. It is wise to set a ruler under each line, read it meticulously, and then put a checkmark at the right of the line to indicate it has been read. Before the proof is returned, inspect it to make sure every line—no matter how widely separated they may be—has been read.

Give special care to the address, phone number, store hours, or similar recurring material that has grown so familiar it is often accepted without reading.

Be particularly careful in reading headlines. Errors in display type—despite the fact that they are so easily overlooked by the proofreader—are especially glaring to the casual reader. Some people will tack proofs up on the wall, step back several paces, and read the display lines from a distance.

Finally, on ads, make sure that the signature cut is included. Without this identification, the ad is worthless; yet this omission is not at all infrequent.

Wise advertising men have checklists of the essential elements in each ad: headline, copy blocks, prices, art, address, phone number, etc., and insist that each be checked off (with the initials of the reader) before the proof is returned.

Proofs must be returned to the typesetter on deadline. If proofs are returned promptly, it can effect savings in money because the magazines may still be on the machine and the stone man is familiar with the style he has just been making up. Late proofs often mean overtime work to make corrections before an inflexible press time. This cost is passed on to the buyer.

Prompt return of proofs assures that the printer will be able to make corrections with at least a modicum of pressureless time. Late proofs just cannot be given that unhurried care that is essential to a perfect job.

The difficulty—and cost—of corrections depend, too, on the job. In book work, the number of corrections will be larger than in a two-page travel folder, and each correction line will cost less proportionately because overhead costs are prorated among many units.

When the proofreader has finished his job he initials or signs it: *OK/ JJH* or "OK with corrections," *OKwc/JJH*. He is the only graphic arts man to sign his work. He does so, not to be identified if an error later becomes visible, but because he is proud of his work.

Printing confers an authority and credibility that spoken words never attain. How many times have you heard, "I know it's so because I saw it in a book!" Or "in the paper" or just "in print." The proofreader is conscientious because he knows that printing is also the art preservative of truth and accuracy.

SUGGESTED READINGS

Lasky, Joseph. *Proofreading and Copy Preparation.* New York: New American Library (Mentor Book), 1954.

A Manual of Style. Chicago: University of Chicago Press, 1969.

Style Manual. Washington, D.C.: Government Printing Office, 1950.

10

Letterpress

The Classic Printing Method

If you have ever used a rubber stamp, you have been a letterpress printer. This familiar gadget is a simple and perfect example of letterpress, the oldest printing method.

Letterpress is the method whereby a relief image of the character carries ink to the paper.

The earliest date we can attribute to printing is about 2000 B.C., when the Babylonians produced playing cards. The Chinese printed from carved wooden blocks by placing paper on the inked relief surfaces and rubbing or brushing the paper until the whole design had been transferred. This is similar to the way youngsters "print" wood blocks by rubbing the paper with the heel of a spoon.

Centuries were to pass before mankind found a method of producing the impression with a single movement. Although Gutenberg would be well enough honored as the inventor of movable type, many observers ascribe to him the first true printing press. This is undeserved acclaim. Wood blocks, which preceded metal type, were printed on a similar, if not identical, press. An ancient engraving of a press shows the date 1420 carved into the wooden structure.

The machine itself was not a drastically new device. As a matter of fact, it gets its name from the prosaic machine long used to press grapes and cheese.

Joining together two massive beams which ran from floor to ceiling was a stout wooden crossbeam. Through it passed a vertical wood screw. A waist-high platform held the type, and the *platen,* a flat plate that impressed the paper upon the type, was forced down as the screw was turned by a long horizontal lever.

The process was entirely manual. Untanned sheepskins, stuffed with wool, and fastened to stubby handles, were the *balls* by which ink was spread on the type. The paper was well moistened, so it would accommodate itself to the often uneven surface of the printing form. These steps were done as the *bed* or form was pulled out from under the platen. Then, after the type was pushed back under the platen, the pressman would tighten the screw to make the impression, pressure was released by a backward sweep of the lever, the form was pulled out so blanket and paper could be peeled off, and the whole cycle started over again—at the frustrating pace of 20 impressions per hour.

This press was standard throughout Europe for 150 years although minor improvements were made: the screw became copper; a sliding bed made it easier to ink the form; the blanket was transformed into a *tympan,* part of the platen; a *frisket* shielded the paper from areas which were not supposed to print. The first press in North America—that of Juan Pablos in 1539 in Mexico City—and the first one in Colonial America—that of Stephen Daye in Plymouth in 1639—were basically the same in design. Daye's press still exists in the state capitol at Montpelier, Vermont.

The first press built in what is now the United States was the product of Christopher Sauer, Jr., in Germantown, Pennsylvania, in 1750. Until that time all presses were imported from England.

The first press to be invented in America was the famous *Columbian,* a name still revered by all printers. Built by George Clymer in Philadelphia in 1813, the new model replaced the cumbersome screw with a system of levers actuated by a long lever, "the devil's tail." (It came honestly by the appellation; if pressure were unexpectedly released, the tail would sweep back like a whip and its heavy iron handle could knock a pressman into oblivion— or even into the obituary columns.)

An adaptation, the *Washington Press,* used a toggle joint instead of a lever complex. Washington presses are still in many a print shop today, most as museum pieces, a few still used as proof presses.

The *platen press* as we know it was born in 1830 in Boston. It is a press with a clamshell motion that carries the platen from a horizontal position, upward from hinges at its bottom, against the printing form which is locked perpendicularly. Its action is similar to that with which the cover of a book is opened and closed as the volume lies stationary and

WOOD PRESS as used in Colonial times in America was hardly changed in the three centuries since its predecessor in Gutenberg's shop. The wood frame had to be sturdy to withstand the extreme pressure that was necessary to impress all elements of the form with an irregular surface.

A heavy woolen blanket was placed between the paper and the wooden platen that was pressed down by the screw. This, too, was to accommodate the pressure to the irregular surface.

Today the covering of the impression cylinder on a letterpress is still called the blanket although it is made of rubber or plastic.

gives the name *clapper*, or *clamshell*, by which platen presses are known familiarly today.

When patents expired, in the 1880's, Chandler and Price entered a market where it is still active. The *C&P* was, and is, the mainstay of many a print-shop, as was the picturesquely named *Colt's Armory* or *Universal Press*.

All these models were operated by a foot treadle which left the pressman's hands free, one to place blank sheets on the platen, the other to remove the printed sheets and pile them up neatly.

Many platen presses today are automatic; mechanical "hands" with pneumatic suckers feed and remove paper. But hand-fed platens are useful for short runs and many an exemplary piece is printed on tiny hand-fed and hand-powered presses that take only a 3×5-inch form. In commercial shops, platens account for well over 50 per cent of all presses in use today although, because so many are used for short runs, they do not produce anywhere near 50 per cent of printing volume.

The second most popular press is the *cylinder press*. The form is placed on a horizontal bed, the paper impressed upon it by a cylinder that rolls across the form. The cylinder touches only a small portion of the form at any given time and thus pressure can be extremely uniform and the result is excellent quality.

A Saxony clockmaker, Friederich Koenig, patented the first cylinder press in England in 1810. He had found references to the use of rollers to print copperplates shortly after Gutenberg's day. He adapted the principle to letterpress, moving the bed back and forth beneath the cylinder, which revolves on a stationary axis. The first cylinder was used by *The Times of London* and performed, to the proprietors' delight, at 1,100 copies per hour. This was improved upon by a Briton, D. Napier, who invented metal *grippers*. These clutched the blank paper, which was then wound around the cylinder during the impression cycle, released, and then clutched by another set of grippers which pulled the printed sheets away from the form and onto the delivery table.

FINNISH PRINTER shows by his costume that he is of the seventeenth century. This stamp marks the centennial of the printing of the first Bible in Finland in 1642. Note the long lever; when this became the "devil's tail" in later versions of a similar press, it met —as shown here—the pressman's head at a most vulnerable place.

On the cylinder press, the bed of the press moves forward and back under a pyramid of rollers that ink the form evenly. During that cycle, the cylinder is raised from the form. Then, gripping a blank sheet, the cylinder drops down to roll across the form as it makes its second back-and-forth motion. As the form is inked again, the lifted cylinder sends the printed sheet to the delivery table. This is the *double-revolution* principle.

The proof press in most composing rooms is a small cylinder model.

Richard March Hoe, whose company built the first American cylinder in 1830, invented the third category of presses in 1846, the *rotary*.

The moving bed of a cylinder press must be massive, and thus heavy, to afford an absolutely smooth surface for the type form. This, plus the not trifling weight of the forms themselves, is a heavy mass to move many feet, stop, and move back again. This places an inherent speed restriction upon all cylinder presses, especially the giants that print newspapers. Hoe looked for a way to eliminate the problem caused by this reversal of direction. His answer was to place the type as well as the paper on a cylinder. V-shaped column rules held the type firmly against the centrifugal force.

This cylinder was large so that each individual line of type stood, in effect, on an almost flat surface. Indeed, the cylinder was so large that four impression cylinders fitted neatly against it. Each of these could be hand-fed at 2,000 copies per hour, making the total production 8,000. Later models added more impression cylinders and increased capacity proportionately.

Again the principle remains today, although one major improvement—curved stereotype plates—makes possible the phenomenal speeds of modern newspaper presses, and curved stereotypes and plastic or rubber plates have many applications.

R. Hoe and Company also invented a cutting and folding machine as an integral part of the *web-fed* press. It cuts the continuous roll of printed paper into proper-sized sheets and folds them into pages. (The principle of printing from a roll, instead of

PLATEN PRESS, shown in schematic form, opens and closes on the hinge at the bottom. The form, held vertically, is inked by a set of rollers that move across the face of a large, smooth disk at the top of the press. It slowly rotates so that its coating of ink remains even.

The printer removes the printed page with one hand and piles it on the delivery table while with the other hand he inserts a fresh sheet before the platen closes again.

single sheets, had been invented in 1865.) These two inventions are essential in newspaper printing today.

Goss Printing Company first built presses that worked together as a team, printing several complete newspapers at one time. As early as 1889, only four years after its founding, the Chicago firm built a sextuple press for the *New York Herald* that printed off a roll unwinding at 25 miles per hour and produced 72,000 complete copies per hour. They were the first to build presses that could be expanded by adding additional units. Today, for instance, the *Chicago Tribune* links 95 Goss units into a single complex that prints two million 20-page papers (or any variation thereof) in one hour.

Most rotaries are *perfecting presses*. That is, they print on both sides of the sheet or paper *web*—the continuous sheet that feeds off a roll—and then fold the pages into signatures. Each *unit* of such a press prints the front and back of two or more pages. The paper must be fed through the press in such a way that the products of all units will fold together properly into a single newspaper.

A *perfector press* performs the same front-and-back printing on a flat-bed press with two cylinders.

Hoe and Goss, along with the Miehle Company, which produces most of the country's cylinder presses, are leaders in the field, although there are many other excellent manufacturers. Among these are Cottrell and Sons, who make the famous McKee rotary. This reverses Hoe's original principle, for it uses a single large impression cylinder and around it banks from two to five platen cylinders, each carrying a separate color so that the entire full-color reproduction can be printed in one revolution. The McKee is credited with making possible such large, huge-volume picture magazines as *Life* and *Look*, which must print precise color work at very high speeds.

The Miehle Vertical is another well-known American press. Its unusual feature is that the type is held in a perpendicular position and moves up

FLATBED PRESS, or cylinder press, in this schematic drawing, shows the two components that give it these names. In simplest version, the cylinder is rolled across the form by hand; often it moves on a cogged track that fits a gear on the axle. This regulates the pressure.

In commercial form, the cylinder is on a stationary axle and the form moves back and forth beneath it. Metal fingers hold the paper to the cylinder instead of having it lie on the form.

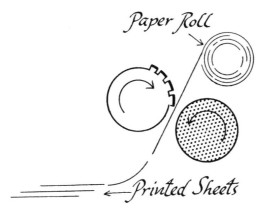

Paper Roll

Printed Sheets

ROTARY PRESS feeds off an end-less roll of paper. It, the type cylinder, and the impression cyl-inder all move in only one direc-tion at a great speed.

The so-called endless roll of paper is practically that. When the roll is just about used up, a second, some 40 inches wide, 6 feet in diameter and weighing a ton, is moved into position. Its leading edge is adhered to the end of the first roll by a mecha-nism called the *flying paster*. All this is done without stopping the press.

The curved printing surface is a stereotype, electrotype, or flexible wraparound plate.

and down to contact the impression cylinder. The Heidelberg press, made in Germany, became very popular in America after World War II. One of the unusual features of this platen press is that its mechanical fingers can pick up two blank sheets and print them, with duplicate or entirely different forms, at the same time. English-made presses are commonplace in Canada although not in the United States.

The pressman is a skilled member of the printing fraternity. He has three ingredients to work with: paper, ink, and the printing form. Each poses prob-lems which require his specialized talents.

He checks all printing elements to make sure that they are exactly type-high. He cannot dampen his paper to make it snuggle down upon a wavy form. Nor can he *sock the type* into the paper. For unlike the thick, almost spongy paper of Gutenberg's day, modern paper is thin, and undue pressure will emboss the paper and make the reverse surface too rough to print upon. For most jobs the pressman seeks a *kiss impression*, bringing the paper and form together exactly close enough to transfer the ink but not to bruise the surface.

To get this delicate juxtaposition, he utilizes *makeready*. If the printing elements are not exactly type-high, he builds them up by applying the thin-nest tissue paper under the low areas. This de-mands skill and care, especially when he must raise

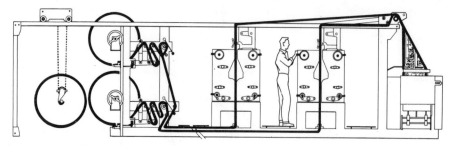

SIZE OF A PRESS is indicated in this drawing of a small rotary press. At the far left, a spare roll of paper has been brought into position by a small crane on a track. The next two heavy circles are rolls from which the web feeds.

The unit the pressman faces— and the similar one behind him— contain the printing and impression cylinders.

The two webs are joined at the folder at the top right and together make the finished job which is folded, ready for saddle binding.

certain portions, sometimes very small areas, in halftone engravings. The pressman may have to compensate in an area smaller than a dime while leaving surrounding areas unaffected.

More commonly he achieves the same effect by building up or reducing the circumference of the impression cylinder. Around this finely tooled metal core are placed several thicknesses of paper, the *packing*, which is then covered by the blanket or a sheet of very tough *tympan paper*. By cutting away or adding to the packing, again in tiny increments of thickness, he can adjust the point at which paper and form meet. Makeready takes time, lots of it, so care must be exercised in keeping type and engravings at precisely type-high to minimize that time.

The pressman must know the intricacies of *imposition* so that after a printed sheet is folded each page will be in proper position (this is discussed in greater detail in Chapter 18).

The pressman must *line up* his forms so that margins are uniform. Hold a newspaper page to the light and notice how the right-hand margin of column 8 on page 1 aligns precisely with the left edge of column 1 on page 2. Line-up, depending on the kind of press, is effected by moving either the form or the grippers which hold the paper.

Similar manipulation creates perfect *register*. When more than one color is used, each must print in exactly the right position, even though one color may be printed days after earlier ones. Perhaps the most common examples of out-of-register printing are seen in the colored comic pages. Often we see the red lips on Blondie's cheek instead of around

her mouth or two sets of eyes, black ones and blue
ones.

Changes in humidity will make paper stretch or
shrink. Impressions perfectly lined up and regis-
tered at the start of a run may be badly off at the
end of the run after humidity has affected the
dimensional stability of the paper. If partially
printed sheets in one or more colors have to stand
for days before extra color is added, the change in
dimension can be irremediable. When paper is fed
off a continuous roll, the weight of the paper *web,*
the tension under which it moves, its momentum,
and the heat generated by friction all contribute to
distorting dimensions. A *web break* is a major
calamity in the pressroom, especially that of a
newspaper where speed is so vital. (It is estimated
that a delay of one minute on the press of a New
York daily means the loss of 10,000 street sales!) To
minimize paper problems, most modern pressrooms
are carefully humidity-controlled.

By manipulating small set-screws, the pressman
regulates the flow of ink into the form. Ink is applied by a series of rollers to assure equal and even
distribution. Where the form contains heavy elements requiring a generous supply of ink adjacent
to light areas, the pressman has a difficult job of
adjusting the ink flow. The heavy element may
print light because its supply is minimized, while
the light areas may be *flooded* and print so heavily
that the ink will ooze and render the image fuzzy.

This problem can be minimized by the way in
which the job is originally planned. When it becomes apparent that any layout will call for elements widely disparate in ink requirements, the
layout man should consult with the printer before
progressing beyond preliminary plans. Simple adjustments at that stage may prevent acute grief at
press time.

After he has performed all his preliminary duties,
the pressman still has an important function
throughout the run. He constantly checks his
printed sheets to make sure the register is holding,
that ink is distributed perfectly (he makes adjust-

ments almost constantly on the flow), and that there are no *work-ups*. Quads, ledds, and other spacing material, because of the pressure exerted at the sides of the form, have a tendency to be pushed upward high enough to accept ink and to print as ugly blemishes. The pressman must watch for these and, when they occur, stop the press quickly, with a minimum of spoilage, so he can hammer the work-ups down below type-high.

To avoid *offsetting*—or *setting-off*—smudging wet ink on preceding or following pages, highspeed presses have dryers built in. Sometimes this is only a row of gas burners over which the paper passes so rapidly that it will not catch fire but which will speed the drying of the ink. By the *spray* method, a fluid—sometimes a simple sugar syrup—or a powder is sprayed over the printed sheet. Immedi-

FORM LOCKED IN THE CHASE. Note the quoins, the wedges in pairs, at the top and left. These are tightened by a quoin key that fits into the cogs and is turned to slide the quoins into a thicker rectangle. This holds the printing elements snugly.

Note how the blank area between the type and the signature is filled with *furniture*, metal elements. This is used by courtesy of Emery Air Freight for whom this announcement, set in Franklin Gothic, was made.

ately the paper passes through intense heat which causes the spray to crystallize. These crystals, although tiny, are thick enough to hold printed sheets far enough apart to prevent offsetting. In some cases a blank piece of paper, a *slipsheet,* is placed on top of each printed page. Any offsetting is thus done on this worthless sheet rather than on the next printed page. This requires low press speed which —along with the extra operation—adds to cost.

Printed sheets are usually conveyed by moving *tapes.* The pressman watches to make sure these tapes don't get dirty and produce smudges on the paper.

For over 300 years, letterpress was the only kind of printing in the Americas. For another century it was barely challenged by the newer method of lithography. But the newcomer developed into off-set lithography and grew to vigorous maturity, and letterpress was slow to react. In 1964, letterpress produced 48 per cent of the dollars in commercial printing's gross, and lithography (some direct, but mostly offset), 43 per cent. By 1966, letterpress had only 45 per cent of the total value, while lithography edged ahead with 46 per cent. By 1968 the ratio had dropped to 43 per cent for letterpress and 48 per cent for lithography, and in 1970 letterpress dropped to 40 per cent with lithography holding a majority, 51 per cent, for the first time. All this while gravure and silk-screen remained stable with 9 per cent of the market.

But while it was losing percentage points, letterpress was showing a substantial dollar growth, if only because the whole printing industry was expanding steadily. And the statistics do not indicate that letterpress is in fatal decline. It still produces more impressions than lithography for the small jobs, a hundred club bulletins, two dozen cocktail invitations, a box of letterheads, all are most efficiently done by letterpress and produce more revenue per impression than the longer runs of thousands and even millions. By any standards, letterpress's $3.2 billion production in 1970 is more than pin money.

Letterpress has a very wide economic base. At least one printing plant can be found in almost every county in the United States, and a majority of these offer letterpress, either alone or with offset. Presses are very sturdy and like the aging Linotype are rarely scrapped but usually find a home in a smaller establishment, thus expanding grassroots facilities not only for productivity but also for training personnel.

But the major reason for an optimistic prognosis of letterpress is the new vigor with which it is meeting competition. Wraparound plates, discussed in the next chapter, and dry offset, discussed in Chapter 14, seem to hold bright prospects for the most ancient of printing methods.

Hailed as one of the most significant breakthroughs in printing history is the *Cameron book production system*. The Cameron is a rotary press, under highly precise electronic control, that prints and automatically collates books as the web travels at speeds up to 1,000 feet per second. This means that a familiar paperback book of 160 pages can be produced at the unbelievable rate of 200 per minute. Book paper from 20- to 80-pound substance may be processed in webs up to 38 inches wide, from mill rolls up to 50 inches in diameter. Printing is from flexible plates; rubber ones were first used but now photopolymers are highly satisfactory.

All the plates for the one side of the paper are carried on a Mylar conveyor belt as one gang from 60 to 378 inches long. The latter is 31½ feet, and obviously no existing press could print a form of that size. So the galaxy of plates, properly inked by passing under a pyramid of rollers, is pressed against the paper web as both move between impression rollers. The galaxy is then rolled around for contact with the next section of paper while the printed portion is turned over and conveyed through the second printing unit, which prints the back in impeccable register.

After the form has been printed front and back, the web is slit into two, three, or four ribbons, each the width of two pages and each perforated exactly along its centerline for subsequent folding.

The ribbons are folded to one-page width (four-page signatures or two-page sheets) and, in a complicated roller arrangement, are stacked in proper signature alignment. Signatures are cut to page-depth dimensions, and the pages are collated in sequence. As pages for a complete book are collected in one of several compartments in the collator, the books are trimmed square.. Gluing, covering, and final trim are done with conventional perfect binding.

Hard- and soft-cover books are being produced by the Cameron system. Advantages are substantial. There is maximum flexibility in the number of pages in a book; the design is not constricted into signatures. There is no costly inventory of work-in-process; within moments after it enters the press, the paper is printed and ready for binding. Plates, right on their conveyor belts, can be rolled up for storage until reprinting—inexpensive now—may be required. Rotary advantages, formerly available only for long runs, now accrue to short ones, too. Labor costs are lowered. Page depth is variable in quarter-inch increments from 6 to 10 inches; widths are infinitely variable from 4⅜ to 8¾ inches, and the book may be up to 2 inches thick, exclusive of the cover.

Letterpress, as the oldest printing method, has evolved specialized subdivisions for its major uses. *Fine printing*, as its name implies, strives for maximum quality, whether its product be a magnificent lectern Bible, reproductions of famous art masterpieces, or letterheads. *Commercial printing* represents the great bulk of work, ranging from handbills for a farm auction to the handsome brochures of Tiffany jewelers. *Book printing* is highly specialized although its products include handsome limited editions and inexpensive paperbacks, as well as everything between. *Periodical printing* represents a large percentage of the astronomical number of pages printed annually.

ROTARY PRESS has just finished printing both sides of the paper web at the top. Now the paper is brought, as a triangular element, to the folder (arrow), then, at the very bottom, the printed paper emerges as a complete newspaper or as single sheets or signatures.

Any of these methods may print direct from type or from plates (the subject of the next chapter). But in all instances, the basic principles of the ancient Chinese block-printing and the ubiquitous rubber stamp are retained. Gutenberg, although he might be amazed, would not be baffled by a modern letterpress.

By its long history, its exemplary performance, and its adaption to changing needs, letterpress well deserves the honor of having its product described simply as "printing."

JOHANNES GUTENBERG himself may be the subject of this woodcut by Jost Amman, depicting a fifteenth-century printer at work. This West German stamp marks the 500th anniversary of type.

Knowledge of the inventor is fragmentary. Apparently he was a most litigious individual, for many references appear in court records.

In Strassburg his name is found on lists of both patricians and goldsmiths. (His sister married the Lord Mayor of the city-state.) A breach-of-promise suit against him by Anna of *Anna of the Iron Door* fame was abruptly ended by threat of a libel suit against the plaintiff herself. Gutenberg returned to his native Mainz in 1444.

SUGGESTED READINGS

Allen, Lewis and Dorothy. *Printing with the Handpress.* New York: Van Nostrand Reinhold, 1969.

Printing Progress. Cincinnati, Ohio: International Association of Printing House Craftsmen, 1959.

Ryder, John. *Printing for Pleasure.* Newton Centre, Mass.: Charles T. Branford Co., 1955.

Long before he wrote words, man "wrote" pictures. And long before he printed words, he printed pictures. Just as pictograms were the ancestors of phonograms, so printed pictures were the progenitors of type.

Wood blocks were the first printing elements. Man simply cut away unwanted portions of a plank, leaving the remainder, in relief, in the form he wanted to print. Many early wood-block prints depicted Biblical scenes and were given as rewards or as reminders to members of the totally illiterate masses.

Eventually words were added to the pictures, like the *balloons* in modern comic strips. Then blocks with only words were cut from wood; from this came the logical step of making words, and their component letters, from more durable metal.

Today it is difficult to think of printing without illustrative material of some kind. From comic strips to road maps, from patterns for sewing dresses to reproductions of the "Mona Lisa," these "pictures" are an important product of contemporary printing presses and certainly offer great enjoyment to their graphic arts producers.

This chapter shall discuss how pictures are produced by letterpress. The principles we shall examine here, mostly in oversimplification—apply to all kinds of printing methods, particularly gravure and offset, which we shall discuss a couple of chapters later.

With negligible exceptions all printing plates used by any printing method are made by the action of light upon photosensitive materials. It is eminently logical, then, that the development of platemaking should go hand in hand with that of *photography*, which is itself a major division of the graphic arts. But let's first look at what the printer did before Joseph Nicephore Niepce invented photography in France.

Wood blocks were carved on the side grain of a board. That made the block fragile; it tended to splinter away with the grain. But the printer's hunger for pictures continued their use, and as

11

Printing Plates

Putting Pictures on Paper

THOMAS BEWICK, inventor of white-line wood engraving, did this charming bucolic scene reproduced here in actual size. The Folio Club of London, through whose courtesy this is used, recently discovered a group of Bewick's original wood plates and printed a limited edition of them which immediately became collectors' items.

early as 1638, the *Weekly News* of London carried a "news picture" engraved in wood. Seeking durability, engravers cut pictures out of metal, usually copper. These took far more time and money than wood blocks, themselves far from cheap.

It was Thomas Bewick, an English artist of the early 1800's, who discovered the *white-line* engraving technique that combined the delicacy and durability of metal with the economy of wood. He carved his plates on the *end grain* of the board and achieved results that are still charming works of art. This method provided most of the pictures that were becoming increasingly popular in nineteenth-century magazines and newspapers.

Sketch artists, comparable to our news cameramen, were sent to cover a story. Their drawings—finely detailed or hasty sketches with marginal notations to help the draftsman at home complete the scene—were rushed to the publication. There highly skilled carvers transferred the drawing to a block of wood and then carved a printing plate. Many methods were evolved to enable more carvers to work on a single picture. The most successful, and merely an improvement on earlier methods, was to bolt several small blocks together to form one large one. The desired drawing was copied onto the large block. It was then disassembled so that as many as 10 or 15 engravers could each carve a small portion. Reassembled, each block fitted in with its neighbors to form the original large engraving. It is amazing that the technique of the engravers was so uniform that each one's work would fit, unobtrusively, into a unified whole.

The Civil War intensified demand for news pictures; in the United States, wood carving reached its height of excellence and volume in that period. Engravers found techniques to simulate the shadings of wash drawings and even photographs in wood. Soon they eliminated the need to trace original pictures onto wood by producing the image there photographically.

The first photograph was made by Niepce in

1826—with an exposure of eight hours! It proved that man could truly "write with light," the literal translation of photography. Two years later he entered partnership with L. J. M. Daguerre, who gave his name to the first practical kind of photography.

The first news photograph, a daguerreotype, showed the ruins of a conflagration in Hamburg, Germany, that raged for three days in May of 1842. Ironically, that was the very time that the first illustrated paper in the world, the *London Illustrated News*, was going to press with an imaginary scene of the fire, copied from an old print, with flames added by the artist, on a wood block.

Photography utilizes the fact that certain substances are darkened by exposure to sunlight. (While these include human epidermis, we cannot term America's suntanning rites as photography.) Silver salts are the most convenient photosensitive materials used today.

The simplest *photoengraving* is the *line cut,* also called a *zinc etching,* or just a *zinc,* because that metal is most commonly used. Tracing the steps in making a line cut is a painless way to learn the basic principles of the process.

As its name indicates, a line cut reproduces black-and-white drawings made up of simple lines and masses and without gradations in tone such as a photograph or wash drawing.

Original *art* is placed before a camera in order to obtain an *engraver's negative.* Let the first example be something as simple as the capital *E* in Example 2. The white paper surrounding the *E* reflects light through the camera lens onto a sheet of film, covered with an *emulsion* of silver salts. The letter itself, because it is black, reflects no light.

In the development process, that area on the film which has been affected by light turns black. The shape of the *E* has not been exposed on the emulsion, the silver has not darkened and it is washed away, leaving the clear film.

This is the *negative.* It is a copy of the original art but with the tonal values reversed: the black letter is white (or transparent) on the negative and

Example 2. LINE PHOTOENGRAVING is shown in schematic form.

LINE ETCHINGS of the photoengraver are made from simple drawings such as this pen-and-ink by Inge Sorenson (above) or the more detailed one (below) by Barry Blackman.

the original white background is now opaque black.

When light is projected through the negative and onto a piece of paper covered with light-sensitive emulsion, the light passes through the E-shaped opening and affects a similar-shaped area on the photopaper. The opaque background prevents light from reaching that corresponding area on the paper. Where the light strikes, the emulsion turns black and the original E is duplicated; where no light has reacted with the silver emulsion, the paper remains white as on the original.

This is the rudiment of all photography.

In the engraving process, a negative is made, as described above. But now, instead of passing light through the negative onto photosensitized paper, it is projected onto a piece of metal covered with a sensitized emulsion.

There is now a black E on metal. A special ink, which adheres only to that portion of the plate that has been struck by light, is rolled over the metal; it refuses to adhere to the unexposed areas but clings to the oxidized emulsion. The plate is washed by running water which removes the unexposed emulsion only. Heating the plate makes the ink tacky. A picturesquely named powder, *dragon's blood*, is sprinkled over the plate and sticks to the inky adhesive. This powder is really a resin—and a good thing, what with the current shortage of dragons. As the plate cools, the resin hardens into a solid, acid-proof coating.

In an etching bath, nitric acid is sprayed against the plate. The covered portion of the metal is unaffected; the balance is eaten away. The original image remains in relief to be inked and impressed onto paper.

What happens when we make our plate as an exact duplicate of our original E? When it is printed, the arms of the E will point to the left instead of the right. So we must produce the printing plate in *mirror form* of the original. That is done simply by turning the negative over before we expose through it onto the metal. This *flopping the negative* is an essential step in all photoengraving.

Occasionally we see a picture in a newspaper or magazine where the "neg" has not been flopped. The result is wedding rings on right hands, men's pocket handkerchiefs on the opposite side of their jackets, and reversed letters on billboards.

By turning the negative so the *E,* in this form, points to the left, we produce a plate with a south-paw *E,* its arms pointing left also. When this plate is printed, the arms will properly extend to the right again.

This simplified description of the etching process ignored a constant danger. As the acid consumes unprotected metal, it will eventually start etching sideways as well as downward, and thus eat under protected areas. This *undercutting* weakens the printing areas which have remained in relief. Under pressure on the press, they crumple, and the plate becomes useless.

To prevent undercutting, the engraver allows the acid to etch only a shallow *bite* the first time. Then the engraver brushes additional resin on the plate to reinforce the original coating and to form new protection on the sides of those areas in relief. (It takes great skill to powder the sidewalls while leaving the bottom of the first bite exposed to additional etching.) Back into nitric acid goes the plate for the second, third, or even more bites.

Depth of the first bite varies from .0001 to .0005 of an inch. Total depth varies with the nature of the copy; it may be as shallow as .001 inch to 10 times that much, with such deep depressions lowered still more by *routing,* grinding them away with a drill.

Having established the classical method, let us now note that improved materials and techniques make it possible to produce the acid-resistant image on the metal and also to prevent undercutting without the use of dragon's blood. Aluminum alloys are often used instead of zinc, but copper remains the favorite material when extremely fine detail must be carried in the plate.

Small imperfections on the plate are cleaned up by hand. The plate is then *blocked*—affixed to a wood base that brings the printing surface to exactly

Example 3. SHADING SHEET, specifically Zip-a-Tone, gives tonal variation to this line cut.

type-high—or it may be delivered unmounted to the printer, who fastens it on a metal base. The cut is usually held to the base by an adhesive or, on special metal base, by small clamps. In newspaper operations the plate is simply laid on the base with no fastening, if stereotyping is to follow.

The film upon which the negative was made consists of a thin layer of sensitized emulsion which is on a thicker, stronger piece of film or glass. This emulsion is peeled, *stripped,* off the reinforcing substance, and then flopped on a glass plate, a *flat,* with several other negatives. For economy, the entire flat is exposed onto a single piece of metal and etched as a single unit.

During exposure, the flat is held by vacuum to the plate so that no distortion results from buckling or warping of the thin emulsion.

Comic strips are a familiar form of line cuts. They are created by simple lines or masses of black and white. But effects of gray tones are achieved by using dots, lines, or cross-hatching. The artist can produce these with his pen or brush. Or he can use a mechanical aid, of which *Zip-a-Tone* is a familiar trade name. This is a *shading sheet* of transparent, self-adhering film upon which is printed a mechanically regular pattern of lines or dots in various combinations. In Example 3 the artist drew his characters in simple line. To produce the gray effect, he chose an appropriate pattern of Zip-a-Tone. He peeled it off a protective paper backing and laid it over the entire cartoon. In those areas where he wanted the tone, he *tacked down* the shading sheet with a *burnisher,* a pencil-like piece of wood with one end cut at an angle. In the other end of the wood is a needle, the stylus. With this, the artist cuts around the outline of the shaded area and lifts off the unwanted shading. Now he rubs the film firmly onto the paper with the burnisher. A waxy substance affixes the film smoothly, tightly, and invisibly, except for the pattern, of course. He can use more than one pattern, and can develop new ones by placing one pattern over another.

There are dozens of patterns available under

many trade names; Zip-a-Tone, *Craftint,* and *Contak* are the most familiar.

The engraver can create similar shading by the *Ben Day* process. The artist makes his drawing as before. In the areas where he wants shading to appear, he paints a wash of light blue, which is invisible to the engraver's camera. In the margin he indicates to the engraver which of the more than 200 Ben Day patterns he wants in the blue area. These patterns are embossed on sheets of thin celluloid. The engraver inks the proper plate; by printing this pattern onto either the negative or the metal and washing away the unwanted areas, he can make this pattern an integral part of the final plate. If he prints the pattern on the negative, it will appear white in the final letterpress reproduction. This technique is often used to *screen type,* placing a fine pattern of white dots on the type area so it appears gray instead of black.

The Ben Day process—named after the inventor—is the older one, but shading sheets are so convenient that they become more popular day to day. Shading sheets, too, come in white as well as black and can be used for graying down type or artwork.

Pen-and-ink drawings (preferably in India ink) are the ideal line copy. But many other media can be reproduced by line etchings and many can by themselves create the effect of shading.

Black *crayon, litho pencil* (which produces crayonlike effects), *charcoal,* and *dry brush* can all be reproduced in line if done on a textured surface. Although the eye seems to detect grays in such original art, it is only an illusion created by tiny areas of pure black on the miniature hilltops of the rough paper while the vast valleys remain white.

Scratchboard, another favorite medium for line cuts, is a paper coated with chalky substance. Black India ink is applied over portions, or all, of the paper surface, and the "drawing" is done with a sharp knife that scratches through the ink and exposes the clean white chalk. *Ross drawing board* is a scratchboard with a built-in geometrical pattern; *Rossco Stip* has similar patterns, in raised stippling

SCRATCHBOARD is an interesting artist's technique. A paper with a heavy clay coating is covered with black ink and the fine lines are scratched through the ink, exposing the white board. Extremely fine detail can be achieved in this way, giving even the utilitarian forms of industrial tooling a new grace and beauty.

on the surface, which appear when the paper is drawn upon.

Mechanical patterns can also be achieved by using *Craftone board,* and this is undoubtedly the most enjoyable to use. A pattern similar to a Ben Day is printed with ink invisible to the camera. The artist draws his picture in ink on that paper. Then, to those areas where he needs shading, he applies a developer solution with a brush. This solution causes the underlying pattern to become visible.

Craftint *Doubletone* is twice as ingenious. It has cross-hatched lines. When one developer is applied, it darkens only one set of lines to create a light gray effect. When the second developer is used, it darkens both sets of lines to create cross-hatching and darker gray.

Line cuts can be printed on any paper, but extremely fine lines or tight cross-hatching should be avoided with unusually coarse paper. Line cuts can be used in any color; the Sunday comics are good examples.

Halftones

The artist and photographer in black-and-white have a full palette to work with. It ranges from pure black to total white, with intermediate tones of gray created by using less pigment on the paper. Take a look at a photograph and notice how the grays vary in intensity as the silver deposit is thick or thin. Such art work is *continuous tone.*

But the printer normally has no grays to work with; he has only black ink and white paper. To reproduce the intermediate tones of a photograph, such as a news picture in your daily paper, he must resort to optical illusion, a *halftone engraving.*

If you look at a halftone in a newspaper with a magnifying glass—or even with the naked eye in some cases—you can see that it is made up of many small dots, ranging from 3,025 to 14,400, or even more, per square inch. Where the dots are large and close together, the eye sees that area as black or very deep gray. Where the dots are tiny and widely scattered, we see light gray and even white.

Between these extremes are varying combinations of dot sizes and dispersal.

This characteristic *dot pattern* is created by the engraver's *screen*. This looks like the one on your front door in the summer. It consists of two sets of parallel black lines, ruled on a glass plate, and crossing each other at right angles. On the plate itself these lines run at 45 and 135 degrees to the edges to make the resultant pattern less conspicuous in the engraving.

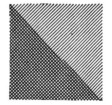
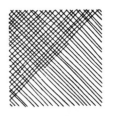
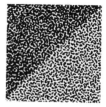
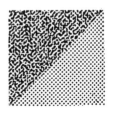

Fineness of an engraving is indicated by the number of *lines* of dots per inch. A 55-line-screen halftone is one made with a screen that has 55 vertical and 55 horizontal lines per inch. This is the coarsest screen in use. Most newspapers use 55- to 85-line screen; most trade publications use 85- to 110-line. For enameled or smooth-finish paper, 120- to 133-line is best suited, and on extremely high-coated paper, 150- to 175 is usable. Two hundred-line can be used only on cast-coated paper—such as Kromecote which has an almost lacquered surface —and then only with extreme care by the pressman.

With one vital exception, halftone engravings are made as line cuts are. That exception is the introduction of the screen between the original art and the negative. The screen is placed a tiny fraction of an inch in front of the film. As the light reflects from the original art, through the camera lens, it passes through the fine openings in the screen, each one of which acts as a pinhole lens itself. Where the light is intense, it casts a bigger dot image on the

DOUBLETONE PAPER comes in combinations of patterns (above). Each half of the pair responds to a different developing fluid.

On such paper the artist makes his drawing in simple line and/or black areas (A). Applying the dark developer with pen or brush, he brings up his dark pattern (B). With a second developer, he makes visible the light pattern (C) and thus has achieved four tones—the two grays, black, and white.

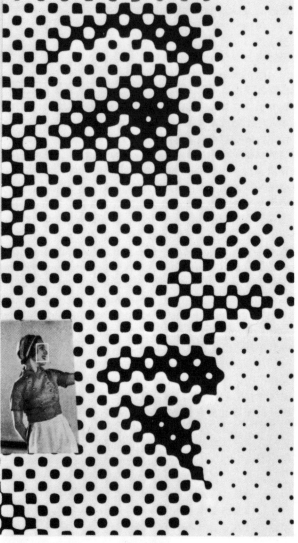

HALFTONE DOT PATTERN is shown in this enlargement. The original engraving at the left is an extremely fine pattern; the area enclosed in the white rectangle is enlarged 31 times lineally. Squinting, or holding the enlargement at a distance, shows it in recognizable form again. The large plate is an example of a blow-up.

negative. Later this large black dot on the negative will, in turn, block light to the metal plate, creating only tiny relief dots on the plate that will deposit a minimum of ink.

Etching is the same as for a line plate, except that one bite is sufficient in most cases. Occasionally a small portion of a halftone must be lightened up. All the other areas are *staged,* protected by an acid-resistant substance, and the dark area is exposed to re-etching which eats down the dots and makes them smaller when printed. This is the *staging and re-etching* process. Re-etching can also be done without staging, by painting acid directly onto the area to be lightened.

Burnishing is the process of making dots larger by rubbing on them with a tool that flattens, and thus spreads, dots which were too small.

The most common of these printing plates is the *square halftone*. This is one that has 90-degree corners whether it is truly a square or, as is more frequent, a rectangle. There are some common variations on this form.

The *silhouette* or *outline* halftone, as its name indicates, shows only an object with no background. A *modified silhouette* has only a portion of the picture in outline.

In a *vignette* halftone, the grays of the picture fade, almost imperceptibly, into the white of the paper. This calls for extremely skillful work from the artist who first creates this blend with an airbrush on the photograph, and from the engraver and the pressman. Because of the problems they present, vignettes are rarely seen in newspapers or magazines using uncoated paper.

A *modified vignette* is one where less than four sides of the picture blend out, the others being squared or silhouetted.

Oval and *circle* halftones are explained by their names.

Mortising is cutting out an area of an engraving so that type or another cut may be placed there. Its most common form is the removal of a rectangle from one corner, an *external* mortise or *notch*. A rectangle mortised out so that three of its sides are defined by the halftone is called a *bay*. *Internal mortises* are those entirely surrounded by the halftone. On rare occasions the mortise may be irregular in shape.

A *highlight* halftone—a *drop-out* or *facsimile*—is one in which the dots are completely removed in certain areas. Dots may be removed by *opaquing* them out with paint, by hand, on the negative. Those areas where the dot pattern is to remain may

VIGNETTE blends the tones of the photograph almost imperceptibly into the white of the printing paper. This is an extremely difficult effect to obtain by letterpress, although relatively easy in offset.

A SILHOUETTE HALFTONE, in which any possible distraction in the background is eliminated, focuses all attention on the subject. The shape of the silhouetted object should be simple; tiny details require undue work, and in a human profile, even a small slip can destroy the likeness.

bay ⌐ ⌐notch

⌐ internal
irregular ⌐

MORTISING may be done in the four styles shown here or with the cutaway portion in free form. Care must be taken that the mortising does not weaken the composition of the picture. In the case of the "bay," shown here, the distance between the standing figures may be exaggerated and thus a false impression given about the relationship of the individuals involved.

Great care must be taken that "the essence of the truth" is never destroyed or altered by manipulation of a photograph.

be protected on the metal plate, while the re-etching removes the unwanted highlight dots. *Tooling* or routing can cut or grind away unwanted dots on the metal plate. Shifting or rotating the halftone screen or moving the engraver's camera diaphragm only a trifle may often eliminate the dots on the negative by photographic means alone.

The *Kromolite process* is a most ingenious method for creating highlight halftones. It is the favorite method for the fashion advertiser who must have drop-outs to reproduce the delicate wash and/or pencil and crayon drawings that lend themselves so admirably to fashion illustration.

Kromolite is a substance that is added to the artist's conventional wash without altering its monochromatic appearance. But when it is sprayed with a developer, the grays turn yellow.

When a yellow filter is placed before the camera, the art work resumes its original black-and-gray appearance to the lens and a halftone negative is made.

Now a blue filter replaces the yellow one and a line negative is shot. The blue filter makes the yellow areas appear jet-black to the camera's eye. On the negative, this area is absolutely clear while the white areas have created opaque black on the film.

When these two negatives are placed together, the clear area of the line negative allows the dot pattern of the drawing to show through, but the opaque areas effectively mask out the unwanted highlight dots in the halftone neg. In actual practice, both exposures are made on the same piece of film so that register of the two images is perfect.

Kemart is a similar process, as is *Maskomatic*.

In the *fluorographic* process a special solvent carries the pigments used in the original art work. Chinese white, dissolved in water, is painted on the areas where the dots are to be eliminated. A special filter is used then, as in the Kromolite process.

Fashion advertisers typically use highlight halftones to show important details of a garment while eliminating or subordinating the others. Another favorite of advertisers, especially in newspapers, is the reverse plate. This is most frequently a line cut which gives the effect of white type on a black background. To create it, the engraver needs a negative on which type is black on a clear background. This he obtains by exposing the original negative—with clear type on black—onto a second piece of film. From this reverse negative the plate is made as any other line cut.

A simpler method is to have a negative Photostat made from the original reproduction proof of the desired type and shot as a normal line cut. This not only may be more economical but also enables the artist to see how the chosen type looks in reverse.

When reverses are used in advertisements, policy of the publication may demand that the black areas be screened to lighten them down to dark gray. This screening is done by use of halftone *screen tints* which are applied by the engraver in a manner similar to Ben Day. Even when a solid black area is desired, it is best to use 90 per cent gray. Excess ink can then run into the tiny depressions on the plate instead of off the edges of the cut, and ink control is much easier.

When lettering is applied directly to a continuous-tone copy and shot in halftone, the dots will hide serifs, break hairlines, and make vertical strokes serrated. In a halftone there are no true blacks or whites; black areas have tiny white shadow dots, white ones have similar small black dots. Type would be gray, too. All this lessens legibility. For this reason, *combination plates* are used when line copy—which includes type—is combined with continuous-tone copy. Two negatives, halftone and line, are shot separately, then printed onto the

HIGHLIGHT HALFTONES like the one above are much used for fashion drawings. They are produced by the Kromolite process.

The picture below is the halftone of a photo in which the whites of the eye have been dropped out by one of several methods.

These highlights, or drop-outs, are among those offered in stereotype matrix form or as repro proofs by Stamps-Conhaim-Whitehead. As copyright holders, they have granted permission for use here.

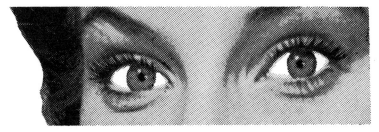

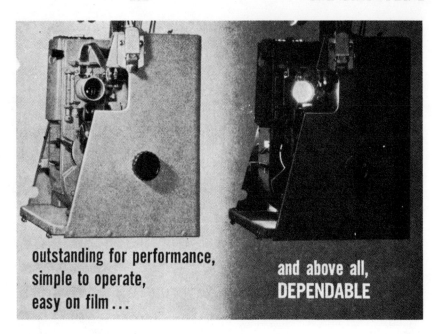

outstanding for performance,
simple to operate,
easy on film...

and above all,
DEPENDABLE

COMBINATION PLATE combines halftone with line material in both positive (left) and reverse form. Line work can be pictorial as well as type and it may project out of the halftone background. But the line work must at least partially overlap halftone to make it a true combination plate.

metal. Combination cuts can carry the line work in black or reverse.

Pre-screening continuous-tone art by the Velox process has many advantages. A *Velox* is a glossy photograph in a dot pattern instead of in continuous tones. It is reproduced as a line cut.

Retouching is comparatively easy on a Velox. Highlight dots may be painted out for a drop-out. The shape and size of dots can be altered by hand; this is easier and often gives better results with poor-quality photographs than to retouch the original. Contact letters may be affixed over a Velox for the effect of a combination cut; silhouetting is simple.

When a Velox is pasted up with other elements, the entire layout is shot as a single-line unit. This eliminates the danger of stripping in a separately screened negative in the wrong place. Being able to handle all the elements of an advertisement as a single engraving saves time, especially for newspapers with tight deadlines.

The most interesting variations on the halftone are those made with *special screens.*

Conventional halftone screens are extremely expensive, made slowly and painstakingly. But recently plates have been made of plastic with the screen pattern made photographically. Their cost is only a small fraction of that of the glass screens, and the typical platemaker can afford a variety of screens.

Each square opening in the regular engraver's halftone screen acts like a tiny lens that takes a square picture. If that screen had only a set of parallel lines, with no cross lines, the picture that each opening would take would be an extremely narrow and long rectangle. This line would vary, not in width and length as the halftone dot does, but only in width. In effect, each one of these lines would be the equivalent of a column of halftone dots joined together.

While some detail is lost, parallel lines can adequately create the optical illusion of intermediate grays as well as reproducing black and white. Similarly the halftone effect can be achieved by using a screen of parallel *wavy lines* or of *concentric circles.* The latter is especially effective when the center of the circles is placed on the most important element in the photograph.

A great many other textures are available by special screens such as the *mezzotint,* which gives the effect of an old art form. So does the *steel engraving* screen, which is made of thin lines of varying lengths and angles to the perpendicular.

Any pattern, however irregular, can be used as a halftone screen. Commercial ones reproduce *burlap, twill, denim, mesh, ring,* and *ringlet* as well as at least 10 different wood grains. Burlap adds a pleasant bulky effect, which is particularly appropriate for heavy stone architectural subjects, and *birch woodgrain,* when used with a highly contrasty photo, converts it into a classical drypoint etching.

Some platemakers even make their own screens. An effective one is made by photographing the irregular pattern created by crumpling the thin foil

Specialized Papers

SPECIAL SCREENS are an invaluable tool in making a photograph a stronger non-verbal communication. It should be remembered that many of the effects shown here may be obtained in two ways: by manipulation of the photograph itself and by using a special screen in the platemaking.

Wavy parallel lines give a pleasant contour to this picture. Note that the dots are dropped out in the model's teeth. (Courtesy Chemco Photoproducts Co.)

HALFTONE DOTS are being used in new shapes to give greater tonal fidelity, especially in the 50 per cent gray range.

From the top, the dot patterns are open, conventional, elliptical, checkerboard, and camera-type dots.

used to wrap food and using the negative as the halftone screen.

Special screens lose detail, and so they are used where the main concern is to create a mood or atmosphere rather than to convey detailed, precise information.

But special screens are also used to sharpen detail. On the conventional halftone pattern the dots vary between tiny, almost perfect circles to large squares with rounded corners. There is a point at about the 50-per-cent-gray value—where half the plate area should be in black and the other half in white to give the effect of intermediate gray—when the tonal value becomes distorted. To correct this, an *elliptical dot screen* makes the white and black dots at the 50 per cent mark of almost identical shape and size and holds the tone very well.

The same effect is achieved with varying success by an *open dot* screen which produces perfect black circles, by the *checkerboard* screen which creates just what its name indicates, and a *camera-type dot* which varies the shape of the dots, from circles to tiny hoods.

All these dots are, for all practical purposes, invisible to the naked eye. At 140-line fineness this is literally true. But occasionally a dramatic effect can be achieved by exaggerating the dot pattern in a *blow-up* plate.

In principle it works this way: a small halftone is made in copper—to hold fine detail—and a careful proof is pulled of it. This becomes copy for an enlarged line cut.

Suppose a newspaper uses 55-line cuts and it wants a blow-up plate 6 inches wide. The engraver would make a 110-line copper halftone 3 inches wide. A proof is pulled. In a line camera, the image is enlarged to the desired 6-inch width. This means that 110 lines of dots that originally occupied a linear inch are now spread out across two inches and the screen is now 55. Before the second engraving is made, on zinc or copper, the proof may be retouched by painting out highlight dots or deepening the shadows.

In practice this can all be done photographically and there is no need actually to make the first half-tone plate.

Striking effects can be created by blowing up the original proof so the ultimate screen is as low as 20 or 25 lines per inch. This technique loses most detail, of course, but where bold effects are desired this is an excellent method of creating unusual impact from ordinary photographic copy.

Just as drama can be achieved by overemphasizing the halftone screen, so it can be done by eliminating it entirely. This is called *linear definition* or *line conversion*. The camera copy is a continuous-tone photograph that has been made as contrasty as possible. It is shot as line work, without a halftone screen. A special film is used that converts everything darker than 50 per cent gray to solid black and everything lighter to pure white. The effect is one of a pen-and-ink or crayon drawing.

LINEAR DEFINITION, shooting a photograph without a halftone screen, gives interesting effects, especially with architectural subjects.

When portraits are made into line conversions, care must be taken that the likeness is preserved in the simple black-and-white pattern. (Courtesy *Print* magazine)

Copy for this technique should be such that deep shadows and highlights alone create a distinguishable image. Sometimes the original photo must be retouched with India ink or white opaque paint to retain necessary definition.

Many other effects can be created by the photographer, in which case the platemaker converts them to printing plates in the conventional manner. *Posterization* is a typical effect in which intermediate grays are all rendered as a single value to contrast against the pure black and white. This is particularly effective in color printing.

All these techniques are especially useful when a typographer must show a familiar scene or product in a fresh new way. Some products, notably heavy industrial machinery, rarely if ever change in appearance. Yet the advertiser insists on showing it and wants it to look different. Ingenious handling can give a dramatically new presentation.

Mechanical Engraving Machines

The many varieties of printing plates we have been considering are all produced by *photochemistry*. These account for the vast majority of relief

CONCENTRIC CIRCLES, used in the middle example here, focus attention sharply at its center. The portion at the left uses a steel-engraving screen, and the one at the right horizontal parallel lines.

plates, but an interesting minority are made by *photomechanical engraving machines.*

Introduced shortly after World War II, the popularity of photomechanical machines zoomed like a skyrocket and was almost as ephemeral as fireworks. Although they have lost much of their advantage to offset, especially among smaller newspapers where once they were a mainstay, the mechanical engravers are still worth examining, for the *scanning* principle they utilize is the same as that used for transmission of pictures by telegraph and even radio.

The grandfather of such devices is the *Fairchild Scan-a-graver.*

The machine produces halftone plates on thin plastic sheets, instead of metal, and removes nonprinting areas by burning them away. There are two identical cylinders on the machine. On one is mounted the copy, on the other the plastic sheet. These revolve at the same rate of speed. A scanning

WEATHERBEATEN EFFECT is produced by the platemaker shooting this subject twice, each time
with a parallel-line screen at right
angles to each other.

MEZZOTINT SCREEN enhances
the texture of this statuary. This
screen is available in several degrees of coarseness. (Courtesy
Consolidated Papers)

eye moves slowly across the copy. As the cylinder
revolves and the scanner moves laterally, every
minute area comes under scrutiny.

On the other cylinder, moving at the identical
speed, is a pyramid-shaped stylus, made red-hot by
electricity. Because their movement is identical, the
eye and the stylus will always be at the same relative position on their respective cylinders.

When the scanner detects a bright white area, it
relays instructions to the stylus. "I see a white
spot," says the scanner. "You, stylus, bury yourself
deeply into the plastic so that you burn away a
large area which then will not be able to receive or
deposit ink."

Similarly, the scanner instructs the stylus to leave
an area unburned, so that it will print heavily or
will create different sized dots for intermediate
grays.

Because of its pyramidal shape, the deeper the
stylus pokes into the plastic, the greater is the area
of surface removed. The stylus oscillates at the rate
of over 10,000 contacts per minute. Its lateral
movement—equal to that of the scanner—is about
one-third of an inch per minute. In that time it has
produced engraving that wide and eight inches—
the circumference of the cylinder—long.

DENIM TEXTURE makes the
middle tone in this posterized
portrait. All intermediate grays
are represented by this single
pattern which functions as a Ben
Day pattern would.

THE ORIGINAL PHOTOGRAPH of a California mission presents an attractive subject in a straight-forward way. (This picture and its variations are used by courtesy of ByChrome Company.)

A PARALLEL LINE SCREEN adds vertical emphasis to this version of the preceding photograph. When this screen is used as a conventional substitute for a dot pattern, it is usually run sideways. This makes it less apparent to contemporary eyes that are used to the parallel scans of their television sets.

To create the necessary mirror image required of a letterpress plate, the stylus moves from right to left while the scanner travels from left to right. A single picture can be converted into a Fairchild plate faster than by photoengraving. But it should be noted that when a quantity of engravings are made, the photoengraver can turn out many times more the area of engraving in a day than the Fairchild can. The standard Scan-a-graver can make 65-, 85- or 120-line screens, but one machine can produce only one screen.

Standard Scan-a-gravers produce only same-size plates; this often requires that a properly sized copy photograph be made from the original art. Maximum size of a standard Fairchild plate is 8 × 10 inches. An advanced model, called the *Scan-a-sizer*, will reduce or enlarge plates. This is only at a fixed ratio, however, and is not as flexible as the same procedure by photoengraving.

Many newspapers leave appropriate areas blank on their curved stereotypes and paste the plastic plates right onto the stereos. Printing directly from the plastic results in excellent reproduction. If care is taken, two or more smaller plastics can be fitted together like a jigsaw puzzle to create a larger plate.

MEZZOTINT special screen.

The *Elgramma,* a Swiss product, and the *Photo-Lathe,* an American machine, are similar in principle. They use two cylinders and a scanning eye as the Fairchild does. But instead of plastic, they use a thin metal sheet. And instead of a stylus, they use a V-shaped cutting tool. As the graver cuts a thin or deep furrow, it leaves a correspondingly thick or narrow printing surface as a series of parallel lines such as the photoengraver produces with his special screen. Reasonably fine detail can be reproduced.

The *Klischograph,* a German machine, also uses a metal plate, but is made of type metal that is non-distributive and can be remelted.

The blank plate is mounted horizontally on a metal table. The cutting tool can best be described as a tiny spade which "digs out" the unwanted metal, leaving the dot pattern in relief.

The three machines that produce metal plates have advantages over the plastic-platemaker. They can make line engravings which cannot be produced on the plastic. The metal plates are so thin that they, too, can be bent and mounted directly on the curved press plate.

As with the Fairchild, the other photomechanical engravers have made their greatest contribution by making it more convenient or economical to use photographs in printing. They acclimated smaller newspapers to the advantages of offset in photojournalism and encouraged letterpress newspapers to use more art. Other printers, in all the methods, began to use illustrations not only more profusely but more effectively. Today the written word is augmented much more frequently with pictures, and smaller publications, especially suburban newspapers, are using photojournalism so expertly that their aggregate circulation is showing a gain proportionately much greater than that of metropolitan dailies.

DELICACY OF A STEEL ETCHING is achieved by using a birch woodgrain screen and dropping out the sky and snow areas.

The original photograph is shown in miniature form.

Duplicate Plates

There is need to make one or more duplicates of an original printing form, whether it is an engraving or a combination of cuts and type, when adver-

TWO TEXTURES are illustrated in this posterized picture. The top portion uses a twill-effect screen and the bottom parallel wavy lines.

tisements and news pictures appear in many publications the same day, or publications are printed in several plants simultaneously. *Duplicate plates* are necessary in such instances.

Often it is not practical to print directly from type. Foundry type wears down quickly on the press and is expensive to replace. Machine-set type is of comparatively soft metal and its life on the press is limited. Engravings wear down and lose clarity. So it is customary, where the run is long as in book work, to make duplicate plates and print from them.

The most common duplicate is the *stereotype*. Stereotyping uses a cardboard-like sheet of paper, a *flong*, to create a mold or matrix of the original type or engraving. The flong, made of cellulose pulp, is placed over the original and subjected to extreme pressure, either by a roller or direct hydraulic press. (In either case, this is called *rolling a mat*. Because "mat" is used to designate both a Linotype matrix or a stereotype matrix, this book will use the term "flong," although technically that is the raw, unmolded sheet of paper.) The flong is pressed onto and around the relief printing surfaces and makes a faithful matrix.

This matrix is light and durable, easy to transport and store. When molten type metal is poured upon it, an exact duplicate of the original form is produced. This is done in a *casting box*, by *flat casting*.

The thickness of the gauges determines the thickness of the cast plate. In some shops, stereotypers prefer to cast type-high. The cut can go directly into the printing form. Others *shell cast* the plate about a quarter-inch thick and then mount it on wood or metal to bring it to proper printing height.

Newspapers, daily or weekly, get most advertising illustrations in mat form either from a service or from manufacturers. Comic strips, panel cartoons, crossword puzzles, and feature pictures are also supplied this way; so flat casting is a familiar chore.

As invented in 1725, the mold was made of plaster of Paris or moist clay. Papier-mâché, introduced in 1829, eliminated the breakage that

plagued users of earlier molding material, but it
required pressure, heat, and moisture—in the form
of steam—in the molding process. *Dry mats* used
today were developed in England and Germany,
and were first manufactured in America as recently
as 1917.

Mats can be rolled at the rate of three to five per
minute and the cost of materials is not significant.
Stereotypes can be remelted along with nondistrib-
utive type.

"Stereotyped material" in the context of the editorial worker takes its name from this mechanical
process. Early in this century, when small papers,
especially weeklies, had a hard time filling their
columns, all kinds of editorial matter was supplied
to the publisher in the form of stereotype plates—
boilerplate. Each week the expressman brought in a
fresh supply of plates. Here were news stories—not
very fresh, it is true, but interesting enough to the
radioless reader—fiction, pictures, puzzles, and
even ads. The editor used what he needed to fill the
holes his handsetting couldn't cope with. This practice continued until after World War II.

Just as vital as stereotyping was to the smalltown
editor, so another version of it is today for all large
dailies. In the discussion of letterpress, it was noted
that rotary presses have printing surfaces on a
cylinder that opposes the impression surface, also a
cylinder. A century ago wedge-shaped type had
been used to create this curved printing surface.
This was not practical for printing today's papers.
There was always the danger that type would be
loosened by centrifugal force and spewed all over
the pressroom. It is hard to make up pages on
cylinders; furthermore, modern presses need duplicate plates to print as many as 20 identical pages at
the same time.

So, how to make up a newspaper page on a flat
surface, then bend it around the cylinder of a
rotary press? Stereotyping solves the problem
neatly.

The page is made up conventionally and a page
flong is rolled from it. This flat flong is then placed

UNLIKELY COMBINATION is this:
an architectural subject and a
burlap texture screen. The rugged
bulk of the building is enhanced
by the special screen. The sky
area has been dropped out.

REVERSE PLATE above is typical of those used for advertising. Below is a calligraphic book jacket. In almost all instances, when white or light letters appear on a dark background, printing is by a reverse plate. The background is printed on; the paper is left exposed to form the white letters.

Artist's copy for reverses is conventional black-on-white.

in a *former* or *scorcher* which bakes it into a proper curve to fit the press cylinder. It then goes into a casting box which duplicates this curve in a printing plate. Most plates today are *half-rounds* that occupy half the perimeter of a 2-foot cylinder. For some presses, they take up about 300 degrees of a much smaller cylinder. Most steps in the casting operation are automatic and four plates can be cast per minute.

While the presses are printing from these plates, the original type forms can be revised in the composing room to correct hitherto undiscovered errors, to include late-breaking news stories, or to vary the makeup for various editions. New flongs can be molded and new plates cast while the presses continue printing and stop only long enough to change plates. *Replating* thus becomes a common editorial term.

A disadvantage is that only coarse-screen halftones can be matted, and sometimes molding pressure breaks down fine details of type.

Another disadvantage of stereotyping has been turned into a virtue. The flong is made up of tiny cellulose fibers in the form of long cylinders that lie parallel to each other. As the flong is dampened to make a true matrix, the fibers swell in circumference but not in length. As they dry—to create a good casting condition—they shrink, again sideways. There is only insignificant vertical shrinkage.

As the fibers change in dimension, so the whole flong shrinks and contracts sideways. This fact has been utilized by newspaper publishers to effect savings in paper.

Newspaper pages are made up in 11-pica columns and then deliberately shrunken down during stereotyping to 10 picas. Because this shrinkage is horizontal, it is possible to print on a narrower roll of paper while still retaining the original vertical measurements on which the price of advertising is predicated. Because the cost of newsprint is about 40 per cent of a paper's expenditure, saving even a tiny strip on the edge of each page can amount to five or six figures annually.

Unfortunately, while publishers were making savings in newsprint, they were squandering readability. Individual letters are distorted in stereotyping, height remaining constant but width compressed. Although type designers have studiedly created letterforms to withstand such distortion, shrinkage is not uniform. The over-all shrinkage of a whole page can be controlled, but column 1 may shrink twice as much as column 7. If too much compensation is designed into a letter, it may look equally as distorted if shrinkage is not up to expectation.

Another hazard of shrinkage is that it produces columns far too narrow for pleasant reading. The optimum line length for typical newspaper body type is 16 picas. When type is set at 11 picas, serious discomfort results to the reading eye. When the column is reduced to 10 picas by shrinkage, it approaches an end to readability.

Fortunately, if belatedly, some newspapers have become aware of this hazard and have adopted the *optimum (op) format* with six columns close to optimum measure on a page instead of the conventional eight narrow ones.

Plastic and rubber plates are used with varying degrees of success; both materials are rapidly being developed today after lengthy periods of experimentation. Advertisers find that plastic plates give good reproduction and, being so light, can be mailed at comparatively low costs to publications throughout the country.

Printing with molded rubber plates is *flexography*. At first the plates could not hold fine detail and a major use was printing bags and carton cardboard. But improvements were made constantly and today much good printing, notably on cellophane and other plastics, is done by rubber plates. The best is when the rubber is vulcanized onto the metal cylinder rather than slipped on as a *sleeve*.

Some of the plastic plates are of rigid materials that are locked up in the page form before stereotyping. Others, like the rubber ones, are highly flexible and are used as *wraparounds*, fastened right onto the curved printing plate for truest reproduction. These may be duplicate or original plates.

Flexible plates are being used instead of stereotypes in some newspaper plants today and they hold interesting promise.

One of the most interesting has been the *Dycril plate*, a product of DuPont. This is a thin, light-sensitive plastic similar to nylon that can be etched by a solvent far less caustic than the engraver's acid. It accepts a fine image, can be etched easily and quickly and then wrapped smoothly around the printing cylinder. The plates are also used flat as conventional printing plates are.

Engravings of entire forms can be made on new metal alloys thin enough to use as wraparounds. Others are bent to the proper arc and mounted like a *saddle* to the printing cylinder.

All these flexible plates take advantage of the high speeds of rotary printing.

The truest duplicate plates are *electrotypes*. These are manufactured by combining a molding process with the same electroplating that puts the chromium on auto bumpers.

The original form—type, engravings or a combination of them—is used to make a mold similar to the stereotype flong. Instead of cellulose of the flong, the electrotyper uses lead, plastic, *Tenaplate*, or wax, although wax is rare today.

This mold must be made electrically conductive, coated with a fine, high-pressure spray of silver nitrate solution. This mold is suspended in an electrolytic tank in a solution of copper salts.

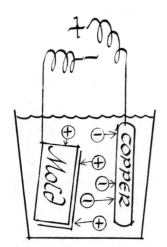

ELECTROTYPES and nickeltypes are made by the electroplating process, shown here in schematic form. Copper ions leave the metal bar and are in solution with a positive charge. This makes them attracted to the negatively charged mold. Negative ions meanwhile travel to the copper cathode and form cuprous salts to replenish the solution.

The mold is given a negative electrical charge. A copper bar hanging in the bath is charged positively. Copper ions in solution also have a positive charge which causes them to seek out the negative of the mold. These ions hug the surface of the mold as they lose their charge and are neutralized. Meanwhile the copper anode slowly dissolves and replenishes the bath with more copper ions. The thickness of the copper coating is determined by

GHOSTING THE BACKGROUND in a photograph eliminates distractions and emphasizes the subject. Ghosting may be done by airbrushing on white paint or by Bourges or similar white shading sheets out of which is cut the area covering the subject itself.

how long the mold remains in the bath. But it is never very thick.

This thin cuprous shell is removed from the mold. It is *tinned* or *plated* on its back and lead is poured onto the back to make a plate about a quarter inch thick. The lead gives strength; the tin assures a strong bond between the copper and lead that would not join each other.

If the mold is of plastic, it can be reused. But the mold is destroyed and a new one must be made if the material is wax or Tenaplate, a thin sheet of aluminum backing the wax.

Electrotypes are carefully finished by hand to correct low areas or defects. They are then mounted on wood by nailing or *sweated* to a block of solid lead with solder. Just as the boilerplate mentioned earlier was mounted on a special base, so electros can be locked into proper position on grooved plates designed for that purpose.

The same electrolytic process is used to make steel or nickel-faced electros. These, commonly called *nickeltypes,* are very durable and are used when long press runs are planned or when extremely rough-surfaced stock will be used. Newspaper name plates are usually nickeltypes.

The use of electros grows constantly. Almost all magazine advertisements are delivered to publications in that form. Because electros hold finer detail than stereos, many advertisers prefer to furnish newspapers also with electros of their ads.

Many good books are printed from electros. Should there be any damage to the printing surface, it is easy to make a new electro. Should signs

GRAY TONES are all of the same value although the fineness of the lines varies to accommodate differing reductions in the plate-making process or different printing processes which will use the plates.

of wear become apparent, new plates can be duplicated. If a new printing of the book is demanded, fresh electros can be made far more easily than resetting the type. And always there are the advantages of printing from a single element rather than from many linecaster slugs. *Curved electros* are used on rotary presses with greater fidelity than stereotypes.

Preparing Copy for the Engraver

While it is the responsibility of the platemaker to produce good printing plates, the man who prepares copy for the camera and specifies plate requirements contributes substantially to the ultimate quality.

It is axiomatic that the engraver can get no better quality in his plates than is in the original copy. While not 100 per cent accurate, the statement stresses the need for good preparation and handling of original art.

The specifier of plates must know those that will best reproduce his original copy. Line etchings are used for pen-and-ink drawings, brush-and-ink, dry brush, wood engravings, linoleum blocks, and scratchboard drawings. Highlight halftones are needed to capture the texture of pencil, charcoal, and wash drawings. Halftones will reproduce photographs and such continuous-tone copy as paintings in oil, watercolor, casein, and other media. Three-dimensional art can often be photographed directly through the halftone screen.

Line art should be done on good-quality white paper, of which every artist has his own favorite brand. Tinted stock should be avoided except that which is blue-white. Ability to erase cleanly is essential. *India ink* is the best medium, smooth, and nonreflective. (Shiny highlights on black areas will reproduce as white.) It can be used with a brush or pen—drawing, ruling, or Speedball.

But India ink has a tendency to thin out at the end of a stroke and, when thin, assumes a brownish cast which results in a weak negative. When used to paint in large areas, it can wrinkle lightweight paper. For large areas, *lampblack* or *tempera* (poster paint) should pinch-hit for India ink.

Most engravers prefer to shoot original art that is larger than the finished cut, so artists consistently work at dimensions larger than the final engraving. Since 1½ times by width seems ideal, to provide a 4-inch-wide cut, the artist does his work 6 inches wide.

Degree of reduction is a factor that must determine the artist's technique. Fine lines may disappear in reduction; so may white areas between lines. Some artists use *reducing lenses* to check on the strength of the reduced picture.

Halftones require glossy photographs for best results. Pictures on *matte paper* will tend to lose crispness in reproduction on the press. Photos should not be too contrasty; deep blacks and highlights must be separated by full gradations of gray. Most photographs are 8 × 10 inches but here, too, original copy should preferably be larger, and certainly no smaller, than the finished engraving.

Photographs often require retouching before going to the engraver's camera. Much retouching must be left to highly skilled artists who work on either the photographer's negative or the photo.

Photos are retouched with brush or airbrush. Four or five tones of gray tempera paint are usually used; pure white and black are sometimes valuable but more often dangerous because the camera sees their extreme values more clearly than most human eyes do. Retouching should always be invisible to the ultimate reader. Retouching paint should be applied sparingly; heavy impasto layers cast shadows that the camera will pick up.

When many photos are cut into irregular shapes to form one large picture, it is called a *collage*. When a similar effect is obtained by printing several negatives onto a single sheet of photopaper, we call it a *montage*. Airbrushing blends tones and hides harsh edges of collages but the technique is rarely if ever satisfactory.

All hand art and retouched photographs must be

A PEN-AND-INK DRAWING, done in the style of a wood engraving, is ideal copy for a zinc etching. If an actual wood engraving had been prepared, it probably could not withstand the pressure of today's printing processes, so a photoengraving would be made from an impression of the wood plate.

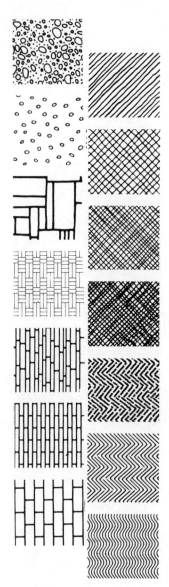

BEN DAY PATTERNS are available in a great many forms. The ones shown here are also made as shading sheets. The ones in the right column are architects' and engineers' symbols showing various construction materials.

protected. The common, and best, method is an overflap. A sheet of soft paper is cut the exact width of and about 3 inches longer.than the artwork. The extra length is folded over the top of the art and fastened to the back with masking tape or rubber cement. It can then be lifted easily, like the page of a book, to expose the art and will automatically fall down to protect it. Some artists use two overflaps, one of tissue and one of strong kraft paper.

Crop marks, which indicate to the engraver the area to be eliminated from the cut, should always be marked outside the picture area. Four crop marks are necessary, two to show height, two for width. If no cropping is indicated, the engraver will shoot to the outside edge of the original. Occasionally the portion of the original to be used is on an axis different from the original. In those cases, one of the horizontal crop marks must be continued to the other side of the picture, and it is wise to mark this "horizontal."

By placing crop marks outside the engraving area, they can be erased and new ones indicated, should the art work be reused. In the case of glossy photographs, crop marks are indicated with grease pencil which can easily be rubbed off.

Sometimes it is desirable to make an overlay of tracing paper and indicate the area to be reproduced. This is most useful in the case of an irregularly shaped cut or *internal mortising.*

If no cropping is required, it is usually best to affix a protruding slip of paper to the back of the picture and on it write directions to the engraver.

Never should instructions be written on the back of a photo. Even light pencil marks may indent the paper and raise the surface of the picture so that the camera catches highlights. Paper clips should never be used on glossies; they also indent the emulsion.

Engraver's copy should never be folded or rolled. Folds cast shadows which the sensitive camera will pick up, and even carefully rolled materials will soon develop tiny ribs or creases.

Instructions to the engraver should be terse and

explicit. The size of the cut should be written between the crop marks, in inches or picas.

Never specify size in words; "reduce one-half" is confusing. Does it mean that the total area of the engraving should be half of that of the original? Or does it mean that the width of the cut should be one-half of the original? In the latter case, the height will also be one-half, so the area will be only one-quarter.

For halftones, the screen must always be indicated. For a square halftone, no express directions are required. But should it be a silhouette, a drop-out, or other less common kind, instructions should be precise.

Specify whether the cut is to be mounted or unblocked. *Flush-mounted* cuts are becoming common; but if it is essential that one or more sides be

CROPPING INSTRUCTIONS are written in the margins of photographs or on overlays. Note that they are necessary only in one margin.

CROPPER'S L'S are valuable tools in helping "find the picture in the photograph."

mounted flush, this should be specifically ordered.

If a number of line cuts are to be reduced at the same proportion—*same-focus*—they can be mounted together and handled as one subject until after the engraving is made. Then they are sawed apart and blocked separately.

Halftones, too, can be grouped into a flat. This requires that they all be reduced at the same focus, of course, but also that their tonal values be identical. It takes an expert to judge these values, and unless you qualify totally it is best to leave this grouping to the engraver.

Good engravings require time. It is wise to schedule work to avoid breathless deadlines. Tell the engraver exactly when you need the cuts. He can then place them into the routine of his shop in such a way as to assure maximum quality, often savings of time and money, and prompt delivery.

While this discussion has been in the context of the photoengraver making relief plates, all the points apply equally to copy for offset or gravure plates as well. So, of course, does the next section on cropping and scaling.

Scaling Pictures

Most art, hand or photographic, is made larger than the finished cut so that the engraver can get sharp focus and so that any slight imperfections will be diminished to invisibility. The layout man must know exactly what the size of the engraving will be to render accurate dummies. So *scaling pictures* is a constant activity.

Scaling may be done arithmetically. The formula

$$W : H = W' : H'$$

simply states that the ratio of width (W) to height (H) of the original art will be exactly the same as that of the reduced width (W') to the reduced height (H').

Suppose we have a picture 8 × 10 and we want to reduce it to 4 inches in width. We have a simple equation:

$$W : H = W' : H'$$
$$8 : 10 = 4 : x$$

If you, as most graphic artsmen seem to, have forgotten your basic algebra, here is the key: The product of the means equals the product of the extremes.

$$8 \times x = 10 \times 4$$
$$8x = 40$$
$$x = 5'', \text{ the new height of the cut.}$$

This was a simple reduction that really did not demand arithmetic or algebra. But it demonstrates the formula.

To avoid this mathematical chore, there are several mechanical devices based on the principle of the slide rule which enables the unknown factor to be found by simply matching up two numbers on a scale and reading the answer opposite the third known factor. These calculators—some like the conventional slipstick, others circular—are inexpensive, accurate, and easy to use.

But the simplest method is to use the *common diagonal*. If a diagonal were drawn from lower left of both the original 8 × 10 photo and the resulting 4 × 5 cut, they would both make the same angle with the baseline. If the small cut were laid on the original, the diagonal of the photo would be an exact extension of that of the engraving.

So, to find the scale for any reduction, or enlargement, this common diagonal is utilized, as shown in Example 4.

In Diagram X a photograph is to be reduced to a specified width. Draw the diagonal AC. Along the baseline AB measure exactly the desired reduced width, E'. At E raise a perpendicular until it meets the diagonal at F. Draw the line FG parallel to the line AB. Then F' is precisely the new height and the area of the cut will be AEFG.

In Diagram Y the new height is known and the new width must be found. Again draw the diagonal AC. Along the side AD measure off the desired height, E'. From E draw a line perpendicular to AD until it meets the diagonal at F. Now F' is no longer the unknown factor; the new width is known and the area of the cut will be AGFE.

On rare occasions you might want to enlarge the area of the original, as in Z. In this case draw the diagonal AC and extend it beyond the area of the original photo. Extend AB to the new required width, E'. At E raise the perpendicular to intersect the diagonal at F and learn the new height, F', and the area of the cut, AEFG.

Often such enlargement is done in planning a printed page, but the photographer is then instructed to prepare a larger glossy so the engraver can still *shoot down* in making his plate.

These diagonals and perpendiculars are not drawn right on the original art, of course; tracing paper is laid over the picture. Care must be taken that the pencil is used so lightly it does not mar the surface of the art.

The diagonal system has two distinct advantages. It avoids cumbersome fractions in reducing the algebraic equation. It enables the layout man to

Example 4. SCALING PICTURES
by the common-diagonal method
is shown here.

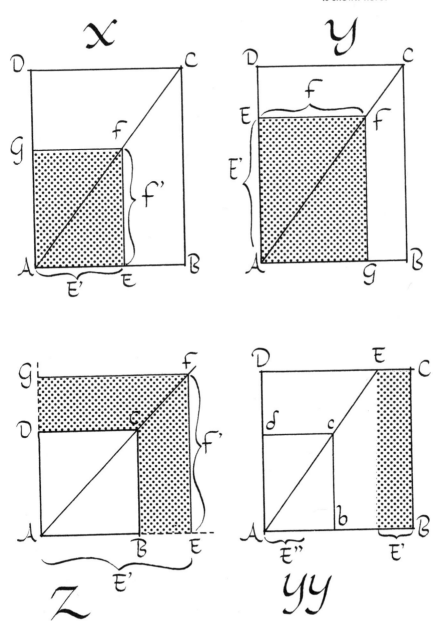

Firmin Gillot

FIRMIN GILLOT, a Parisian lithographer, made the first photoengraving in 1850. He used sensitized *asphaltum,* the same material used by his countryman, Joseph Nicephore Niepce, in photography. The inventor called his process *panicography* but, perhaps because it was so long, it was changed to *gillotage.*

The first line cut printed commercially appeared in a French photographic journal, *La Lumière.* It was a picture of Gutenberg: Hooray!

This picture is taken from a series of old drawings of prominent graphic arts personages, entitled *Valhalla of Printers.*

It was several years later, in 1869, that the first printed half-

visualize the photograph in its reduced size. For he sees its new dimensions imposed upon the original one and can thus gauge the approximate reduced size of any element within the picture. This is difficult to do when given only a set of numbers: just how big is $2\frac{7}{8} \times 5\frac{3}{16}$?

Often the use of the overlay and diagonal will suggest a more effective way to crop the original.

The diagonal also shows where a picture must be cropped to fit a specific area. Example 4, YY shows a photograph ABCD which must be cropped and reduced to fit an area Abcd.

Over the photo, draw the new area, Abcd, and extend the diagonal Ac until it intersects DC at E. Immediately you know that the original picture must be cropped the equivalent of E' to give it the proportions to reduce exactly to the required area. It's then easy to decide whether to crop off E', slice the same amount off the left at E" or divide the required amount, in any proportion, between both sides of the picture.

In all cases, care must be taken to draw the diagonals and perpendiculars accurately. In diagram YY, for instance, if the diagonal from A does not hit the corner c precisely, the error grows and E' is not correct.

Cropping photographs to maximum effectiveness is an exercise in discernment. The picture editor says, "I get the picture out of a photograph." He distinguishes between a photograph, as a technical product, and a picture, as a communication.

His basic axiom is: Crop ruthlessly. All elements that do not contribute to conveying information—especially those that confuse or distract the eye—should be eliminated. To show a watchmaker at work, the editor would probably crop down so that the timepiece, his hands and his tools occupied the whole picture area. But if his workshop were photogenic or the subject of the picture, the editor would use far more of the photo.

Cropping ruthlessly gives assurance to the reader that it was done on purpose. To slice off just the top of a man's head, like a surgeon trepanning a skull, makes the reader uncomfortable. When the photo is cropped to just above the eyebrows, he knows his attention is being directed to the face. Never crop a standing figure at the ankles; cut him at mid-shin or mid-thigh or, better yet, just below the rib cage.

It is almost impossible to crop too tightly; the reader's mental eye will fill in details.

Cropping is also done to enhance a mood. The vastness of the ocean can best be conveyed by a very shallow picture; a tall vertical composition lifts the eye and mind like a rocket.

Cropper's L's are useful tools for determining how a photo can best be cropped. These are L-shaped pieces of paper or plastic, usually 2 inches wide and 12 to 24 inches long on each arm, with inch or pica increments indicated on the edges. With one guide in the position of a normal *L* and the other one upside down, they can define any area of a photo and show its dimensions.

If areas of a photo are confusing, but cannot be cropped out because of the shape required by a layout, the background may be *ghosted,* covered with a dimming layer of thin white paint or Bourges sheets or darkened by the same processes. Depending upon the intensity of the toning, the main features may still be recognized but annoying details are melted away.

Working with illustrations is one of the most satisfying phases of the graphic arts. The designer should learn the technical aspects so thoroughly that he can perform them instinctively and not diminish his pleasure or effectiveness by having to divide his attention between picture and procedure.

SUGGESTED READINGS

Cardamone, Tom. *Advertising Agency and Studio Skills.* New York: Watson-Guptill, 1958.

Line, Halftone and Color. Chicago: American Photoengravers Association, 1961.

Maurello, S. Ralph. *Commercial Art Techniques.* New York: Tudor Publishing Co., 1958.

Nelson, Roy Paul, and Ferris, Byron. *Fell's Guide to Commercial Art.* New York: Frederick Fell, 1966.

tone appeared in the Canadian Illustrated News of Montreal. Apparently it was the work of William Leggo.

But many people may claim to be the actual inventors. William Henry Fox Talbot, who discovered the *latent-image* principle in photography, used two layers of tulle—a gauzy fabric—as the first engraver's halftone "screen."

An American, Frederic Eugene Ives, played an important part in advancing halftone techniques when he used a wood engraver's ruling machine to make the crossline screen in 1885.

It took only one more year for Max Levy, like Ives a Philadelphian, to find the way to make such screens commercially. The lines are etched into fine glass by hydrofluoric acid and then filled with an opaque pigment. Two such plates, at right angles, are fastened together with Canada balsam, an invisible bond. Levy and his brother Louis —and their descendants today— have long been leaders in photoengraving.

12
Color Printing

The Rainbow on the Page

Ever since early cave dwellers rubbed tinted earth into the drawings they made on rocky walls, color has been a close companion of the written word.

Egyptians painted their hieroglyphics; Gutenberg *illuminated* his Bible, as scribes had been doing for centuries; Currier & Ives tinted their engravings by hand. Today color makes rainbows of printed pages, with magazines producing exemplary work on high-speed presses and newspapers constantly expanding color on their forbidding paper.

Color has many important functions. It amplifies communication by giving information black and white cannot convey. It sets a mood that makes the reader more receptive to the message or makes the message more meaningful. It provides accent or contrast that makes reading more pleasurable. It helps direct the reader through the printed page. It can give identification as instantaneous as a trademark.

Color should be used only when it serves at least one of these functions. Color cannot—nor should the designer try to make it—hide poor typography, layout, or printing.

The theory and use of color have intrigued the creative mind since history began, and probably before that. In this generation we have added volumes to our knowledge. Here we shall not discuss more than the fundamentals necessary to understand the value and application of color in graphic arts. Much of this can be done by defining terms.

All color comes from sunlight. When white light is broken into its components, we have the rainbow. *Reflection* and *absorption* of sunlight produce the effects we know as color. A lemon is yellow because it absorbs all colors except yellow and reflects that to stimulate our nerves of vision. In an unlighted room a lemon is not yellow; it is not visible at all. Under dim light, the yellow rays it reflects will be so weak we see it as gray.

There are two kinds of color: *chromatics* are all the true colors—the rainbow and all its mutations; *achromatic* colors are black, white, and grays.

Black and white are, theoretically and commonly, not classed as colors. Black is the absence of all color; white is the presence of all; grays are mixtures of black and white.

Hue is that quality which creates color as we know it. It is the element that makes red red.

Tone or *value* is that variation of hue resulting from the addition of a small quantity of black or white. Adding black to color creates a *shade*. Addition of white makes a *tint*.

Adding one color to another creates a *hue*—note the difference in meaning from "hue" as a quality. Jade green or peacock blue are hues made by mixing different proportions of blue and green.

Chroma—the *intensity* of a color—is its strength and brilliance. A "bright green" has higher intensity than a "dull green." Acute lack of intensity is referred to as *muddy* or *washed-out* color.

Despite contrary theory in physics and psychology, the printer classifies red, yellow, and blue as the *primary* colors. With these he can produce any of the others. *Secondary* colors are the product of any two primaries. Red and blue make violet; red and yellow, orange; blue and yellow, green. Mixing two secondaries gives a *tertiary* color: green and violet result in olive; violet and orange, russet; orange and green, citrine. Mixing primary and secondary colors creates *intermediate* colors.

Beyond that, possible combinations—each creating a new hue—are staggering to contemplate, and when the shades and tints of varying degrees are created for each hue the peacock pales in comparison.

There are *warm* and *cool* colors, so named for their natural associations. Fire and sunshine naturally make red, yellow, and orange the warm colors; water, sky, and the shadows of deep forests make blue, violet, and dark green cool. Warm colors are gay and exciting; cool colors are calm and collected. Some colors are on the borderline; green can be cool or warm depending upon its hue and intensity.

Painters use this "temperature" of color to create effects of distance. Cool colors recede; warm colors

MAINZ PSALTER, probably the second book printed with movable type, was certainly the first printed in color. This *B* is in red with the ornate background in blue. It's 3½ inches square.

The book, of which only 10 copies are known to exist, was printed on vellum. It used two sizes of type, the *lettre de forme* similar in design to, and about the same size as, that of the 42-Line Bible, and its main text, which is about a 40-point type by modern measurement.

It is believed that a single psalter was held up in front of the choir and therefore the characters had to be big enough so even the bass in the back row could read it.

The relief letter itself fits precisely into a recess in the background block. It was lifted out and inked in red. Then the block with the background was lifted out and inked in blue. The type, meanwhile, was inked in black. The three components were replaced, and all colors printed in a single impression.

(The United States Bureau of Printing and Engraving uses a project themselves closer to the viewer. Taking this effect into consideration, the designer prefers to use cool colors as a background on which to surprint black type; they recede and do not detract from the type.

Warm and cool colors can be used together with pleasant effect. But the designer should use one kind of color sparingly, as an accent or contrast, rather than use equal amounts of cool and warm colors.

Color combinations add to the legibility of type. It is because black type on a yellow background has the highest legibility that highway traffic signs were long painted in that combination. Black on red has the lowest legibility. Certain red-green combinations set up such dissonance that the eye is actually pained.

Psychological effects of color are strong. Of pure colors, women prefer red, blue, violet, green, orange, and yellow in that order. Among both tints and shades, they prefer violet. Yellow is preferred in tints far above its pure color or shades.

Blue is the favorite color of men, then red, violet, green, orange, and yellow. Blue is also preferred among tints and shades.

Children, as well as people and peoples whose educational and cultural development is not far advanced, prefer bright primaries and secondaries. Older persons prefer softer color, just as they prefer softer music.

Bad psychological effects come from the unnatural use of color. Printing a steak in green not only fails to add to communication, it actually detracts from it by creating a strong sense of repulsion on the part of the reader. Such distortions as yellow skies are exaggerations, not perversions, of natural phenomena and so do not disturb the reader.

Red is the color of boldness and power. It can easily become overpowering and then banal. But used sparingly, like red pepper in cooking, it gives lift to a page. As a background, red must be reduced to a pale tint to counteract the forward movement of warm colors. In pure form, red is a good background for white type (in a reverse cut), if the type is large and devoid of thin hairlines.

Blue, with its intimate association with sky and water, is a quiet color of hope and patience. As the favorite color of the majority of people, it can be used with no fear of adverse psychological effects. Its coolness makes it a good background color, in tints for black surprinting, in full strength for reverses.

Yellow generates the buoyant happiness of a sunny day. In large masses it lights up a page, but it is too weak to provide legibility to type unless it is on a black background. Yellow on black has legibility almost as high as black on yellow.

Orange is a happy color, too. Its resemblance to gold gives overtones of money and prosperity. Its use should be in the same manner as that of yellow.

Brown, a shade of orange, is a most versatile color. Its shades have enough body to carry type; its tints are never anemic. Men associate it with wood and leather, women with fine furs. Like blue, it has no inherent weaknesses and so can be used in a wide variety of jobs.

Green is another universally popular and widely

variation of multiple-color printing today. Various portions of a plate for postage stamps are inked while the rest is blocked out by a precisely cut *frisket*. Several inkings are made, and all the colors printed at one time.)

Peter Schoeffer, who printed the *Psalter*, was an illuminator of manuscripts in Paris, and there still exists one he signed and dated in 1449. Soon after this he became an employee of Gutenberg. When Johannes Fust sued for recovery of loans, he took Schoeffer as a partner in order to have the technical knowledge required to continue the printing business. Soon thereafter, Schoeffer married the boss's daughter.

Schoeffer was a good printer and produced many fine volumes including some, as early as 1465, in Greek characters. He is credited with improving on—or even inventing—the hand-held mold in which Gutenberg's type was cast.

used color because the grass and foliage it suggests
are universal. Like brown, it can be used in large
masses, in small accents, or for type.

Violet, especially its shade of purple, suggests
robes of royalty, the dignity of church vestments,
and the pomp and splendor of high ritual. It can be
used in many ways, but its lighter tints, although
popular with women, are too reminiscent of
lavender-and-old-lace to appeal to men.

The human eye can distinguish about 10 million
variations in color. Of these, 17,500 have specific
names listed in various dictionaries. The average
person probably uses no more than several dozens
of these; the rest are mainly the coinage of fashion
publicists: Shocking Pink, Eleanor Blue, or Kelly
Green. Many of the coined names compound confusion. "Football" is a blue, so is African Green;
Swedish Red is orange to the average man's eye.

In 1899, A. H. Munsell, a Boston teacher, began
research that resulted in the *Munsell system* of
noting color. Starting with 10 hues, he charted
values on a numerical scale of nine steps ranging
from black, 1, to white, 9. Chroma is shown on a
similar, but longer scale.

A bright, strong red is *R 5/12*. The *5* indicates
that this red is halfway between dark and light and
the *12* that it is a dozen steps away from neutral
gray in intensity. Maroon is designated as *R 2/6*,
with low value and chroma. Pink is *R 8/4*. (*Five
value*, the halfway point on the tonal scale, is that
level to which the eye unconsciously and constantly
adjusts itself. The most successful use of color—in a
painting, a package, or a piece of merchandise—is
usually at this intermediate, five value.)

After 28 years of labor, the National Bureau of
Standards, early in 1962, announced a new method
of designation.

Charts with 28 familiar colors and modified in
value and intensity yield 267 different color names.
These names are prosaic in contrast to the advertiser's Lilac Champagne or Hot Tomato. But the no-
nonsense scientific attitude that devised such names
as light-grayish-yellowish-brown, vivid red, or mod-

erate pink does create a reasonably accurate vocabulary for describing colors verbally. While the new system was greeted with pleasure by people who must work with colors, the general public will still call pink just "pink" for at least as long as they call a flower a daisy instead of a *bellis perennis* or *chrysanthemum leucathemum*.

But the average printer, like the average person, has not developed or been born with such acute color perception. So the printer has devised a color wheel whereby he can reassure himself, when combining colors, that he will create acceptable harmonies.

Around the wheel, in a triangle, are placed the colors comprising the *primary triad*. Halfway between them come the secondary colors produced by each pair. In the remaining blanks are the intermediate colors, named by combining the name of the primary, first, with the secondary: red-orange, for instance, never orange-red.

Color Combinations

There are six basic color combinations.

Monochromatic uses two or more tones of one color. In practice, this is produced by using one color of ink and screening some of the elements to tints; or the color of ink in a deep value may be printed on paper in a lighter tint of the same color.

Analogous harmony comes from two colors, primary and secondary, that are adjacent on the color wheel.

Complementary color combinations are made from colors directly opposite each other on the wheel: blue and orange, red and green, and yellow and violet. This combination always consists of a cool and a warm color. The result is a dramatic combination in contrast to the genteel softness of analogous combinations.

In the beloved Yule combination, green is best in large masses with red as an accent. In the blue-orange complement, often considered the loveliest of all combinations, blue should dominate.

Yellow and violet are the calmest of the comple-

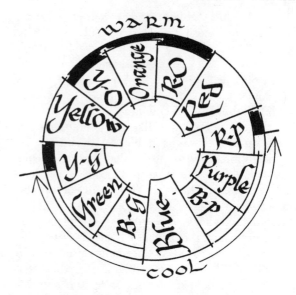

COLOR WHEEL shows relationships of various hues. The large areas show primary colors. Halfway between the primaries are the secondaries, while the tertiaries are between each of them and a primary. Note that the primary color's name is always first in designating the tertiaries.

COLOR HARMONIES can readily be determined by using the color wheel.

mentaries; here either can dominate, but never should both be used in equal quantity. Combinations of complementary intermediate colors are more subdued, but all complementaries are striking. One color should be a shade, the other a tint, never both pure.

Split complements are found by choosing any color on the wheel, determining its complement straight across the wheel, and then using a color adjacent to it. The split complement of blue, therefore, would be yellow-orange or red-orange, the nextdoor neighbors of the complementary orange.

The *triad* is a combination of three colors. Visualize a triangle that connects the primary colors; as you turn this triangle to any position, its points will designate the triad.

The triad of primaries is primitive and almost brazen. The triad of the secondaries is more refined, that of the intermediates is the most delicate.

The triads should consist of one strong color, one light in tone, and the third one about halfway between. Always use just one color in large quantities, with the other two in definitely smaller amounts.

T-harmony also uses three colors; its other name,

complements and a third, describes the method. Choose your complementary colors and draw a line between them; at the center of the circle draw a perpendicular line in either direction. It will point to the third color.

Any of these combinations can be created on white stock with colored inks. The paper, on the other hand, may furnish one of the colors, or the combinations, in ink, may be printed on colored stock, thus adding yet another color. When colored paper is used, it should be a tint of one of the inks for harmony, although it is possible to use an adjacent color to any one of the inks with pleasing effect.

Black, white, and gray are not colors in the strict sense, yet any one of them will harmonize with all other colors. Black and red is undoubtedly the most widely used of any combination; red-orange affords more contrast than pure red in this case. Gold and silver are not true colors either but also harmonize with all others. Gold and purple produce the richest, most elegant of all combinations.

Red and blue do not harmonize by any mathematical scheme. Yet in our flag the combination satisfies not only our patriotic but our aesthetic values. The reason is that the colors are separated by white bands. In a layout also, nonharmonic colors can be used pleasingly, if they are kept well separated by white paper or by bands of the "noncolor colors" we have just discussed.

Wisely used, color is a powerful tool for the designer. For this reason, and also because it is exciting to work with color, the typographic designer should study it and experiment with it enthusiastically and thoroughly.

Complementary

Triad

Analogous

Color Printing

By reversing normal procedures and considering the more complex use of color first, we can actually simplify an interesting subject. So we shall discuss *process color,* a more sophisticated form of the sleight-of-eye that the platemaker produces in halftone reproductions.

Process color is that printing in which primary colors interact to create the impression of all other colors. It may utilize two colors or many, although three are adequate to reproduce the full spectrum.

The chemist's *analysis* and *synthesis* is a close analogy to the work of the engraver and printer in reproducing a picture in full color.

By electrolytic analysis the chemist breaks water into two parts of hydrogen and one of oxygen. By synthesis he combines these two gases, in proper proportions, to make the familiar fluid. The engraver analyzes full-color copy by breaking it down into the three basic colors. The printer puts them together again to make the original, chromatic image.

Imagine, for example, a picture of a red barn standing on the crest of a green hill with orange foliage and a blue sky behind it. This is to be reproduced by printing in any of the methods.

The engraver places the picture before his camera, just as when making a black-and-white halftone, for all process printing uses halftone plates. But he adds one more factor, a *filter,* a sheet of colored gelatin sandwiched between glass.

If he places a red filter between copy and film, red reflections from the picture will be absorbed by the filter. If he also places a blue filter before his lens, all blue rays will be absorbed. Then only the yellow reflections from the picture will pass through to affect the negative in his camera.

In practice, he combines red and blue filters into a single sheet of violet for convenience.

Now he has a halftone negative which represents only—and all of—the yellow in the original picture. There is a large amount of it in the orange of the trees and also in the green of the grass, lesser amounts in other areas of the picture, probably none in the sky.

By using a green filter, he bars all yellow and blue reflections and captures only red reflections from the original. In the barn of the picture, red will be intense. It will be lighter in the orange areas and in other places will be so faint the naked eye does not discern it as such.

PROGRESSIVE PROOFS begin with the yellow plate and the red plate, proofed separately.

Because the dots of all colors are printed on white paper and don't generally overlap, the order in which they are placed on the paper, either in proofing or in printing, has little bearing on the final image.

Red has the longest waves we can see, 33,000 per inch.

RED AND YELLOW plates are proofed together to make the third proof in the set of seven progressives. These two primary colors, plus the orange they create—a secondary, or binary, color—are on the warm side of the spectrum.

THE BLUE PLATE is proofed separately. Blue and red light rays don't focus at the same point within the eye so printed images in these two colors when touching seem to vibrate physically and the eye is strongly discomforted.

ALL COLORS of the spectrum have now been produced by optical mixing of images as the three plates are combined into this, the fifth progressive.

This painting is *Wivenhoe Park, Essex,* by the English landscapist, John Constable, (1776–1837).

Examined under magnification, this picture shows dots of all three colors in all areas. Even the sky, which at first glance seems to be merely a tint of cyan, has red and yellow dots. Nowhere in the picture does any primary color appear alone.

The screen used here is 150-line and the paper of this insert is, obviously, coated stock. The insert, like the book itself, is printed by offset.

The nature of color has intrigued both scientist and artist for centuries. As early as 1660, Sir Isaac Newton, of law-of-gravity fame, discovered that sunlight passing through a prism is broken into a tiny rainbow. He theorized that light is a series of atoms, moving in a straight line, and that their varying sizes made the hues.

Light is a form of radiant energy carried as electromagnetic waves. We can see only those waves that form the spectrum but we can feel—as heat—those below red. But visible waves can have a tactile effect, too. A red flannel wrapping around a sore throat, for instance, will raise body temperature more than the same fabric in white will do.

Colors are detected by *cones,* nerve endings in the center of the eye; *rods* around the circumference of the retina can see only in black and white. If you hold a piece of paper behind your head and slowly move it forward around your shoulder, you will "see" the paper before you can detect its color.

THE BLACK PLATE is proofed as the sixth prog, above, and then combines with the primary colors in the final, complete full-color reproduction, below.

The black sharpens detail and creates shades of the colors pro- duced by the first three plates.

Black has no effect on the actual colors of the picture. It does, however, mold the image and, as comparison with the fifth prog shows, seems to change hue as well as value.

Blocking out red and yellow light with an orange filter allows only the blue to create a halftone negative.

The filters actually used in color separation are *magenta,* a slightly bluish red used instead of violet, *cyan,* a greenish blue used instead of pure green, and *yellow,* used instead of orange. These three filtering steps are *color separation.*

From each of these three negatives, the engraver makes a halftone plate. The analysis is complete.

Life magazine's research department pioneered a machine that produces color separations by scanning original copy much the same way that a Fairchild scans black and white; today there are several such machines on the market. Typically, the machine scans colored opaque pictures or transparencies—the familiar slides of the home-movie fan (and some scanners even handle color negatives). A beam of light, reflected off opaque copy or projected through transparent, is broken into its three primary-color components and projects them onto *photomultipliers,* each of which makes one of the separations on film.

Computers make color correction—a tedious and difficult manual task—as well as prepare the black-plate copy and memorize data so that original copy may be enlarged.

Diascan and *Magnascan,* made by Rutherford, *EPOI Color Repro Control* and the *Mergenthaler Linoscanner* are some of the trade names. A similar device combines with the Klischograph and immediately produces printing plates for each of the separations.

This brief description is adequate for the generalist in the graphic arts, but the subject is so fascinating that more detailed study will appeal to many, even though they are not technicians themselves.

Now the printer performs synthesis. By printing each plate in the proper color, he produces the original in all its hues. The red plate has re-created the barn and blends with the yellow to make orange. The yellow has combined with the blue to reproduce green grass. The blue makes the sky and blends with the red to make deep shadows under the eaves.

This is *three-color process.*

There are important points that have been left out in this simple explanation. The inks do not mix physically to create secondary and subordinate colors; the reader's eye does this mixing. As each separation negative is shot, the screen is rotated slightly. The yellow plate is made with the dot pattern running perpendicularly and horizontally. When the red negative is shot, the screen is rotated 15 degrees to the right; for the blue negative, the screen turns to the left, from 90 to 105 degrees. The result is that the halftone dots are not superimposed in printing but lie side by side. The reading eye sees not a tiny blue dot snuggling up to a small yellow one, but one large green one. Occasionally two dots will overprint, but their effect is negligible; the eye does the vital mixing.

The engraver proves his plates individually and in combination, in a series of *progressive proofs* or *progs.* He prints the yellow plate in yellow ink and the red in its color; then he combines the two. Next he pulls the blue plate alone and then over the yellow-red combination. These proofs serve two purposes: they indicate needed color correction, and they show the printer the proper inks to use.

This proofing is time-consuming, and two alternative methods have been developed. In the 3-M *Color-Key* method, each of the separation-negatives is exposed upon a sheet of film of the proper corresponding color. On the b&w negative of the blue separation, for example, each transparent dot will eventually make a relief dot on the printing plate which will deposit a spot of blue ink on the printing paper. When the negative is exposed to a sheet of blue proofing film, the dot remains on the film, the unexposed color is washed away. When the transparencies of the three colors and black are superimposed, they show how the final synthesis on the press will appear.

The *colography technique* is employed by the

Colex 520 of Staley Graphics Company. To a sheet of special paper, a coating of photosensitive emulsion is applied and exposed to the separation negative of one color. A dry powder of the appropriate color is then applied and the photo image becomes visible in that hue. Unexposed emulsion is washed off. The paper is dried and a new coating of emulsion applied. The second color is placed on the paper in the same steps, then the third and fourth. The whole production of four-color proofs up to 25 × 38 inches takes only 20 minutes.

Color correction is made on the plates by staging and re-etching, burnishing or even making dots smaller physically by hand. Another correction method is to make continuous-tone *positive separations*. These are, in effect, a black-and-white photograph of the yellow—or the blue or the red—components of the original art. These can be retouched by conventional methods before they are made into screened negatives.

These methods obviously require an unusually keen sense of color, acute eyesight, and skilled hands. Correction is one of the factors that makes process color costly.

Register must be precise in process color. *Register marks* are drawn on the original at at least two points. The most common form is a cross centered on a circle. Even minute deviation in position is readily measured and corrected. It is easy to overprint these marks precisely and assure perfect register. The marks are removed from the plate before actual printing begins or printed in the margins, which is later cut off.

Three-color process is most common in newspaper work, although it has many other commercial uses. But it lacks the strength and sharpness of *four-color process*, the most common.

In four-color, a black plate is added. This gives definition, produces intermediate grays that cannot be achieved by mixing primaries, and adds strength to the shades of other colors.

There are seven proofs in a set of four-color progs: that of the black plate and of the black on

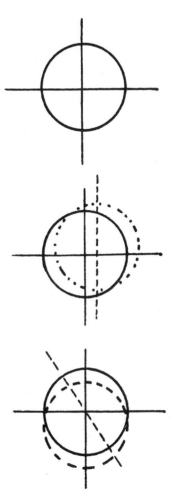

REGISTER MARKS are most commonly used in this form although there are several variations. The distance by which an impression is off register, vertically or horizontally, can easily be measured and proper correction made. When the second impression is tilted in relation to the first, the angle of mis-register can also be determined easily.

top of the three primaries in addition to the five of three-color process. Progressives are usually pulled yellow, red, blue, and black, the same order in which the printer normally uses them, though it is not necessary to follow this sequence because each set of dots lands on white paper anyway.

By showing the printer exactly what color ink to use, progs assure faithful reproduction of the original. A chemist must use the same two gases for synthesis that he obtained from analysis; if he mixes hydrogen with nitrogen he will not produce water. Similarly, if the printer does not use exactly the colors produced by separation, his printing will not be true. If the engraver breaks down the green grass to a mixture of lemon yellow and robin's-egg blue, but the printer uses chrome yellow and Prussian blue, the grass on the printed page will be far different from that of the original.

To avoid this obvious danger, most process color is printed in *standard process colors,* cyan, magenta, and yellow, that are precisely compatible with the standard filters used.

In a great deal of process work, the first color is allowed to dry before the next is run. But for magazines and other high-speed work, *wet printing* is necessary; there is no time to wait for drying. This requires special inks, but the principles remain unchanged.

Sometimes, especially in offset, more than four colors are used for utmost fidelity, and in letterpress six are not unusual.

Two-color process does not even attempt to reproduce full color although some recent experiments with red-orange and blue-green inks give surprising chromatic range. Generally two-color is used for paintings—typically magazine covers—that have been done in only two colors.

Fake color is an interesting process whose most familiar product is the old-fashioned picture postcard which depicts items of local pride. Today souvenir cards are usually four-color process, but the older version well explains color faking. Suppose an engraver were handed a black-and-white photo of the West Siwash city hall and asked to prepare color plates.

He would shoot four black-and-white screened negatives. One he would arbitrarily designate as his "yellow separation." He knows that the grass and foliage in West Siwash is green, so he would leave yellow dots in those areas and also in the building which is orangey brick. But he would remove all the dots in the sky.

On his "red separation" he would leave small dots in the building and in the stripes of the flag and perhaps to indicate crimson blossoms, but again would remove them from the sky area. On the "blue separation" he would leave large dots in the sky and smaller ones where they are to mix with the yellow in the grass. But he would remove them from the building.

When the job is printed, the foliage is green, the sky blue and the building brick red. These colors would not be exact reproductions of the original, but they would be close enough for the purpose.

Fake color is often useful in catalogues. A manufacturer might be bringing out a line of colored plastic wastebaskets. Rather than shoot several color photographs, he can make one black-and-white and fake the color to show the complete line long before all the colors had come off the assembly line. Fake color is far less expensive than full color in this and similar cases.

Correcting fake separations can be done on the negative or the engraving.

Flat Color

Flat or *spot color* is best defined as "any use of color that is not process." This is a broad definition, but so is the use of flat color. There are several loopholes in the definition even beyond the lexicographer's plaint that definitions should not be phrased negatively.

We might say that in spot color the proper hue is provided by the ink rather than by the optical illusion of process color. This simple statement masks a most intricate chain of cooperation. For instance,

before each Christmas, fashion designers have decided on what the popular colors will be for Spring
styles. Suppose it's "passion-fruit purple." Manufacturers of every kind of fabric, synthetic and natural,
of plastic, of leather, and of hat straw must duplicate this hue precisely. So must the maker of
printer's ink. Then, months later, when a merchant
wants to advertise a coat or dress in passion-fruit
purple, the printer has the exact ink ready for use.

Flat color is usually printed from line plates. So
there is no gradation of color value. If a screen is
used, the whole area will be lighter than the solid,
but it will be of the same tint throughout, without
the modulation of halftone dots as in process color.

Note the exception: a halftone may be printed in
color instead of black and is considered spot color.
The effect is usually not very pleasing, however;
halftones are best printed in black.

Of course, flat colors can be combined to form
new hues. The Sunday comic strips are excellent
examples. There black and the primary colors are
used in solids, screened down to tints and combined with each other to create new hues. But these
new colors are flat colors, too; they are of arbitrary
hue and value that only suggest, never re-create,
the color and tonal gradations of nature.

A headline printed in color is spot color. So is the
picture of citrus fruit printed in orange ink instead
of by red-and-yellow process. So is a panel of color
on which black type is printed or a reverse plate in
color. So are *tint blocks*, a simple yet effective
means of using color. A tint block is a mass of color
that carries no detail or tonal variations. It may be
in full value or lightened by a Ben Day, in which
case it is often called a *screen*.

A common use of a tint block is as a background
upon which type is *surprinted*—overprinted—in
black or dark ink. This adds interest, emphasis and
sometimes even legibility to the type.

Such all-over backgrounds can enliven black-and-
white halftones, too. A fire scene gains excitement
from a red tint block; light blue can make a winter
scene look even colder. Sometimes a tint block

makes only a *silhouetted background* for a halftone. In such use, color does not run behind the halftone and its highlights expose the white of the paper. This is more striking than if highlights showed the color of the tint block. Silhouetted tint blocks can be run in far heavier colors and 100 per cent intensity, while over-all blocks must be screened to well below 50 per cent, for most colors, lest they drown details of the halftone.

Tint blocks in deep colors may carry reverse type or, when screened, letters in full, unscreened values. Purists insist that these are technically not tint blocks because they then carry detail. But for practical uses, we would call tint blocks "those areas of color which are in simple shapes, if there is no gradation in tone." A silhouetted jack-o-lantern which ran under part of a full-page ad, for instance, would function as a tint block even though it carried detail at its outline.

Any engraving that does not meet the definition of a tint block is called a *flat color plate,* whether or not it is surprinted by another element.

Not quite spot color nor process color, the *duotone* is a common and useful bridge between the two. Printing one requires two colors, a dark and a light one. (In periodical work, the dark one is usually the always-present black.) Both plates are made from a single black-and-white continuous tone picture. One plate is exposed for the highlight detail; this is the one to be printed in light color. The other, exposed for shadow detail, is printed in dark ink. The finished printed picture appears to be totally in a new, third color; the eye does not see the original hues anywhere. Almost any combination of colors may be used; yellow and black, creating a sepia, is a common combination.

Duotones give a sparkle and feeling of depth that cannot be achieved by printing, let us say, in sepia ink alone. Preparatory cost is low in money and time, and printing poses no problems.

As with all printing, the paper must pass through the press for each color used. This may be once, to print an auction handbill in red; twice, to print a letterhead in black with a trademark in blue; or a couple dozen times to show each available hue for a new line of dinnerware. The number of colors or the elaborateness of their use has no bearing on their definition as spot color.

The product is called a *three-color job* or a *four-color job,* etc. The word "job" always designates it as spot color.

Whether the paper goes through a simple press more than once or through a multi-cylinder press only once, spot printing requires a separate plate or form for each color. These are prepared, not by the filtering that creates process-color separations, but by physically separating the various color components in *mechanical separation.*

When spot color is to be used with all type, there are several methods to make the separation. In the simplest, the form is made up with all the elements as for a one-color job. Then those which are to be in color are removed by the compositor and placed in an adjacent form in exactly the same position. The space left vacant on both forms is filled with quads or furniture. Printing is done from original type.

A mat may be rolled from the original form and two stereos cast from it. On one all the color elements are routed out; on the other, routing removes all elements to be printed in black, leaving only those to be in color. The same technique is used with two electrotypes. Or the artist can take a black-and-white proof, cut out the elements, and mount them separately as copy for two line cuts.

Of course, these techniques can be used only when the components do not overprint each other. You might physically separate thin rules that will print intersecting lines of two colors, but you could not separate large overlapping elements, a headline overprinted on a Halloween pumpkin, for instance. For such separation, the artist prepares mechanical separations by the use of *overlays.*

Suppose the artist is doing a Christmas card which shows Santa Claus trimming an evergreen. He draws the basic picture, the *key plate,* on drawing board. (The key plate will usually, though not

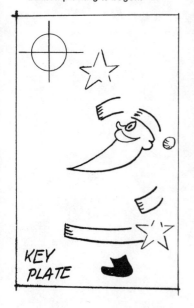

MECHANICAL SEPARATIONS for a three-color job. The key plate, which will be printed in black, was drawn on board or heavy paper. Green and red portions were drawn on overlays. The red overlay was hinged at the top, the green at its left edge. Register is maintained by superimposition of the conventional circle-and-cross mark. This is removed from the plate before the actual production printing is begun.

KEY PLATE

necessarily, be printed in black.) Over this he *flaps* a sheet of acetate. This is clear enough so he can see the key plate easily and its matte surface has enough tooth to make a good drawing surface. On this he draws those areas which will be printed in red: Santa's suit, cap and gloves, his lips and the glow on his cheeks. (This drawing, as are all of them, is done in black India ink for the benefit of the platemaker's camera.) Some of the areas—Santa's cheeks, for instance—may be screened down to a tint by Ben Day or shading sheet. Or both red and black areas may be screened so that when they overprint they'll create the brown of his boots.

Now a second flap, hinged on a different edge, is used for the drawing of those areas which will be printed in green. If the card is to show golden ornaments being hung on the tree, a third overlay will carry those areas in gold.

On the key plate and each overlay the artist draws a register mark so that each printing plate will be in exact relation to the others.

The various color components have now been mechanically separated, to live up to their name, at a cost far less than that of the filter separation. Note that, in both separation processes, the components are in black and white. Color comes into the scene only on the printing press.

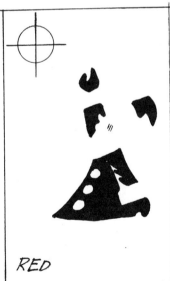

To the platemaker's camera, black and red are identical. So sometimes a clear red acetate is used instead of black India ink. (This is most common when a large area must be filled in and also when the artist needs to discern lines of the key plate through this mass.) But the camera cannot see light blue; so all guidelines the artist uses are in this pale color. Often they need not even be erased after the final drawing.

These techniques for handling color are used identically for letterpress, offset, gravure, or other printing methods and techniques for preparing off-set copy, discussed in Chapter 14, are applicable in many phases of color work.

The *Bourges* (pronounced Burgess) *process,*

which has recently been developed as a versatile tool for color work, is far too broad for more than cursory inspection here. Basically, it consists of transparent plastic sheets in 10 standard printing colors, each in five values from 10 to 100 per cent, that duplicate standard printing inks.

When the artist prepares overlays, he uses the same colors the printer will use. Thus he can see just how the finished job will look. Such sheets are valuable, for the same reason, in preparing roughs and comps.

The sheets are augmented by pencils and inks, again exact matches to printing inks. White, grays, and black are also available; these have great value in ghosting backgrounds on photographs but this is by no means the limit of their functions.

The Bourges method is also used for process color, most notably in pre-correction of color separations.

Reference books are also available that show the results of overprinting tint blocks of various values. If the artist wants a dark green fir and a lighter green pine, he finds the proper hues on a chart. This tells him that the darker one requires 90 per cent blue and 40 per cent yellow while the lighter uses 40 per cent blue and 10 per cent yellow. He specifies this for Ben Day or uses his own Zip-a-Tone of proper value.

To save time, labor, and money, a single piece of art is used for more than one color. By shooting a negative for each color and eliminating areas within each—just as in breaking down a hot-metal form as discussed a few paragraphs back—the platemaker does the mechanical separating.

Suppose the artist wants the word "SALE" to print in orange on a blue background, both colors to be provided by ink, not paper. He letters the word in black on white paper. Over this he places a *tissue overlay,* a sheet of tissue or tracing paper. On it he lays orange crayon over the letters and blue on the background. The engraver shoots two negatives. One makes the orange plate. The other negative must be reversed to leave "SALE," in white, on

KEYLINE DRAWING is used for making both plates for a two-color job.

The background will be printed in blue, the letters in orange.

The platemaker shoots two negatives of this copy. On one he removes the background. This is easy as he need not work down to a fine line but only to the area left blank outside the line. What's left makes the plate for the letters.

In the same way, again with no close work necessary, he opaques out the inside of the letters to make the plate that will print in blue.

The original lines that show the letters are common to both plates and provide the overlapping for lap register.

This process is *painting up*.

the blue background. The orange "SALE" prints on this white area.

The engraver may have to touch up his negatives to give proper register by one of three varieties.

Loose register is used for decorative color where its position need not be precise. For newspaper work and other processes where register may be a problem, loose register is often chosen because it does not lose effectiveness even if its position shifts as much as a pica or two. *Hairline register* brings two colors up to each other with no overlap and no gap. This is the most difficult for artist and pressman to achieve. *Lap register* provides a small area —about a thirty-second of an inch—where the colors overlap. This is the easiest for every craftsman involved.

With the exception of layouts using only type, color is used in half a dozen basic categories:

1. Full-color paintings, in oil or watercolors of various kinds; drawings in crayon, pastel, or colored inks; combinations of line drawing with color wash.

The engraver may encounter some difficulty with highly varnished oil paintings that reflect light. But special filters control the situation and most oils reproduce well. Watercolors must be painted either in transparent or opaque paints; mixing the two creates difficulties in the whites because white paper will not affect the engraver's film exactly as white opaque paint will, even though they look the same to the eye.

2. *Photographic color prints* produced by any commercial method. These are still the favorite copy for most color separators. But there is a growing use of:

3. *Photographic color transparencies.* Brilliant results are obtained from such copy. But transparencies have disadvantages: they are difficult to retouch, to handle in collage, or to letter over.

4. *Hand-colored photographs.* These must be light in the original black-and-white so that colors laid over the image will be captured clearly by the engraver's lens. Brilliant colors are hard to achieve from such copy, but art with delicate hues makes good plates.

5. *Line drawings with color added* by Ben Day (or Zip-a-Tone) or in simple areas.

6. *Continuous-tone* black-and-white photos or wash drawings, with Ben Day adding color.

Newspaper Color

In newspapers color is designated as *ROP, run of the paper,* to distinguish material which is printed on regular newspaper presses from that produced on special color presses.

Newspapers use both process and spot. The pioneer *Milwaukee Journal* ran its first ROP color January 5, 1891; to herald the inauguration of a Wisconsin governor, it printed groups of horizontal lines in red and blue across page one. But not until 1937 did the first ROP ad run in that paper.

The *New York Journal* in 1897 reproduced sketches drawn by Frederic Remington in Cuba as the earliest use of true color for editorial purposes.

Three-color process is a favorite with newspapers. Pages can be made over between editions without changing register of color plates, because news type is all in the black plate which is entirely independent. Where time is short, as in a newspaper plant, it is also advantageous to eliminate the black plate which, because it carries the heaviest color, requires the most hand work by the engraver.

The Milwaukee paper's case histories testify to the power of color in advertising. Typical is that of a stove manufacturer who found that, although color advertising costs were 70 per cent higher than black-and-white, it drew 395 per cent more returns. A full-color ad sold 500 per cent more merchandise for a department store than did black-and-white.

In reporting its own story of developing ROP color, the *Milwaukee Journal* preached the definitive sermon on the use of color: "Experience [showed] that color added to a poor black-and-white ad made it worse, not better. Improperly used, color could often make a good black-and-white ad bad. Good layout men, thrilled with the opportunity to use color, concentrated on it and sometimes forgot their fundamental training and knowledge of good design, headline- and copywriting."

While the reference is to newspaper advertising, it applies to all areas of the graphic arts. Color must be used functionally, and only to make a faster, clearer, and more pleasant transmittal of information.

The function of color is to capture attention, give information that words alone cannot convey, guide the eye in reading, and create a mood that makes the reader more receptive to the printed message. Color should perform at least one, and preferably more, of these functions. It cannot—and should not be used to—disguise unsound layout by mere dazzle.

The hallmark of a good designer is not only how he uses color but how he does not use it. Color adds expense to printing; extra engravings must be used or a form must be broken down into two or more parts. And there must be at least one extra press run. So there is always strong temptation to "get your money's worth." The mediocre designer will start on a two-color ad by putting an illustration or headline in red, let's say. Then he will decide, "I've already paid the surcharge for this red. If I set the signature in color, it won't cost me a penny more." So the sig goes in red. By the same logic he makes the prices red . . . at no extra cost! Then he uses his—absolutely free now!—color for the border. Soon the eye cannot tell whether this is a black-and-white ad with red added or a red-and-white with black.

Color should always be used functionally. It should also be used sparingly. Color is an accent, just as spices and herbs are. If a cook uses just a pinch of paprika, his goulash is a gourmet's delight; if he uses too much spice, the whole dish is spoiled. So it is with color; it should just bring out the flavor of the typographic design, never supplant it.

SUGGESTED READINGS

Birren, Faber. *Principles of Color*. New York: Van Nostrand Reinhold, 1965.

Itten, Johannes. *The Elements of Color*. New York: Van Nostrand Reinhold, 1969.

Maerz, A., and Paul, M. Rea. *Dictionary of Color*. New York: McGraw-Hill Book Company, 1950.

Paschal, Herbert P. *First Book of Color*. New York: Franklin Watts, Inc., 1959.

Sipley, Louis Walton. *Half Century of Color*. New York: Macmillan Company, 1951.

One of those folk tales that no one cares to disprove because it is charming tells the origin of *intaglio* printing.

A knight, off to fight a dragon, stopped to embrace his fair lady. His varlet had just polished his master's suit of armor, but had neglected to wipe the dirty fluid out of the fine, ornamental designs that were incised into the metal suit of every well-dressed knight. So, as the dragon-slayer pressed his beloved to his steel-encased chest, her white dress absorbed the cleaning fluid and the design in the armor was thus printed on her frock.

This is truly how intaglio printing is done. The printing surface is *incised*—that is what intaglio means—into a metal plate. Ink is spread across the entire plate, then wiped off the top of the plate, leaving only that within the incised depressions. As paper is pressed against the plate, the ink transfers from the incisions onto the paper sheet just as it did on the lady's dress.

Intaglio printing derives in fact from the armorer's craft. It was fashionable to decorate armor, shields, and swords, and the handles of other lethal instruments with intricate engravings, which were sometimes inlaid with enamel or precious materials. When the engraver achieved an especially successful pattern, he would actually print it for future reference.

It was only a short step from this process to true printing, and the earliest known intaglio print is a German copper engraving dated 1446—the period when Gutenberg was holding forth.

The purest form of classic intaglio today is encountered in engraved wedding invitations, formal invitations, announcements, and stationery. The most common is the rotogravure magazine of Sunday newspapers; not common enough is paper money.

The intricate design of our currency is incised, by a team of craftsmen, into steel. After hardening in potassium cyanide, this plate is pressed into a softer steel. This in turn is hardened and pressed into soft steel plates, which do the actual printing in sets of

13

Intaglio Printing

Legacy from the Armorer

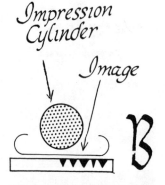

INTAGLIO PRINTING is shown in schematic form. In *A*, the ink roller has covered the face of the plate and the incised image with ink.

In *B* the ink has been wiped off the face of the plate, and the paper is being pressed into the incisions to lift the ink out.

12. These dozen plates, and those to replace worn ones, can all be made from only one original engraving. The formula of the ink is so secret that at the end of each day all leftover ink is gathered and stored under guard. (Ink on our money never dries completely. You can test this by rubbing a bill—especially a green area—over a sheet of clean paper.)

Engraving like this, especially when several men work on different areas, cannot be duplicated by another hand or even by the camera. This is the bane of counterfeiters and a consolation to the legitimate earner of money.

The *etching* is an original art form that employs chemicals—specifically acid—to incise the design. (It should not be confused with the photoengraver's line etching, a relief plate.) A thin plate of copper or zinc is coated with a *ground*, a mixture of wax and mastic. With an etcher's *needle*, the artist draws his design through the wax to expose the plate. He need not draw thick or thin lines; the acid will ultimately create the desired weight of stroke.

The back and sides of the plate are protected by an acid-resistant *stop-out varnish* and the plate is immersed into a *mordant*—usually nitric acid but sometimes potassium chlorate, iron perchloride, or a mixture of two. The etchant bites into the metal only where the protective ground has been removed by the needle. Fine lines are then *stopped out* (as for re-etching of photoengravings) and the plate is re-immersed to bite deeper in other lines. Another method is to scratch in only heavy lines, etch them, remove the plate, and scratch in lighter lines. The heavier ones are re-etched as light ones are subjected to the first bite.

Etchings are printed in a press that resembles an old-fashioned clothes wringer. It is customary for the artist to number each print he pulls; their value often depends on the number of copies that have been made. Then he may destroy the plate by gouging a large X across the plate. He pulls a print of this, too, as proof that the limited edition will not, some time in the future, become unlimited.

Etchings can be recognized by running a finger across the printing. It will be raised, not only because the ink lies high on the paper but also because the printing process slightly debosses the reverse side of the paper as it is forced into the incisions of the plate. The obverse side is then embossed into slight relief.

Other variations of etchings are properly discussed in Chapter 21 under "fine art." But an understanding of the principle helps in examining commercial intaglio, *gravure.*

Although two kinds of such printing are designated as *sheet-fed gravure* and *rotogravure* (from rotary gravure), both are produced on rotary presses. Because the paper must be squeezed onto and into the incised ink bearers, extreme pressure is required, and gravure presses must be husky and heavy. Sheet-fed gravure is usually produced from thin copper plates which are wrapped around a cylinder. Rotogravure plates are themselves heavier copper cylinders. Both are produced by the same photographic method.

The curved-plate principle is old; it was used as far back as 1785 to print intaglio designs onto textiles. The gravure principle was invented around 1879 by Karel Klic in Vienna.

Gravure is a complete screen process. There is no line art; everything, including type, is screened. Thus gravure is a medium ideally suited to reproducing art and far less ideal for type or other line. The printing surface of a gravure plate consists of a vast number of tiny holes or wells, at least 22,500 per square inch. They are all of identical size but vary in depth, and hence in the amount of ink they carry.

Though no one can learn to make these intaglios by reading a book, a knowledge of the basic process is necessary to assay the strengths and weaknesses of this printing method.

All the elements of the page—body and display type and illustrations—are pasted into position. (Although photographs are the ideal original for gravure reproduction, any medium that can be

KAREL KLIC, also known as Karl Klietsch, the Germanized version of his Bohemian name, invented the gravure process around 1878.

At first kept a deep, dark secret, details of his invention were brought to the United States by 1903, but the process didn't become popular until after World War I. Its most familiar form was the sepia-colored Sunday pictorial sections of newspapers. This was 25 years after the first rotogravure press was installed in Lancaster, England.

Although Klic's name, incidentally, seems to be perpetuated by that of the Klischograph, a mechanical engraving machine, actually the machine owes its name to the word *cliché,* used in Europe not for "an overworked phrase," but as a synonym for photoengraving.

This drawing is from *Valhalla of Printers.*

photographed can be reproduced.) This exact-size paste-up is photographed without a screen.

It must be kept in mind that, when the printing plate is etched, intaglio is exactly the opposite of letterpress. In photoengravings, the nonprinting areas are eaten away by acid; in gravure plates, the printing areas must be exposed to the etchant. Therefore a *film positive* must be used for gravure plates. To make such positives, the negative from the camera is simply printed on film instead of photopaper. Retouching may be done on either the negative or positive film.

Meanwhile the screen pattern has been printed onto a *carbon tissue*. This is a sheet of paper (whose only function is as a bearer) covered with sensitized gelatin. The gravure screen is similar to the photoengraver's with two notable exceptions: (1) It is finer (150-line) than most letterpress screens, and (2) it is positive rather than negative —instead of black lines crossing to form small transparent windows, the gravure screen has transparent lines enclosing small black squares.

The sensitized gelatin hardens to the degree of light to which it has been exposed. The white lines of the screen allow maximum light to hit the gelatin, with the result that the entire surface of the carbon tissue has now been cross-hatched by strips of gelatin which is so hard it will not allow penetration by the etchant.

Now the transparent positive is printed on this gridded carbon tissue. Light, varying in intensity of white and dark of the positive, reacts upon those little squares of gelatin that were protected during exposure of the screen.

Deep blacks of the original photograph, and of the film positive, allow little if any light to pass through onto the gelatin. This unexposed area is entirely soluble; it will allow the etchant to work unimpeded and create a deep well. This will hold a maximum quantity of ink which will print heavily. On the other hand, highlights in the positive will allow a great deal of light to strike the gelatin and harden it. There the etchant will be able to eat away just a shallow well holding only a small amount of ink and printing only a small highlight dot. In printing the screen onto the carbon tissue, those intersecting lines create the sides of the little wells.

Now the carbon tissue, face down, is squeegeed onto the copper plate or cylinder (face down is the equivalent of flopping the negative). Moisture makes the gelatin adhere to the plate; the paper, its job done, is stripped away. Etching done with perchloride of iron, a mild etchant, requires 20–30 minutes to do its work, in from three to six bites. Type matter, which only needs half as much etching time as pictures, is staged out until the last portion of the etching period.

On the press the cylinder dips into an ink reservoir, and each of the millions of tiny wells picks up its full capacity of ink. A *doctor blade* wipes away the ink from the outer surface of the cylinder, and the paper is then impressed into the wells to pick up their contents of ink.

Gravure can be recognized by the screen that covers the entire printing area and by the uniform size of all dots, shadow or highlight. In a modification of the basic gravure principle, the *Dultgen* (sometimes called Dultgen-News) *process*, tonal values are controlled not only by the depth of the ink wells but also by their area.

Color gravure has advantages inherent in the method. Whereas in letterpress only the full strength of the ink can be printed, in gravure different quantities of ink are deposited; in one printing 15 different intensities of ink can be transferred to the paper. Gravure ink is transparent. The white of the paper shows through to lend luminosity; the color of the lower layer of ink will shine through that of a superimposed color to create very subtle gradations in color and hue. Black-and-white gravure has a richness unmatched by any other printing process. The extremely fine screen also contributes to fine gradations.

That screen, however, is also a liability in printing type. Being broken by a screen, no matter how

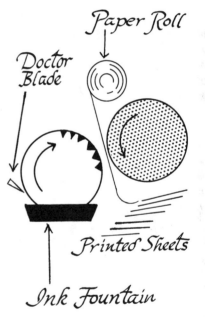

Paper Roll

Doctor Blade

Printed Sheets

Ink Fountain

ROTOGRAVURE is shown in this schematic. The revolving cylinder at the left turns through the fountain. The surface of the plate and incisions are covered with ink. That on the surface is wiped off by the doctor blade. Paper, fed off an endless roll, is pressed against the plate cylinder for the actual printing.

fine, destroys the sharpness of type. If the hairlines are extremely thin, they may be completely severed. If the type runs as a reverse, fine lines may fill in.

Fortune magazine solves the problem neatly. On many pages it prints illustrations by gravure and type by letterpress. But, as this doubles the press run, it is not a panacea for most printers. If more than one color is used, however, it is comparatively easy to combine gravure and letterpress at no extra cost if the color can be run from gravure plates and type from relief.

To minimize the dangers of screening, no type smaller than 8-point should be used and 10-point is the desirable minimum. A full-bodied face—one without fine hairlines or marked difference between thicks and thins—should be selected. Monotonal Sans Serifs or Gothics are best for gravure work despite their basically lower readability.

Photographs are the ideal copy for gravure. Line work should not be the open, sketchy kind; this wastes the resources of gravure. Instead, line art should have a wide tonal range. Pencil, charcoal, and crayon work should have well-defined middle tones and wash drawings are best in flat, posterlike technique. Oil paintings must be done in smooth technique; conspicuous brush marks or *impasto* effects will be exaggerated in reproduction.

Non-contrasty photographs reproduce best. Soft-focus photos will become even softer in gravure and thus should be used with full realization of such added diffusion.

A major asset of rotogravure is the ability to reproduce fine detail on inexpensive paper. There can be no better example of this than Sunday newspaper roto sections. The quality of their color work, especially, is a wonderful demonstration of the worth of this ancient printing form that has nobly weathered the transition from knights to satellites.

SUGGESTED READINGS

Cartwright, H. M., and MacKay, Robert. *Rotogravure.* New York: David McKay Co., Inc., 1951.

The invention of *lithography* is so recent (1799) that not only can we credit it to a well-identified individual, we also have his own journals to document the extraordinary labors that preceded its birth.

Lithography is called *planographic* printing, printing from a flat surface. The printing image is neither raised, as in letterpress, nor incised, as in gravure; it lies on the same plane as the bearing surface. It sometimes is referred to as *chemical printing*.

The inventor was Aloys Senefelder, like Gutenberg and Mergenthaler, a German. Like them, he had an almost unbelievable tenacity—and needed it. Also like theirs, his invention so thoroughly covered all the basic principles involved that subsequent changes have been only refinements.

The son of an actor in the Royal Theater of Munich who died and left his family destitute, Senefelder wrote for amateur theatricals, one of which made for him a substantial profit. Like most authors of that time, he had to publish his own works; when he ran out of money, he decided to print his own plays. This objective was soon forgotten as Aloys began to encounter difficulties. For he was a man who apparently derived great satisfaction from solving insoluble problems and the game soon became more important than the prize.

First, he attempted crude stereotyping by punching letters of steel into hardwood and casting from the wooden matrix. Then he trained himself in mirror-writing so that he could make gravure copperplates. But copper was expensive and he owned only one plate, which had to be reground after every experiment. Eventually it became too thin to work on. Looking for a cheaper substitute, he caught the idea of using a slab of stone on which he mixed the various inks he concocted for his experiments. This was Kelheim, a variety of Bavarian limestone from Solnhofen which polishes down easily to a smooth, silky surface excellent for making intaglio plates.

Lithography means *writing by stone,* and now

14
Lithography

Oil and Water
Don't Mix

Senefelder had the material for his great invention.
But his experiments, now only in intaglio, still had
to go through letterpress before he found the third
major printing process.

Then came one of those happy, illogical occur-
rences that have led the way to many a great invention. One day his mother sought throughout the
house for a piece of paper on which to make a
laundry list; Aloys had used it all up. The washer-
woman grew impatient with the delay and Frau
Senefelder was more than a little annoyed with her
son. She stalked into his laboratory and demanded
that he find something on which to list the laundry.

Somewhat desperately, he took the newly
polished slab of Kelheim and wrote the list on it
with a new ink he had mixed consisting of wax,
soap, and lampblack.

When the laundry was safely returned and he
could wash off the stone for new experiments, Aloys
suddenly decided to use it, just as it was, to test
another thought. He built a wall of wax around the
stone and onto it poured a solution of *aqua fortis*,
nitric acid and water. The acid ate away the bare
stone but the ink protected the stone it covered.
The result was a relief plate, very shallow but sufficiently in relief for careful letterpress printing. This
process was good enough to set Senefelder up in
the business of printing sheet music.

Aloys had long since mastered mirror-writing but
his workmen had not. So the process of transferring
music from the composer's right-reading copy onto
the wrong-reading image on the stone was laborious and prone to errors. Again, faced with a problem, Senefelder bulldogged it into submission. He
found an ink with which he could write normally
on paper and then *transfer* onto the stone. In fact,
he could print right from paper to paper. Great care
had to be taken to avoid tearing the original sheet,
however, and he sought a more durable printing
surface. Again he turned to his stone.

During these transfer experiments, he noticed the
inherent repulsion between grease and water, and
after countless steps harnessed this principle.

This is how he printed from his stone: he wet the entire stone with water, which was repelled by the greasy ink but attracted by the gum-washed blank stone. Then he rolled an inked brayer across the entire stone. The water on the stone repelled the ink, but the image he had drawn was most receptive to it. When he laid a piece of paper against this image, it was transferred perfectly. Subsequent impressions required only additional wetting and re-inking.

This is the process of lithography for which, in 1799, King Maximilian Joseph of Bavaria granted a patent, whose principle remains intact.

Senefelder even discovered the variations which are used today. He found that copper or zinc plates could be used as well as stone. He invented a press which automatically dampened and inked the plates. He wrote a manual, published in 1818, so lucid and comprehensive that it remained the definitive textbook for decades after his death in 1834.

Like Gutenberg's, Senefelder's invention spread rapidly.

The inventor himself used color and, as early as 1806, banknotes were lithographed in color in Berlin. French artists, such as Toulouse-Lautrec and Daumier, found it a perfect medium for their work. Music, always a problem for the typesetter, was produced economically by the new method. Johann Andre, an intimate of such great musicians as Mozart, became a business partner of Senefelder at Offenbach, Germany, the same year lithography was invented, and soon branches were opened in London, Paris, Vienna, and Berlin.

Lithography flowered in the nineteenth century. By 1870 it was common to have up to a hundred high-speed lithographic presses, printing from stones, in one plant. Posters, labels, maps, packages, pictures of all kinds, and reproductions of famous paintings could be produced in this manner with exemplary results. In the United States the most famous lithograph was a painting, *Custer's Last Fight*. (This was among the first, and certainly

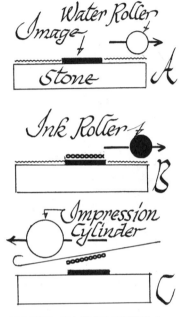

PROCESS OF LITHOGRAPHY is shown in this schematic.

In A the roller has wetted the stone, but the greasy image has repelled the water. In B the ink roller has passed over the stone. The water-wet areas have repelled the ink, but it has been attracted to the image itself. In C the layer of ink is being lifted off the stone onto the paper. Note that the image itself is not depleted.

The thicknesses of the various layers has been greatly exaggerated here to make the process visible. In actuality the lithographic image is so thin that it has no more three-dimensional characteristics than the printing on this page.

the most popular, of advertising giveaways. Anheuser-Busch Brewing Company has distributed over a million copies since the early 1880's. Today it is a classic of the naive genre paintings of a simpler era. When it was first produced, by hand lithography, the picture required 33 colors—and 33 hand-drawn plates. Today it is reproduced by 11 colors and travels six times through a two-color offset press; the twelfth application is a coat of varnish. Using newer techniques, the painting could be reproduced in eight colors without appreciable loss of quality.)

One more step was required, however, to make lithography into *offset lithography*, its contemporary form. Offset lithography can, in simplest terms, be demonstrated by an ingenious technique used by forgers in America when ballpoint pens first came into use. The forger would obtain a genuine signature, written by ballpoint, and press his thumb firmly upon the writing. The signature was thus "lithographed" from the paper onto his thumb. Then he would press his autographed thumb onto a blank check. The signature would transfer from his skin onto the check paper. This second step is the "offset" process used in modern offset lithography. (Lest any reader be tempted to a life of crime, it should be noted that manufacturers changed the ink in their pens so that this method is no longer feasible.)

In modern offset the stone has long since been replaced by a metal or paper plate, but the same grease *vs.* water principle is maintained. Instead of lithographing the image on paper, it is first transferred onto a rubber roller from which it is offset to the paper.

The elasticity of the rubber offset plate enables it to take the ink off the image plate faultlessly and to transfer it perfectly onto any stock, combining finest gradations with sharpness and color intensity. Only minimal pressure is required, and the image, therefore, can be transferred cleanly onto rough or hard paper, cloth, and metal.

Patents for offset were granted in France in 1881

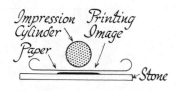

OFFSET PROCESS is shown in these diagrams. Above is the process of lithography, the image transferring from stone to paper.

Below, the image is lithographed from the metal plate—the equivalent of the original stone—to the rubber blanket and, from there, is set off to the paper.

and eight years later in Germany. But it was not
until 1905 that the first offset printing on paper was
done in the United States, and that same year it
was used to print cardboard cartons in England. It
followed by just a year the accidental discovery of
the offset process by Ira W. Rubel, an American
zinc printer. Casper Herman, who had lived in the
United States for several years, is credited with
influencing the growth of offset more than any
other individual. He was the first German offset
printer and the first in that country to build an
offset press (in 1906). Coincidentally, he died just
a hundred years after Senefelder.

Today offset is used in many forms. The simplest
is exemplified by the small office duplicators using
paper plates. At the other end are huge four-color
presses that will print 6,800 sheets—each sheet
almost 4 feet long and over 5 feet wide—per hour,
and newspaper presses that feed from rolls at much
higher speeds.

Growth of lithography and offset was greatly
stimulated by the development of photographic
process, and most plates used today are prepared
by photography.

Good old-fashioned lithography—using the traditional stone—is still used for one contemporary
product, though. It's the *decalcomania,* a name
almost unrecognizable to most Americans because
its abbreviation *decal* is so much easier to say.
Decals are composed of several layers of colored
ink, faced with an adhesive to make them cling to
windows, doors, truck panels, or practically any
surface, and a protective paper coating which is
peeled off after application. Decals are usually
printed from stones on flatbed presses.

The most common offset plate today is the
albumen or *surface plate,* used for runs up to
25,000 impressions. Of grained zinc or aluminum,
this plate is flexible and durable. It is coated with a
photosensitive solution, either by the platemaker in
his own shop, or by the manufacturer as *presensitized* plates.

The image to be printed has been photographed,

and the platemaker uses a negative just as does the photoengraver. He exposes the plate through the negative and by photochemistry creates, not an acid-resistant image, but a water-repelling one.

It should be noted that the offset platemaker need not flop the negative. For the offset plate is a *right-reading positive*. The mirror-image needed for printing is produced when the image is lithographed onto the rubber transfer blanket.

For long runs, a *deep-etch plate* is used. It prints by planography but is made, in part, like an intaglio plate. There are two versions, *bimetallic* or *trimetallic plates*.

Each plate is a sandwich of thin metals. Chromium, stainless steel, or aluminum is on the face. Then comes a layer of copper and then—in the trimetallic kind—one of steel or other metal to give strength. The image is etched right through the facing metal, in intaglio form. But then the incisions are filled with a grease-attracting substance so it levels off with the water-attracting surface of the facing metal. By providing a metal container for the greasy image, deep-etch plates reduce the erosion of the unprotected image on the albumen plate. (It should be pointed out that the lithographic image is not consumed by printing as is the one on the familiar *Ditto* machine. But the friction of contact with the blanket and action of the water that worms its way between the image and the plate eventually wear it away.)

The facing metal of the deep-etch plate has an affinity all its own for the dampening agents, while the copper has strong attraction for the ink-receptive substance. Thus a minimum of water is required, solving many press problems. The face is ungrained and its smooth surface provides better printing of fine type and halftones.

Bimetallic and trimetallic plates have a long press life, often exceeding runs of nearly a million. Because they will not corrode, they can be stored for future use.

Multimetal plates are exactly opposite to deep etches in two ways. While acid etching is still used, copper is now the top layer, and the printing image, instead of being incised, is left in relief. But the image is raised so slightly, only .0002 inches, and is made grease-attractive, so for all practical purposes the plate remains planographic.

Dry offset—sometimes called *letterset*—combines two classic printing methods. Regular letterpress is used to print images on the rubber blanket from which it is offset to the paper. Originally it was used to print safety paper such as that used for checks. The printing elements were kept in such low relief that the blanket picked up not only the full value of the raised image but also the lighter ink deposits in the shallow depressions. This created the familiar two-tone effect.

Today dry offset has been expanded greatly because it eliminates one of the weaknesses of lithography, the need for water and the attendant hazard of its affecting the paper. The printing surface may be right-reading plates or right-reading Linotype slugs which are cast from *patrices* instead of matrices.

Direct-image plates are those in which photography is not used. The printing image is placed on the plate, usually of paper—*paper masters*—by a typewriter using a special ribbon or by writing or drawing in special ink or pencil. Most of such plates are used in office duplicating machines which are really simple offset presses. Senefelder had predicted this development in his famous manual and the process is hardly different from his own paper-to-paper experiments.

Electrostatic plates are made by a Xerox or similar machine, which we shall explore in Chapter 17. These represent only a tiny percentage of offset plates in use today, but their share grows constantly and it is anticipated that this method will give further impetus to the growth of offset.

That growth has been dramatic. We have already noted in Chapter 10 how it has nosed out letterpress as a dollar producer in general printing. But it is in newspaper printing that the most telling statistics appear. In 1950 there was exactly one offset

daily newspaper in the country, the *World* of
Opelousas, Louisiana. In the next 20 years that
number rose to 5,069 weekly and 583 daily papers
—61 per cent of the total.

Obviously there must be many advantages to
offset. A major one is the speed of printing. Indeed,
newspapers can be printed so rapidly that few
papers can use their whole capacity. So it is common now for a fairly large group of weeklies to be
printed in one plant. The only reason dailies don't
do the same is that they would all need the presses
at the same time.

Because the printing plate is so light, offset
presses need not be as sturdy and heavy as letterpresses of comparable size; there need be no
rugged construction to prevent disintegration by
centrifugal force while running at high speeds,
especially when web-fed.

There is no makeready process which often adds
substantial costs to letterpress.

Because they are so light, the plates—or the
negatives, which are even lighter—can be conven-
iently filed and stored.

Relatively inexpensive strikeon composition is
ideally suited for offset work, and other cold type,
too, is usually lower in cost than relief type.

Reprinting material is quick and inexpensive; the
printed piece itself becomes camera copy.

Offset can print on almost any surface, even
curved ones. Metal, glass, and plastic containers in
kitchen and medicine chest testify to that. (Printers
sometimes show off by printing small type on sandpaper!) The hortatory slogans on sweatshirts are
usually placed there by offset. But the surface that
has been most responsive is the rough and un-
accommodating one of newsprint. By letterpress,
this, the cheapest of regular papers, can accept
halftones only in 55- to 85-line screens. By offset,
120-line pictures will print beautifully and on fine
papers screens up to 300-line are not rare and 200-
line is common.

And those pictures are inexpensive. Line art costs
nothing to add to a job; halftones require a

screened negative but the second, costly step of making the photoengraving is eliminated.

By its nature, offset is a "soft" medium, ideal for reproducing delicate art; watercolor paintings, for instance, are duplicated so faithfully by offset that often they are almost indistinguishable from the original.

Equally obvious, there are disadvantages to offset, too. But most of these are being overcome.

The gravest problem was one of waste. The pressman has to keep two factors, the amount of water and of oil, in perfect balance. This is difficult as both are variables. With the great speed of the press, many sheets of paper could be spoiled while adjustments were made.

Another was the need to expose paper to moisture. This could cause the edges to curl and make it difficult to feed through machinery. And, as paper absorbs moisture, it swells; its dimensions change and it becomes difficult to register color planned for the unswollen size. Folding, binding, and cutting may also be adversely affected by the increase in area of a sheet.

But this problem is constantly diminishing. Offset paper is *sized* with a thin coating of glue, invisible but adequate to keep water out of the fibers of the paper. This does not add significantly to the price of the paper, be it of high or low quality.

But more important, the amount of water required is constantly being reduced. Senefelder had found out in his early experiments that he could further the mutual repulsion of grease and water by the similar antipathy of acid to alkali. His greasy image combined with the calcium carbonate of the stone to make a fatty acid that was increased by washing with weak nitric acid. He washed the stone with soapy, alkaline water and then coated it with a vegetable *gum* to enhance its acid-repelling characteristics.

Today, emphasizing the acid-alkali feud has enabled constant decrease in the amount of water needed. The plate is merely dampened rather than made sloshing wet.

Offset ink must be much thinner than that for letterpress and so it cannot give the same richness of color. This disadvantage is often overcome by running more than the four standard colors. Often pinks, grays, or blues of varying hues and tints are added to maintain true tonal values; sometimes several additional colors are used. Eight-color offset is far from rare. The cost of extra plates is usually not an inhibiting factor because much of this work is done on inexpensive albumen plates; deep-etch plates carry more ink and require supplementary colors less frequently.

Another disadvantage was overcome so thoroughly no one even thinks about it any more. Color correction cannot be done on the printing plate as with halftone engravings. But *dot etching*, discovered in 1920, took care of that nicely, and now color correction is done on the platemaker's negative.

Each tiny dot on that negative has a *core* that is denser than the *halo* around the edges. By exposing the dot to a solvent, the halo can be dissolved to leave the dot at the size desired. The solvent—a *reducer*—can be applied after staging or directly, with a brush, for very delicate manipulation.

Dot etching is most frequently used with deep-etch plates made with a screened positive. This gives the added advantage of making it easier for the retoucher to see the tonal changes his etching is effecting.

A disadvantage applying mainly to newspapers is the waiting period, the time during which negatives dry before the plate can be exposed. This is all the more distressing because it usually comes just before deadline time when clock hands race with manic speed. Again there is a solution.

The *Itek* system removes the need for a negative. Original copy, let's say a newspaper-page paste-up, is used as *reflecting copy* to create an image on a sheet of special photopaper. Its whole surface turns black; the image can be seen only by a difference in glossiness. This black *photo matrix* is pressed against the sensitized offset plate and the conventional ink-attractive image formed there. This whole process compares favorably in speed with stereotyping.

Itek also has a machine that puts the reflected image right onto a coated plastic plate which becomes the printing surface. It takes less than 2 minutes to make a plate and the maximum size is 20 × 28 inches. Du Pont has a *Lydel processing machine* which—totally automatic—produces a pressready photopolymer lithographic plate up to 59 × 78 inches in three minutes. That speed is phenomenal by all industry standards.

Two more developments suggest even more enticing prospects. The 3M company has announced a *driography* plate that does not require any water to keep nonimage areas free of ink. At this writing there is little field experience for evaluating it.

Even more exciting are experiments being conducted at the research center of the American Newspaper Publishers Association. The object is to print by direct lithography, not offset, from a rubber instead of a metal plate. This would have the same resiliency as the rubber blanket of the offset press and would accommodate itself to rough newsprint. Implications of this are awesome. Observers believe that this would enable the conversion of rotary letterpresses to lithographic presses with relative ease and low cost. (They couldn't be converted to offset presses very handily; there isn't room for the required blanket cylinder on the typical newspaper press.)

Rotary letterpress in newspaper plants represent an investment of billions of dollars. Reluctance to scrap this expensive—and usually still satisfactorily producing—machinery is a major factor in keeping larger dailies from offset. Comparatively easy conversion could open up this huge field to lithography.

That would leave only one vexing problem for newspapers to solve: remaking between editions. A completely new paste-up is required when a page is remade. This takes time, of course, but the real nuisance is re-using cold-type material. If on the

first paste-up a story under a 2-column headline
had 23 lines in one leg and 24 in the other and, for
the remake, it requires 19 lines in the first and 28 in
the other, a 4-line block would have to be moved
from one column to the other. An element as small
as this is awkward to handle and often difficult to
square up. If only a single line need be moved,
aggravation resembles that brought by a swarm of
blackflies. This might be solved by having the story
reset or photocopied.

It might be possible to hold elements down by
static electricity rather than adhesive—wax is commonly used—and that could speed the process. We
can be sure, though, that if the big breakthrough is
made in direct-printing rubber plates, the minor
ones will follow almost automatically.

Pasting-up for Platemaking

The economics of offset printing are discussed in
Chapter 20, but there is one obvious advantage that
directly concerns the designer. *Copy* for platemaking or *art*—they are synonymous—can be prepared
in final form on the drawing board instead of in the
composing room; this gives the obvious advantage
of having make-up done in the studio instead of the
print shop. (Many offset printing plants do not
even have a composing room.)

The letterpress compositor makes up a form in a
chase; the offset compositor *pastes up* his form at
his drawing board or on a light table. Instead of
metal type, the paste-up man has *reproduction
proofs* of hot metal, cold type in film or paper,
strike-on, or just plain typewritten copy, produced
with a fresh ribbon—preferably a silk one—on
good white paper.

Display lines come from similar sources or may
be hand-lettered. His "cuts" are original art, line or
continuous tone, proofs of engravings (often cut
out of other publications), or Veloxes.

He works in exact size in most instances because
it is easier to see what the completed job will be;
reduction is possible if not too extreme.

Reproduction proofs are usually pulled on dull-coated paper (although every lithographer has his own ideas on the subject and unanimity of opinion is nonexistent), but much fine work is done on *acetate* or *Kromecote,* an extremely high-gloss paper. Ink cannot be too stiff lest it cause *picking* of the paper surface, which makes white spots appear in the type. Too-soft ink will spread and cause soft halos around the letters. Impression must be completely even; high letters will punch into the paper and the camera catches shadows on the shoulder of the impression indentation.

Repro proofs must be thoroughly dry, of course, to avoid smudging in the paste-up. A clear fixative can be applied as protection.

Paste-up is done on a sturdy, hard, smooth-finished board—4-ply Bristol, 182-pound index, or illustration board. Cold-white stock, without a trace of yellow or cream, should be chosen.

Rubber cement is a good adhesive. It lays the paper flat, without wrinkles; it permits paper to be lifted easily, yet holds it securely; excess adhesive can be rubbed off easily with a finger. Instead of rubber cement, a thin layer of wax may be applied to the back of the material. This, too, allows the paper to be removed and repositioned, yet holds it firmly in place. Wax has a distinct advantage where speed is essential, as in a newspaper; it eliminates the danger of the rubber cement container being spilled, and there is no excess adhesive which must be cleaned off.

With a light blue pencil, invisible to the camera, the paste-up man draws the outer dimensions of the job. Then, using a T-square constantly, he places all type in the proper position. He uses meticulous care for, once the platemaker's negative is shot, it is expensive to straighten up a line of type.

Newspapers and magazines paste up on sheets especially prepared for them. The exact page and column dimensions are printed in the "invisible" light blue and the whole sheet is covered with a grid of 1-pica squares. Elements may be aligned by means of these grid lines and that minimizes the

S/S   BROWN PLATE   BB 139-52

MECHANICAL OR PASTE-UP for a two-color job. This is the key plate and will be printed in brown. The symbol S/S means "same size."

A yellow-orange was used as a tint block behind the sun in the headline and behind the human figure and the signature in an irregular band across the bottom of the layout.

Shadows have been exaggerated to distinguish the various elements of the mechanical. Before actual platemaking they would have to be opaqued out.

need for checking with the T-square. This speeds up paste-up, a desirable situation for tight deadlines.

If his art is also the same size and, in the case of continuous-tone pictures, has already been screened as a Velox, he pastes that into position, too.

If illustrations must be shot separately, to screen or reduce, the paste-up man indicates their position in one of several ways. He may have a Photostat made of the art work in the proper size and paste that into position; in this case he must plainly indicate "for position only" so that the platemaker does not use it for actual copy. He may use a blueprint proof of the platemaker's screened negative. These methods are most frequently used for *outsize* art (which must be reduced) or for irregularly shaped pictures.

For square halftones, two common methods are: to rule the exact-shaped rectangle in red ink, or to mount a rectangle of black paper into position. (On the negative this black square becomes a clear "window" into which the platemaker can strip the screened negative.)

A variation of the latter is used when there is more than one picture of similar size, shape, and subject which might confuse the platemaker. A

properly sized Photostat is pasted into position and
then covered with red acetate. The red photographs
as black and creates the clear window for stripping.
Yet it is transparent, enabling the platemaker to see
exactly which screened negative he should place
into the opening.

When the copy is delivered to the platemaker, it
is an exact replica of the final job except for
stripped-in art. The platemaker's "proof" is a *blueprint, silverprint, brownprint,* or *Vandyke,* inexpensive photocopies using the negative from which the
offset plate will be made. These are "wet processes." The negative is laid over the blueprint or
brownprint paper and exposed to ultraviolet light
for 2 to 5 minutes. Then the proofing paper is
treated with a chemical solution for another 2 or 3
minutes and hung on a line to dry for about 10
minutes more, during which the paper often curls,
wrinkles, or even shrinks. Du Pont's *Dylux* reduces
the time to 30 seconds. It is a paper made photosensitive by organic compounds. The negative is
laid on the Dylux and exposed to ultraviolet light.
Immediately, with no developing chemical, a blue-
on-white image is formed. The image can be fixed
by deactivating the Dylux; this is done by exposing
it to bright white light for several seconds or just
leaving it in room light for about an hour.

More than one negative can be exposed to the
same piece of paper. Because the intensity of the
image depends on the length of exposure to the
ultraviolet, negatives for different color plates may
be used to show their images in varying values of
blue. While the actual hue isn't shown, of course,
relationship of color elements can readily be
checked. Dylux is also available sensitized on both
sides. Usually when a booklet is shown in proof
form, two pieces of blueprint paper must be pasted
together to show front and back. Now mock-ups of
books are only half as bulky with images on both
sides of a single piece of paper.

All these methods can be used for proofing negatives for photoengravings and positive transparencies for rotogravure. (Many large newspapers
use cold type and paste-up for advertising and

combine the resulting photoengravings with Linotype slugs to complete the page.)

If the reflex Itek method is used, there is, of
course, no negative to prove. In that case the paste-
up itself may be inspected. If, as is customary in
newspapers, proofs of an ad must be sent to the
advertiser, regular photocopies by Xerox, Thermo-
fax, etc., are made from the paste-up.

Before the plate is actually made, the negative
must be *opaqued*. Shadows cast by too-thick pasted-
on materials or specks caused by dust or improper
developing procedures must all be painted out with
a dull red, flat paint.

When repro proofs and line art are pasted up,
they should be surrounded by at least one-eighth of
an inch of the paper. If the pasted-on paper casts a
shadow, the platemaker can retouch it out of his
negative without hitting type matter. If thick sheets
or board must be pasted up, edges should be
beveled to avoid heavy shadows and time-
consuming opaquing. An extra set of repro proofs
should be kept on hand in case type in the paste-up
is accidentally damaged.

Corrections are made on the original copy. A
word or line is reset and simply pasted over the
error line. The negative must be reshot.

Copy for offset color is prepared as for letterpress.

When it is required to gang a job so that several
copies of the same material are printed on a single
sheet, the platemaker uses a *step-and-repeat*
camera. By this device it is possible to expose the
same negative to more than one location on the
plate rapidly and accurately, by moving the negative through a system of gears and cogs. The device
is also used when a repetitive, over-all pattern is
required over a large area.

Offset Conversion

The growth of offset printing, especially in book
publishing, has occasioned a new need, converting
standing letterpress material to offset plates.

Book publishers have literally millions of pages in

original type or in electrotypes. The space they occupy is huge and their weight is awesome. If nothing else, *offset conversion* to negatives or litho plate reduces a vexatious storage problem. The making of an offset plate is so simple that often it is economical to file only negatives, making plates anew as they are needed.

The simplest conversion method is to pull a repro proof of the standing relief elements, usually on coated paper, either glossy or dull finish, which is then photographed as regular platemaker's copy. This is not always simple. If the metal has been worn, it may be difficult to get an even over-all impression. Impression may be required so heavy that it may distort letters, slur halftone dots, create a halo or fuzzy edges or emboss the proofing paper so much that a shadow will be cast under the camera lights.

So several methods have been developed to overcome these handicaps without the need for much time-consuming makeready before the proof is pulled.

All these methods will duplicate halftone dots or lines as readily and sharply as type itself.

The *Kalvar* method heats the metal form and presses it against a piece of opaque film. The heat causes a reaction—not burning—which creates a clear, negative image of the characters. This is similar to the process by which white subtitles are placed on dark areas of foreign motion-picture film.

In the *Direct-Image—DI*—process by Mergenthaler the standing relief matter is used to print directly upon the metal offset plate and the image is heat-set in an oven. To make sure that all areas of the type form have printed properly, the impression is made so firmly that some parts are punched right into the plate. The plate is releveled by sandwiching it between two thin plastic sheets—to prevent surface scuffing—and placing it on a revolving cylinder of a *debosser* where a series of small air-activated rollers smooth the plate without distorting the image.

The *Cronapress* technique requires no proof-press, camera, or darkroom. A sheet of Cronar film is placed on the relief form and a legion of tiny steel or lead balls are bounced on the film to bring it in complete contact with the printing surface no matter how irregular it may be. Where that contact is made, minute cells of the film coating are collapsed, leaving a clear negative image. The rest of the film, where no pressure has been applied, is made opaque as the uncollapsed pores accept a liquid dye. A newer model uses a series of narrow brass fingers to provide the multiple impacts required.

In another method, repro proofs are covered with a sheet of *instant negative* film and heated briefly. This transfers a latent image to the film which, upon being wiped with a clearing solution, creates a conventional negative for platemaking.

Brighttype, a product of Ludlow, is an ingenious system. The letterpress printing form is sprayed with a coating of nonreflective black paint. Rubbing the dried surface with a soft rubber eraser clears just the printing surfaces. The result is already in negative form, the black background and the shiny metallic plane of the type. A special camera with a rotating light that gives equal illumination to every area produces a film or paper positive.

Scotchprint is a 3M conversion method. A repro proof is pulled on a special ink-receptive mylar film. The film accepts the heavier proofing impression that might be required without distortion, fuzzy edges, or embossing. Because it is transparent, the film can make a negative by contact printing on regular film.

Some other uses for such conversions: some advertising agencies send the conversions—at reduced postage cost because of the lightness of film—to publishers who can make relief, offset, or gravure plates as needed therefrom. Extra conversions can be made for protection against loss of the originals. Hot and cold type can easily be combined into one piece of film.

Because the functions of "setting type" and of locking up are so often moved from the composing room to the studio or office or even the home of the amateur, the typical typographic layout man comes in closer contact with offset processes than he may with others. So there is an added need—and incentive—to master the medium to use it most effectively for communication.

Aloys Sene-felder

ALOYS SENEFELDER is the first major figure in the graphic arts whose likeness is preserved in contemporary portraits. Most are more flattering than this one. In a mild irony, this picture of the inventor of lithography was originally done as a steel engraving.

It's interesting to note that Senefelder's first commercial lithographing shop, at Offenbach, was only a short distance from Mainz, where the first letterpress shop had opened some 350 years earlier.

SUGGESTED READINGS

Cleeton, Glen U., and Pitkin, Charles W. *General Printing*. New York: Taplinger Publishing Co., Inc., 1958.
Strauss, Victor (ed.). *The Lithographers Manual*. New York: Waltwin, 1958.
Tory, Bruce E. *Offset Lithography*. New York: Pitman Publishing Corp., 1957.

15
Paper

The Wrapping of Culture

It is mildly ironic that the subject that provides half the title of this book should occasion only a brief chapter therein. But it has been said that you should approach the study of paper as you would a trip to Paris: "Spend a weekend there . . . or a lifetime."

Obviously we can't spend a lifetime on one topic in a book like this, so this chapter will be a weekend visit, noting only a few things of interest and a few more of utility that the graphic arts user of paper should know about this tool.

Paper derives its name more directly than its composition from *papyrus*, the writing surface developed by the Egyptians about 3000 B.C. Papyrus was not truly paper; it was made by weaving the stalks of a reedy plant, pasting them together with fruit juices, then pounding the sheet to proper thickness and smoothness.

Paper as we know it was first made in China by Ts'ai Lun early in the second century. He floated vegetable fibers—inner mulberry bark and bamboo —in a bath of water and allowed them to settle and dry into a sheet. Six hundred years later, when the Arabs conquered storied Samarkand deep in Central Asia, their prisoners-of-war included two Chinese papermakers. Via North Africa papermaking came to Europe, reached England in 1494, but took until 1690 to come to America.

Technically, paper is a web or mat of vegetable fibers—cellulose. All growing plants contain this fibrous substance, but cotton and wood are the main substances used for papermaking today. Some special papers are made of rice, corn straw, or grasses, and constant research goes on to seek new raw materials. Experiments with wheat straw show promise. But wood remains an excellent source of cellulose.

Growing interest in ecology often results more in enthusiastic emotion than in rational thinking, and a vociferous if small group is demanding reduction in the use of paper in order to "save our trees." Appealing and noble as this sounds, it is hardly logical. Papermaking has actually saved more trees than it has used. It has brought the continuous-crop system that has encouraged reforestation and biological care of woodlots. Pulpwood is a crop. It makes as little sense to "save our trees" by not using paper as it does to "save our wheat" by not using flour or breakfast cereal. Forests—with the knowing help of man—replenish themselves faster than the lumberjack fells them. So our supply is able to meet constantly growing demands for paper, and wood remains the best source of cellulose.

Late in 1970 it was announced that paper had been made in the laboratory with "synthetic cellulose." So man may have another source of raw material, unless the inorganic compounds become more rare than organic cellulose.

Paper remained an expensive product for several centuries because it was made slowly, sheet by sheet. Mechanization came to the industry with the invention of a papermaking machine in 1798 by Nicholas Louis Roberts, an employee of the famous Didots. But he sold the patents to the *Fourdrinier* brothers of England, and it is their name that commonly designates all such machines today.

Paper is an essential ingredient in all printing. Its color, surface, and physical characteristics are as important as the shapes ink places on its surface. Because of this, the designer must have at least a cursory knowledge of paper.

To oversimplify the manufacturing process: Wood or cotton rags are ground or *cooked*, with chemicals, into pulp. The fibers are beaten in water to soften them and to extract a gelatinous substance that causes the fibers to cling together. This creamy soup is further diluted with water, which makes up 90 per cent of the mass.

This solution is strained through microscopic slots onto an endless conveyor belt made of a finely woven screen, with 60 to 80 horizontal—and the same number of vertical—wires per inch.

The fibers all tend to float parallel to each other; this gives the *grain* to paper. Short fibers, such as those produced by grinding wood or cooking it with caustic soda, provide the smoothness neces-

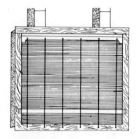

PAPERMAKER'S MOLD was used when papermaking was a hand operation. The familiar pattern of laid paper is created by the wires on which the pulp lies during its forming.

The heavier vertical lines show the *chains* and the thinner, more numerous ones, the *wires*. The pattern is duplicated in machine-made paper by using a dandy roller.

Papermaking was first done commercially in Baghdad in A.D. 795. That was about the time the Moors were conquering North Africa and Spain, and they may have brought the secret to Europe with them. But other observers believe this didn't happen until the Crusades, which were staged intermittently from 1096 to 1192.

For it wasn't until the late 1100's that paper was made on any appreciable scale in Europe. It was expensive and, until printing, was in slight demand.

Paper was handmade until 1750, when a Dutch machine successfully broke rags into fibers, made mass production possible.

sary for good printing. Long fibers, from pulp cooked with sulfites or sulfates, give strength. The skill of the papermaker is demonstrated in the way he mixes the two lengths.

Papermaking machines are behemoths. They are several hundred feet long, depending upon how many drying rollers they have, and produce paper from 6 to 20 feet wide in continuous rolls. The screen conveyor is up to 50 feet long. As the paper mash moves onto the screen, water drains off by gravity and by vigorous sideways shaking that throws out the water and causes a lateral interweaving of fibers which increases paper strength. Paper at this stage looks like a thoroughly wet piece of blotting paper.

By this time water represents about two-thirds of the mass. By squeezing, blotting with felt rollers, and applying heat, the paper is finally reduced to only 7 per cent to 10 per cent water content, its final form, and is wound onto rollers.

There have been several other steps during the process. Some will be discussed as they effect differences between kinds of paper; others can be safely left to the papermaker.

Watermarks, if any, have been produced by a *dandy roll,* a wirecloth roller, just after the paper has left the screen. The design is created by compressing some fibers in the very wet paper as it receives its first surface pressure. The paper itself is not thicker or thinner there. Watermarks are primarily used as trademarks of the manufacturer or the user. The watermark can be read from the "right side" of the paper (a term soon to be explained).

Extra materials are added to paper pulp to perform specific functions. *Sizing* helps hold the fibers together, makes book paper repellent to the dampness which might cause pages to wave or wrinkle, and reduces the absorbency of writing paper so the ink doesn't blur or feather.

Loading agents, or *fillers,* are mineral substances added to fill the spaces between paper fibers and to give solidity and a smooth surface.

Similar mineral smoothing materials are used to make *coated paper;* one or both of its sides are surfaced very smoothly for better printing. Although the term "coated papers" usually refers to glossy stock, dull or semi-dull finishes are also available and are often used because by eliminating glare they are easier on the reader's eyes.

Calendered, or *machine finish,* is produced by running the paper between smooth metal rollers that press and polish it. In *super-calendering,* pressure, steam, and friction "iron" the paper to glassy smoothness, just as a housewife irons a shirt.

Four major divisions of paper commonly used in printing are newsprint, book, writing, and cover stock. Many others come to mind instantly—kraft paper for heavy wrappings, cardboard, oiled paper, tissues, for instance—but these are handled by specialized printers, if they are printed upon at all. The paper used for a printing job is the *stock,* and that word is used constantly as a synonym for paper.

Newsprint

Newsprint is the cheapest paper used for common printing. It must be stressed that price does not necessarily make a "poor" paper; if it does the job it is supposed to, paper is "good." Newsprint does that. It furnishes an adequate printing surface that satisfactorily takes type and halftones in 65- or 85-line screen in letterpress, 120 in offset, and 150-screen in rotogravure. Its color, though grayish, is bright enough to lend reasonably good legibility.

Its permanence and strength are low because of its high content of short wood fiber and large proportions of filler. Because the whole log is ground up to make newsprint, vegetable resins and gums remain in the paper, causing it to yellow and discolor. Newspapers overcome the short life of newsprint by microfilming pages or printing a few copies, for permanent records, on rag-content paper. A newspaper is not reread so often that its brittleness is a grave disability.

Roto paper is a smooth-finish newsprint.

Newsprint, in addition to its common use, is chosen for handbills and other advertising material of a very ephemeral nature.

Book Papers

Categories of *book papers* are as varied as those of type faces; many stocks have characteristics of more than one classification. Yet we must have some pigeonholing in order to discuss them logically. Arbitrary but useful subdivisions are *textures*.

Antique is a loose term applied to papers that are soft, comparatively rough-surfaced, and *bulky*, relatively thick sheets in relation to its weight. Antiques, as the name indicates, resemble paper used in the early days of printing.

Text paper is high-grade uncoated antique, often with considerable rag content—cotton fibers—for greater permanence. *Vellum* finishes are in this same broad grouping.

Eggshell antique is named for the texture of its *felt side* which strongly resembles that of a shell.

We must digress for a moment to define "felt side" and its opposite, *wire side*. As the paper moves through the papermaking machine, that side which rests on the wire conveyor receives a faint pattern of the mesh. The top side, which has been pressed only by the felt rollers, is smoother. For printing on only one side, as on a letterhead, the impression is made on the felt, or the *right*, side.

Antique paper is either *wove* or *laid*. The first is so named because the textures of both the screen and the felt are combined to create a comparatively smooth paper that looks like a woven fabric. Laid stock purposely resembles handmade paper. Laid stock is not only a little rougher than wove, there is also a more marked difference between the felt and

EARLY WATERMARK is this one (shown in two-thirds its original size), which was used in the early 1200's in Italy.

In 1797, Louis Robert, a Frenchman, invented a papermaking machine. Six years later the Fourdrinier brothers—Englishmen with a French name—financed Robert's work and even-

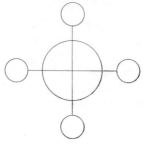

wire sides, and therefore it is commonly used for letterheads, which require printing on only one side.

Offset stock is smooth, uncoated, and sized with extra care to minimize the effect of the dampening agent of an offset press.

English finish—E.F.—is given its smooth surface because its relatively high content of clay filler is heavily machined. The clay filler gives a rather suede-like finish; it can be detected by the slight pull as fingertips are brushed across the surface.

Super-calendered stock—just plain *super* to most printers—is given a very high finish by running it through a separate machine which continues and intensifies the results of calendering rolls on the Fourdrinier. Super is the slickest of the uncoated books.

Coated stock goes through a supplementary process whereby a substance consisting of clay, whitening agents, and casein glue surfaces the paper. Coated finishes range from *dull*—very smooth but not glossy—to the extremely high luster of *enamel* which has been super-calendered.

Writing stock subdivides into three groups. *Flat writing* is a calendered, well-sized paper of wood pulp. *Bond*, the most important group, usually contains varying percentages of rag content and is often sized with animal gelatins. The sizing not only gives the proper surface for writing but also contributes to the *rattle*, the crispness and snap that distinguishes good bond.

The finest bonds, made entirely from new cotton or linen rags, closely resemble the stock of paper money. Bond gets its name because it was first developed for printing bonds, stock certificates, deeds, and other documents which require maximum durability. Bond is closely associated with quality in the public mind.

Ledger, the third writing category, is smooth-surfaced for ease in writing, specially sized to resist erasure, and made with long fibers to facilitate fold-

tually took over patents for the machine. It is still named for the brothers, not the inventor!

The first papermill in the United States opened in Germantown, Pennsylvania, in 1690. Later it was the British nuisance tax on paper that to a large extent exacerbated colonial feelings to the violence of the American Revolution.

Today's tremendous paper industry was spurred by two major developments. In 1840, a German, Herman Keller, made a machine to grind logs into fibrous pulp, and, in 1867, George Tilghman, an American, found he could separate cellulose fibers by cooking wood in sulferous acid. This gives its name to *sulfite paper* which is so prepared.

Tree farms which produce pulpwood as a regular crop are credited with being a major factor in the recent economic growth of the South.

Writing Papers

ing. Often it has high rag content. As its name
indicates, it is largely used for ledgers and other
records, but has many other uses, often for letterheads, and—of special interest to designers—for
line drawings and for making dummies.

Cover Stock

Cover stocks are made in the same way as book
and writing stocks but are usually considerably
heavier to withstand the wear that their name
indicates they will receive.

Cover is available in a very wide range of colors
and finishes, ranging from laid and wove through
velour, imitation leather, and fabric, to paper faced
with foil.

Finishes

All papers can be finished in a variety of textures,
but offset is used in the widest range of finishes
because the printing process of that name can print
on irregular surfaces.

Cockle finish has surface ripples caused by
shrinkage under little or no tension during drying.
It is popular in writing paper. *Pebble* and *ripple*
finishes are placed in the paper by textured rollers
in the manufacturing process. *Stucco* and *fabric* are
other popular textures.

Ivory finish is produced by calendering between
rollers coated with beeswax. Its tactile effect is like
that of the substance that names it.

Deckle is the irregular, feathery edge produced
by contact with the walls that confine paper pulp
during manufacture or by jets of water or air.
Handmade paper is deckled on four sides; machine-
made, on two. Imitation deckle is produced by saw-
ing, cutting, tearing, or sandblasting finished paper.

Specialized Papers

There are a few of the myriad papers that we
ought at least nod to in passing. They mostly concern designers who specialize narrowly.

Bible or *India paper* is extremely thin but strong,
opaque, and permanent. It is used for printing, in

addition to Bibles for which it was developed, any book with so many pages that bulk becomes a problem.

Cardboard is a thick, heavy paper made by pasting together several *plies* of cheap filler with one of coated or calendered paper on the outside.

Bristol board is a thin—.006 inch—cardboard with an excellent surface for printing, writing, or drawing. Often several sheets are pasted together to create two- or three-ply or even heavier boards.

Kraft—German for "strong"—is usually identified as familiar brown butcher paper. It is also called *sulfate* from the manufacturing process that uses caustic soda to cook pitchy woods such as pine. This produces the longest of all chemically refined pulp fibers and gives unusual strength to the paper. Therefore kraft is often used to reinforce other papers. Although it is most commonly unbleached, it can be manufactured in colors suitable for gift wrapping.

Manifold is commonly known as *onionskin.* Strong and durable, it accepts carbon-paper typing well and its low bulk is an asset where many records must be kept. Onionskin is used for airmail stationery.

Safety paper is made by adding certain chemicals to the pulp, by bathing finished paper in chemicals, or by printing an all-over design in special inks. These methods make the paper sensitive to erasure, bleaching, or other attempts to delete or change the writing on checks, money orders, tickets, or other negotiable papers.

Blotting paper, made without sizing, is soft, absorbent, and bulky. (Incidentally, white blotting paper shows clearly the difference between wire and felt sides.) Blotting paper to which a harder-finished paper has been pasted is *porcelain.*

Qualities of Paper

The buyer of printing and the designer of printed jobs must specify the paper. He is usually concerned with the weight, finish, and color, but there are other factors he cannot overlook.

Opacity, the quality which prevents *show-through* of printing from one side or leaf to the other, is important. Bulk and weight must be considered, the first in relation to ease of handling and storage, the latter in regard to cost of mailing or shipping.

Color is, of course, a basic element of the over-all appearance. Wide ranges are available and that choice is made by the artist who designs the piece.

Color of paper is as useful as color of ink. Recent use of the color of paper to substitute for a colored ink in process-color printing has resulted in dramatic effects well worth studying. When colored stock is used, its selection must be preceded by careful thought. There must be enough difference in value between paper and ink so that the type will be strong enough for readability. Especially small faces, or those with very thin hairlines, can lose readability dangerously on an unsuitable color stock.

Always the ink should be of strong value. Black is best for printing on colored stock, but other deep colors can be effective.

Two-tone coated papers have a different color on front and back. Their use, especially when folded or cut in unusual fashion, gives a multicolor effect with only one trip through the press.

Sizing is important, especially as it affects the receptivity of paper to moisture. Addition of moisture can cause an unhappy increase in weight. Large catalogues, such as those of Sears, Roebuck or Montgomery Ward, are printed and stored in humidity-controlled rooms; an increase of 1 or 2 per cent of moisture in a million or more books can add hundreds and thousands of dollars to postage.

Paper can never be entirely free from moisture, though, because it would then lose pliability.

The *grain* of the paper must be considered, especially for folding. It has been seen how the cellulose fibers in paper float endwise during the manufacturing, just like logs floating down the river. When paper is folded against the grain, these "logs" are broken and the folded edge is harsh and irregular.

The heavier the paper, the worse the results of folding against the grain.

For many kinds of printing, especially color offset, the relation of the grain to the direction in which the paper is fed into the press has a distinct effect on the quality of registration and impression. This must be considered when planning how the stock is to be cut out of the basic sheet.

Direction of the grain can be determined by three methods. The first is to tear or fold the paper; it tears more easily and folds more cleanly with the grain. Often, however, the difference is too slight for anyone but an expert to detect.

Sized paper can be wet on one side only and it will immediately curl into a semi-cylinder whose long axis runs with the grain.

The *strip test* can be used for any paper, sized or not. Two strips, about ½ inch wide and 6 to 8 inches long, are cut from the stock, one in each direction. They are held, horizontally and side by side, at one end. One strip will droop considerably more than the other. This is because in it the grain runs sideways and allows the strip to sag, while on the other strip the fibers run lengthwise and give more support.

The advice of the pressman can always be sought before an unusual stock is selected. He is well able to judge whether a stock is best adapted to the specific needs of the particular job and printing process. It is wise to leave many technical decisions to the pressman; but the designer should know the basic strengths and liabilities of those papers which he most frequently uses.

Newsprint's ability to take line and halftones in proper screens has been noted. A good range of colored news inks has been developed and newsprint itself comes in a few colors. The growth of comic books has opened this art form to advertising and instruction; newsprint thus becomes a more useful tool in many areas of communication.

Adaptability of antique papers depends so much upon texture that generalizations are hard to come by. Generally they have a natural affinity for Old

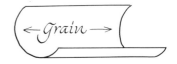

GRAIN OF PAPER can be detected by these methods. When water is applied to one side of sized paper, above, it curls into the start of a cylinder whose length is in the direction of the grain.

When two strips are held horizontally, below, the one that bends the least will indicate that the grain is running in its longer dimension.

Style Roman type and for line cuts in letterpress. They will accept coarse halftones—65- to 85-line. Sometimes solid tint blocks are printed to smooth the surface and over them finer screens or type can be used. But it is never wise to force a medium to do a job which it is not supposed to do. It is far more honest, and results are happiest, when any material can use its true resources.

Antiques—indeed, any textured paper—are well suited to offset if properly sized and add interest and appeal to printed jobs. Gravure also easily adapts to textured surfaces.

Offset stock is comparable to the antiques for letterpress work; for offset litho, it is ideal; for gravure, its hard surface may create problems.

English finish takes up to 120-line halftones by letterpress and is well suited to intaglio and planographic printing. Transitional and Modern Romans, Sans, and Gothics are its most compatible types. Its easy-on-the-eyes, glossless surface makes it a favorite for a wide range of printing.

Super-calendered stocks will easily take up to 133-line, so fine that the human eye is unconscious of the screen. Often super is equivalent to coated stock with the added advantage of lighter weight.

Coated stocks will take up to 150-line screens and, in some cases, as fine as 200. It is ideally suited to Modern Romans because the fine hairlines print sharply and cleanly. Coated stock gives extra sparkle to the thinner inks of offset but it is seldom used for gravure.

Writing papers are generally difficult to print on by letterpress, although as countless letterheads testify, they will accept type and line. The better the quality of bond, the more difficult letterpress printing becomes. It is necessary to use inks that dry by oxidation rather than by penetration, which is difficult or impossible with the hard surface of bond. Letterpress halftones should not be attempted on bond. But offset gives excellent quality on this paper and it is common to combine the two processes: letterpress for type, offset for illustrations. Steel engravings are ideally suited to bond.

Ledger accepts offset beautifully and accepts letterpress better than bond. In many cases ledger will give the same effect of quality associated with bond and without the cost and many of the problems of high-grade bond.

Because the range of cover stock is so vast, any statement about its adaptability to printing must be made with reservations. Generally covers will not take letterpress halftones, although there are exceptions, but will accept offset screens. Covers are often designed for special functions. Thus catalogues which must take heavy usage or those which will be used by people with greasy or dirty hands can be covered in extremely tough or grease-resistant stock.

Paper is sold by *weight*. That is about the last simple statement that can be made on the subject. For, as in so many printing terminologies and systems, things get complicated from here on in. A printer is not interested in buying 87 pounds of bond; he wants enough for 5,000 letterheads. So there must be a combination of weight and *count*.

To add confusion, there are still two systems in use.

In the first, paper is designated by size and *substance*. The latter is the weight of 1,000 sheets of paper in the basis size. So an antique designated 25 × 38–70M weighs 70 pounds per thousand sheets in that size. (Printers use the Roman numeral M for "thousand"; when written, it carries a horizontal stroke through its middle.) If one of the dimensions is underscored it shows that the grain runs lengthways on that dimension.

But all papers are available in other than base sizes. To convert odd weights and/or sizes to standard, we use the formula:

$$S : B = S' : B'$$

S is the square-inch area of the basis size; B the basis weight. S' and B' are the same factors in the nonstandard sheet. While this formula is simple and accurate, it is far better to ask a paper salesman to read the answer off a conversion chart he always carries with him—or to give you a spare copy of it.

An older system, but still in use, is based on the *ream*, 500 sheets. When the printer talks of "60-pound stock," he means that is its weight in 500 sheets, only half of the "substance weight." It is well worth defining terms before you get too involved in discussing paper purchase or selections.

The basis size varies among various categories of paper. Thus a single sheet of basis-size 100-pound cover stock will not weigh as much as a basic sheet of English finish of the same weight, for cover is based on a 20 × 26 sheet, E.F. on 25 × 38.

Another confusing practice of paper merchants creates the pleasant paradox that often you can buy more paper for less money than a smaller quantity costs. Flat papers are packaged in several standard quantities; if you buy less than this amount—a *broken-package lot*—you pay a *penalty* of as much as 25 per cent for the extra effort of opening the original package, rewrapping it, and storing the remainder in a less convenient form.

For a round-figure example, let us assume that you can buy 1M sheets of cover for $20 at package price. If you bought only 900, you would pay $18 plus a penalty of $4.50, a total of $22.50. By buying the extra hundred sheets for $20, you save $2.50. This anomaly often makes it practical to print extra copies of a job if they can be distributed usefully; paper savings may well be greater than the cost of the extra presswork.

Remember about paper that its use is far more important than details about its manufacture or characteristics. The choice of proper paper can effect savings in press and bindery work, in distribution and storage, as well as lifting any job from mediocre to outstanding.

Paper is more than "the wrapping of culture"; it is an indispensable tool of civilization. Each American uses over 530 pounds of it annually; it surrounds us—literally, as wallpaper or even as *nonwoven fabric* of paper clothing. We use it from tissues at our bedside to sleeping bags under a

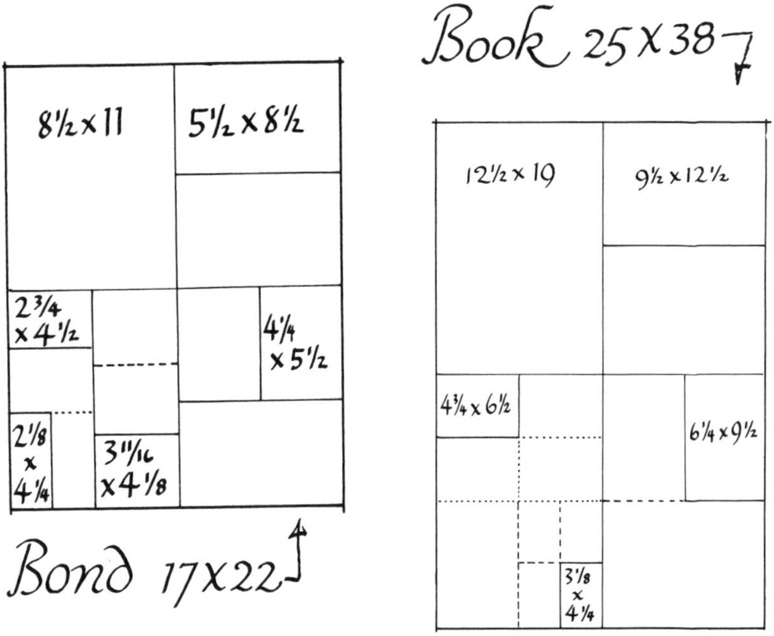

Book 25 × 38 →

8½ × 11	5½ × 8½
2¾ × 4½	4¼ × 5½
2⅛ × 4¼	3¹¹⁄₁₆ × 4⅛	

Bond 17 × 22 ↲

12½ × 19	9½ × 12½
4¾ × 6½	6¼ × 9½
	3⅛ × 4¼	

COMMON PAGE SIZES used today are based on standard paper sizes that can be cut without waste. Notice that the common 8½ X 11 letterhead size is a quarter of the regular sheet of bond paper.

paper tent, from theater tickets to computer cards, from motor oil "cans" to coverings for entire agricultural fields. Add to that all the products of the printing press . . . maybe this chapter should have been longer!

SUGGESTED READINGS

Ainsworth, John Haworth. *Paper, The Fifth Wonder.* Kaukauna, Wis.: Thomas Printing and Publishing, 1961.

Hunter, Dard. *Paper Making.* New York: Alfred A. Knopf, 1947.

Norris, F. H. *Paper and Paper Making.* New York: Oxford University Press, 1955.

16
Ink

The Lifeblood
of Printing

More than a billion pounds of printing ink is used every year in America . . . and hardly anyone ever sees it. The typical reader looks at a page and sees words and pictures, not ink. He doesn't even know what printer's ink is like. If he were to guess, he'd say it's like the liquid that was used to fill old-fashioned fountain pens or like the drawing ink used by draftsmen or even like the food coloring his wife uses to tint cake icing. And he'd be wrong.

But so would many graphic arts workers whose duties are not in the pressroom. For the selection of ink is based on a few obvious characteristics. The invisible ones the typographer is quite willing to leave for the printer's decisions.

The first "inks" were juices—of fruit, vegetables, or sea creatures. These were both *inks,* used for drawing defined forms, and *dyes,* which colored a whole area indiscriminately. The first man-made ink was probably that developed in Egypt around 2500 B.C. for writing or drawing on papyrus; animal or vegetable charcoal was mixed with glue. The Chinese used—and refined—the same recipe. Their carbon was lampblack, the best of which was the soot of burning tung oil, mixed with gum. Today's *India,* drawing, *ink* is basically the same.

It was Gutenberg who invented printer's ink, and some observers believe that invention was as great as that of movable type itself. But then, one could not have existed without the other. Gutenberg— and letterpress printers today—needed a substance that would stick evenly to the face of the type, transfer just as evenly to the surface of paper pressed against it, then stick to the paper indefinitely. The specifications are deceptively simple. The answer is more difficult.

Gutenberg, whether knowingly or not, concocted an equivalent of the oil paints that artists had been developing over centuries. (Letterpress ink is still by definition the same as prosaic house paint.) He mixed carbon lampblack with boiled linseed oil, and the results were practically perfect. If we inspect his Bible or the *Mainz Psalter* today, we'll find the letters are as black and perfect as they were 500 years ago when ink and paper first wedded.

For centuries each printer made his own ink—
today he may still mix inks to get an exact color he
needs. The first factory for printer's ink was established in America in 1742.

Ink is, with paper, the flesh and blood of a
printed piece and thus must be selected with as
much care as the type, illustrations, and paper.
Many factors in the selection of ink are highly
technical and are best left to the pressman. But
every graphic designer must be familiar with some
basic characteristics of ink in order to base his part
of the selection on sound logic.

Ink consists of three components. The *pigment,*
minerals or metals, gives ink its color. The *vehicle,*
or *solvent,* converts the powdery pigment into a
liquid that can be easily distributed over a printing
form and deposited onto the paper. The *binder*—
oils or mineral compounds—causes the ink to dry
rapidly enough so it will not smudge.

In ancient days the blood of 1,200 small shellfish
was required to make a gram of the famous royal
purple of Tyre, and Cicero wrote with ink made
from the pouch of a cuttlefish. Gallnuts, a parasitic
infection of trees, are still used today for making
black writing ink, and animal or bone black is used
for black printing inks, but most printing inks use
inorganic pigments. These are usually identified
with familiar chemical names: cadmium yellow,
chrome green, iron blue, molybdate orange, and
lithopone, used for white inks.

Pigment must be powder or easily powderable; it
must have coloring and/or opaquing qualities; it
must form a homogenous paste when mixed with
the vehicle. If ink isn't uniformly smooth and
strong, the printed image will be unsatisfactory.

Gutenberg's old linseed oil is still used commonly
as a vehicle along with the less familiar oils of soy-
beans, perilla, castor beans, and china wood. Other
categories are animal, mineral substances, and the
misnamed "synthetic oils," which are really processed natural oils, dehydrated castor oil, and
esterified fish oil. The vehicle must hold the pigment
either in solution or as a suspension in an emulsion.

The binder, as its name indicates, bonds the

SIGNATURE HAND STAMP, shown in enlargement here, was done in a forerunner of printer's ink in China in the second century B.C.

Writing ink had been used for one hundred years before. The ink was made in the shape of a thin stick. This was ground in the hollow of a stone, water was added, and calligraphic characters were painted.

Today in the United States nearly a million formulas for printing inks are compounded annually.

pigment onto the paper so strongly it will resist water, acid, alkalies, melted paraffin, and heat, not to mention other solvents, including the oils in a reader's fingers, as well as flexing of the paper and friction of objects moving across the page. The binder also influences the way in which the ink dries.

Ink dries by one of several processes. Linseed-oil-based inks dry by *oxidation,* which solidifies the vehicle. Oxidation is speeded by subjecting the printed sheet to heat. The paper may be passed through a gas flame (a process that requires care lest the paper catch fire) and then over chilled rollers. It may be wrapped around a steam drum or pass under infrared heat lamps. Metallic "soaps" made by the reaction of a fatty acid upon cobalt or lead will catalyze and speed oxidation.

Inks with alcohol or petroleum solvents are dried by *evaporation.* Heat, applied by any method, evaporates the vehicle in less than a second. (It is interesting to note that rotogravure plants, which use petroleum vehicles, have recovery systems so that the evaporated solvents can be distilled and reused.)

Absorption is used in newspaper printing and is not actually drying. News-ink (so thin it is transported by tank truck and pipes) is absorbed by the inner fibers of the paper. There it remains, still damp, during most of the transitory life of the newspaper—and smudges off on the fingers of the reader. Complaints about this grubby-hand syndrome are considered so seriously that the industry is researching a cure—perhaps the use of water-based inks.

Drying may be by *polymerization.* Induced by heat or catalysts, small liquid molecules combine to form larger solid dry ones. By *gelation,* a highly complicated process, the ultimate effect is for elements of the vehicle to form into a solid gel by exposure to oxygen.

Opposite to oxidation inks are those which dry when cooled. Basically solid ink is used, "melted"; heated beyond its low melting point, it flows like normal ink on the press. As soon as it touches the cooler paper stock, it "freezes" solid again. This is useful with low-grade papers which normally would absorb the ink.

Selective precipitation is used on medium- and low-quality printing. Many vehicles contain resin. A spray of water or steam causes the resin to come out of solution while the rest of the solvent is absorbed into the paper.

Consistency of ink varies by the printing process used. Letterpress requires a fairly *tacky* ink that will not run into the counters of type or the etched depressions in engravings. Offset ink must be greasy so that the dampening agent repels it. Because it is deposited in a very thin layer and without pressure, its pigment must be strong. Gravure ink must be very fluid in order to fill the tiny wells, and therefore its solvent must be highly volatile so the thin ink will dry rapidly enough. In fact, its volatility is so great that the ink fountain on a gravure press must be enclosed. The solvent is almost like gasoline and when stagnant in a press room can explode as in an auto cylinder. Despite efficient air exhaust systems, the danger is always real and such explosions have caused the greatest disasters connected with the graphic arts since a century ago, when printers were unwitting victims of lead poisoning from fumes of type metal.

Aniline ink, which meets all the definition of a dye, is widely used for printing food wrappers, bags, and cellophane. It has given its name to a rapid and simple method of lower-grade letterpress work. Aniline is carried by resin-alcohol vehicles that dry rapidly, a necessity when printing on impervious surfaces such as metallic sheets or plastics.

Silk-screen uses both inks and paints, transparent and opaque. Variations are many, and each ink must be carefully chosen for the particular function of a specific stencil.

Inks used in process colors must be used according to color specifications of the platemaker as has already been noted. Flat colors come in a wide spectrum. When the exact shade of merchandise is to be shown in flat color, it is not uncommon for the printer to send a sample of the merchandise to the ink-maker, who mixes a batch to the exact color required.

But the printer must often mix his own inks to the customer's specifications. As he mixes, he painstakingly notes the addition of even the smallest ingredient. His "recipes" are carefully recorded and are usually kept attached to the sample printed sheet so that he can match the mixed color exactly should additional press runs be required.

In mixing for a tint, the printer adds color to white inks; for a shade, he adds black to the color.

Even that old standby, black ink, has many variations. It has various degrees of, or lack of, gloss; it has different textures when dry; it has different hues, blue-black, brown-black, and red-black to obtain special effects.

Fortunately, the designer need not know all about the composition or physical properties of ink. But he should have a collection of ink catalogues for constant reference. Not only will they show the wide variety of optical effects possible through the use of ink, but the rainbow-bright pages of ink catalogues make wonderful browsing material.

The planner of printing should be aware of the many special inks that are available: glossy and dull and many intermediates, nonscratch and non-rub, rain- and paste-proof for outdoor posters, with special vehicles and binders for printing on any kind of surface from fabric to glass.

Inks used for food wrappings must have many special characteristics. They must conform to federal pure-food specifications. They must be odor- and taste-proof to avoid contaminating the food and colorfast to avoid discoloring the contents. Ink for butter and oleo wrappers must be impervious to grease. That used for frozen-food packages must be resistant to marked temperature changes.

There are inks that change color under varying atmospheric pressures; they are used for souvenir weather predicters. There are invisible inks that appear when the paper is wet or exposed to black light. (If you are still a child at heart, you can make your own invisible ink by dissolving cobalt chlorine in water. Writing is invisible until the paper is heated, then it turns blue.)

For real children, invisible inks make self-contained coloring books. The visible image is a simple outline drawing in black. When clear water is applied to the enclosed areas, they become red, blue, yellow, or green from hitherto invisible ink.

Visible ink that glows or changes color under infrared or ultraviolet light is used for the psychedelic posters so popular in the Age of Aquarius.

There are slow-drying, fast-drying, and instant-drying inks. The fabrics that make most dresses and draperies are printed in *textile inks*. Leather and wood require special inks. Electrical circuits in radios, television sets, bombing computers, and countless other appliances are literally printed, with electrically conductive ink.

One of the newest inks is that sold under the trade name of *Day-Glow*. It is so bright that it seems to have a fluorescent quality.

Also new is *encapsulated* ink. This is a conventional ink in which are suspended microscopic capsules of perfume. When the reader responds to the printed invitation to scratch the printed image, the scent breaks out, as pure and stimulating as when a perfume bottle is opened. Manufacturers of cosmetics or any product where olfactory appeal is important—bread, new autos, leather, or liquors—can add a new dimension to their printed advertising. Perfumed inks, where the scent is dissolved with the pigment, have been available for years. Bread wrappers were often printed in such ink so that the shopper could be tempted by the artificial bakery smell even though the real scent was sealed off by the container. But in some instances perfumes were poured right into the ink fountain; often unexpected reactions between it and the vehicle created a new and unpleasant odor that offended readers rather than delighted them.

Magnetic ink has tiny particles of iron substances that have been magnetized to activate special

PRINTER'S INK must stick, in proper thickness, to the metal printing face of type, then transfer smoothly to the paper. The bottom Q shows a proper image. The top character is pitted either because it wasn't inked sufficiently or, more likely, didn't transfer cleanly off the metal.

The middle Q was overinked and, during the impressing, the excess ink squeezed out to create an irregular outline.

sensors. This has saved incalculable hours of accounting time in the nation's banking system.

More spectacular is the metal in *metallic inks*. They come in gold, silver, copper, bronze, and aluminum "color." Almost like alchemy, gold is simulated by a brasslike copper alloy and silver by aluminum. The gold comes in several gradations from that near pure gold in appearance to the more reddish shades of low-carat jewelry.

The metals are beaten into thin flakes which, upon printing, float or *leaf* to the surface of the binder where the bare metal gives the proper luster. Because the cuprous flakes of gold ink will tarnish if kept too long in contact with the varnish, such ink is separated into two components that must be mixed just before printing.

Metallic inks, although constantly improving, are still disappointing on occasion because of their weakness of color or lack of luster or covering ability. Some gold inks require more than a single layer—and thus extra passes through the press—to give even a passable sheen.

These inks are more practical than the older method of *bronzing*, or *dusting*. Here a very tacky ink was printed and onto it was applied the metallic powder. This required a special machine or slow hand work. Today dusting is never used for silver, except for a very small run, and for gold only when it is desirable to have maximum brilliance. This is achieved by bronzing, in part, because larger metallic flakes can be used than those in ink.

Aluminum ink is useful when a light ink must be printed on a dark background by letterpress. The elements are printed in aluminum which completely opaques off the undercolor. When dry the aluminum accepts the regular ink of the lighter color which itself could never cover the dark background.

Two major goals being sought by researchers for ink manufacturers today concern the graphic arts worker only as a concerned citizen rather than because of his vocational involvement. The first is finding an ink that can inexpensively be bleached

INKING THE FORM during the period of incunabula was done by ink balls fastened to wooden handles. The printer at the right is pounding the sheepskin instruments onto the form.

The man at the left is lifting the printed sheet off the platen. The frame standing at an angle at the far left holds the *frisket* that is laid over the fresh paper so that the sides of the type form, although inked, will print on the stencil material rather than the printing paper.

out of paper so it can be recycled. It does not—as we discussed in the last chapter—appear to be necessary to reuse wood pulp to protect our forests. But if it were economically feasible to recycle paper, it would help solve that most prosaic of civic problems: how do we get rid of waste paper?

The second research goal is to find new solvents that will not contribute to air pollution when they part company with printed paper. This does not seem to be an acute danger for any one printing plant . . . but neither does the pollution from any one automobile.

General Printing Ink has developed *Thermofast*, which is described as a "solventless web ink." In effect the binder replaces the solvent, and the elimination of the solvents which would otherwise be discharged into the air is cited as a major advantage of this ink which otherwise meets all specifications for the more conventional ones.

Ink is a most important tool of the typographer. Even if he doesn't "have printer's ink in his veins"— the ultimate compliment for a graphic artsman—he must always have it on his mind as he designs a printing job.

SUGGESTED READINGS

Printing Ink Handbook. New York: National Association of Printing Ink Manufacturers, 1967.

Wolf, Herbert Jay. *Printing and Litho Inks.* New York: McNair-Dorland, 1949.

17

The Specialists

Methods for Specific Needs

The level and life of civilizations depend on how easily and permanently they can duplicate written messages. In a society as complicated as ours, graphic arts has grown into a sophisticated complex that is involved in every facet of human activity—cultural, social, political, and economic. It is not surprising that technological progress in fields as spectacular as space travel and heart transplants should be reflected in parallel advances in graphic arts and that specialization should be advanced.

These are, at the moment, deeply subordinate to the three major fields of printing. Offset and letterpress represent 91 per cent of total dollar volume in 1970. Gravure represents about 4.5 per cent and silkscreen process about 3.5 per cent. That leaves a very small slice of the pie for the innovative or well-established specialties.

Let's first look at some minor methods that certainly cannot be called experimental.

The principle of *debossing* is ancient; a monarch pressed a signet ring or the throne's great seal into wax, creating an image only by the change in plane. The process continues today; called *stamping*, it depresses an image into paper or, most frequently, in the cloth or leather binding of a book.

Stamping into leather or fabric of fine binding is done with special foundry type or Linotype slugs. Type-high for these is .950 and the shoulder or neck of the characters protrudes .075 inches above the shoulder, .032 more than on regular slugs. Brass dies are used for tradebook cover designs.

If the stamped material is thin enough—an ordinary sheet of paper—*embossing* occurs on its reverse side. The only difference between debossing and embossing depends on which side of the paper is being "read." If the image is depressed in the printing—and viewing—surface, it's debossed or stamped; if the image is raised, it is embossed.

Embossing is used primarily on letterheads and booklets covered in paper. There are two kinds of embossing—as there are stamping. *Blind* embossing or stamping is that in which only the difference in plane defines the image; *brilliant* embossing or stamping is one in which the image is defined in ink in addition to its contour.

Embossing—blind or brilliant—is further subdivided.

Plane embossing is that in which the image is raised to a flat, single plane above the surface of the paper. *Modeled* embossing creates a bas relief in the paper with several planes, like those of the bust on a coin.

In each process a pair of dies is used. The *male* or *impressing* die pushes the paper into the matching receptacle of a *female* or *receiving* die. For plane embossing, the dies can be made by photoengraving; for modeled embossing the original art is a piece of sculpture. For stamping, the materials are usually accommodating enough that no receiving die is required.

Using inked elements, stamping and inking can be performed in the same operation. *Foil stamping* is a variation. Metal foil—often pure genuine gold—is punched into the material by relief elements that are heated electrically; a heat-set bond seals the foil to the fabric or leather and the depression protects the metal against abrasion.

Metal appliqué is a newer variation. A piece of metal foil, much heavier than that used for stamping, is adhered to the paper at the same time both are embossed. The effect is rich and handsome.

Because the element that comes in contact with the "reading" side of embossed material is depressed, it is impossible to ink it. So for brilliant embossing, the image in ink (often metallic) must be printed separately before embossing.

Another way of raising an image is by *thermography*, which was developed to simulate the slight embossing of intaglio printing. Printing is done with a highly tacky ink. While it is still wet it is dusted with a powdered rosin; that which doesn't adhere to the image is blown away. The job then passes under heat which causes the rosin to liquefy. In cooling, moments later, it fuses into a solid, raised image. Thermography powder is available in

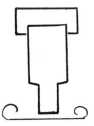

STAMPING is shown in this schematic. Type—foundry or Linotype—or engravings are used to punch the image into a soft material such as the fabric of a book binding. Type-high for such elements is .950 inches; the neck of the printing element projects .075 inches from the shoulder, .032 more than regular relief elements. Note that there is no receiving element against which the fabric is punched.

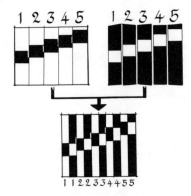

BINOCULAR VISION, parallax, gives the third dimension to the image the human sees. This schematic illustrates the principle.

One eye sees the image represented by the white rectangles at the left. The other eye sees a slightly different view (represented by the black rectangles) because it is separated by a slight distance from its companion.

The brain mixes the two images. The left-eye view, symbolized by the white rectangles, and the right-eye view, the black rectangles, are broken up into strips which then are interlaced to form the stereogram, as suggested by the lower diagram.

This is done optically on the camera which is fitted with a *lenticular grid.*

The grid has over 100 lines per inch and the halftone screen with which the photo image is converted to a printing plate itself has 300 lines per inch. The dots are practically as fine as those of the silver salts that make a photograph, and the printing must be done on a paper surface almost as smooth as the surface of a glossy photograph.

The ratio of distance between the eyes and the range at which a scene is viewed affects the degree of "roundness" in which

gold, silver, and many colors as well as in clear form that enhances the color of ink.

Seeing an image through colorless material is also the secret of three-dimensional printing, called *Xography.* (It's always capped because it's a trademark, not a generic term.) The X stands for *parallax,* a phenomenon remarked on 2,000 years ago by Euclid and referred to, in 1584, by Leonardo Da Vinci as *binocular vision.* Each eye sees a slightly different "picture" which, when combined in the viewer's brain, tells him something about the roundness, the third dimension, of the original scene.

Shortly after the Civil War this was the operating principle of that nostalgic favorite, the stereoscope. Two photographs, taken by a pair of cameras mounted apart, like human eyes, were held in front of a viewing device so that the human left eye saw what the left camera had seen and the right eye saw the other picture. This gave a marked 3-D effect that had viewers oh-ing and ah-ing right through the turn of the century.

Printers used the *anaglyph* in the same way. Two printed images, one in green, the parallax one in red, were superimposed on each other. The reader wore a pair of glasses, one lens in red, the other in green, so each eye saw only one picture (of the color opposite to its lens), which was blended mentally with the other. (Movies used the same device with polarized and normal light.)

By 1940, *parallax panoramagrams* printing gave the effect of 3-D printing without the need for special glasses. The viewer looked through a thick pre-embossed glass or plastic screen in front of the picture. But this was too cumbersome for mass production and too bulky for periodical distribution. Three big graphic arts names—*Look* magazine, Harris-Intertype, and Eastman Kodak—joined forces led by Arthur Rothstein, a great *Look* photographer who had wrestled with the problem for 13 years.

The answer became public in a 1964 issue of the magazine.

Shooting through a screen in front of the special camera divides the resulting picture into hundreds of tiny vertical parallel strips, each showing a slightly different view as the camera moves on a track to take exposures from different angles. From this, fine-screen halftones are made and printed by letterpress or offset—in black and white or, usually, color. The press, immediately after the last ink impression, adds the key element: hot-melt, chill-embossed clear plastic formed into a myriad of narrow, vertical half-cylinders.

Each of these semi-tubes acts as a lens that allows each eye to see only one set of the strip images in the familiar stereoscope method.

Xographs have been used for magazine ads and covers, record album covers, postcards, and wall placards . . . and scores of other uses, even as pasted-on elements of outdoor billboards to give illusions of motion as well as depth.

A far more astonishing three-dimensional image is that produced by *holography*. "Holo" comes from the Greek word "entire" and the process does "write" an entire object. It uses *lasers* that emit light that is phased in steady and regular pulses. In a highly complex manner, phased and unphased light create interferences which are recorded on photofilm. When similar light is projected through the negatives, the entire image is re-created, not on a screen but out in open space. It is truly the "entire" image. If the viewer shifts his position, he can see the front and left side of an object instead of front and right. He can move further and see the back or kneel and see the bottom, then stand on a chair and see the top of the photographed object.

Holography is as definitely a part of the graphic arts as photography is. Yet it involves so many other sciences that it will probably never be more than a well-liked cousin to the conventional graphic arts. Probably its holographs will be packaged as negatives with books or magazines. Of course, because it requires laser projection, it can't become an integral part of a magazine as can Xography, for instance.

an object is seen. If the object is viewed at a distance of only a few inches, the difference between the two images is marked. Objects viewed a mile away are seen in images so nearly identical that it is impossible to tell the space between a barn, for instance, and a grove behind it.

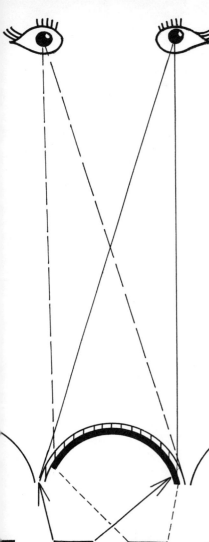

Another X name is *Xerography,* also trademarked and capped. This is the newest of graphic arts methods; the first automatic *Xerox* copier didn't appear until 1960. "Xero" means "dry," incidentally, because the process is also known as "inkless printing."

If the field ever becomes large enough to require a generic name, it might be called *ionography* because it utilizes the action of electric ions to create the image.

A plate coated with selenium, a nonmetallic element, passes under a field of electrically charged wires. This coats the plate with a layer of positively charged ions. Now the image of the copy is projected—by reflection or through a negative—onto the plate. Where areas are exposed to the light, the charge is drained away.

Pigment powder so fine it is sometimes referred to as "smoke" is given a negative charge. As it swirls over the plate—because opposites attract electrically as well as romantically—the minus-charged powder adheres to, and only to, the plus-charged

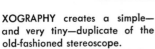

XOGRAPHY creates a simple—and very tiny—duplicate of the old-fashioned stereoscope.

The alternating black and gray rectangles at the bottom of this schematic illustration represent the alternating images of the parallax stereogram.

The arcs represent tiny semicylinders—just 1/112 inch in diam-

latent image on the plate.

A sheet of paper, given a positive charge, is placed over the selenium. It attracts the negative pigment from the plate and finally the pigment is fused to the paper by heat. While the steps are many, they are swift and automatic, and so the machine is simple in actual operation.

The Xerox is still primarily used for a relatively short run. Its greatest graphic arts application is in the making of offset plates. The "smoke" is now particles of acid-resist which adhere to a zinc or copper plate, ready for the etching step of photo-engraving. Or the smoke may be of a technically "greasy" substance which is placed right on a lithographic plate. Because this process does not require a darkroom or developing fluids—and because the "coating" of ions is applied swiftly just before exposure and therefore doesn't deteriorate as the emulsion on packaged pre-sensitized plates might—the new method offers many advantages to platemakers.

LDX (long-distance Xerography) is a system for transmitting visual copy electronically . . . across a corridor or a continent. A scanner reads the documentary image, converts it into electrical impulses which, at a receiving station any distance away, actuate the ions of the Xerox to re-create a visual image. The *Wall Street Journal*, for example, sends facsimiles from its San Francisco office to its printing plant in Riverside, California. McGraw-Hill transmits 8½ × 11-inch copy from its New York offices to its Albany, New York, plant in five seconds.

RCA has a device that could produce a daily newspaper—or a supplement thereto—right in the reader's home by facsimile. They have even considered having advertising pre-printed on the back of the rolls of paper on which the reproduction will be done. Performance is "technically excellent" and it would be feasible to send newspapers and magazines around the world. It ought to be noted here that the need for functional and attractive typographic display would be as great for *fax* material as that printed more conventionally.

High transmission costs have inhibited rapid expansion of the principle. But ingenuity again sets in. Much of the cost of transmission, American Telegraph and Telephone explains, is spent on blank spaces on a page. The *Telikon* selectively skips such blanks, shortening transmission time and cost.

Communications satellites are used to carry written messages now. Of course, they carry TV images, too, so soon they will be transmitting con-

eter—of plastic which are laid onto the paper immediately after the images are printed. Each of these arcs acts as a lens. Both the left- and right-eye images are projected to the surface of the plastic. (They are not identical in form, of course, and their position varies, too. The drawing below suggests—in great exaggeration—how the images occupy a different arc on the lens surface.)

The gray rectangle is the left-eye image. Arrows extending from it show how that image is projected onto the lens so the left eye can see it. Similarly the right-eye image is projected so that organ can see only its own image.

The images and the lenses are so tiny that the three-dimensional image is produced over a 90-degree viewing range. If the eye looks at the image at a greater angle than that, the right eye will see the left image and vice versa. This will make the image jump suddenly. This principle is used to create a moving image, in a size small enough for a tiny pocket card or large enough to give motion to an outdoor billboard.

ventional word-and-picture facsimiles. This will be even more commonplace when they are combined with the constantly expanding technology of laser-beam transmission.

A handicap to a truly major communications breakthrough—and consequent application to the graphic arts—is the incompatibility of computer language. Each company guards its software and speaks in its own language. The result is a latter-day Tower of Babel where the Univac can speak to the IBM 360 no more intelligibly than Trobiander could to Lapp or Masai. But many people still alive today can remember when they couldn't telephone their neighbors who were hooked into an alien system. Public demand and plain common sense have linked practically all phones and phone systems in the world into a single operative network. So, soon, either the industry or legislation is going to impose uniformity of input, output, and language upon all computer phases, including that of the graphic arts.

We have mentioned inkless printing; now comes the most intriguing and truly revolutionary of all the blue-sky projections of the 1970's: typeless printing, no less!

This process—called *ink jet, non-impact* or *digital press*—"prints" by spraying ink on paper. A metal plate, perforated by hundreds of tiny holes, extends across the width of the paper. By signal from a computer, some of these holes are closed. Those remaining open form letters in the same way that bulbs on an electric scoreboard or display clocks-thermometers create letterforms and numbers from spots of light.

The result then is a form of the pinprick stencils used by signpainters to transfer drawings from paper to walls or billboards. When a whole line of characters has been formed in this way, fine ink is forced through the openings and the characters are "spray-painted" onto the paper.

At this writing, typographic quality is poor; but that can undoubtedly be improved. Speed of the process is so high that it is being used—competitively to the Teletype—for the transmission of stock-

"I have to reset the whole job; I received the copy from the wrong communication satellite."

(Courtesy of American Press magazine)

market reports. The Teletype Corporation, A. B. Dick—best known for another stencil-user, the Mimeograph—and Stanford Research Corporation have developed very similar applications of the principle.

After this quick look at A.D. 2001, let's come back to the most prosaic of present machines, the *duplicators*. (There is no common definition of this term. Sometimes it is used synonymously with "copier." Generally, a copier does not require a printing plate or its equivalent. The *Thermo-fax*, which copies a page by reproducing the image in the carbon "ashes" of a burning process, is a typical copier. All its functions are automatic, requiring nothing from the operator except feeding in the material. A duplicating machine usually needs a specially prepared intermediate object between the original copy and the finished product. But the difference between the duplicator and a printing press is so slight that many cannot detect it and fewer can agree on definition.)

Most printers refuse to recognize office duplication as printing, and commonly, often inaccurately, consider it of submarginal quality. But, within their capabilities, these processes can produce quality dependent primarily on the craftsmanship of the user. At any rate, they do have a definite and useful place in reproduction of the written word.

The simplest *fluid duplicator* is the *hectograph*, from *hectare*, "a hundred," that indicates the very short runs it is used for. You are probably most familiar with its aggressive purple ink from materials teachers prepare on it for class work. Onto a gelatin slab, treated with glycerin, the image is written directly (in mirror form) or by transfer from paper. The plate is not re-inked; each impression removes a tiny layer of the image. Several colors may be used at one time by using different hues in the original ink or pencil.

The principle is mechanized in the *Ditto* machine. The paper master consists of a sheet of high-finish coated stock backed by one of special carbon paper. As the copy is typed on the face of the master, the face-up carbon creates a mirror image on the back of the master. Drawings or signatures done right-reading on the face of the master are also mirror-imaged in the same way. The master is placed on a drum and reproduced by depletion of the image.

These two methods are inexpensive; materials other than paper cost less than .2¢ per copy. They require only a modicum of skill for passable work. Ditto copy may be prepared and stored for a period of up to a year. Often the method is used to prepare accumulative copy as it becomes available and then duplicate it when material is complete.

The *Mimeograph* (a trade name which is fast becoming as generic as Linotype) is a machine that reproduces copy by forcing ink through a stencil as paper passes under a drum. It is thus related more closely to silk-screening than to the common printing methods.

The stencil, the equivalent to a printing "plate," is the key to good reproduction. It must be cut on a clean typewriter in good condition and with an even, firm stroke. Electric typewriters, because of their mechanical uniformity of stroke, are best suited to stencil cutting.

Illustrations and ruling are done by hand with a stylus, formed as a loop of wire or a needle with a tiny ball at the tip. By a *shading wheel* or screens, Ben Day-like tones may be added. It is possible to place an image, even halftones, on the stencil by photographic means. Color is possible. Normally the ink feeds from inside a drum around which the stencil is wrapped. An oiled-paper cover may be placed over the inking pad and a fresh pad with another color placed over that. Color may be applied by areas to the fresh pad so that more than one color can be reproduced at the same time or a two-color job can be done as in other processes, by two press runs.

Wax stencils can reproduce up to 400 copies, dry stencils up to 5,000 with care.

Letterpress duplicators become more rare. Type is set into segmented channels as with the earliest rotary newspaper presses. Cuts, electros, or stereo-types are curved, or rubber plates are used as wraparounds.

Offset presses have been adapted for office use. Many have ingenious devices such as automatic wash-up and plate changing for specialized work. The plate may be conventional metal or a *paper master*, prepared by typing with a special ribbon. Masters do not have a very long life, but it is pos-sible to run one or more masters off the original and thus the image bearers can be self-reproducing. The improvement of *pre-sensitized* plates broadens the use, not only of office duplicators, but of all smaller offset presses or any offset press in a smaller shop. Presensitized plates are prepared, packaged, and sold like camera film and eliminate time and equipment needed to coat plates in the shop.

The only true limitation on office offset is size and, sometimes, a more rudimentary ink distribu-tion that precludes large areas of solid masses of ink. Color is easy and even some excellent four-color process work is done on these small presses.

Duplicators, except for the hectograph, have rated speeds of 1,000 to 5,000 impressions per hour. They are commonly used for internal distribution of transitory material where quality is not essential, for outside distribution where quality is not of paramount importance, or where informality and spontaneity have virtues. Higher quality is possible on many machines; but a factor in their economics is that semiskilled personnel is often assigned to the operation and the lack of skill is apparent in the product.

One more major, and several minor, printing processes are discussed in Chapter 21. And we ought to note in passing here that there are other specialized printing methods that are interesting although their products are credited to industries other than the graphic arts.

Three-dimensional contour maps, which used to be regally expensive, are now almost impulse items thanks to combining printing on and modeled em-bossing of thin plastic sheets. Printing of clothing fabrics create seasonal rainbows. Woodgrain printed on a cellulose-composition pressboard is handsomer than plywood, veneer, or even quarter-sawn wood. Wallpaper printers have left us gorgeous antiques. Their printing "plates" were wooden cylinders about 6 inches in diameter into which were driven brass strips to form the relief elements. These are truly *objets d'art*.

Graphic arts gets hectic at times, as does any activity where immediacy is vital. But it is rarely dull. And the prognosis is that this field will be no more boring in the sixth century after Gutenberg.

PLANE EMBOSSING is done, as this schematic shows, when the paper is pressed between the male die (shown in white) and the female die (black). The resulting image is on one single, unmodulated plane.

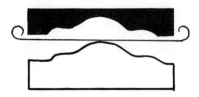

MODELED EMBOSSING creates a bas-relief image, as shown in this diagram. Both the impressing die (in white) and the receiving die (black) are reproduced from a piece of sculpture.

A small cutting tool, mounted on a *pantagraph*, cuts the dies to the much smaller proper size as a stylus travels over the surface of the sculpture. Cutting with a pantagraph is also used for making punches for Linotype matrices.

SUGGESTED READINGS

The same comments and suggestions made for Chapter 6 apply to this chapter, too.

18
The Bindery

Packaging the Written Word

The final step in converting a piece of mineral from a potential commercial tool to a coveted and costly gem is putting the diamond ring into a little satin-lined box. No one would even think of just dropping it into a brownpaper sack and twisting it closed.

After a piece of paper has been printed, its effectiveness depends on the way in which it is presented to the reader and how he uses it. This "packaging" is done by cutting, folding, fastening, and covering the paper, the function of the *bindery*.

Most of our printed matter is packaged as a *book* or some variation thereof. This is such a familiar form to us that often we fail to realize that there are "books" other than the kind we use.

The name comes from the Phoenician city of Byblos, whose merchants bought papyrus in Egypt and sold it throughout the Mediterranean basin. The Greeks transmuted the name to *biblos*, "book," and the most famous of all books is called just that, "The Book," the Bible.

Books were once just long strips of parchment, papyrus, or paper wound onto two wooden rolls. The reader rolled the material off one spindle and onto the other as he read. The sacred writings of Judaism, the Torah, are still preserved in scrolls for ceremonial occasions. In the South Pacific a book may be a tall stack of bamboo boards, kept together by loose cords that pass through parallel holes in the wood.

A very few of our books still retain the traditional *portfolio* design, a series of loose leaves stored in a specially made box.

Conventional books are too familiar to need description but it should be pointed out that when a letter or an advertising piece is folded, it forms a small book. In all countries except the Soviet Union, nothing with less than 48 pages is considered a book. Reducing that minimum explains why the Russians are credited, in academic statistics, with producing so many more books than the decadent democracies.

Other confusing terms include: *leaf* or *sheet,* a

single, flat piece of paper; *folder,* a leaf folded a few or many times; *leaflet,* a leaf folded only once or twice; *broadside,* a large leaf—customarily at least 15 × 22 inches—made into a folder; *French fold,* a leaf printed on only one side, then folded twice so the unprinted side is the inner one of a 4-page folder; *booklet* or *pamphlet,* a book form of less than 48 pages with a paper cover; *brochure,* a booklet of very high quality.

A *broadsheet* is the size of a normal 8-column newspaper page approximately 15 × 21 inches, and a *tabloid* (*tab*) sheet is one half that size.

To learn how to manipulate printed pages most effectively, we can do no better than to consider each of the functions of the bindery.

Cutting

The first bindery job is *cutting.* Most paper is made in sheets much larger than the customary printing sizes. Before or after printing, these large sheets must be cut to the proper dimensions. In specifying this process the graphic arts buyer can effect substantial savings or create monumental waste.

As has been seen, paper is manufactured in almost endless sheets and wound into rolls. These are then cut into flat sheets, some roughly as large as 4 × 5 feet.

Basic size for book stock is 25 × 38 inches; writing, 17 × 22; cover, 20 × 26. Although larger sheets are usually available, they are all in multiples of these sizes unless a special *make order* has been manufactured to special specification. This is done, of course, only when the quantity is sufficient to retain the economies of standardization.

When a printing buyer specifies a sheet, he is charged for the total amount of paper including that wasted in cutting down to his size. To *cut without waste* is a skill that must be learned early. Cutting depends on three factors, only one of which is variable: specified size of the printed job, press capacity and *imposition,* size of available paper stock. The latter two usually cannot be changed, but by modifying the first, waste can be minimized or eliminated.

Some jobs, like a letterhead, for instance, can go through the press one small sheet at a time. Any page of a book or booklet must be printed with an opposing page against which the first page is folded. Actually, all except very small books are printed on far larger sheets, with as many as 64 pages or more at a time. When such a sheet has been folded into pages, it is called a *signature*. (With the misuse of terms so common in the graphic arts, the printed, but not yet folded, sheet is sometimes called a signature, too.)

The obvious advantage of printing many pages per sheet is the reduction of the length of the total press run as well as the simplification of later bindery operations.

The capacity of the press determines just how large each signature will be, so does the number of pages in the book. For a 70-page book, for example, the pressman would run a 64-page signature plus an additional one of eight pages. Two pages in the last signature will be blank but they are necessary to fold the printed pages into the book. Or the press capacity might dictate two 32-page signatures.

Consider a simpler printing job to see how waste can be avoided. Assume a 4-page folder, each page 6 × 9 inches. This must be printed on a 9 × 12 sheet containing two pages. Perhaps the original sheet must be even larger to provide room for the grippers on the press or for trimming, especially when there are *bleed cuts*. (*Bleeds* are cuts that run off one or more sides of the paper. They require an extra ⅛-inch margin of paper which is trimmed off after printing. In planning bleeds, attention must be given to their position. Should a bleed run off the edge which the grippers grasp on the press, additional margin must be provided. This adds to waste.)

Book stock is available in 25 × 38-inch sheets. Some printers use what they term the *gozinta system*. They divide the job size into the stock size, one dimension of the job into one of the stock, then

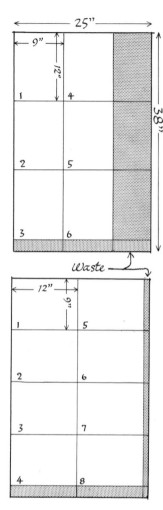

Example 5. CUTTING TO WASTE of various amounts is shown on this diagram.

the other job dimension into the second stock measurement.

Dividing 12 inches into 38 inches shows that the printer can get three lengths of the job from each length of stock and have only 2 inches left over. He will probably need this much for trimming so he doesn't consider it waste. Then, dividing 9 inches into the width of the paper, he finds that he can get two pieces crosswise for a total of six pieces from each sheet of stock. But now he has real waste, a 7-inch strip across the whole 38-inch height, as shown in Example 5.

So he tries again. He divides 12 inches into 25 and finds he can cut two sheets crosswise. Then, 9 inches goes into 38 four times. Now he has left over a 1 × 38-inch and a 2 × 24-inch strip, just about the amount needed for normal trim.

By cutting the original sheet advantageously, he gets eight desired pieces instead of the six that the first method produced. Because he had to pay for the entire stock sheet, he thus saves 25 per cent of the paper cost.

Suppose this same job had been specified for 7 × 9½-inch pages. That would require 14 × 9½-inch pieces. Using the same division method, 14 goes into 25 once, with 11 inches of waste, and 9½ goes into 38 exactly four times, without trim margins, for four pieces per sheet. The other way: 14 goes into 38 twice with a 10-inch waste, and 9½ goes into 25 twice, with 6 inches of waste, and a total of four pieces per sheet again.

In both instances, 44 per cent of the stock is wasted. This would add an unconscionable burden on paper cost. It is apparent, then, that by reducing the size of the printed page only a trifle—from 7 × 9½ to 6 × 9—substantial savings can be made without destroying the effectiveness of the printing job.

The good designer will determine what size stock is available and try to design his job to cut without waste. Working with standard sizes, he knows automatically those dimensions which cut advantageously. He is also assured that the proportions of such cut sheets will be harmonious; that is why standard paper sizes were established at those particular dimensions.

Sometimes it may be possible to cut one or more sheets in the opposite direction out of the original trimmed-off paper to reduce waste further.

With some paper the direction of the grain becomes a factor. If the press must be fed, or if the job must be folded, *with the grain,* this will affect the cutting-out pattern and must be considered in planning. Sometimes the watermark, too, must be taken into account. Is it imperative that it read right or can it be ignored?

It is wise for the beginner with any problem, or the experienced layout man with a more complicated one, to draw a rough sketch as he works the solution. Visualization often enables maximum utilization.

There are times, of course, when waste stock can be used for other jobs. Often one or several smaller pieces can be *ganged* with a larger one and run through the press at the same time for the same or different customers.

Often it is possible to obtain striking effects by cutting at other than right angles. This is especially effective when two colors of ink are used, one on each side, or when a two-toned paper is used. Example 6 shows how a piece of paper is cut with the upper edge at an angle. In an accordion fold, the back of the paper makes each alternating triangle at the top. Variations on this method are many.

Although the process is done on a press, *die cutting* is so closely related to bindery cutting that it should be considered here. *Dies* resemble cookie cutters. They are made of thin, sharp-edged steel strips that can be formed into countless patterns, simple or quite complex. On a platen press, the die takes the place of the printing form. A mirror die may be placed in the platen to assure a clean cut. Envelopes and boxes are made this way.

By die cutting, it is possible to make the piece of printed paper, or a whole booklet, assume an appropriate form. Or a *window,* of any shape or size,

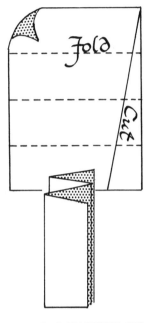

Example 6. DIAGONAL CUT and straight fold creates pleasant effect.

Example 7. DRILLING, a version of die cutting that produces only circular holes, is used here as an attention-compellor. (Courtesy *Show* magazine)

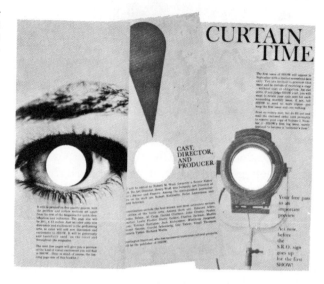

can be cut into one page to show printing on the third page. In such cases the third page must be so designed that the exposed portion harmonizes with the front-page pattern as well as that one on the page on which it is printed.

Example 7 shows several pages from a handsome booklet for *Show* magazine. A large circular hole was drilled through the entire booklet. On the cover, the hole made the *O* in *SHOW*. On inner pages it made one lens of binoculars, the halo around a light bulb, and similar circular shapes.

Dies are available in a great many standard shapes and sizes. Rectangles, circles, ovals, and stars are favorites. Standard dies are inexpensive. Special dies can be made to almost any desired shape; while they are expensive, cost is a relative standard; often a special die is an excellent investment.

Simple dies can be used on regular platen presses, but most often such cutting is done on special, heavier versions of platen presses.

Scoring is the process of creasing paper or cardboard to facilitate folding with less cracking or breaking. The *score* is impressed into the paper by plates or rollers consisting of a raised metal tongue that presses the paper into a recessed groove on a

DIE CUTTING is an effective tool to solving an immediate problem of a printed folder: getting the reader to open it up and consume the message inside.

In this example the message is on the area occupied by the Sphinx. The die-cut triangles fold over to create a square folder so intriguing that it would be a rare reader who could resist the urge to open it up and see what's inside.

metal surface behind the sheet. The score marks the line on which the paper will be folded. A common example is the box used by clothing merchants. Boxes are shipped flat, then folded by hand as needed.

Scoring may be done as simply as by raising a plain rule a little higher than type-high. The crease is not deep but is adequate for light stock. (If the fold is a permanent one, as that on a 4-page folder, scoring may be done during the printing process. The line printed by the scoring rule will not be visible on the fold. But most scoring is done with blank, uninked elements.)

Perforating is done by a mechanism attached to a press or a separate machine. Check and receipt books are common examples of perforating, while in advertising it is frequently used to make it easy for the reader to detach a coupon or return postal card.

The most common perforation is a line of small holes although there are variations, such as *serrated* incisions.

Scoring and perforating are commonly considered bindery operations although they may be done during the printing operation. *Numbering* is often grouped with the other two processes, but it is definitely a printing, not a binding, operation.

Many jobs—checks, receipts, tickets, etc.—require consecutive numbers which are imprinted by a *numbering machine*. This mechanism is contained in a type-high unit that is locked into a printing form just as a piece of furniture might be. Pressure of the printing impression moves the next number into printing position, just as the numbers on an automobile odometer rotate into view.

Numbering machines can be set to move up one or more numbers after an impression. If a printer were producing a checkbook with four checks per page, he would set his first numbering machine to imprint #1 on the first page, #5 on the second, and so on. The next machine would begin at #2 and move to #6 for the next sheet, etc.

Tipping-in is a bindery operation that can be done by hand, by a special machine, or by an

ROUNDING CORNERS of cards makes them easier to handle and sometimes more attractive to the reader. Various corner-rounds are shown above.

Below are shown some standard dies for edging paper. Both these processes are done by dies, like cookie cutters.

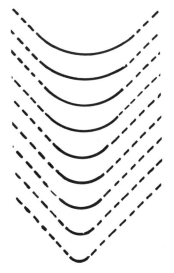

attachment to a press. This is simply pasting a single sheet, a *tip*, into a book or magazine, or onto another page. Often inserts of pre-printed material, or on special stock, are pasted into books or magazines. It used to be a common practice to produce illustrations for books by lithography, then tip them onto a blank page of a letterpress book. This method is still used, especially for books of art reproductions in full color.

Folding

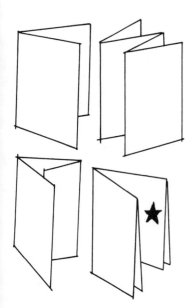

FOLDING BY MACHINE can produce all these variations and many more. The starred example is a *French fold*. If the inner pages were only half as tall as the outer ones, it would be a *short fold,* a very effective technique.

The one directly above the French fold is an *accordion fold,* and the one to its left is the conventional two-fold letter.

Origami is an ancient Japanese art form that has had recent revival and popularity in the United States. An amazing variety of three-dimensional objects are created by folding a single piece of paper. Graphic artists especially find it fascinating; it challenges their creativity and utilizes a common material that is always in abundance in any of their working places.

While it is not necessary to master paper folding to this advanced degree, every designer and printer should know how to enhance the effectiveness of a printed piece by proper folding.

The simplest fold is to crease a piece of paper down the middle and thus convert it into four pages. A series of such folds can be inserted into each other to create a sizable booklet. (The designer must remember, when using this method, that eventually the inner set of pages will protrude considerably past the outer ones. So he must leave a generous margin for trimming.)

Books as large as 80 pages are folded from a single sheet of stock and pages are cut open after binding.

The double fold of a regular business letterhead gives six "pages." If the second fold is made in the same direction as the first—instead of backwards to form an enclosure—it is an *accordion fold.*

There are some 40 or 50 standard folding patterns, all of them possible on automatic folding machines. A few of them are shown here and it is easy to see how these can be expanded upon.

Paper grain is a decisive factor in all folding and

must be considered as early as the first rough dummy.

Fastening is the part of its work that gives the bindery its name. *Binding* paper together into a convenient and durable book or booklet is an important function.

If we consider the ways in which a book may be bound, we shall also learn those methods acceptable to booklets.

Books are usually bound so that pages are vertical rectangles. But occasionally, most usually for advertising booklets, they may be fastened along a short side to open horizontally.

When a printer specifies the size of a book, he gives the width first; so a 6 × 9-inch book is a vertical rectangle, the conventional size and form. The binder, however, gives first the size of the binding edge. To describe the normal book he would call it 9 × 6. To him a 6 × 9 book is *landscaped,* the term applied to a book in horizontal form.

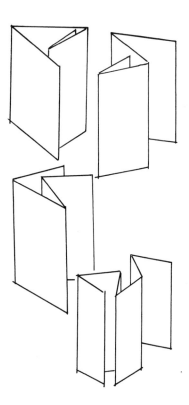

The simplest and most widely used form of permanent binding is *saddle stitching* or *sewing.* "Stitching" refers to the use of wire fastening—regular staples for simple jobs, or short pieces cut from a roll of wire for longer ones. "Sewing" indicates that thread is used, by a device just like the familiar family sewing machine except that it is a little sturdier.

If the binder took our first folding example, two pieces of paper, each creased to make four pages, and slipped one inside the other, then fastened them with a long-armed paper desk stapler in the fold, he would produce a perfect example of saddle wiring. Commercially, the folded sheets rest on an inverted V of metal, the saddle.

Saddle stitching is suitable for books from 8 to 32 pages. Beyond that number the book will gape open and the inner pages will be noticeably narrower than the outer. But the book lies flat for easy reading; inner margins may be quite narrow; bleeds may run across the fold.

Saddle Stitch

Side Stitch

Sewed Soft Cover

Case Bound
(Sewed)

BINDING METHODS most commonly used are the four shown here. These are all permanent bindings.

Usually two stitches are used on smaller books. For larger pages, three or more may be required. The number, and the size of wire used for staples, depends on the page size, thickness of the book, kind of stock, and the kind of usage it will receive. Many magazines are wire-stitched and it is annoying to have the centerspread part company from the rest of the book on the first reading because the paper has torn away from the staples.

Now if the binder takes those original two folded pieces, again one inside the other, and staples them at the fold but from the outside, and sideways, he produces an example of *side wiring* or *side stitching*. This method is simple and inexpensive. The cover is usually pasted on in one piece, front and back. This creates a *backbone*—which saddle stitching does not provide—that may be printed on for identification.

Side wiring can be used on books up to about a half-inch thick and up to 9 × 12 pages. Unless it is very large, a side-wired book will not lie flat. Inner margins must be wide enough to compensate for that strip which is invisible under the staples.

The simplest binding is *padding*, which is commonly seen on scratch pads. A suitable quantity of single sheets is squeezed under pressure. An extremely flexible adhesive is brushed onto one edge. When dry this holds the sheets into a quite permanent pad from which a single sheet may easily be removed.

This method is much used to bind inexpensive paperbacks. They are printed in signatures and are padded after being trimmed into single sheets. Around this pad is placed the one-piece wraparound cover, which also adheres to the adhesive. Sometimes a loosely woven fabric is placed between the pad and the cover to add a little strength, or the edges of the pages may be striated to absorb more adhesive. Books bound this way—in *perfect binding*—open flat.

Recent introduction of the Cameron system—discussed in Chapter 10—has made it possible to use perfect binding, in a way that makes its name almost 100 per cent accurate, with regular hardback books.

Sewed softcover books are gathered in signatures, usually of 16 pages, which are sewn down the fold as in saddle stitching. Now, however, thread replaces the staples and the stitches are many and even, just as in a garment. Each signature is tied, in loops from a continuous thread, to the one over and under it. This process is more expensive than the previous two but it has many advantages. It is strong. It can be used for any size books, up to the largest. It lies flat when opened, and thus the inside margin can be small and bleeds can be used through the gutter. It has a backbone, of course, which may be printed. The cover is glued on, as with side stitching.

In *sewed-case binding*, signatures are sewn together as in the method just examined, with all the enumerated advantages. But now the cover is made separately. Fabric, paper, or leather is pasted onto the *boards*, two stout pieces of cardboard, with the edges overlapping and turned over on all the outer sides. The backbone, with no board behind it, is sturdy but flexible to protect the sewing. Tough paper, the *end papers*, is then glued—tipped—to the outside signatures and pasted to the boards. The result is a cover of great durability that can be decorated in many ways. The simplest is printing, the most elaborate, hand-tooling of leather, perhaps with gilt added. End papers are often decorated, too.

This book you're now reading is an example of the process.

Books bound in these four methods are permanent. But for many uses, books must be bound so that pages can be added or replaced. These are *loose-leaf* books and they are of three general kinds.

The most common form is the simple *ring binder* such as students use for class notes. Pages lie flat when opened and inner margins can be small. This is the best binding when pages must be changed quickly and frequently.

Binding posts are like staples in side stitching

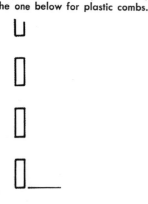

PUNCHING holes in paper is necessary for several kinds of mechanical bindings. The ones shown above are for post binders, the one below for plastic combs.

except that they are metal "bolts." Posts are inserted through pre-punched holes and a flat nut is screwed on the end to prevent the post slipping out. To change pages is possible but it requires unscrewing the top, sliding the pages off and sliding them on again with care. Pages do not lie flat and the exposed ends of the posts preclude handsome covers. This binding is used on journals and ledgers where changes must be made, but only on occasion.

Tongue covers are used to hide binding posts. Here the covers—front and back are separate—have a short extension through which the post fastens and then the cover itself is folded over to hide the post. Except that the cover is more attractive, this binding has the same assets and liabilities as that with naked posts.

Mechanical bindings that have become popular in recent years are *plastic* and *spiral*.

Plastic bindings are *combs*. They have many short, wide teeth fastened to a wide backbone. The teeth are inserted into pre-punched slots and the whole comb encircles tightly into a cylinder. In spiral binding, a continuous length of wire or plastic spirals through pre-punched holes.

Mechanical bindings have many advantages to outweigh some obvious disadvantages. Books need not be run in signatures, each 2-page sheet can be fastened separately. This is a great advantage in color work. Color pages can be ganged and printed without regard for their ultimate position in the book and thus press runs can be reduced though hand-gathering is then required. Odd-sized pages can be inserted, again by a manual operation. Margins can be small; the entire page is always visible.

Mechanical bindings are generally rugged and therefore are good for catalogues and other books that must constantly be referred to. The book lies perfectly flat.

Plastics and spirals come in a wide range of colors, and handsome effects are possible. Comb backbones can be printed on.

The main disadvantage is that mechanical bindings do not convey the impression of quality that sewn books do. New sheets can be combed into plastic binders but this is a painstaking job and the added sheet does not hold as well as the originals. Pages cannot be added to spiral binding. But in both cases pages may be torn out without affecting the remaining ones.

Spiral binding requires stiff covers; combs do not. Facing pages will register perfectly in combs; they cannot in spirals. Spiral-bound books will fold over on themselves for ease in reading (and also in writing; that is why stenographers' notebooks are so often bound this way).

Variations of these mechanical bindings are flat metal or plastic *rings*, comb teeth without the backbone; *wire loops* at close intervals, which resemble spirals; metal rings riveted to a backbone; *overwire*, a spiral hidden by a separate cover.

Much of the function of covering has been discussed. The simplest form is a *self-cover*, which is the very same paper as the rest of the pages.

Then comes the simple *stock cover*. This is a four-page single fold of cover stock, which is just placed around the outer pages and bound by the same stitching that holds the pages. Sometimes heavy paper is folded to double thickness for a cover before stitching. Covers for mechanical binding are single sheets, front and back, and so two different stocks can be used.

Note that cover stock has a different basic size than book stock. This is to allow the cover to extend beyond the pages for protection.

The choice of binding and cover stock should be made on a purely functional basis. Normally it would be foolish to case-bind an advertising piece. This has been done, though, when the value of making an impression outweighed the extra cost. It would not be wise to side stitch a dictionary; outer pages would be torn off, inner pages would have deeply hidden inside margins.

The choice of cover material is also based on function. Cookbooks and reference books used in a garage must be impervious to grease. Dark covers

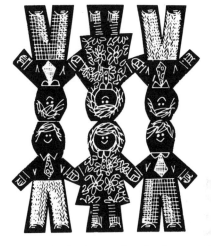

DIE CUTTING produced the paper dolls above. On the inside is a most effective advertisement for a back-to-school promotion.

More conventional—and considerably older—is the jointed doll below. Paper dolls were first made in France in the early 1700's. The *pantin* was a card on

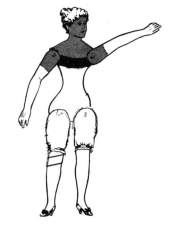

which was printed the "exploded" figure of a child. The parts were cut out and joined to make a doll from 12 to 15 inches tall.

In 1790, the English developed the *fashion doll*. A die-cut cardboard figure, dressed in under-linen and corset, was provided with a complete paper wardrobe which fastened to the torso by means of folded-over tabs.

Even in today's sophisticated age when three-dimensional dolls not only speak but perform more metabolic functions, paper dolls are a favorite toy.

hide black fingerprints. Fine books deserve handsome bindings.

With the extremely wide selection of cover stocks, it is possible to create the important first impression and to carry out the basic feeling of the contents. In color, covers can contrast or blend with the paper or ink inside. A catalogue for a sporting goods dealer can resemble wood so closely it is often difficult to detect the difference. For a jeweler, a cover can simulate mother-of-pearl or gold.

Sometimes unusual materials can make covers. Wallpaper is often striking. Metal foil or fabric is often usable. (Aluminum foil is pasted on paper, on one or both sides, and gives striking effects. Special techniques must be used to print on this metal but the end result is often well worth the extra effort.) Genuine wood or veneer, sand- or emery-paper or -cloth, butcher or gift-wrapping paper, anything which combines flexibility and durability can be used for covers.

Cutting, folding, and binding is the packaging of printing. It is as important as packaging is to the purveyor of soap powder, soft drinks, or diamonds. Precious stones are not sold in kraft bags; good printing should not be presented to the reader in any way other than that which will make the message more easy, convenient, and pleasurable to read.

The bindery is an important ally to the graphic designer; he should learn its potentials well.

SUGGESTED READINGS

Groneman, Chris. *General Bookbinding.* New York: Taplinger Publisher Co., Inc., 1958.

Stanley, Thomas Blaine. *The Technique of Advertising Production.* Englewood Cliffs, N.J.: Prentice-Hall, Inc., 1954.

Layout was no problem to the old country printer. He had an axiom that handled the situation nicely, thank you: "When in doubt, set it in Cheltenham and center it."

Today layout is recognized as being far too important to be produced by this old home recipe.

Layout is the disposition of various printing elements—display and body type, illustrations and ornamentation, white space—in a pattern that is pleasant and attractive to the eye and that makes reading easy and convenient. It is an art, just as much as the disposition of oil paints on canvas or sounds upon human eardrums is an art. But it can be learned; individuals this side of genius have been taught to paint a picture or compose a singable tune.

A good layout should be *organic;* it must be *functional;* it must be *invisible.*

Organic layout "grows" from the materials the designer has to work with. As he looks at the type, headlines, and art that must be used, these elements will often "make themselves up." Of course, it is not that easy, otherwise we could develop a layout machine and we would all be out of work. But as the trained eye of a layout man first sees his materials, it will tell him almost unconsciously how these elements should be arranged in relation to each other. This last phrase must be stressed. A picture that would occupy 80 per cent of a page with a certain head and block of type might be reduced to a tiny rectangle if combined with other pictures or with a different message to convey.

Functional layout is layout that is studiedly utilized to further the primary job of all printing: carrying a message. Anything that the layout can do to lift the message off the page, through the reader's eye and mind, and into his comprehension is functional. Anything that layout does to impede this flow of information is certainly nonfunctional and, in the graphic arts, most nonfunctional elements are automatically malfunctional. Anything that does not speed reading usually impedes it.

A good layout should be invisible. The reader

19

Layout

Patterns to Serve the Reading Eye

should never be aware of the layout. As soon as he is conscious of it, his attention is distracted from the message. In all arts invisibility is important. When you look at a Corot painting, you want to see the picture, not an S-pattern or thrusting diagonals. When you listen to a *Brandenburg Concerto* you want to absorb the total music, not count off the beats or become aware that now the bassoon has modulated to a new key.

If we accept the yardstick of functionalism, we must first determine the job of layout.

First, it must attract or hold attention. There is a great difference between the function of the dust jacket on a book, its title page, and its 102nd page. The cover must compete for attention against many other gay designs that decorate other books on a shelf. The title page must attract the browser, give him a foretaste of the flavor of the book. Inside pages need not attract attention, but they must hold it.

Layout must make the message easy to read. All the techniques of readability talked about in Chapter 7 must be put into practice. Ink and the paper must give maximum legibility. Type blocks must be given enough elbow room. It is especially important to insulate them against other elements which might dilute or absorb all the reader's attention.

Layout must arrange our elements so that the reader can consider and digest each one in a logical progression. Reading is no longer convenient if the reader must ask himself, "Where do I start reading?" or "Well, I've read this; where do I go from here?" Then danger rears its ugly head; the reader may decide to dispense with this chore, and our printing becomes useless—worse than useless, in fact, because it has become an immoral economic waste, a form of creative "featherbedding."

Finally, layout must make reading satisfying. This does not mean that the reader must obtain conscious sensual satisfaction or exclaim between paragraphs, like the fun-loving Rover Boy, "What a jolly good time!" But the process of reading must be pleasant, and the reader must derive some satis-

---

you are cordially invited

TO THE

OPEN ☆
☆HOUSE

AT OUR *NEW* PLANT,

35th and Capitol Drive
in Springfield Heights

JANUARY 22   4:30 - 7:00 P.M.

---

you are
cordially
invited
to the

OPEN HOUSE

at our new plant,

35th and Capitol Drive
in Springfield Heights

4:30-7:00 p.m.
January 22

SIMPLICITY IS THE KEY to any good layout. The one at the top is distracting. Five different type faces are used and one of them —NEW—is staggered. There are no common axes for alignment and the top line is too far from the next element.

In the revision, only one typeface has been used. Most of the elements align on a common left-hand margin and the eye flows from one line to the next in easy rhythm.

faction, however unconscious, from the page as well as from the content. A child can gain this satisfaction from the drawings in a Dr. Seuss book, the attorney from the information he receives from a stark page in a law book. But this satisfaction, or realization of reward, must be present—or else the reader will not be.

The layout man has a big job on his hands. Possible solutions are endless.

Give the same raw material to a dozen layout men and you will get a dozen different layouts, just as the same scene would be rendered differently by El Greco, Utrillo, and Grandma Moses.

If the designers are all of equal talent, it will be impossible to say, "This is the best layout." All we can say is, "In my opinion, this will do the job best," or simply, "I like this one." For, just as the creation of art is subjective, so is its evaluation.

But a few elementary principles can be formulated that will enable us to discuss, evaluate, and create sound layouts.

Equipment

Before embarking on the creative aspects of layout, we should consider those that are purely mechanical. The tools of the layout man are important. The layout man should have adequate equipment, and it should be of good quality. The difference in initial cost may be marked but, amortized over many years and many jobs, it is wise economy to buy quality in the first place.

Some items are basic necessities—a drawing board, for instance. It should be of medium size and nonwarping. Most artists prefer to rest it against a table or desk at an angle; some prefer to work on it flat. A more elaborate table-type drawing stand may be convenient as progress or volume of work advances.

Thumbtacks should not be used for holding paper to the drawing board. After a few months the surface becomes so pitted that its usefulness is impaired or destroyed. *Masking tape* is best to hold your work.

A sturdy, accurate *T-square* and a right-angle *triangle* are essential to assure perfectly horizontal and perpendicular lines. *French curves* and 60-degree triangles have many uses.

Writing tools are essential and pencils are the foremost among them. Soft lead, in the B grade, is practical. Drawing pens should be at hand in good assortment, varying from the delicate *crowquill* to the broadest *Speedball*. The latter are used in C shapes, broad and narrow, for Roman lettering and in *B*, ball, for monotonal letters.

Brushes are used constantly; *flats*, corresponding to C Speedballs, are good for laying in large areas; *brights*, sharply pointed, execute finest detail.

Black India ink is the classic medium.

For color, *opaque tempera, showcard paints*, are ideal. Their range of color is wide and they mix easily to produce new ones. They can be used in ruling pens and compasses when properly diluted.

Some designers use colored pencils, colored India inks, or *pastel crayons*. In the latter case, a clear *fixative* must be used. In the popular "bomb" cans it comes in a variety of finishes.

Erasers, alas, are a human necessity. Two kinds are generally employed: *art gum* is useful for cleaning large areas; *plastic rubber* can be delicately manipulated.

Tracing paper is most popular for it is easy to use to trace the exact outline of drawings, trademarks, or other elements. If a layout is generally satisfactory, but some element must be changed, tracing paper can be overlayed and units easily shifted, resized, or changed. By rubbing the reverse of the paper with a soft graphite pencil, then tracing on the face with a sharp pencil, it is easy to transfer any element.

A wide assortment of printing papers of various colors, textures, and weights should always be at hand, and the designer must learn to work on all of them. Many paper manufacturers prepare portfolios of their various products for use by layout men.

Rubber cement is indispensable. When one coat

is applied, paper may easily be lifted and shifted. When both the paper and the surface on which it is to be mounted are coated with cement and it is allowed to dry almost completely, an absolutely permanent bond is effected.

A pair of good scissors, at least 6 inches long, is a constant necessity and razor blades are good for straight cuts. Never use a blade against a triangle, T-square, or other valuable instrument; it will nick even hard metal. Instead, cut against the metal ferrule of a cheap ruler. Many designers use single-edged razor blades without a handle. This can result in cut fingers; they heal—but bloodstains can ruin a layout!

The artist's "reference library" consists of type specimen books or sheets, especially from the printer with whom he works most often. Specimen sheets showing a variety of halftone screens, Ben Day tints, Zip-a-Tone, Artype, and ink catalogues should be within arm's reach.

The *morgue,* or clipping library, is irreverently called the *swipe file.* This consists of clippings or specimens of printed matter, filed in as casual or elaborate a system as the designer desires or finds time to do. The swipe file should contain examples of all media of original art and all engraving styles.

Catalogues are good morgues themselves, especially those for merchandise with which the designer must work frequently. A two-drawer filing cabinet is the most convenient storage place. As they are desk high, they make a handy *taboret,* a table alongside a drawing board for holding tools and materials.

Some of the finest layouts have been done with a ballpoint pen on scrap paper. The beginning designer really needs only paper, a pencil, and a straight edge. Other tools need not be added until the need arises, or when the frequency of a task makes it impractical to make-do with a tool that is adequate but inefficient.

Dummies

With this hand he can lift the world

MAGAZINES GIVE PEOPLE IDEAS

THUMBNAILS, shown same size, preceded the designing of the ad, which was 10 X 14 inches in actual size. The starred one was the basis of the finished layout.

The layout man's first efforts are *thumbnail sketches*. These are small—1 × 2 inches can visualize a 24-sheet poster—and are hastily drawn. They are "notes written in shorthand."

One of the most useful exercises in learning layout is to make thumbnails of all the ads or pages in a magazine, newspaper, or book. As hand and eye are trained to reduce a finished layout to a quick sketch, they are also trained in the reverse of this process, visualizing the completed layout from a few hasty notes.

Dozens of thumbnails will be scribbled as the designer experiments with patterns. This is an essential process, for ideas proliferate in a chain reaction; the more thumbnails he makes, the more possibilities the designer visualizes.

When he has arrived at a satisfactory one, the designer expands upon the thumbnail in a *rough*. This is also "shorthand, but written in complete sentences." The rough is the same size as the finished job. While it is not sloppy or amateurish, the rough is casual, with an incisive, quick character.

Thumbnails are sketched on anything from the backs of old envelopes to restaurant tablecloths. Roughs are done on tracing paper, bond, or ledger.

Illustrations are merely sketched, but they indicate the tonal value. Headlines, too, must show the weight of the type although the letterforms are not polished. Body type is suggested by parallel lines. Color is added by any convenient means; if there are large areas, such as backgrounds or panels, a piece of colored paper may be pasted on and lettered over.

As work progresses, refinements are added, and

by the time the third step—the *comprehensive dummy,* the *comp* or just the *dummy*—has been completed, it will be an accurate blueprint of the finished job. The comp has two purposes: (1) to show the printer exactly how to make up the form and (2) to show the client exactly how the finished job will look. It is the latter function that requires the most work.

Headlines are carefully drawn or traced. Tracing letters from specimen books or cards especially prepared for such use is another useful exercise. No other method teaches the eye to learn identifying characteristics of a type face as thoroughly, quickly, and painlessly. Niceties of letterspacing become apparent and the hand is trained to swift deftness. The ability to trace letters is not as childish as it seems; it will pay good dividends in those cases where dummies must be very detailed.

Body type is indicated in several ways. Pairs of parallel horizontal lines or single wide pencil lines of varying density can show both texture and approximate point size. *Greeking* is simulating type by random assortments of straight and curved lines; it is used for both body and head type. Greeking is available as Copy Block by Craftype and in other shading sheet material in various "point sizes." If art is already available, *Photostats* will be made to the desired size and mounted.

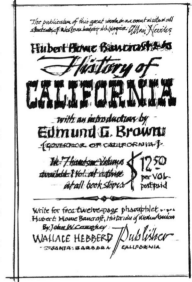

ROUGH DUMMY for an all-type layout shows great spontaneity of the designer, Raymond DaBoll. Although obviously done in haste, the letterforms are authoritatively shown and the flavor of the type is successfully transmitted.

COMPREHENSIVE DUMMY is same size as the finished piece. Illustrations are exact in size and show most detail of the finished art. The headline is a Photostat of very informal calligraphy and copy blocks are indicated by Copy Block by Craftint.

If this were to be done in color, hues would be indicated by crayon, ink, tempera paint or color sheets.

SLICK COMPREHENSIVE carries detail much further than in a regular comp. Here the arrows, in black, red, and brown, are shown by color sheets. The headline is transfer type and the body and signature are Copy Block. The original was in the same size the ad would appear, 8 X 11 inches. This was done by John Mehall, a typographic designer.

Reverses are shown in the negative stats. Colors are applied in exact chroma and intensity.

If the art work has not yet been done, the layout man may produce a miniature of such high quality that the casual observer may think that it is the finished job. When the author of this book directed advertising for a manufacturing company, he often used art from the comp or even the rough because it had a spontaneity that was sometimes lost in a picture more painstakingly drawn.

The comp should be prepared for the use to which it will be put. If it is an in-plant job—the dummy of a newspaper page, for instance—it can be sketchy, but should be accurate, of course. If it is for a client, he is the determining factor. An old customer may be willing to entrust details to the taste and skill of the designer. A new customer, or a prospective one unfamiliar with your work or who must be impressed, will receive an extremely high-gloss comp. In the case of a booklet, it will be prepared on the same cover and inside stock as will be used in printing. Sometimes more than one comp must be prepared—if the elevator operator, the vice-president's mother-in-law, and the stock clerk must approve, as happens in too many companies. Often additional comps are assembled from photocopies, if various details must be checked by different departments.

Photocopying is valuable when the same basic layout or material is to be used in different forms. A newspaper ad may be revised for magazine use, as the cover or page in a catalogue, as a direct-mail piece, or a poster.

The *mechanical* is an exact replica of the finished piece. Usually the same size as the final job—sometimes larger, but never smaller—the mechanical may be used as copy for making plates or as a guide to assembling an engraving, form, or negative which has been made in several units for reduction or special effects.

Making layouts and dummies is like playing golf: you can learn the basic principles in an afternoon, then spend the rest of your life mastering details.

This discussion does not pretend to cover everything a layout man must know about his craft, but it is adequate as a sound foundation.

Design

Having given attention to those mechanical or technical aspects of layout work that can be well defined, let us embark now into an aspect which defies such specificity—the creative.

Every creator has his own method and often it is not apparent even to him. There must be a period of gestation, a subconscious process that goes on while the designer works on another job, on his thumbnails, or just plays poker or sleeps. A serendipitous journey through the swipe file often switches on the light of a bright idea. This is a process that must be developed, not taught.

The following steps may be taken as a point of departure only. They are benchmarks from which each individual must blaze his own trail of creativity.

The designer should read the copy carefully to obtain the over-all impression of the piece. Is it

ROUGH DUMMY (left) was converted into the finished layout (right). Note how slight are the changes that were made in the final art. (Courtesy Arthur L. Koop, Jr., the designer)

corona builds reader traffic

B *1* D

B' = determined by designer

B'

$C' = \frac{1}{2}B$

C'

A

Gutter

A'

A' = ⅛ page width
$C' = A' + \frac{1}{6}A'$
$D' = C' + 2$ picas

C'

D'

2

Example 8. MARGINS may be established by mathematical formula.

calm, as the title page of a book of poetry? Is it rugged and masculine, a catalogue for a manufacturer of road graders? Is it traditional, a program for the consecration of a bishop? Or dynamic and modern, to announce a new jet plane schedule?

Then he must decide whether the type or illustrations will dominate the layout. Is the art already at hand? Which pictures are musts? If art must be commissioned, will delicate pen-and-ink or a bold oil painting best harmonize with the general tone—and aid communication? Type faces, colors, and paper will be chosen the same way.

Then the designer must decide on the size and shape. Often this has already been done. A client will tell the layout man to design an ad 5 columns wide by 17 inches deep, or a publisher will have decided on the size of the pages in a book. If the choice is the designer's, he weighs the factors of paper sizes and press capacities.

His proportions will usually be close to the *Golden Rectangle*. Its proportions were established by pragmatic artists centuries ago. By rule of thumb and their own aesthetic appreciation, they established its ratio as *one to the square root of two* (1:1.414). This has been modified to 3 × 5 (close enough to the mathematical 3 × 4.24 for all practical purposes). A *regular oblong*, 2 × 3, is often used.

Mathematical formulas developed from instinctive solutions include the *line of golden proportion*. This establishes that a single unit within an area is best displayed on a horizontal plane three-eighths of the whole height from the top. Book page margins can also be established by geometry. The first method allows the designer to establish the outside margin, B', himself, as in Example 8. One half of this distance, C', becomes the inside or *gutter* margin. At B and C perpendiculars are drawn and then the diagonal, AD, is drawn. Intersections with the verticals mark the top and bottom of the type area.

The second method is entirely mathematical. The gutter is one-eighth the width of the page, A'. The top margin is the same. The outer margin, C′, is A′ plus one-sixth; the foot, D′, is C′ plus 2 picas.

Having determined the size of the printed piece, the designer must choose between vertical or horizontal rectangles. The use of the piece is a determinant. We are used to vertical books and tend to read large masses or many pages most comfortably in this form. On the other hand, desk blotters or business cards are customarily used or read as horizontal units.

There may be shock value in using an unaccustomed shape, size, or axis. This should never be overlooked but must be used warily; too much shock may repel the reader and hamper communication.

Many publications require vertical composition in ads, restricting them to no shallower than a square.

If he decides on a horizontal rectangle, the designer soon finds he must subdivide the area in most cases, because his lines of type will usually be too long if they carry clear across. Or, if the type is large enough so that readability is not sacrificed by using them that wide, the resultant design is apt to be squat and stolid. There are exceptions, of course, but in most cases the vertical rectangle allows for more dynamic layouts.

Now the designer is ready to begin his composition. Because he appeals to the reader's eye, it is necessary to know a few things about eye movement in reading. From long habit, we look first at the upper left corner of any page or area, just as you looked first at that area on this page. We have been taught that this is the starting point for writing or reading and go there instinctively. There, in the *primary optical area* or *focal point*, we must place something attractive to the eye at first glance.

When you get to the lower right corner of this page you will automatically turn the page; you know that that area is the end. The eye keeps that goal in mind always and thus the basic movement is a diagonal from top left to bottom right, the *terminal area*. The eye does not follow this line like

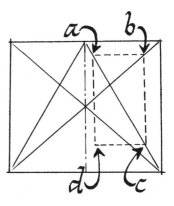

MARGINS MAY BE DETERMINED by this geometric method, but only if the page is—or is nearly— the Golden Rectangle.

Diagonals are drawn for both the double spread and for each page. The inner, gutter margin is arbitrarily fixed by the designer and drawn to intersect with the page diagonal at *a*. From there the top margin is drawn till it hits the diagonal of the spread at *b*.

From *b* a vertical is drawn to hit the page diagonal at *c*. The line *cd* marks the bottom margin.

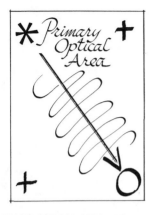

PRIMARY OPTICAL AREA—POA— is the top left corner. The instinctive path of the reading eye is from this starting point, marked by the asterisk, to the terminal area, marked by the circle in the lower right. The opposite areas are the *fallow corners*, marked by the plus signs. The swirling lines indicate how the eye courses over the page; it rarely moves in a straight line of the reading diagonal.

NEWSPAPER PAGE LAYOUT seeks to place a strong attention

a honey-laden bee but more like a beagle puppy in the park. It courses back and forth—the more flowing the loops, the easier the eye is working— but always toward the goal.

That pull toward the terminal area is so strong and so constant that we might liken it to that of gravity. While we can modify it, we can't ever eliminate it. We must modify it at least by placing strong optical magnets in the *fallow corners*, top right and lower left.

The eye always wants to move downward. To attract it by an appealing element, and then to expect the eye to backtrack and read something higher on the page is just not understanding human nature. If the eye should back up, it has been subjected to undue effort and irritation and the result is apt to be that the eye will stop reading before the whole page or area has been covered.

The eye, while small and delicate, is willful. It can be coaxed but it cannot be forced. It is susceptible to suggestion, and so designers try to cajole and guide it into covering all parts of a layout. Suggestions may be obvious: an arrow or pointing finger. They may be less apparent: the direction of an automobile or of fork tines, the gaze of a model in a photograph. Or they may be very subtle: the shape of a word or the sweep of a hilltop in a drawing.

A layout is a whole network of lines that the eye may subconsciously follow. The designer must make sure that the dominant lines lead the eye where he wants it to go. This is the *rhythm* a designer seeks in his layout.

Just as these suggestions can entice the eye to a path the designer wants it to follow, so they may distract him in other, undesirable directions. The eye will follow any motion, real or implied. If a layout shows a child running with his dog, the eye will follow the projected path of the youngster. The layout man must make sure that this projection does not lead the reader right off the page or out of the printing area. Even motion implied as gently as that of a human profile or the direction of his gaze can urge the eye off the page. That is the why of an axiom: pictures should always face into the page or composition.

Any nonparallel lines that would eventually meet to form an arrowhead will carry the eye in that direction, even if the lines would have to be continued far beyond the boundaries of our layout before meeting.

An excellent means for training your eye to detect these subtle lines of direction is to draw them, with heavy or grease pencil, on advertisements or other layouts. As you learn to detect these "magnetic forces," you will also learn to harness them to your own needs.

There are many signposts that can be erected along the path to direct the eye. Initial letters are good. Decorative *paragraph openers* are good guideposts; most common is the *bullet* or large period.

The layout must arrange each element so that the eye will reach it in logical progression. There must be distinct but unobtrusive order and neatness; the eye does not enjoy a jumbled page any more than we like a cluttered room. The designer may well heed the Japanese as they furnish a room: they use little furniture and few ornamental objects, because in simplicity is the neatness we all enjoy. So typographic layouts should be simplified. For another exercise, take an ad or printed piece and, with white poster paint, eliminate as many details as you can, borders, ornaments, rules. It is surprising how much can be taken out of a layout without loss.

Always apply to every element in a layout the criterion of functionalism: does this do a good job? If not, throw it out.

As the layout man plans his patterns to attract the reading eye and make its task lighter, he uses contrast to give it pleasure. Here we may draw an analogy from music. Think of the opening four notes of Beethoven's *Fifth Symphony*. It opens with three authoritative G's and then, just as the ear has grasped the pattern, it sings out with a startling E-flat. To mix metaphors, it is like the boxer who jabs three times with a left and then crosses with a right.

Contrast gives emphasis that perks the ears and

compellor in the POA. Note how the fallow corners and the terminal area are anchored by strong display elements and how placement of the headlines accentuates the reading diagonal.

LINES OF FORCE are within almost every picture. Here they are indicated by arrows. Note how each one is used to direct the reading eye into essential type elements.

perks the eyes. It may come from shape, size, or tone of any elements. It may be a big picture breaking forth from a group of smaller ones. It may be an Italic in the midst of a forum of Romans. It may be a vertical element rearing among horizontal ones.

When contrast is used, it must be marked. You cannot contrast Caslon with a Garamond; a 3×5 picture is little contrast against a $3\frac{1}{4} \times 4\frac{1}{4}$.

Remember that all emphasis is no emphasis. Designers who use more and more black type find their message no longer carries; typographically it is the boy crying "Wolf!"

Layouts may be categorized as *formal balance* or *symmetrical,* and *informal balance,* also called *occult* (heavens knows why) or *dynamic balance.*

In symmetrical layout, everything balances on a vertical axis down the middle of the page. (For the rest of this discussion, we shall refer to the "page" as any area the layout man has to work with, even a business card or an ad which will be only part of the whole newspaper or magazine page.) In its simplest form it follows the old printshop dictum that opened this chapter: Center everything.

A trifle more complex is the layout in which identical cuts or type masses are mathematically balanced against each other. Occasionally a fillip of

SYMMETRICAL LAYOUTS may be centered, left; be made of two vertical mirrored forms, center; or be diagonally mirrored as at right.

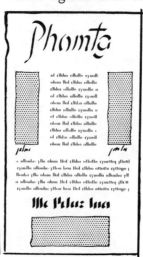

contrast may be added by some element that does not balance mathematically but does balance optically.

Formal layout has the dignity and stability that its name indicates. That stability is its main weakness; such layout is far too static for many needs. But symmetrical layout is ideal to express formality —as in wedding invitations; dignity—as in documents or the pages of a Bible; stability—as in an advertisement for a bank or a funeral home.

Dignity need not equate with stodginess and, while formal layout is solid, it need not be stolid. Its simplicity pleases the eye.

Informal layout balances its elements in a less rigid manner. The designer should imagine a pivot at the *optical center* of the page, about one-tenth the height of the page above the mathematical center. Then he should envision each element as having physical as well as optical weight. He pastes these onto an imaginary board that hangs on this pivot in such a way that the board hangs almost, but not quite, straight up and down.

Elements balance like children on a seesaw; a fat little fellow has to get close to the bar to balance his skinny chum at the end of the board. But in this case, we do more than merely balance two children against each other—we scatter many of them around in the cars of a Ferris wheel.

If you will take another look at your favorite picture, physically or by mind's eye, you will undoubtedly discover that it does not quite "hang straight." There will be some diagonal movement that takes it off the rigid 90 degrees. A good example is the portrait photographer who poses his subject or prints or crops the picture so the head or torso tilts a little. This slight imbalance is pleasing to the eye; it suggests interest and motion. This the designer should seek in most of his layouts.

Tall and thin pictures tend to swing the layout away from the pivot more than square or flat pictures. Dark backgrounds outweigh light ones; square halftones are heavier than silhouettes. Boldface outweighs lightface, and Condensed or Ex-

SYMMETRICAL LAYOUT in a distinguished form is this handlettered presentation plaque for a library wall. Bruce Rogers truly was—as the copy puts it—a "distinguished typographical artist & book designer."

Note the formality of "handlettering" with its "drawn" forms as compared to the freer forms of calligraphy which is basically "written" by the artist.

BRUCE ROGERS
Distinguished
Typographical Artist
& Book Designer

CLASS OF 1890

tended weigh more than the normal letterform. Ultimately, the designer's eye must determine when all elements are in balance; this comes from trained or experienced instinct. A picture with strong motion will tilt the board in the direction of that motion no matter what its tonal weight may be.

While you do not want your layout to stand as stiffly erect as a cigar-store Indian, neither do you want it to lean so far that it may fall on its face. It should be almost, but not entirely, perpendicular.

Within an already broad classification of informal balance, we establish subdivisions that are equally elastic; most layouts combine one, or even several, characteristics of these groups.

Classic layouts are those in patterns of composition that were well developed by the great artists of centuries ago. They are not necessarily stilted. Durer's illustrations of Dante's *Inferno* are eminently classic in composition; they are certainly not stodgy.

The most famous of the classic patterns is the S or *reverse S*. The latter is extremely useful; it begins at the primary optical area and carries the eye, not only down the basic diagonal, but also into the opposite corners in the flowing curves that the eye loves. The *pyramidal* pattern of Da Vinci's *Mona Lisa* lends itself well to typographic layouts as does the reverse L of Whistler's portrait of his mother.

Geometric layout is an extension of the classic forms. It uses pictures or blocks of type to define geometric shapes more definitely than the classicists did. The simplest is to *anchor the corners*, place a strong element in each one. Common patterns are the *triangle*, facing up or down; a *T, U, Y,* or *L,* facing in any direction. *Bands—braces* or *brackets* —can run vertically or horizontally. A pair of *L's*

CLASSIC PATTERNS for layouts are suggested here. At the top is a reverse-S pattern. The middle one is a triangle. The lower one is either an L or a C, depending on how heavy the headline is made.

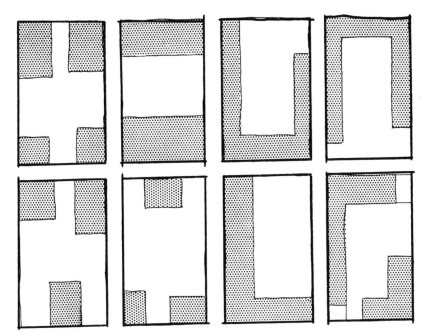

can be arranged like hands to hold other elements.

Rectangular layouts are "the poor man's Mondrian paintings." Here a large area is broken up into smaller units of varying shape and size and harmoniously related to each other. Sometimes these areas are defined, boldly or delicately, with rules or decorative border material. Sometimes, they are merely suggested.

Dutch artist Piet Mondrian's paintings are amazingly, deceptively simple. It is only when you attempt his design style that you realize the genuine artistry and delicate manipulation of areas that is involved. There is only one piece of advice that can be formulated for these layouts: subdivision of areas should never be obvious; no line should be drawn at the half-, quarter-, or third-way mark. No area should be a third, quarter, or half of the whole, and none should be exactly the dimensions of another. Beyond that, the designer's experience and discernment must stand all alone.

Rectangular layout takes a long while to master. But long before the designer produces masterpieces he can create functional and pleasing layouts by this method.

GEOMETRIC LAYOUTS are done by placing pictures in patterns similar to the ones shown here.

RECTANGULAR LAYOUTS—also called Mondrian—are a version of geometric ones. This advertisement of United States Lines—through whose courtesy it is used here—shows application of the principle.

VERTICAL AXIS layouts are suggested here. The headline treatment below is an interesting variation that not only suggests the vertical axis but makes it strongly visible.

The

and

Bill
Dwiggins

EXPANDED LAYOUT uses suggestion to please the reading eye. As the rectangle formed by the type is expanded by the projecting picture, the whole area of the layout seems to grow larger.

The picture should bleed to the margins toward which the lines of force move. This is an exception to the axiom that pictures should face into the page or layout.

A variation is the *modular* or *Swiss grid system,* a good example of functional design. Only a part of the philosophy is the basic method of dividing the "page" into grids and playing dark against white masses. Unlike the Mondrians, the grids do divide areas into obvious fractions. This is too fascinating a subject to dismiss in one paragraph and the reader is strongly urged to read some of the excellent books about it.

The *vertical axis* layout is sometimes called the *totem pole* or *Christmas tree* to distinguish it from symmetrical balance; which is also on a perpendicular. The totem pole is not symmetrical; rarely, if ever, does the axis run along the center of the page. Projecting from the axis—which is usually imaginary but can be defined—are lines and blocks of type. Those at the left of the axis are flush right; those on the other side are flush left. Their inner margins, then, align along the axis; their outer margins may be ragged and, certainly, the margins of the whole layout are ragged, for the projections are usually deliberately made of varying length.

The *oblique axis* is a variation of the totem pole. In one form, the entire layout is tilted. This is poor; the eye is accustomed to reading on horizontal planes and may become irritated by having to establish a new horizon. This danger can be mini-

mized by tilting the top only between 30 and 40 degrees to the left. This is approximately the angle at which paper is held in writing, and the reader is not as aware of the angle as he would be if he had to cock his head to the right.

The danger of irritation is increased when only some elements of a layout are tilted. Varying horizons discomfort the eye.

The reader can be given the convenience of reading on the accustomed plane if the oblique axis is achieved by stepping type down to create a diagonal block but keeping each line horizontal.

Expanded layouts create an optical illusion that enlarges the layout area.

Within the entire area of the layout, a smaller rectangle is drawn to leave a generous frame of white. The rectangle is well filled to define it sharply. Then a large picture breaks out of this area to touch one or two sides of the outer edge of the layout. The feeling of motion expands the entire layout and makes it appear larger. Because the thrust of the picture shifts considerable weight with it, other display elements must be placed to make the composition hang almost straight.

A large headline can expand a layout but far less effectively than a picture does.

Connotative patterns are also called *jazz layouts*, because they take their method from the Dixieland

OBLIQUE AXIS LAYOUTS in three variations. The left one runs all the type, body and head, at an angle. Tilting to the left is the best method, for that's the way the right-hander tilts a piece of paper when he writes . . . or, to a lesser degree, when he reads.

In the center example only the body block is tilted. This is less than desirable because now there are two horizontal axes to which the reader must orient himself.

On the right example all elements are horizontal. Body type is *stepped down* to create the diagonal effect. If the indent for each line is the same as for all preceding ones, the eye unconsciously "sees" a diagonal axis of orientation to which it will return automatically and with ease.

Notice how headlines are greeked.

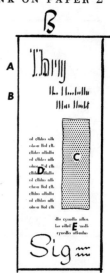

Example 9. JAZZ LAYOUT principles are demonstrated in these diagrams.

jazz band. The band plays a chorus or two of a familiar melody to establish it in the listener's mind. Then each soloist embroiders a harmonic pattern around the now unplayed melody. His music line may approach the melody but never follows it exactly. So the listener supplies the "lead" and the soloist the "tenor."

In a jazz layout, the pattern is suggested but never totally defined. Again a rectangle is drawn within the area of the layout to provide proper framing. (This technique should be used with any layout; the frame of white space is as important as the mat on a watercolor. The frame is not the same width all around. Tops and sides are equal; the bottom is 50 per cent wider.) Now he alludes to the rectangle by suggesting each of its four sides by one or more elements. One element may suggest more than one side, but usually no more than two.

The principle is demonstrated in Example 9. In Sketch A, a picture (A) defines the top and left margin. The headline (B) and a block of type (D) mark the right; another type block (C), the left again, while a shallow illustration (E) suggests the bottom margin. In Sketch B, the principle is used for a tall composition. Now the top is defined by a line of display type (A) and the right margin by a subhead (B), a type block (E), and a cut (C).

Another mass of type (D) establishes the left margin, while the signature sets the bottom and both side margins.

The most frequently seen advertising layout is called *Ayers No. 1*. Named for the first advertising agency in the world, the layout well demonstrates the axiom: *Pictures above type*. The illustration is at the top of the layout, then the headline, body block, and signature. There are countless variations but each one is good in that it places each element exactly where it will be read pleasantly and effectively.

In any informal layout, the *orientation system—* also called the *buddy* or *no-orphan—*may be used to insure a sense of orderliness. We have discussed

AYERS NO. 1 is a favorite pattern for advertising layouts. These four—all typical—were only a few of the many found in a single issue of *Newsweek* magazine.

The GIANT-KILLER ad is the conventional one. The picture bleeds and the layout is symmetrical. The ad is black-and-white.

The NOVA SCOTIA ad is also symmetrical; the shape of the map at the right is balanced by the ragged-left setting alongside it. The picture is four-color process; the map, spot color in tans and blue. The name of the province and its flag are in blue.

CONSOLIDATED PAPERS gets informal balance by playing the flush-left head against the trademark. While the circular picture is centered, the figure is to the left of its vertical axis, thus adding weight to the headline as well as giving room for the action of the golf swing.

The HEART FUND is interesting. In the big black mass appear the musical notes for a trill. In the lower left is the "headline": *You're Whistling in the Dark . . .* which reads right into the positive type of the copy block.

These ads, which are used by the courtesy of the advertisers, show only four of the almost countless variations of the Ayers pattern.

292 on left, INK ON PAPER 2 on right.

how this quality puts the eye at ease and makes it more comfortable to read a layout. The eye wants a definite, even if most unobtrusive, orientation point for every element, the *axis of orientation,* the *A/O*. It constantly asks: "Why is this picture (or headline or block) here instead of somewhere else?" If the designer cannot answer this question—even though it is rarely articulated—his layout has a dangerous weakness.

By this orientation system, every element is placed at some logical reference point vertically and/or horizontally. Each element has a companion piece, a buddy, just as a swimmer has at a Boy Scout camp. No element stands alone, hence no orphans.

Look at Example 10, a layout for a newspaper ad. This is the kind of layout that often consists of many different elements, each of which must have its own readership yet be integrated with all others.

The dominant feature is a large picture of the product (*A*), a new sailboat. To position it, there are three basic orientation points: flush left or right (on the white frame, not the outer edge of the layout), or centered. Let's center it. The headline (*B*) can also be placed at any of these three benchmarks, and for this demonstration it is placed flush left. Now comes a copy block (*C*); it, too, can go to any one of the three basic points, but now two new orientations are possible; it may align to the right or left of the end of either line of the head. Here it has been lined up flush right. The price (*D*), a separate element because of its size, also aligns at the right.

Two smaller pictures (*E*) and (*F*), show close-

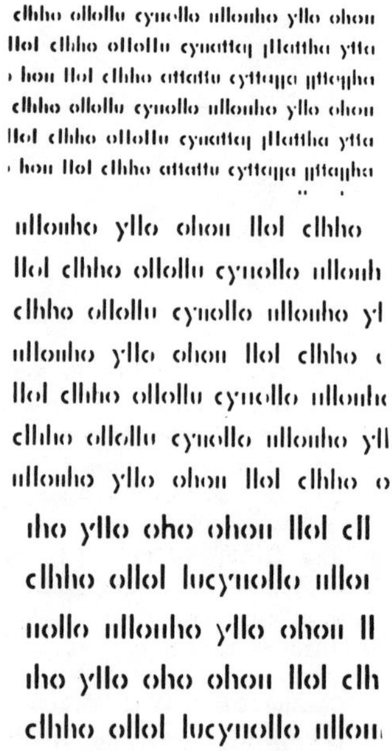

GREEKING shows the texture of a block of body type without distracting the reader by its often inappropriate verbal content. Three sizes of Copy Block, on self-adhesive plastic, are shown above.

Below greeking is done by pencil. The size of the proposed type and/or its approximate texture must be suggested.

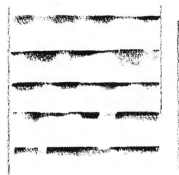

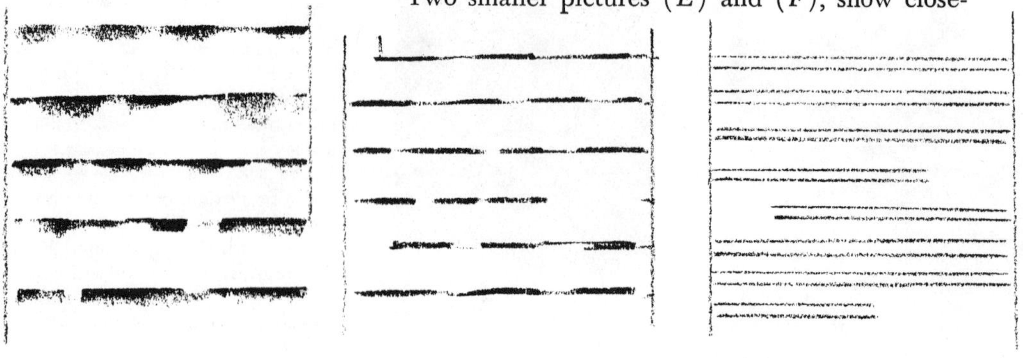

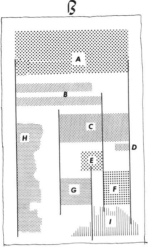

ups of optional equipment which is described in (G). Picture F is pushed flush right and E aligns with F at the left.

Now there are several possibilities for G. Every time a new element is placed, at least one new orientation point is gained, unless that element only marks previous ones. Having placed E and F, G can align with the left, right, or common axes, or with the top or bottom of either picture. Or it can align with the left margin of D, or, as here, with the left margin of C. It also lines with the bottom of F.

Most ads carry one or more subordinate items; in this case H is a whole list of sailing accessories, set flush left and aligning with the bottom of C. The signature I lines up with the right margin of G.

Now every element has a buddy: A, B, and H share the left margin; A, C, D, and F the right; E and F buddy up, so do C and G; I teams with G. Not even the bone stands alone. (Notice that this has created a jazz layout.) Also note that in Example 9 everything is paired with the exception of the shallow picture at the bottom of Sketch A, which is nonetheless well oriented by being so definitely centered.

The same orientation system is used in Example 11, a double spread for a magazine. Here the elements are more closely tied together by subject

Example 11. ORIENTED LAYOUT used for double spread of magazine.

matter and the problem is not as acute as in advertising layout. But the principle remains valid.

Again a large picture is centered (not because this is the only orientation but because it seems best). The subhead (*B*) buddies, not with the picture but with an element therein, the stripped-in head *The Bleeding Land*. A silhouetted picture (*H*) also aligns with an element in the top picture, a windmill. Another square halftone (*G*) aligns with the right margin of the subhead.

Columns of type are rather definitely oriented by the format of the magazine, but we buddy them vertically. Column *C* aligns at the bottom of the type page and *D* aligns at the top with column 1; *E* and *F* align with the bottom of the subhead, and *E* at the bottom with the shoulder of the standing figure; *F*, of course, ends to allow plenty of breathing room for the cut *H*.

In all layout systems, the initial placement of elements is just that—initial. Once the pattern has been established, elements must frequently be moved around a bit to create the optical effect that matches the mathematical effect we seek.

To demonstrate the optical manipulation required, let's look at this word:

MOTEL

The letters appear to be perfectly aligned, don't they? Yet if you lay a straight edge, or squint from the side along the bottom, you'll see that the designer has made the O and M extend below the baseline. He has deliberately drawn these letters in such a way that they seem, to the casual observer, to be lined up properly.

The shape or color of a typographic element or the lines of motion within it, which have been discussed, may create an optical center of gravity that does not coincide with its mathematical center. It must then be moved a trifle to place it in proper optical reference.

In Example 11 the weight of the top picture is toward the right. If it were not for the added weight of the surprinted head, we would probably have to push the cut a little to the left to make it look centered. The shapes of words affect optical balance. Look at these two:

thin
milt

Although both are centered, the top one leans to the left and the lower one to the right, because of the position of the ascenders.

All-cap words must frequently be *optically spaced* to make them look as if they are evenly spaced. Two straight lines, side by side, look closer together than a straight line—like the edge of an M—at the same distance from the outer segment of a circle, as O. The built-in white space under the shoulder of a T, below the diagonals of a W, or above those of an A must frequently be compen-

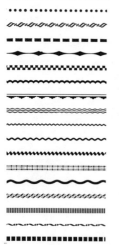

CARAVAN DECORATIONS were designed by William Addison Dwiggins and harmonize nicely with his Roman typefaces, notably Caledonia and Electra.

RULES are available in literally hundreds of varieties, both in hot metal and in cold, and in the form of stick-on, transfer, or tape.

The distinction between rules and borders is slight, but generally borders are heavier and often more intricate than rules.

sated for by adding extra space between the straight letters, as discussed in Chapter 5.

Only the designer's eye can tell him when, and how much, an element must be shifted to make it align properly.

The designer's eye may be all the authority he needs in any layout. To the question, "Why is this element here?" a perfectly valid answer might be, "I like it here," or "This is where it looks right to me."

The systems outlined here are useful only as points of departure. They are not insurance policies, but they are good icebreakers. When a designer sits at his drawing board and ideas are conspicuous by their absence (a state of affairs that, sadly, does sometimes occur), he can say, as he otherwise would not, "Now I shall design an expanded layout." Often he will soon abandon his first attempts, but the mental log jam has been broken. For the person whose layout sense has not been well developed, following these systems will assure him of workmanlike results even though they may lack the spark that makes a truly outstanding layout.

There are no "rules" in graphic design, even if they are usually referred to as such. If there were rules, they would be meant to be broken. But when you break a rule, do so deliberately for a well-thought-out reason.

Today's typography stresses functionalism and simplification. "Throw it out if it doesn't do a good job," the designer is told. "Simplify your layouts to the essentials." It is no wonder then that we hear an occasional wail, "Can't I use *any* ornamentation?"

Of course you can; much ornamentation is functional. Ornaments are an integral part of the type library and many great type designers have drawn ornaments that are happily wedded to the alphabet font of type. W. A. Dwiggins designed a pleasant repertoire of florets and decorations—his *Caravan series*—that go with his type faces as tonic goes with gin. Rudolf Ruzicka has eight handsome Fairfield decorations.

Since Gutenberg's Bible, decorative initials have

been grown like flowers on the vine of type. Today they are abundant and useful; so are paragraph marks, most designed with a specific font.

Borders and all rules except the straight line are ornaments.

How do we use them?

1. Ornamentation should be used with restraint.

2. It should be unobtrusive, felt more than seen.

3. It should never outweigh the type; it must harmonize with the other elements in weight, form, and feeling.

4. If color is used for ornaments, or solely as ornamentation, it must be chosen so the final chromatic ornament will be of the same tonal value as the basic black type. This often requires a heavier weight of ornament than if it were to be printed in black.

5. Ornamentation must be functional.

This statement is often unbelievable to the mind that stripped serifs off the Roman alphabet and porches off Victorian homes. But the initials in the Mazarin Bible do a job. And how better could one convey the flavor of the halcyon 1910's than to use a wide, ornate Jenson border or an intricate Cheltenham initial?

The function of ornament is to convey a mood, direct the eye, or to add to the pleasure of the reader. The initials on a Gutenberg Bible do all three. They create a mood of dignity, awe, and authority; they attract the reader to the primary optical area or to major starting points within the page; they certainly delight the eye with their exquisite detail and rich color. Modern ornamentation must serve at least one, and preferably more, of these basic functions.

Ornaments should never be used just to fill space!

A simple stick-up initial or a bullet to start a paragraph is ornamentation. The designer might choose the complex *Raffia* initial in type or have an artist hand-letter one. In any case, he can combine mechanics and aesthetics without loss of either one.

Borders must meet the same functional stand-

ORNAMENTS can be as classical as the pen flourishes at the top, as contemporary as the Christmas motifs, or as antique as the animals. All are in type form. The bottom design is a *floret*, a little more realistic than most ornaments of that category.

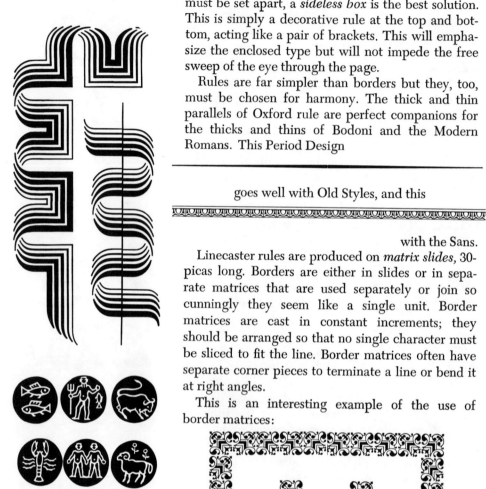

ards. Rarely is a border, other than a hairline, necessary to separate elements in a layout or on a page such as a newspaper's. If a portion of a layout must be set apart, a *sideless box* is the best solution. This is simply a decorative rule at the top and bottom, acting like a pair of brackets. This will emphasize the enclosed type but will not impede the free sweep of the eye through the page.

Rules are far simpler than borders but they, too, must be chosen for harmony. The thick and thin parallels of Oxford rule are perfect companions for the thicks and thins of Bodoni and the Modern Romans. This Period Design

goes well with Old Styles, and this

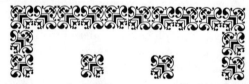

with the Sans.

Linecaster rules are produced on *matrix slides,* 30-picas long. Borders are either in slides or in separate matrices that are used separately or join so cunningly they seem like a single unit. Border matrices are cast in constant increments; they should be arranged so that no single character must be sliced to fit the line. Border matrices often have separate corner pieces to terminate a line or bend it at right angles.

This is an interesting example of the use of border matrices:

Notice how right-hand pieces and southpaws tie in so tightly that they seem to constitute a single linear unit and form neat corners that turn the design without apparent break. The eye doesn't discern that this border is made up of 14 matrices.

If all advice on layout had to be summed up in two words, it would be: Have fun!

All creative work is fun; it satisfies the soul even

ORNAMENTS in type form can add pleasure for the reader and make him more receptive to a printed message. The swirling borders at the top are Ombree. (Note how they harmonize with Ombree letters shown in Chapter 3.) The other specimens here are Troyer decorations; directly above are the ever-popular signs of the zodiac, whose acceptance has though it has its moments of travail. When the designer has had fun and satisfaction in creating a layout, the odds are long that the reader will gain fun and satisfaction, too. If he does, he is in perfect receptivity to information.

Book Design

Just as a football player must learn the fundamentals of tackling and blocking, so there are fundamental layouts that the designer must master. If he can solve these problems well, he can handle most others.

The first is designing a book. Some critics sneer that books are no longer designed today, they are canned, like sardines. The truth is not quite as dour. The number of books published every year, like the soaring total of the national budget, increases constantly. Some books are canned; many, fortunately, are designed. Often the finest designed books are of such limited circulation that they are overlooked in the flood of cheap paperbacks.

To understand book designing, we must know something about the anatomy of a book.

The first a prospective reader sees of most books is not part of the volume at all, it is the *dust jacket*, more commonly today, the *jacket*. This is, in effect, a poster. It must give the name of book, author, and publisher, and must convey, or at least suggest, the subject matter or flavor of its contents. The jacket has three parts: the *spine* or *backbone*, the *front cover*, and the *back cover* (often used as an advertising area). The jacket *flaps* (which fold around the cover) usually carry a synopsis of the book and biographical data on the author.

Rarely does the reader see more than one cover and the spine at one time, and usually only one cover. Thus each subdivision can be treated as a separate unit. Because the jacket folds over in a roll instead of a crease, there is no sharp definition of area, and there must be a physical blending of the two units as well as one of feeling and treatment.

The cover, or *case*, of the book itself, while often not seen until the dust jacket disintegrates, also identifies the book, author, and publisher. Defi-

reached new heights in the 1970's. The ones below are strongly calligraphic in style, showing the thicks and thins of the broadnibbed pen.

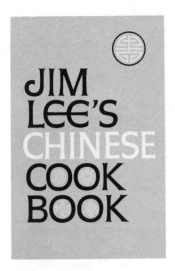

BOOK JACKETS
On an (appropriately) Chinese-red background, the key word is in reverse, the rest of title in black and ideograms within O's in yellow.

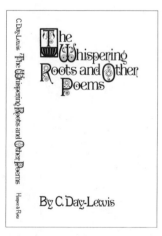

Cover design, though simple, is actually in four spot colors. Victorian type is black with ornamentation within bowls in blue, yellow, and green. Background is chaste white.

nitely, but subtly, it must contribute to the over-all impression which the author seeks to make.

A long-term debate about the direction of the printing—when it runs lengthwise on the spine—has apparently been settled, although there are still unreconstructed rebels. Such titles are now printed —in America but not in England—so that when the book stands on a shelf, the reader must tilt his head to the right to read the backbone. Or, to visualize better, when the book lies flat on the table and printing on the spine is right-side-up, the front cover will be visible.

The book itself consists of three parts: *preliminaries, text,* and *references.*

The first loose page in a book is half of the *end paper;* the other half is pasted on the cover. The first page on book stock is the *half-title page* or *bastard title.* This is unnumbered and carries only the name of the book. This is backed by a blank page, although sometimes a list of the author's other books is given here.

The *title page* is backed up by the page proclaiming the *copyright.* The *dedication,* if any, is the next right-hand page and it is backed with a blank.

Dedications were rare for a decade or two; they were too sentimental for a culture that allows such indulgence only on such peremptory occasions as Mother's Day and Christmas or others set by commercial calendars. They are coming back, though, a happy practice.

None of these pages has been numbered. When pages are numbered, remember that right-hand pages are always odd numbers. That means that Page 1 always faces a blank.

But before we find Arabic numerals, we may have Roman ones. The *preface* and/or *foreword* come after the dedication and are numbered in lowercase Romans. Thus, the first page of the preface is, in this case, *vii,* for it is the seventh page even though the first six are unnumbered.

The next right-hand page carries the *table of contents* and a printed page number or *folio.* A *list of illustrations,* if there is one, runs on the next right-hand page and, on the next odd number, the *intro-duction*. (The preface and introduction are written by the author; forewords by another person.)

All these pages are preliminaries. Not all of them appear in every book. Sometimes, to gain a vital page that would otherwise add a signature, two or more items may appear on the same page. Or, if a required signature contains blank pages, they may be interspersed in this section. Preliminaries may take through *page xiii* or more.

The first page of "reading," Chapter 1, begins on a right-hand page. It carries the chapter number and/or title. This is the first page designated by Arabic numerals. It starts with 1, even though it may be preceded by many preliminary pages of "front matter." It may start with page 3 if the main body of the book is introduced by a *part title* page.

Page 2 is the first to carry the *running head*. Outside the main type area, the name of the book runs on even pages, of the chapter on odd pages. If chapters are not titled, the name of the book runs on both pages. Folios—page numbers—usually occupy the same space line as running heads to save space and simplify make-up. They should be at the top of the page; this is the easiest area to uncover as the reader thumbs through to find his place where he had stopped reading.

Succeeding chapters may start on odd or even pages.

Reference pages contain one or more of the following: *appendix, supplement, bibliography, glossary, vocabulary, index.* They are usually set in smaller type than the text but should harmonize, and so are usually kept in the same face.

Occasionally a designer will use two pages for the title. This can be very effective, and one wonders why it is not a more frequent device. The title page is probably the most important page in the book; it sets the key in which the book is played.

The title page carries the name of the book—and perhaps some descriptive matter or subtitle; the name of the author—again with descriptive matter or identification if this is pertinent; a series title;

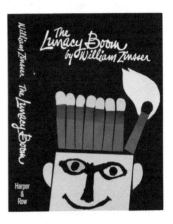

Carefree spirit of book is reflected in zany, casual drawing and informal Script. Background is black; face and match heads, red; matches, blue; flame, yellow, as is author's name in spine.

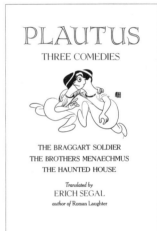

Classics need not be boring; earthy Plautus demonstrates that. Top two lines of type and author's name in green, rest of type black, against white background.

Design wraps around spine to back cover. Top panel is orange, lower one green, both have bright chroma. Type is black and brown; author's portrait in black-and-white. (All book jackets courtesy Harper & Row, Publishers)

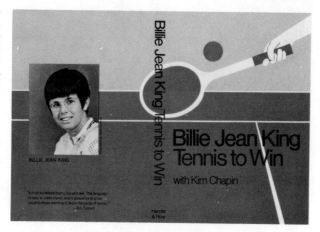

COLOPHONS, trademarks, of publishing houses trace their ancestry to guild marks of the earliest printers. Gutenberg had none, as far as we know. But his successors, Fust and Schoeffer, used the joined shields, above. Today this is the insignia of the International Club of Printing House Craftsmen.

From the top, and from the left, colophons shown below are those of Oklahoma University Press, World Publishing, Viking

name of collaborator or illustrator; previous books; the name and address of the publisher, and sometimes his *colophon* or trademark.

The colophon is the ancient mark with which every craftsman identified his product. (In silver we call it the hallmark.) Manutius made his, the anchor and dolphin, a respected symbol. Fust and Schoeffer, successors to, or grabbers of, Gutenberg, used two shields on a branch which today has become the insignia of the Printing House Craftsmen. Modern colophons are handsome—the torch of Harper & Row, the borzoi of Alfred Knopf, and the house of Random House being among the more distinctive.

The designer has more freedom with the title page than with any others, and more display material to work with. Restraint is therefore a laudable virtue. Type need not be the same family as that of the text, but it should either harmonize closely or contrast markedly.

Because white space represents such a large portion of the title page, its disposition is critical. Instead of dispersing type all over the page, those elements which logically go together should be grouped: the title and subtitle, or the title and author. The principle of rectangular make-up which we have discussed applies to the placement on title pages; no line or ornament should be placed to define halves, quarters, or thirds of the page. The mass of weight is always high, well above the optical center. By custom our eyes are used to this; title pages with the mass below the optical center disturb us.

Chapter headings are the bridge between the title page and text. They must harmonize with either or both. Their typography is purely organic. If chapters are only numbered, treatment is different from that of chapter titles. Decoration is often used, but it must be subdued. Often when there is little material for attractive display—and other times, too, of course—the head may be *sunken,* dropped to the line of golden proportion or even lower. Or the head may be at the top of the page, with the body beginning at the line. Distance from page-top to the first line of body type is the *sinkage.*

We have already discussed margination. The method of binding must be considered. If it is side stitching, for instance, we must widen the gutter because so much of it will be hidden in the binding.

On text pages the designer's major decisions involve determining type specification, running heads and folios, and treatment of illustrations. After that, pagination is mainly the compositor's job. The very finest books do not begin or end a page with a widow and copy is sometimes rewritten to eliminate short lines. In *trade editions* these niceties are often ignored, because of their additional cost and of the American theory that it is better to make a book a little less than perfect available to a great many people than to restrict, by price, a perfect book to a small audience.

In children's books especially, illustrations are an integral part of the page design. The illustrator works closely with the author or book designer and type is set and paginated around the art. As most such books are now printed by offset, the artist prepares the mechanical for each page—or at least specifies how it is to be arranged.

The growing popularity of *paperbacks* has opened a new field of book design. Here the cover combines the function and design of the jacket, the cover, and the title page. Such books do have title

Press, Oxford University Press (New York Division), Random House, and University of Texas Press.

CHAPTER HEADINGS are de-
signed with utmost simplicity.
Note different ways of handling
chapter titles and various depths
of sinkage. Only one uses rising
initial. Page for chapter titled
"1963" has type set at 16 picas,
all other pages in book are in
24-pica measure. (Courtesy Harper & Row, Publishers)

3

The Last Day of Love

In the morning he felt the need of action, action that would make
the happenings of the night irrevocable. Boats must be burned,
bonds cut. He ought to speak to Coldharbour, speak to Max, tell
them that he wanted to accept the American offer and was going
to resign from the firm. A shrinking from action went with this
desire for it. He felt that if he let the past come into contact with
the present it would destroy the world in which he was going to
live with Anna. It was with reluctance that after breakfast he
made a call to Max in Sarajevo, with relief that he learned that
all the lines were engaged. Afterward he looked for Anna, and
found her in the foyer with Briars, the Strong/Longs and half a
dozen others. The English contingent was in a rebellious and in-
harmonious mood. Fat Briars, no longer jolly, was their spokes-
man.
    "It's a bit much, don't you agree? One of the best hotels in the
place, or supposed to be. You would think they might make an
effort." He appealed directly to Gilbert.
    "What sort of effort?"
    "Eggs and bacon. Bacon and tomato. Something more than
the old bread and marmalade."
    "You must understand that they don't eat things of that kind

.1963   There was no hail and farewell when
President Lyndon Baines Johnson returned to Washington on November 22,
1963, with the body of his predecessor.
That night at Andrews, the air force base
outside Washington, one was hardly aware
of the new president as the coffin and pall-
bearers were lowered from Air Force One
on a fork-lift truck. Those who were there
must have known that power had passed
from John Fitzgerald Kennedy, that the
former vice-president was now the thirty-
sixth president of the United States, but
the grief and shock of the senseless assassi-
nation was such that there was no immediate recognition of his new authority.
Somehow it was still assumed to belong to
the dead man. Nor was there an assertion
of authority. Johnson stood back modestly
after being rudely thrust aside by some of
the Kennedy men. Eventually he went to
the microphones and said, "This is a sad
time for all people. We have suffered a loss
that cannot be weighed. For me it is a
deep personal tragedy. I will do my best.
That is all I can do. I ask your help—and
God's."
    It seemed that few were listening. The
country had not accepted the death of
Kennedy, let alone the succession. The

3

pages, but they are often treated very simply, almost like the conventional half-title.

There are legions of good paperbacks whose
covers are among the freshest designs of the
graphic arts. Like dust jackets of trade books, these
may use art work but many—and good ones—use
only type.

Letterheads

The next test of a layout man is a letterhead. On
the face of it, this appears to be an easy job.
Actually it is anything but easy. For the letterhead
stands out like a matador in a bull ring, surrounded
as it is with a wide arena of paper.

Functions of the letterhead are: to identify the
sender; to connote the kind of business, especially
when the name is ambiguous; to suggest the per-
sonality of the business; to create a pleasant page
after the letter has been written.

It is wise to design the letterhead and to present
the comp with typing in the conventional style because this is the way most people will see the
finished job.

Typographical elements of the letterhead are
the name, address, phone number, cable address,
and locations of agencies and subdivisions. These
are the essentials.

2

A Short Symphony

a. First Movement: G8

The work accomplished so far has made it possible to bring together a great many myths. But in my haste to strengthen and consolidate the most obvious connections, I have left a number of loose threads hanging here and there; and these must be tidied up before I can assert my belief that all the myths so far examined are part of a coherent whole.

Let us try, then, to take an over-all look at the tapestry I have been putting together piecemeal, and let us behave as if it were already complete, without bothering for the moment about the gaps that still exist in it. All the myths with which we are here concerned divide into four big sets, which subdivide into pairs characterized by antithetical forms of behavior on the part of the hero.

The hero of the first group, on the one hand, is incontinent: he does not refrain from laughter when dealing with someone who makes ridiculous gestures (M₁₀, M₂₀, M₃₀) or speaks in a ridiculous tone (M₄₀). He cannot control himself when tickled (M₄₀). Alternatively, he cannot avoid opening his mouth when eating and so chews his food noisily (M₇₀); or he opens his ears when listening and so hears the ghosts call (M₈₀); or again, he cannot refrain from releasing his sphincter muscles, either because he laughs too hard (M₄₀, M₅₀), or because, as in the key myth, his fundament has been eaten up (M₁₀); or lastly, because he breaks wind with deadly effect (M₂₀).

Continence and incontinence, closing and opening are therefore contrasted, in the first place, as manifestations of our control and excess. But we immediately note two further sets, complementary to the preceding ones: in these, continence takes on the character of excess, since it is carried too far, and incontinence (if not carried too far) seems, on the contrary, to be a controlled form of behavior.

Excessive continence is characteristic of insensitive or taciturn heroes (M₀₀, M₀₀, M₀₀) and of gluttonous heroes who are incapable of evacuating the food they "contain" normally, and therefore remain closed (M₀₀) or doomed to a lethal form of evacuation (M₂₀); or again of imprudent or indiscreet

134

one: *Greenville, August 8*

1.   He drove into Greenville with the sun climbing over his left shoulder and burning his eyes through the rear-view mirror while he shivered and heard howling in his ears. This time of morning, even in August, the sun was more white than yellow, more light than heat, as the blade of air cutting into his face from the slitted side vent proved. Later on the day would be hot enough, when the sun climbed higher in its slice of sky and settled in for itself; it would make up then for the struggle to overcome the chilled morning air that never turned warm without having to, and it would burn then with light *and* heat, and everyone would broil the rest of the day for having had the privilege of being cold in the morning.

Or maybe it was just that he was moving. He shivered from the air that was hitting him, though he was wearing a jacket over his short-sleeved shirt and arms deep-tanned from three months of outdoor work. The light hurt his eyes and made him squint. He scrunched down in his seat a little, but refused to close the window or touch the rear-view mirror. If he did that he would have to adjust it again; instead he took the green sunglasses out of his shirt pocket, where he had put them

4

THE DISTANT MIRROR

Naming the still tiny colony of unowned Negroes "Liberia" was validly motivated, but calling it a commonwealth was still premature. The colony was able to fulfill a basic definition of "commonwealth" in that it was a "body of people constituting a politically organized community," but it was not a sovereign body politic.

Technically Liberia remained a ward of a still highly controversial and alien nonprofit corporation which claimed ownership of all lands of the colony, selected and appointed its senior officials or "agents," and otherwise sought to dominate the colony and direct its destinies.

Liberia remained and gained significance as a most remarkable American phenomenon, but it was not yet an African nation. American Negroes had clashed with the African tribespeople yet had succeeded in establishing friendships and certain correlations of common interest between themselves and the neighboring aborigines. But even while gaining some degree of African rootage, Liberia had not gained convincing status as an African nation. Even more disappointing, despite its valorous stand against the continuing slave trade, Liberia was being used as a ploy and an inexpensive *pièce de resistance* by one of the most blatant and cynical lobby forces that had ever befouled American government.

The secretary-general of the American Colonization Society was

43

To these are added the *mosquitos*, the plague of the designer. The trademark is one, especially if it is not a good one. Officials of the company may individualize letterheads with the addition of their name. Organizations list all officers. Some companies have slogans of which they are inordinately, and sometimes undeservedly, proud. The worst of the skeeters is the picture of *Our Founder* or *Our Plant*. (If you listen carefully now, you may hear a sound like a distant surf. This is the sound of all the letterhead designers in America shuddering.)

On conventional letterheads (and woe to him who would change them), everything is centered at the top of the page. Modern letterheads often carry material at the bottom of the page and sometimes group long lists of names into thin panels that run

LETTERHEAD DESIGN is a fine test of the designer. Here the designer makes a visual pun upon Fox River Paper Company (by whose courtesy this rough is used). The little fox and the second line of type are in light brown; the rest in black. Note how both lines of type are greeked.

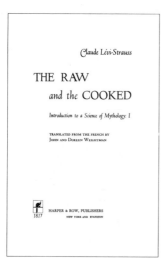

Claude Lévi-Strauss

THE RAW
and the COOKED

Introduction to a Science of Mythology: 1

TRANSLATED FROM THE FRENCH BY
JOHN AND DOREEN WEIGHTMAN

HARPER & ROW, PUBLISHERS
1817   NEW YORK AND EVANSTON

Oriented layout aligns *T* and torch of colophon on their vertical strokes, other elements on ends of lines.

down one or both sides. Color, in paper and ink, becomes more accepted every day.

Letterheads should be so designed that they can be used—as-is or with slight modification—on billheads, invoices, statements, and other business forms. The value of identifying all written matter from one source, by color of stock and ink and typographic treatment, is substantial.

Often the letterhead is reduced and used on envelopes, sometimes sideways to make it fit. In this usage only the name and address are necessary. The Post Office prefers the return address on the face of the envelope and its advertising value suggests this is the best location. By postal regulations, no printed matter can be placed closer than 3½ inches from the right edge; this assures room for postage and postmarks to be easily seen.

Most business letters are typewritten; they look best when margins of the typing align with those of the letterhead. The designer must keep this in mind. When window envelopes are used, it saves time if there is some device which will tell the typist where to begin the name and address. This can be unobtrusive, an agate period, for instance. Or it can be made highly visible, part of the total design.

Some letterheads combine inked or blind embossing, letterpress, offset, or Thermography in various combinations. Others use two-toned stock folded over an inch or so at the top with the letterhead printed on the side opposite that on which the letter is typed. If the letterhead performs its necessary functions, the only limit on its design is expense and good taste.

Business Cards

Business cards contain most of the information of a letterhead plus the name of the individual presenting it. They must be businesslike, attractive, connotative, and above all easy to read, so that the recipient can grasp the entire message at a glance or use it as a convenient reference.

Business cards are small: 3⅛ × 1¾ inches is

THE GREEN HOUSE

by Mario Vargas Llosa

Translated from the Spanish by GREGORY RABASSA

Books by Mario Vargas Llosa
THE GREEN HOUSE ● THE TIME OF THE HERO

Harper & Row, Publishers
NEW YORK AND EVANSTON

Summer's Lie   Summer's Lie   Summer's Lie   Summer's Lie

A   N O V E L   B Y   *Alan Boatman*

HARPER & ROW, PUBLISHERS

NEW YORK
EVANSTON
AND LONDON

LIBERIA

BLACK AFRICA IN MICROCOSM

Charles Morrow Wilson

Introduction by J. William Fulbright

HARPER & ROW, PUBLISHERS
NEW YORK, EVANSTON, AND LONDON

Double-spread title pages grow slowly in popularity. Connotation of typefaces is important in conveying flavor of nonfiction as well as novels.

THE MIRROR OF INFINITY

A Critics' Anthology of Science Fiction

edited by
Robert Silverberg

HARPER & ROW, PUBLISHERS
New York, Evanston, and London

Mirror image, in screened type, gives visual repetition of verbal title.

The
Grandees

AMERICA'S SEPHARDIC ELITE

by
STEPHEN BIRMINGHAM

HARPER & ROW, PUBLISHERS
New York, Evanston, San Francisco, London

Classical centered layout is reinforced by elegance of Script title. (All title pages courtesy of Harper & Row, Publishers)

common. All elements, therefore, must be scaled down in proportion. There is not much room for maneuvering in an area this small; the designer must be surefooted.

It is said that if the layout man can handle letterheads and business cards successfully, nothing can daunt him thereafter. There is enough truth here to be an incentive to any designer to hit these tackling dummies at every opportunity.

One thing is sure. In most cases he cannot help but improve the present product. As a group, American letterheads fit the summary, "The average quality is well below average."

With the treasure chest of materials available, and the greater freedom being given to designers today, layout work is one of the most gratifying of all phases of the graphic arts. Not the least of the contributing factors is the fact that this job, unlike so many others in graphic arts, is not done backstage; it always plays to an audience.

TRADEMARKS or company symbols are among the most interesting assignments given a typographer. This is a very happy solution. The pictorial element is obviously a roll of paper, but it might also be a lowercase r for "Roosevelt" or a cap P for "paper."

SUGGESTED READINGS

Carter, John. *ABC for Book Collectors*. London: Rupert Hart-Davis, 1961.

Cataldo, John W. *Graphic Design*. Scranton, Pennsylvania: International Textbook, 1966.

Lee, Marshal. *Bookmaking*. New York: Bowker, 1966.

Levarie, Norma. *The Art and History of Books*. New York: James Heineman, 1968.

Morison, Stanley, and Day, Kenneth. *The Typographic Book*. Chicago: University of Chicago Press, 1963.

Nelson, Roy Paul. *The Design of Advertising*. Dubuque, Iowa: Wm. C. Brown, 1967.

Tschichold, Jan. *Designing Books*. New York: George Wittenborn, Inc., 1949.

Wills, F. H., *Layout*. New York: Sterling, 1965.

Wilson, Adrian. *The Design of Books*. New York: Reinhold, 1967.

Gutenberg, Senefelder, and Mergenthaler were not seeking permanent abode in the graphic arts Valhalla; they were looking to make an honest dollar, thaler, florin, or guilder. Their incentive, like that of graphic arts people's always, was economic; aesthetics were secondary.

The typographer prides himself on getting maximum communication out of his customer's budget and the printer is unhappy when his work goes unread and unused, even though he has been paid for its production.

If the typographic designer realizes that every printing job is custom-built, if he uses a simple checklist conscientiously, he can effect major savings on many of his projects, real savings in all of them. There are eight major areas that he must consider. In each one he should not be ashamed to go through the actual mechanics of a checkoff list just as does the captain of a 747. The more we can commit to paper, the more brain cells we leave available for important creativity.

On any project, the very first step is to ask: "Is this job necessary?" Too many things are printed simply because the inventory is getting low, the budget has got some unallocated money, somebody has a bright idea he'd like to see preserved in ink on paper. Graphic arts people are kept busy enough doing necessary jobs; there is no need for featherbedding.

Have the actual users of the proposed job been consulted for improvements, additional requirements, possible eliminations?

Can data provided in this job be combined with some other? Or can that in other pieces be combined into this one? Has everyone responsible for the content, distribution, use—or payment—of this job given approval?

Does this job, by title and appearance, clearly indicate its purpose? If this is a revised form, can it readily be distinguished from the previous one? Is there proper space for date, TO and FROM; number-

20

Planning Printing

Economics and the Budget

Planning and Scheduling

ing; address if used in window envelope; code designation for inventory needs?

If the reader must fill in anything by hand, has that been kept at a minimum and is there enough room for it? Is there enough room for a signature, if needed? Is spacing correct for typewriter or hand-writing?

Has consideration been given to the number of copies really required? Will there be possible changes soon? Will the piece remain useful during the time estimated for its consumption?

Is the size of the printed piece proper to: carry all necessary information? Cut without waste? Get proper attention? Fit into filing cases or envelopes?

Should the job be on colored paper to speed up writing, distributing, sorting, and filing? Is it advantageous to use colored paper to designate departments or branch offices? Days, months, or years? To differentiate between multiple carbon copies? To identify rush orders?

(Aesthetics and communicative functionalism of paper and color are considered, of course, during the creative, designing process.)

Is proper weight of paper specified for original and various carbon copies?

Can other jobs, printed on the same paper as that chosen, be ordered now to cut production costs? Have requirements been estimated correctly and is the quantity ordered the most economical considering probability of revisions and rate of use?

There are usually alternative sources for materials and services. The typographer should know these so well that he can choose between and among them on the basis of constantly changing requirements. As soon as other craftsmen become involved in a project, chances for costly misunderstandings proliferate. So be precise and detailed in all instructions whether on estimating sheets, requests for bids, printing order or contract. Take nothing for granted. Minimize verbal instructions; get everything possible in writing. If any instructions are changed—especially by cancellation—be sure that everyone involved knows they are. Follow up on all instructions, spoken or written.

Several or many craftsmen will be working—
often simultaneously and at distances varying from
feet to miles—on a single job. Each one should get
all—but only—the instructions he needs. The typesetter needs specific instructions about composition
—but it doesn't matter to him whether a block goes
under a picture or alongside it. The lockup man
doesn't care whether an engraving is 85-line or 120;
but he has to know whether the 2 × 5 cut on page 2
is of a two-suiter bag or a vanity case. If instructions are given clearly—but on the wrong piece of
paper—the loss in time and money can prove
mortal.

Time is always an important factor in the graphic
arts. Advertising prepared for periodicals must
meet press times for the publications. Direct-mail
advertising may become useless in a matter of days
if the merchandise is of especially ephemeral popularity. Printing equipment is large and expensive; it
must be kept in almost-constant use. Your job can't
be printed at any moment you decide; it must fit
around other commitments made for men and
machines.

A very early step in planning and job-letting is
establishing a timetable. This should be realistic,
then policed as if it were the implacable laws of the
Medes and the Persians!

Determine when the job is needed. Be utterly
truthful here; cushions will be built into the schedule later. Then work backward. How long will it
take to deliver the job from the printer or bindery?
When must the pressman have the final okayed
proof? How much earlier must the lockup man
have all components? How long will it take to set
type? When do we need dummy and copy?

Usually the answer to that last question is
"Yesterday!" But if we find the schedule is unreal-
istic or even impossible, we trim down the job,
consider overtime, or break it into separately produced sections.

A realistic timetable will build in a little insurance against the horrors of the unforeseen. And it
will allow enough time—and proper time intervals
—for each job. There is no point in having proofs

delivered at 4 P.M. Friday with a promise to return
them by Monday at 9 unless someone works over
the weekend. There is no point in allowing a half
day for pasting up a 48-page brochure; there isn't
enough room in your art studio for all the people
needed to do all that work.

Schedule so that as many jobs as possible are
done simultaneously; the engraver can do his work
while the typesetter does his, then the printer need
not wait for the components of his job.

So he can build in enough time for coping and
follow-ups, the designer must know all processes
involved well enough to anticipate emergencies and
to recognize key stages. (This is the reason for this
book, incidentally.)

Cliff-hanger deadlines should be avoided. A rush
job or a missed deadline produces costly and pain-
ful chain reaction.

Let us suppose that you have a job that just has
to get out by Thursday or you will lose your job—
and maybe your life. The printer will accommodate
you. He takes his compositor off another job to
work on yours. He schedules yours onto the press
or bindery ahead of the one that would normally be
there. Your job is completed during normal working hours.

But, to meet delivery dates on the displaced jobs,
the shop must work overtime. Who gets charged for
this time-and-a-half? Not innocent Customer X—
you do!

Unfortunately, so many printing orders are
marked RUSH that these get only normal treatment.
In order to warrant even a second glance, a job
ticket must be marked CATACLYSMIC! ! ! ! The buyer
who sets a realistic delivery date and gives the
printer maximum time to meet it will always be
rewarded with a better job.

For two factors are invisible but essential in any
printing process: time and craftsmanship. You can't
buy time; if you try to cheat the clock a little on the
press, you may find your spoilage mounting because the ink hasn't dried completely and there is a

lot of set-off. *Railroading* copy through the composing room lowers quality; the comp will have to let loose word spacing go through because he just doesn't have time to go back and manipulate spacing by hand.

Craftsmanship cannot be measured by the arbitrary figures of estimate, bid, or bill. But it is the final difference between mediocrity and excellence.

Craftsmanship is linked with time. A good compositor gets type to the stoneman on time, and he, in turn, delivers forms on schedule to the pressroom. A less competent man, then, takes away irretrievable time from succeeding operations and quality inevitably falls.

Somewhere along the line we must assume, of course, that the comprehensive dummy meets all the criteria of functional typography.

Printing Processes

It has been said that planning a printing job is like doing a jigsaw puzzle on the turntable of a record player. Every time a new piece is added, every time the table turns, a new situation develops. In planning printing production, an old-timer once observed that "The first thing to do is . . . everything!"

It is difficult to define any step as the first one to take. And even, having taken a step, made a decision, in any area, it is often necessary to back up and revise it in the light of decisions made afterward. But the printing process is certainly a major factor that will determine any other corollaries and is at least a starting point.

Again it must be emphasized that every printing job is tailor-made. Every one is unique. Every one must be analyzed individually. So there is no "best way" to print it. Because of the many obvious advantages of offset, many people think this is "the most economical printing process" and specify it as a reflex action. This just isn't so. Every process has advantages—as well as disadvantages—or they would long have gone the way of the dinosaurs.

There are a few criteria which enable us to make a preliminary, starting evaluation. We remind ourselves that this is a temporary premise that may—or must—be changed any time that later evidence warrants.

Letterpress is indicated for work on tight deadlines—no other process can go from copy to printing as quickly; short runs—100 to 25,000—with all type or few cuts; reprints of standing type, especially in complicated forms; finest detail possible in halftones; good, even black tones with a crisp effect; long runs of halftones on coated stock; envelopes in runs up to 10,000.

Offset should be considered first for runs up to 10,000 when the ratio of illustrations to type is high; reprints when good camera copy is available; ruled work; halftones on rough paper; envelopes in long runs that are printed before they are cut and formed; soft illustrations as vignettes, washes, fine stipple, and crayon.

Gravure has natural advantages for long runs—above 25,000—with relatively many pictures; fine details and color on low-grade paper; jobs which contain little type; reproduction of fine art work without an apparent screen.

If your schedule—or budget—is very tight, press speeds are significant. How much time will your job require for printing? This determines press costs. Gravure presses are generally fastest, offset next, and letterpress third. If you want the speed of rotary letterpress you must make curved plates.

Press speed is indicated by *impressions per hour*. The quoted speed must be discounted to get true production speed. On small presses, cruising speed is 40 per cent less than maximum; on large presses 30 per cent. A press cannot operate at maximum speed all day long any more than your car can travel 100 miles per hour all the way from San Francisco to New York.

No one can argue with these basic assumptions but not even these apply all the time. The economics of the individual printing plant enter now.

Suppose a plant, by any process, prints several

publications every month. The *Gadgeteers Journal*
is off the press by the nineteenth of the month but
the *Forbisider Bulletin* isn't scheduled until the
twenty-first. Letting the press stand idle is sheer
waste; overhead, depreciation, and wages continue.
It is wise to take a one-day job at 6 per cent profit
instead of 8 per cent, and keep the press running.

Or suppose you have a 4-hour job that does not
have to meet a tight deadline. And suppose the
printer also has an 8-hour job to get out. If he does
yours in the morning, he has to split the longer run
between this afternoon and tomorrow. This may
mean additional wash-up time or complicate storage of the incomplete job under humidity control.
It is advantageous to him, and to your price, to do
your job tomorrow.

Or suppose his bindery is occupied by a big job.
It is better to keep your forms lying unprinted than
to store printed sheets while they await binding.

Or the printer may say, "Look, you've got a
simple spot color on this job. If you can wait a
couple days, I'll have orange in the fountain for
another job and can put yours on without extra
washup." In all these cases, the ability to adjust
your schedule may mean savings.

Composition

The designer has several basic choices of composition, with the printing process a determining factor, of course. If standing type is to be used, either
as-is or with rearrangement of elements, it may
need only be locked into the new form for letterpress or repro-proofed for offset or gravure. If
many but minor changes are required—changing a
lot of prices in a catalogue—hot metal is ideal. (Or
maybe an existing job is of camera-ready quality.)

Is the copy available in cold-type input, as punch
cards or tape used for another job? If strikeon is
used, how good must it be? Will copy batted off on
the ad manager's 20-year-old portable be adequate?

No matter what method is chosen for setting
type, one thing applies always: good clean copy is
least expensive to set. So any manuscript edited to

any extent ought to be retyped. It is far less costly to have a stenographer do that job than to tie up, and pay for, a man and machine while the Linotype or Photon operator deciphers a mass of changes scrawled between lines.

Time can be saved if all copy instructions are written plainly and unmistakably. Ganging-up copy speeds operations, too. Put all 8/9 x 14 pica copy together, then that set at 11 picas, 27 picas, etc. Then keep all your 12-point together. All headlines should be grouped by face and size. This avoids the necessity of the operator thumbing through the copy or changing magazines too often. This ganging must be done with intelligence, of course. It's false economy to set a single one-line 14-point Italic subhead separately and make the stoneman look through a dozen galleys of body type to find where to insert it.

Type should be chosen to provide the proper duplexing. It wastes time to have to set boldface on a second machine because your basic body type is duplexed with Italic instead.

Of course, the obvious economies should have long ago been built into the dummy: no run-arounds, no butted slugs, no free-fall setting, no complicated use of initials, no specification of exotic type faces whose setting may have to be subcontracted.

On rush jobs do not specify rare types which must be electrotyped or photoengraved. Printing directly from type or slugs will save at least a half day, usually more.

All editing should be done on the manuscript; every author's alteration should be taken as a personal insult to the typographer. Copy should be double-spaced, with generous margins on only one side of the paper. A fresh ribbon is always a good investment.

Check that all specifications for typesetting match with the dummy. Headlines, especially, need this scrutiny.

Mark type face, size, ledding, and measure plainly. Key it clearly so the copy block *A* doesn't appear three pages too late. If the job is in sections, number each page as *1, Chapter V; 2, Chapter V,* etc. Sometimes copy for each section is typed on a different-colored paper. (This is fine only if the typing is perfectly legible.) If the whole job is of one parcel, it is wise to number sheets as *Sheet 1 of 7, Sheet 2 of 7,* or even as *1 of 7, 2 of 7,* etc. Should one get lost, it will be spotted easily and at a time when finding or replacing it will be relatively simple.

Proofreading

Allow adequate time in your timetable for proofreading; it is a vitally important part of the long chain of processes.

If there are more than a single proof, mark one as MASTER PROOF and number the others. Consolidate all corrections to the master.

Before reading proof, look at the dummy for pencil marks, marginal notations, attached memos. Get the previous proof, if any. Question all doubtful points! It is far better to check a hundred things that have been taken care of than to overlook one that "I assumed you were taking care of."

Artwork

Check against the dummy that all artwork is at hand and approved by necessary supervisors. (In many instances the patent and legal department as well as engineering must OK pictures.)

Check against dummy that scaling has been properly done. It can be a costly embarrassment to hold presses because a late photoengraving was an inch too long—even if it was "only on one end." Make sure that the size of the plate is properly given on the art and that all necessary instructions —cropping, screen, stripped-in type, reverse, etc.— are clear and complete. (You would previously have checked to see whether your platemaker prefers glossy or matte photographs.)

Protect all artwork with overflaps and use husky stiffeners to prevent folding.

Code each picture to its proper position in the

dummy. This is particularly important when many pictures of the same size show the same subjects. A catalogue may have a dozen 2 × 2 halftones, each of a pattern of dinner plates or of silverware. Opportunities for misplacement are far too numerous.

If a choice of color prints or transparencies is available, let the platemaker choose the best one. Often his loupe (magnifying glass) will detect flaws, especially in small 35 mm. transparencies, that your naked eye didn't see.

Major savings can be effected if same-focus material is shot at the same time. Line art should all be done at one and a half times the linear dimension of the plate; this copy can actually be mounted on a single board and shot as one element. Halftones may similarly be ganged if their tonal value is the same. But color work will rarely be shot at the same time because of compensations the cameraman must make in exposures to correct for varying color value. But even if the cameraman must shoot each piece of art separately, he saves valuable time if he need not change his focus for each shot.

Check engraver's proofs and plates against copy for size. Be sure to go beyond the proof and examine the plates themselves against scratches that may have marred them after proofing.

Have all relief materials checked for type-high uniformity and have necessary makeready of engravings done long before lockup.

If engravings are to be delivered to the printer, be sure the address is clearly indicated; give a particular person's name to whom delivery is to be made and alert him as to when he should expect it.

If the job is unusual in production or if highest quality is demanded, include a sample of paper and ink that will be used on the press.

Duplicate Plates

Determine which duplicate plates are most efficient for the job. If they must be mailed, stereos or plastic plates use the least postage. Electros hold the finest details; nickeltypes have the longest life, so use them for runs longer than 500,000. When sending original halftone plates for duplicating, do not mount them. And leave dead metal around the sides of all plates as *bearers,* to protect the plate against an oblique pressure at the edges of the form.

Presswork

Here is a key factor in the quality and economy of a job. Many designers are less careful in this final checking than otherwise, sometimes because of fatigue or time pressure, often because they don't realize its importance.

Make certain that the dummy is clear and complete. If spot or process color is involved, make sure all dummies coincide. Turn over a complete set of engraver's proofs.

If more than one form is involved, get and give OK's on as many as posssible at one time. If the printer for any reason needs to change forms or if he finds unexpected open time, he will have something ready to put on the press.

If possible, check press proofs at the printer's instead of having them sent to you for approval. This is the costliest waiting time in the whole chain and the only one for which the customer pays almost totally.

Potential savings on the press are great and would have been anticipated in the earliest planning and layout steps. But this is a logical time to consider them here.

There is little that can be done to affect makeready other than to buy composition and engravings from sources of high standards. Cheap engravings may be cheap because they are mounted carelessly on poor blocking material. Then the dollar saved on them is erased by two dollars' worth of makeready time as the pressman attempts to bring them to uniform type-high.

There are some techniques of presswork that can effect substantial savings. Printing may be *sheet-wise;* one sheet—although it may contain several or many individual pages—is printed on one side,

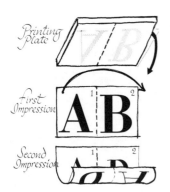

Example 12. WORK-AND-TURN technique is shown in this diagram.

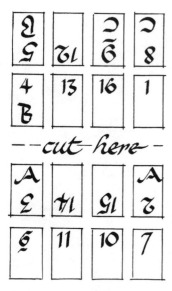

Example 13. IMPOSITION PATTERN for 16-page booklet.

allowed to dry, then printed on the other. Or it may be printed *work-and-turn*. Example 12 demonstrates this technique.

The front form (A) and the reverse (B) are printed at the same time, side by side on one double-size sheet. Then the paper is turned lengthwise. The printed side A now lies, face down, under form B. After B is printed there, the printer need only to cut the paper on the dotted line to have a completely printed job. He gets one whole piece with each press impression. Note again that this piece may be a single page or a complete signature, depending on the size of the job and press.

Work-and-turn, *w&t,* has many advantages. With quick-drying ink and a fairly long run, the first piece can be *backed up,* printed on the reverse side, as soon as Piece No. 10,000 comes off the press. There is no additional makeready; the process continues without pause. No changes are necessary on the grippers or side guides on the press.

Work-and-tumble is the variation in which paper is turned sideways before backing up and then is cut lengthwise to get the two separate pieces. One disadvantage of work-and-tumble is that the gripper edge of the paper is changed, unlike the work-and-turn process. This means extra adjustments on the press because paper cannot be cut in a perfect rectangle, the drag of the knife produces deviation from right angles. Even with this extra work in adjusting for the difference in gripper edges, work-and-tumble often has economic advantages.

A two-color effect is obtainable by the simple expedient of washing up the press and changing inks before backing up. Thus half of the job would be printed with A in blue and B in red, and the other half with A in red and B in blue. Not every job lends itself to this treatment, of course. But often the color for any given form does not much matter; the over-all effect of two colors, no matter on what pages they may appear, may be desirable and functional.

Another way of obtaining two colors with one

press run is the *split fountain*. The ink fountain and the inking roller are divided so that the form is inked in two or more colors for each impression. This means that the form must have some division there, too, for any typographic element that passed under the separation would be uninked in a thin strip. Sometimes two colors are placed in the same, unsplit fountain. The colors remain true at opposite ends and *blend* together in the middle. The longer the run the wider the area of blending. Neither of these methods can control color critically but both have advantages similar to those of work-and-turn with two colors. Split fountains and blending can be done only on presses that have fountains; platen presses with their ink plates cannot be used.

Interesting effects can be obtained with single runs by utilizing colored inks on colored paper. Blue ink, applied full intensity or screened in various degrees, will produce pleasant effects on a light green stock, for instance. Two-tone papers give a multicolor effect to a single-color job, especially with unusual folding or cutting.

Utilizing the imposition scheme can reduce color cost when it appears on only some pages. Example 13 shows the imposition scheme for a 16-page booklet, printed sheetwise. If all color can be placed on one side of the sheet, it need go through the press only three times, front and back in black, front *or* back in color. The designer must lay out his pages in such a way that he does not bleed cuts at the gripper edge.

Press time can be reduced by printing more than *one up* and by *ganging*. One up means printing from a single form, sheetwise or work-and-turn. By making duplicate plates we can print the same form twice in one impression; this is *two up*. Depending on size, jobs may be printed with any number up, sheetwise or w&t. For large quantities the cost of duplicate plates is trifling compared to press savings though extra cutting costs do decrease savings to some extent.

Ganging is printing several forms on the same sheet with one impression. A letterhead may be

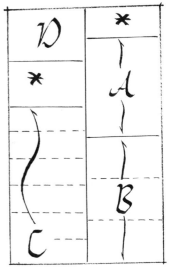

GANGING JOBS reduces press time markedly. In this example, A is a letter on an 8½ X 11 sheet and B is a two-fold folder. C is a broadside, five-folded, and D will be die-cut. The two areas marked with asterisks can be used for something as simple as a memo pad and still not cost anything.

ganged with invoices, memo sheets, and billheads, for instance. Any one of these items may be printed two or more up to establish the proper ratio of printed pieces. Odd areas, which otherwise would be trimmed to waste, can be utilized for small advertising pieces as envelope stuffers. All these pieces will be printed on the same stock, of course. Often the economy of gang runs makes it feasible to use higher quality paper for some of the items than would be practical were they printed separately.

Mail-order printing firms are able to offer extremely low prices on standard items by ganging dozens of letterheads and scores of business cards, for many different customers, into one run.

Bindery

Binding economies can be built in in original dummies. Suppose you have a halftone or headline that runs across the gutter from page 6 to page 7. A look at the imposition scheme shows that the sheet must be folded precisely along the horizontal line that divides the two pages. If the fold is off only 3 points, the cut on one page will be lowered that much and on the other raised the same amount so that registration will be off by 6 points. If the fold between pages 10 and 7 is off, a portion of the cut on one page may be hidden under the stitching or it may be moved away from the gutter, leaving a blank strip. In any of these instances, the two halves will not match properly. The only way in which to assure necessary accuracy in the folding operation is to reduce the speed of the folding machine. This increases the time, and cost, of the operation.

So it is wise to minimize such close folding-registration. When this is impossible, care must be taken that within the gutter area there is no fine detail that might be destroyed when registration drifts.

Typical of the interlocking of decisions is the need, while paper was being selected, to designate the grain so it runs parallel to the binding edge of the sheet. Folding should be with the grain, too.

Most of these economies can be effected in all

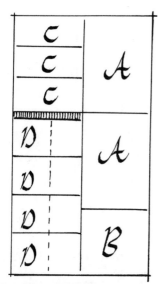

GANGING DIFFERENT JOBS is also possible when different quantities are required. Assume that a thousand impressions will be made on a sheet of this size. This will yield a thousand copies printing processes but there are some that are inherent in each method. This is one of the factors that determine the choice of basic processes.

Paper

Decisions involving paper are one of the major economic factors in printing. We have considered the most important ones already in Chapter 15, and here we need only a couple of simple reminders.

Paper should be selected to fit the maximum capacity of the chosen press and, of course, so it will cut without waste. The kind and weight of paper depend on the function of the job; if minute detail must be shown by letterpress, it is economical to choose very smooth stock, no matter what its price. If printing is on only one side of the paper, opacity becomes a minor factor, and so on.

Paper is a decisive factor in postage costs, especially when large quantities are involved. It is wise to prepare a dummy of the finished job, using the same stock and binding and placed in the same envelope that will be used for mailing. If, on weighing this package, you find it has just edged over into the next postage bracket, you might save tidy sums by making the pages just a trifle smaller, even though that does mean more paper waste.

Envelopes

Just as a job should be planned to utilize standard paper sizes, so it should fit into standard envelopes. Special sizes or styles can be made to specification, but unless the quantity is very large, costs mount prohibitively. There are sufficient standard envelopes so that it is a mighty rare job which cannot be designed to use one of them.

The No. 10 envelope, called *official*, is the common business size, 4⅛ × 9½; it takes a two-fold 8½ × 11 letterhead. *Commercial* sizes—No. 6 envelopes, 3⅝ × 6, or No. 6¼, a trifle smaller—take invoices or small letterheads.

Growing in popularity are *baronial*, 4⅛ × 5⅛, and *monarch*, 3⅞ × 7½, which were once exclusively social correspondence.

of B, a point-of-purchase (POP) display, but 2,000 letters, A.

Envelope stuffers, C, will number 3,000, and folders, D, 4,000. Again there may be enough paper, shaded area, for small "free" phone pads.

This technique will not work with all jobs, of course, unless they can use the same paper. But often it is economical to use a better quality paper—for inserts, let's say—so they can be ganged.

Other standards that have wide use are the 6 × 9 and 9 × 12 *catalogue* envelopes and, in the same size, *clasp* envelopes. These open at the narrow dimension. *Postage savers* have a deep, ungummed flap on one side so they can be opened for postal inspection and go at rates lower than sealed first class. *Window* envelopes in many sizes and styles save addressing time and also enable a modicum of personalization in direct-mail advertising.

Selection of an envelope should be an early, not deferred, decision. Cases are far too numerous when a printing job has been completed and only then did the user discover that a special envelope would be required or else the piece would rattle around in a standard size far too large.

Delivery

Transmission of materials to and from the printer and supplier poses a constant threat of loss. Even the United States mail, once of Jehovan assurance, now manages to lose crucial matter at the most crucial time.

When sending multiple-page jobs to the printer, materials for each spread may be gathered into a single large envelope. In all instances, the contents of each package should be noted on its face—and a duplicate kept by you. If any copy is missing from the matter you are sending in that listing, note its absence and indicate when the printer may expect it. If anything is missing in material he is sending to you, get Lost-and-Found on it immediately.

Be sure to open all packages from the printer soon on arrival. Many a typographer has wasted hours looking for a missing galley proof . . . which was in an envelope he was sure contained nothing but dummies from a previous job!

All details of packaging and delivery should be specified. Crucial time may be lost if the printer delivers a job to the customer's office instead of to the letter service that's supposed to address it. And if the job is to go to the customer's warehouse instead of his main office, failure to notify the deliveryman may lose less important but yet costly time. It is disconcerting for a stock room accustomed to storing letterheads in packages of 500 to be confronted by 100,000 pieces in a big wooden box. If the printer stores the job for you, he must charge rent—even though the item may be disguised on the bill. Labeling is often important; no one wants to open three identically wrapped packages to find letterheads instead of second sheets.

Spoilage is a factor that grows more important with the size of the run. Even though the percentage drops, numbers get larger. On short runs, 250 and under, allow 10 per cent spoilage for one color, 5 per cent for each additional color and 5 per cent in the bindery. This is cut in half on runs of 500 to 1,000. Between 5,000 and 10,000, spoilage is 3½ per cent for the first color, 2½ per cent for each extra color and 2 per cent for binding. Over 10,000, it is 2 per cent for each category.

Because it is most difficult for a printer to produce a job in exact amounts, contracts customarily specify a leeway of 10 per cent over or under the order. The price is adjusted to the actual number delivered. Spoilage is an important factor in estimating costs and cannot be overlooked.

Letting the Job

The final, and constant, decision is "Who shall print our job and how do we choose him?" The answer is far from simple. Even for companies that have their own printing plants, there come occasions when it would be more efficient and economical to farm out certain jobs.

There are no hard-and-fast rules and two schools of thought can muster convincing arguments.

Says one buyer: "Printing is a very competitive business. By letting plants bid on each job, I get advantage of the economic situation in each one. If a printer wants my business badly enough to shade his profit a little, I wouldn't be doing my job properly if I did not take advantage of these savings."

Says another, just as sincerely: "No buyer can expect a job less than cost plus a fair profit. The

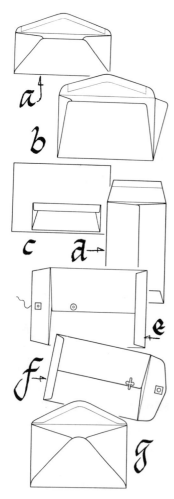

STANDARD ENVELOPES come in a great variety of shapes, sizes, styles, colors, and paper. Among the most widely used are:

a. *Number 10,* 9½ X 4⅛ inches, or *Standard 6¾,* 6½ X 3⅝ inches;

b. *Penny-saver,* which looks like a first-class letter but, because the side flap is not glued, takes a lower postage rate;

c. *Duo style,* the smaller envelope, carrying a letter at first-class rates, is attached

lowest price is not always the best price; cutting corners to be competitive and still solvent may be done by increasing efficiency, but most of the time it's done by lowering quality. I actually save money by staying with one good printer. He knows my problems and what I like. We save a lot of time in communicating therefore. The printer is a backstop against errors; he knows my line well enough to question me when something doesn't look quite right. If I used a low bidder each time, I'd be working in a new shop with new people most of the time."

When competitive bids are sought, indeed on any job where an estimate is required, detailed information must be given. Paper should be specified by kind and weight, or by a trade name or "equivalent thereof." This phrase, however, might lead to disappointment; products "just as good as" often are not, except by the flexible evaluation of a biased person.

If the printer is to buy plates, this must be specified; this is often wise because the printer has no alibi, then, if reproduction is unsatisfactory. Printers usually buy paper stock for everything except very, very large jobs. Even here there are advantages to have him do so. The buyer need not coordinate schedules or seek storage room for tons of paper until time for its use.

The wisest procedure is to stick with one printer and to have him bill you on a cost-plus basis for each job. There will be times when emergencies run up the price on a job; but when the printer makes a firm estimate, he must include a sum for contingencies and the buyer pays for unusual costs anyway.

The buyer must have confidence in the efficiency and integrity of his printer. And he must have a general knowledge of average costs in his area. Some buyers put up an occasional job to competitive bidding, both to keep their information up-to-date and their regular printer on his toes. But a close, continued working arrangement between buyer and printer makes a strong team that is more efficient than a pick-up team.

Printers are businessmen; they must have repeat business. Their efforts to keep the customer happy will usually result in arrangements that are of mutual economic advantage.

Public agencies, by law, must give orders to the "lowest or best bid." They are not synonymous. A big job should never be given to a company that will have to steam under forced draft to meet deadlines or standards of quality. Craftsmen who have to work longer shifts and over weekends will eventually become too fatigued to continue doing good work. And emergencies hit harder at smaller organizations. A plant that has only two presses loses 50 per cent of its capacity when one breaks down or its chief pressman becomes ill; in a plant with 10 presses, the loss of one is relatively much easier to overcome.

The printing buyer must know his field well. He must know which printers specialize in small while-you-wait jobs and which are geared to large and long-run jobs. Each is most efficient within his specialty.

Graphic arts developed for economic—rather than aesthetic—reasons. Demand for multiple copies also required not only fast but economical production. The economics of printing are still a major influence on all graphic arts design and methods.

If the criterion of functionalism is consistently applied, common sense will determine which process and technique will produce the best printing at maximum economy.

to the larger envelope which—because it's un-sealed—takes a lower rate;

d. *Open end*, in several sizes for booklets, catalogues, etc.;

e. *String-and-button*, usually made of heavier paper for bulky and/or heavy enclosures;

f. *Clasp*, often made of kraft paper, and

g. *Side opening*.

Envelopes are die-cut before folding and pasting and, in large-quantity jobs, after they have been printed. In smaller lots, the manufactured envelopes are printed. Care must be taken that the additional thickness of overlapping paper does not affect the makeready so that elements print more heavily on such areas.

SUGGESTED READINGS

Arthur, Paul (ed.). *Handbook for Printing Production.* Ottawa: E. B. Eddy Co., 1967.

Auble, J. Woodard. *Arithmetic for Printers.* Peoria, Ill.: Chas. A. Bennett Co., Inc., 1955.

Latimer, H. C. *Advertising Production Planning.* New York: Art Directions Book Co., 1969.

Melcher, Daniel, and Larrick, Nancy. *Printing and Promotion Handbook.* New York: McGraw-Hill Book Co., Inc., 1956.

21

The Fine Arts

The Craftsman as an Artist

This chapter is the last in this overview of the graphic arts, not because it is of least importance, but to emphasize again that "art" is more than a meaningless word in the title. Art plays as much a part in graphic communications as do skill and science. The art preservative not only nurtures all the arts, it is a legitimate, interesting, and satisfying one itself.

The "graphic arts" of the fine artist are the "fine arts" of the printer.

If this sentence is confusing, it is only because the terms are. Confusion can be dispelled at least a little by a closer look at these dual-named processes.

From the point of view of the fine artist, his "graphic arts" are *printmaking:* lithographs, woodcuts and wood engravings, linoleum blocks, etchings, aquatints, mezzotints, dry points, and serigraphs. These all utilize the three basic printing processes, except serigraphy, which is a stencil process. Therefore, they all fall within the vast area of the graphic arts as defined by the printer.

The artist considers his "graphic arts" as fine art because no mechanical or photographic process intervenes between the creator and his creation. Every etching or lithograph is as much an original work of art as a painting by Rembrandt or a violin solo by the composer himself.

Wood was the original printing plate. Although the mechanical age has replaced it with metal, wood remains a favorite vehicle for the artist.

The difference between a *woodcut* and *wood engravings* is slight but distinct. A woodcut is made in the grained side of a plank, using knives and gouges. Its basic effect is of large black figures on a white background. Wood engravings are cut with *burins* and *gravers* into the end-grain of a wooden block. It produces white lines on a black ground or thin black lines. Wood engraving reached its zenith with Thomas Bewick, whom we met a few chapters ago. Unlike most other art forms, it has not been improved upon by later generations. John DePol, one of the few artists in this medium today, did the

charming picture (Example 14) in two colors, black and yellow. His personal style is distinctive.

Linoleum blocks are but a variation of woodcuts. Battleship linoleum is worked just as a wooden plank would be. It is cheaper and easier to handle and, though its plebeian name may flare the nostrils of the dilettante, it is an honest and vigorous medium.

Purists are also disturbed because some contemporary artists use such unartistic materials as masonite or plastics—any surface that will yield prints—and work them with a flexible drill. As if this were not disquieting enough, these contemporaries nail wire screen or paste string, barley,

Example 14. WOOD ENGRAVING by John DePol, a famed American artist who is one of the few who work in this classical medium. It shows Whitelaw Reid, successor to Horace Greeley, inspecting the first Linotype slug which had just been produced by Ottmar Mergenthaler, seated, at an 1886 Linotype. This is used by courtesy of Mergenthaler Linotype Company which issued the original print to mark the 75th anniversary of the invention of the machine. This reproduction was made from a copy of the original wood engraving.

cheesecloth, and other prosaic materials onto certain areas of their wood block to create unusual textures and printing effects. They puncture large areas with nails of various sizes, or harry the smooth wood with rasps, files, or screwdrivers.

The classical *etching* has been examined in discussing intaglio. It has long been a favorite art form and continues to be today. Probably the most famous etcher is Albrecht Durer, whose work packs the same potency today as it did in his heyday in the early 1500's. Rembrandt loved etching, and it is interesting to note that Rembrandt is Rembrandt with a burin as well as with a paintbrush.

William Hogarth's biting satire of eighteenth-century England combined etching and engraving; Goya could protest against "Disasters of the War" or exult in Spain's pageantry. William Blake used etching to create his soaring illustrations of Biblical themes and America's Whistler found the acid as delicate as his watercolor.

Dry point is another of the many confusing terms in the graphic arts. It is considered an etching, yet there is no "etching" process involved. Instead of using acid to incise his lines, the artist cuts them with a metal, diamond, ruby, or sapphire needle. Actually, he plows a furrow and the displaced metal piles up along the sides of the line. This *burr* catches the ink that, even after the plate is wiped, gives drypoint its distinguishing flavor and mellowness.

Close cousin to the drypoint is the *mezzotint*. Its entire surface is covered with burrs, produced by a *rocker,* an instrument with many small teeth, that is rocked across the plate. The burr acts as intaglio wells. In desired areas it is either removed entirely with a *scraper,* or flattened out with a burnisher to create lighter areas of gray.

Another of the intaglio art forms that adds texture to etching is the *aquatint*. In this technique a ground of resin dust is sprinkled on all or certain areas of the etcher's plate and heated to make it adhere. The etchant penetrates between the fine grains to bite countless tiny intaglio wells that print

OLD ENGRAVINGS not only convey the flavor of much simpler days and of lustier patriotism but are the subject of many a collection. Old illustrative material like this can be used effectively with more modern elements for striking contemporary layouts.

in a soft texture. Salt and sugar are also used for aquatints, and sometimes sandpaper is pressed into the ground before etching. Aquatint is usually combined with bitten lines and so the texture must be applied after the linework has been etched.

The resin technique of aquatints is used in *photogravure*. Powdered resin is applied to a metal plate as in an aquatint. A carbon tissue, just as in rotogravure, is exposed to a film positive. But no screen is used; the minute granules of resin, with tiny areas between them, act as the screen, of a pleasant irregular pattern, somewhat like that of a mezzotint. Except for the one photographic step, the making of a photogravure is entirely a hand process. Printing, after hand-wiping, is manual, and 500 prints a day is maximum production, striking contrast to that of roto.

Photogravure is practically never printed with more than one plate. But the artist may carefully apply different colored inks to various areas of the same plate and print several colors at one time. This is not "color printing," though, in the accepted sense of the word; each print is an individual, and variable, product of the artist. (This same color technique is utilized with mezzotints also.) Sometimes photogravure is printed in a light ink and the print tinted with watercolors. This harks back to the days of Currier & Ives.

The fine-artist lithographer works directly upon a stone that he has himself ground down to a smooth surface. He can use lithographic crayons and pencils; he can apply a greasy liquid, *tusche,* as in a wash drawing; with his fingers he can apply *rubbing ink*. He may apply large areas of ink and scratch, rub, scrape, or burn (with mild acid) designs or texture. It must be kept in mind that this "lithographer" does not reproduce other people's work; he creates his own. Lithography has been a facile medium for such famed artists as Goya, Daumier, William Gropper, and Diego Rivera, to mention only a fragment of the roster.

Letterpress and intaglio printing began as fine-art tools and then were broadened to commercial use.

But *stencil printing* went from commerce to art to commerce to art to commerce . . . and much of it in the memory of living persons.

We have already noted that printers refuse to give Mimeographing, a stencil process, houseroom within their craft. But another stencil process known by several names—*silk-screen, screen,* or *process printing*—is accepted as a full, dues-paying member of the graphic arts.

Stencils made as tiny holes in heavy paper or similar material, even before the Renaissance, were beaten with bags of powder to transfer drawings to walls and ceilings prior to painting frescos there. This was commercial, it saved time. Painters picked up this device from China where it had been used as early as 1000 B.C.

Another form of stencils, the complete cutout, was used by heralds during the Crusades to place red crosses on banners, clothing, and armor.

In simplest of forms, a stencil is a hole in some protective fabric through which is brushed, dabbed, or smoothed a coat of paint that will replicate the shape of the stencil. The Crusader's cross is a good example. Circles, squares, and similar shapes were used, often like a cattle brand, to denote ownership. It is a logical and short step to make the stencil in the shape of a *T, V,* or *M.* In theory, then, we can stencil any written message.

Unfortunately, too many of our Latin letters have bowls. Suppose you want to make an *O* in a stencil. As soon as you have cut the outer edge, you have a bullet, this ● instead of an O; the center has just fallen out. To make a distinguishable *O,* we need to connect that "island" to the "mainland" of the stencil by means of a narrow "isthmus" or two. So a stencil-form *O* looks like two semicircular parentheses ( ) almost but not quite touching.

Now comes the material that gives silk-screen its name. This is really silk (no fiction as with dragon's blood!). The only purpose of the silk is to connect "islands" to the "mainland" of the stencil.

The silk is stretched tightly to a wooden frame to become the surface on which the image is painted

STENCIL
TEA

STENCIL STYLE TYPE shows—especially in the A—how the voids within a letter must be attached to the background. This is the principle used in the Mimeograph stencil where tiny cellulose fibers support the voids in the waxy stencil and in silk-screen printing where the thin white lines shown here are replaced by fibers of silk. The top type is—appropriately enough—called Stencil and the lower one, Tea Chest.

with tusche. After it has dried, the whole area is painted over with a mixture of glue and water. Later the silk is washed with kerosene which will dissolve the tusche but not the glue. The result is that the image area now shows raw silk while the rest of the screen is covered by the glue.

Paint is squeegeed across the screen. The silk allows it to penetrate as if there were no barrier. On paper or fabric under the screen, the original tusche-defined image is now reproduced in paint.

The silk-screen technique was invented in England in 1907 and used for fine-art painting. It came to America in 1914 and was used only for signs and—shades of the Crusades!—for banners and flags. Even invention of an automatic press in 1925 did no practical good, for there was no quick-drying paint.

In 1929 came two contributing events, the Wall Street crash and the invention of *Profilm*.

Profilm is a thin emulsion of lacquer or similar substance on glassine backing. The design is cut around with a sharp knife and peeled off. The silk is placed over the film which is adhered to it; the glassine is stripped away and the stencil is ready.

During the Great Depression of the 30's, there wasn't much demand for commercial printing of any kind. But the WPA Federal Arts Project sought an inexpensive medium, revived the fine-arts technique of the tusche method, and called it *serigraphy* (*sericum* is "silk" in Latin).

Artists experimented with transparent and opaque paints, the latter in degrees of consistency and thickness, and found a wide range of striking effects. The public happily accepted serigraphs, which, like other prints, are originals. This acceptance gave a boost to the commercial adaptations and the development of photographically-made stencils was the final stimulus. Serigraphy, the fine-arts form, flourishes today with many galleries devoted exclusively to that medium, and commercial applications continue to grow.

Screen printing has been adopted for block covers and dust jackets, for 24-sheet posters, for beer cans, for athletic sweaters as well as for ceramic ware, wallpaper, and decals.

An unusually felicitous marriage of art and commerce is in its reproduction of classical oil paintings. Actual brush strokes can be duplicated, not only in shape by the stencil but in thickness by controlling the amount of paint. The result is a practically exact replica of the original. It is expensive—dozens of stencils are used and often lithography is combined—and is not to be confused with the inexpensive "brush-stroke reproductions" which are simply offset onto randomly and irregularly embossed surfaces.

Collotype and *aquatone* are two interesting printing processes that use gelatin as a printing surface. Technically speaking, these are not "graphic fine arts" because they are commercial processes. But as a major use, especially in color, is to reproduce art works, it seems more logical to discuss them here than in the chapter on lithography, which they resemble. Both rely on the mutual repulsion of grease and water.

Collotype, also called *photogelatin,* was first produced in England in 1865. It uses no screen but produces continuous-tone copies of continuous-tone originals.

A thin layer of sensitized gelatin is exposed to an unscreened negative. Then it is thoroughly dampened with water and glycerin. Those areas which were light in the copy will absorb most moisture; those dark portions, which were exposed to maximum light through the negative, are almost dry. All the intermediate tones of the original are reproduced, in varying degrees of dampness, on the gelatin. The gelatin plate accepts ink in close ratio to its dampness, taking the most where the gelatin is most nearly dry.

Only four colors are used: gray, yellow, red, and blue, usually printed in that order. The transparent inks and the unscreened surface give finely diffused layers of color that reproduce art work in beauty and richness. Dependent as they are on moisture, gelatin plates must be made and printed under

strictly controlled humidity. No retouching is possible on the plate; it must all be done on the negative.

Commercially collotype is used, in monochrome usually, where fidelity of reproduction is required, but only for short runs. For longer runs, new plates must be made; this slows down an already slow process to the point of impracticality.

Familiar examples of monochromatic collotype are the large posters used by theaters. Because it has no screen, the process is useful in making blowups from smaller copy. Lobby posters are often several-diameter enlargements of smaller ones that have been produced by other processes.

Aquatone combines the principles of gelatin printing with that of offset. Here a screen is used, but the interrelation of the smooth gelatin and the

WATERCOLORS—such as this, *The Lighthouse* by Frank Wagner, can be reproduced with utmost fidelity by offset printing. This is shown by courtesy of the 3-M Company which uses it, in about four times this area and in full color, to demonstrate the abilities of its offset materials.

rubber offset blanket is such that 400-line screen can be used. Like collotype, aquatone is handicapped by its slow rate of production.

Aquarelle, although similar in name, has no relationship to aquatone except that it, too, teeter-totters across the line dividing the fine from the commercial graphic arts. An aquarelle is a printed picture to which color is added by applying water-color through stencils, one for each color. This is a slow, manual application. The skill of the painter has noticeable effect on the quality of the added color and this pushes the process toward the fine-arts category.

Products of the fine-arts processes discussed in this chapter are known generically as *prints.* This is unfortunate; for the public associates "prints" with cheap reproductions of other art forms. So it must be stressed again that these prints are original works of art. Many an art collector has begun by acquiring prints. The price is low; an original Picasso can be bought for $10. This appeals to young connoisseurs, especially, whose beer budget will not permit the acquisition of champagne-priced oil paintings.

Printmaking also appeals to the creative instincts of many people who long for the relaxation and satisfaction of creating something with their hands after a day of mental work. Materials are inexpensive; few tools are required (the heel of a spoon, or even of your hand, makes a satisfactory "printing press"); the basic technique is quickly learned. Once it is mastered, there are enough challenges in any of these media to intrigue an artist for the rest of his life.

The graphic arts has produced art forms peculiarly its own. Printing done before A.D. 1500 is known as *incunabula* (from the Latin term for "cradle" or "swaddling clothes"). An incunabulum is a collector's item of great beauty and interest. Although the true graphic artsman would no more cut a page out of a book than he would remove the arm from a baby, dealers have in the past disassembled books and individual leaves are on sale today at prices unbelievably low . . . or high.

THE TYPOPHILES, an informal organization of people in, or enamored of, the graphic arts, has produced a series of chapbooks, each of which is a collector's item. This is one of the marks the society uses. The symbol changes with the whim of the editor or when a member designs a new one.

Graphic arts people are notably sentimental. An old tradition is the *wayzgoose,* a festive affair that used to be the apprentices' salute to the master once they had passed out of their indentures. It continues today on the slightest excuse, usually to mark some anniversary of a colleague. On such an occasion a *chapbook* is customarily prepared. Once these were small books hawked on street corners or rural countryside by chapmen, peddlers. Today they are still small books but produced with a loving care that makes each an impeccable work of art. Notable among them are the series produced by the Typophiles and the Christmas cards of Tommy Tommasini, the typographer who designed and printed the original charter of the United Nations, the copies actually signed and sealed.

Amateur printers—many who are members of formal groups—print various forms of *ephemera,* with varying degrees of skill but always with obvious affection.

"Ephemera" is printing deliberately designed for a short life: direct-mail *envelope stuffers,* handbills, business cards, shipping tags, and a marathon-long list of similar items. Ephemera of the nineteenth century have become collectors' items.

Whether a person wants to be a creator or a user, a sender or a receiver, a doer or a viewer, an amateur or a professional, the aesthetic side of the graphic arts is a vast and truly fascinating one.

PRINTED EPHEMERA delights many a collector. This is a small piece that advertised a tobacconist.

The one below is a label for a vintner. Printing like this is expected to have a short life, being discarded as soon as it is read or the merchandise to which it is attached has been used. This contributes to a rarity that gives it far more value as an antique than it had when first printed.

SUGGESTED READINGS

Bockus, H. William. *Advertising Graphics.* New York: Macmillan Company, 1969.

Heller, Jules. *Printmaking Today.* New York: Henry Holt & Co., Inc., 1958.

Knigin, Michael, and Zimiles, Murray. *The Technique of Fine Art Lithography.* New York: Van Nostrand Reinhold, 1970.

Schwalbach, Mathilda V. and James A. *Screen-Process Printing.* New York: Van Nostrand Reinhold, 1970.

Strauss, Victor. *Modern Silk Screen.* New York: Pied Piper Press, 1959.

Glossary

A.A. Author's alteration, editorial change made in set type.

absorption. Process whereby ink dries by soaking into fibers of paper.

accent face. Type used for marked contrast to predominant typographic color of page. In newspaper usage, face used for kickers, catchlines, etc., often exaggerated weight of basic head letter.

accordion fold. Series of folds in paper, each in opposite direction of previous fold.

acetate. Transparent sheet placed over art work to effect mechanical color separation (*which see*) or to carry directions to platemaker.

achromatic. Black, white, and gray. Called "colors" but technically they are not.

ad alley. Portion of composing room devoted to preparing advertising.

agate. 5½-point type; as unit of measuring depth of newspaper page or advertisement, 14 agate lines equal one column-inch.

albumen plate. Surface plate; most common kind used for offset lithography.

alignment. Regular placement of characters on a theoretically straight line.

American. Ethnic of Square Serifs with serifs heavier than main strokes of letterform.

analogous. Color harmony using two colors adjacent on color wheel.

analysis. Chemical action of breaking down substance into components, analogous to color separation (*which see*).

anchor corners. Make-up pattern—especially on newspaper page—in which heavy heads or cuts are placed in or near each corner of page.

aniline printing. Relief process on paper bags, envelopes, food wrappers, etc., using quick-drying alcohol-based inks or dyes.

antique. Soft, bulky paper with comparatively rough surface, similar to old handmade papers. Also (capitalized), Gothic letter.

apex. Top juncture of diagonal strokes as in A.

aqua fortis. Mixture of water and nitric acid.

aquarelle. Printed picture on which color is applied by hand through stencils.

aquatone. Method of printing combining extremely fine screen on gelatin plates with offset lithography.

area printer. CRT machine that composes entire area of type in proper position.

arms. Elements of letters that protrude from stem as in *K* and *Y*.

art. All illustrative material, lettering, and ornamentation prepared by an artist. Also, original copy for platemaking, especially for photolithography.

art lining. System of aligning letters with long descenders. (*See* lining.)

Artype. Black or white letters on transparent, self-adhering plastic.

ascenders. Portions of a letter that rise above the mean line; also those characters themselves, as *b, d, f, h, k, l,* and *t.*

automatic typesetting. System in which the keyboard of a typesetting machine is actuated by a mechanical device directed by electrical impulses.

backbone. Portion of the binding that connects the front and back covers of a book.

backing up. Printing reverse side of sheet of paper which has already received an impression on the obverse.

ball. The finishing element on the top of the strokes in *a* and *c.* Also, untanned leather wrapped around pads of wool with which early printers applied ink to type.

bank. Cabinet or bench on which is stored type awaiting make-up.

bar. The horizontal stroke in *t, H,* and *A* and in many forms of *e.*

baseline. Horizontal line upon which stand capitals, lowercase letters, punctuation points, etc.

basis weight. Weight of 500 sheets of paper of standard size. Basic size for writing papers, bond and ledger is 17 × 22; for book papers, 25 × 38; cover stock, 20 × 26; bristol 25½ × 30½ inches.

Bauhaus. German school of architecture and design that originated Sans Serif letterform.

beak. The serif on the arm of a letter such as *K.*

beard. The side between the shoulder and the face of a piece of type. Also the cross stroke on the stem of the *G.*

beaten proof. Stone proof (*which see*).

bed. Flat surface of cylinder press upon which type stands during printing.

Ben Day. Trade name for a pattern of lines or dots used in photoengraving to provide shading in line drawings, as background for photos or type, or to cut down the tone of type, rules, or solid areas in cuts. Named for the inventor. Patterns are identical with those achieved by Zip-a-Tone (*which see*).

b.f. Boldface.

Bible paper. Thin but strong and opaque book paper.

big-on-slug. That quality in a type face which is effected by using maximum of body area for x-height (*which see*).

bimetallic. Offset plate combining aluminum and copper.

binary. Computer capable of giving only off-on signals.

binder. Craftsman who works in a bindery, especially those who bind books. Also oils or mineral compounds used to speed drying of ink.

binding posts. Kind of loose-leaf binding in which pages are held on metal pegs inserted into pre-punched holes.

Black Letter. Text or Old English, race of type based on letters of early handwritten German manuscripts.

bleed. To place a cut so it runs off one or more edges of the paper.

blind embossing. Impressing a design into back of paper so it appears in bas-relief on front side. No ink is used.

blow-up plate. Halftone engraving made in small size with fine screen then enlarged, by line engraving, to larger size and coarser screen.

blueprint. Photocopy process used to provide proofs for cold type.

boards. Stiff material in the cover of a book.

Bodoni, Giambatista. Venetian printer and type founder who designed type face bearing his name.

body. Metal block that carries printing surface of a type character. Also regular reading matter of a newspaper, book, or advertisement as contrasted to display lines. Body type is that face in which such material is set, usually through 12-point.

boiler plate. Printing material supplied to newspapers in the form of stereotype plates. Also editorial material so printed.

bogus. Type uselessly reset after being printed in other form, e.g., stereotype or electro.

bond. Rag or sulphite paper of hard finish used for writing and stationery forms.

book. A basic category of printing paper.

booklet. Folded printed matter with less than 48 pages, each as part of facing pair.

book system. Method of proofreading which requires two marks for every correction. One mark designates place of error; the other instructs how to make correction.

bounced type. That set on irregular baseline and sometimes irregular vertical axes.

Bourges. (Pronounced Burgess), coloring materials, especially thin acetate sheets—keyed to standard printing inks—for preparing art and dummies and modifying photographs.

bowl. Curved lines that create circular or semicircular shapes in letters such as *c*, the lower portion of a, the right-hand portion of *b*, etc., and the upper portion of *g*.

box. Unit of type enclosed by a border. Modern, or sideless, boxes have border only at top and bottom.

brace. A bracket.

bracketed serifs. Those which connect to the stem by a curve that smooths the angle of juncture.

brackets. Typographic devices used to set off matter grammatically in apposition.

Braille. Dots in code embossed in paper for reading by blind.

brayer. Roller to apply ink to type by hand.

Bristol board. Thin cardboard with smooth surface ideal for drawing, writing, and printing.

broadside. Large leaf of paper, at least 15×28 inches, in folder form.

broadsheet. Newspaper format on page approximately 15×21 inches.

brochure. Folder of high quality in design and/or production.

broken package. Quantities of paper less than normally wrapped amounts. When sold, broken packages carry penalty price.

bronzing. Applying metal powder to sticky ink to create metallic effect or perfect opacity on reproduction proofs.

brownprint. Photocopy process used to provide cold-type proofs.

Bruning. Photocopy process used to prepare cold-type proofs.

buddy system. Orientation system of layout (*which see*).

bug. Printers' union label.

bullet. Large period used for decoration.

burin. Pointed steel cutting tool used by engravers.

burnish. To increase area of halftone dots by flattening them. Also, to smooth down self-adhering letters and shading sheets.

butted lines. Two or more linecaster slugs placed side by side to create one line of type.

c. & s.c. Capitals and small capitals, style of composition in which each word starts with a capital and other letters are in capital form in the height of lowercase letters.

calendered. Paper which has been given a very smooth surface by passing it between polished steel rollers during manufacture.

California job case. Receptacle in which foundry type is stored and from which it is hand set.

caliper. Measurement of single sheet of paper expressed in thousandths of an inch.

camera-type. Halftone pattern where random dots are sliced off at one side.

Cameron machine. One for printing and collating entire book in two steps.

caption. In newspaper usage, display line above a picture; not cutlines, explanatory matter under the engraving. In advertising and magazines, any explanatory matter that runs with an illustration.

Cartoon. Very casual letter form in Script or Cursive style.

carbon tissue. Gelatin sheet through which a mordant etches a rotogravure plate.

cardboard. Stiff, sturdy sheet consisting of several layers of low-quality paper pasted together.

casting box. Receptacle in which stereotype flong is placed to cast a printing plate.

casting off manuscript. Copyfitting.

cathode-ray tube. CRT. Typesetting method in which letterform is defined on television-like tube by digitized instructions.

center spread. Double truck; the two pages at which a newspaper, magazine or booklet is folded. Advertising or editorial matter may occupy that space which is normally devoted to the gutter. (*See* double truck.)

chain marks. Watermarks on laid paper that run parallel to grain and about an inch apart.

chapbook. Small book, often handprinted, usually produced as keepsake.

chapter heads. Display type that begins a chapter of a book.

characters-per-pica. Cpp, system of copyfitting (*which see*).

chase. Metal frame into which page form is locked before printing or stereotyping.

checkerboard. Halftone pattern of perfect squares alternating between black and white.

chemical printing. Lithography.

Christmas tree. Layout pattern in which components project to one or both sides from a vertical axis.

chroma. That quality of intensity of a color.

chromatic. True colors.

circulating matrix. Mold, in a brass body, from which Linotype and Intertype cast type. Matrices are automatically returned to proper receptacle for reuse.

clamshell. Colloquialism for platen press.

clapper. Colloquialism for platen press.

classic. Layout pattern based on geometric forms to create rhythm.

claw. Projection from stem of *r* and from bowl of *g*.

coated paper. That covered with a smooth layer of mineral substances.

cockle. Paper finish with surface ripples.

cold type. That set photographically or by means that do not utilize metal, hot type.

Colex 520. Machine used for colographic proofing.

collage. Picture or design created by pasting various elements onto common background.

collotype. Method of offset printing of continuous-tone copy utilizing an unscreened gelatin plate.

colography. System of dry color proofing using powder of appropriate color to give hue.

colophon. Originally the mark whereby a printer identified his products, now the trademark of a publisher. Also, that part of a book that specifies types used, designer, and/or artist.

color job. Printing which uses flat color (*which see*).

Color-Key. System of color proofing using overlaid transparencies in each color.

color separation. Breaking down full-color copy into its component proportions of the primary colors. Also, black-and-white negative which shows amount of one primary color in a full-color original.

color, typographic. Devices to alter overall tone of masses of type. Also, apparent tone or density of printed matter on a page as affected by various types, borders, decorations, etc.

color wheel. Diagrammatic arrangement of primary and secondary colors as a visual aid in determining relationship and harmony among colors.

Columbian. First printing press invented in America.

comb. A series of prongs connected by a spine, used for loose-leaf binding.

combination cut. Printing plate consisting of line and halftone.

combo. Combination, a group of pictures arranged into and used as a single unit.

ComCom. Method of computerized composition using RCA machine.

common diagonal. Visual method used to determine size of reduced or enlarged picture.

complementary harmony. Color combinations using two colors directly opposite each other on the color wheel.

composing room. Area where type is set and made up.

composing stick. Metal receptacle into which type is placed when set by hand.

composition. Typographic material that has been set and/or assembled.

compositor. Craftsman who sets type or assembles it into printing form.

comprehensive. Compre or comp, complete and detailed dummy.

concentric circle. Halftone screen using parallel-line technique.

connotative. Jazz, layout pattern in which rectangular areas are suggested but not defined.

continuous tone. Photographs or painted pictures that utilize varying values of color.

control information. That coded into tape which determines machine functions other than character selection, e.g., paragraphing, line erase, setting duplex, etc.

controller paper. Wide perforated tape which actuates casting mechanism of Monotype.

conversion, offset. Turning letterpress standing matter into camera-ready plate-making copy.

cool colors. Those which tend to recede from the viewer, usully greens and blues.

copy. Material which the compositor sets in type or from which a platemaker creates printing plates.

copyfitting. Determining the area to be occupied by type set from given copy.

copyholder. Proofreader's assistant who reads original copy to compare to proof.

counter. Areas within and around the printing surface of a piece of type which are depressed to prevent contact with ink rollers and paper.

cover. A heavy paper such as used for covering books and booklets.

Craftint. Patterns similar to those of Ben Day which are applied, on thin plastic sheets, onto original art.

Craftype. Trade name for letters printed on transparent, self-adhering plastic.

Cronapress. Method of offset conversion using pressure of tiny steel balls to force opaque film evenly upon relief printing elements and creating clear areas where contact is made.

crop. To eliminate unwanted portion of photograph by actually cutting away or indicating, by marginal lines, that platemaker should ignore it.

cross stroke. Horizontal stroke of *t* and *f*.

CRT. Cathode-ray tube (*which see*).

cuneiform. Early form of writing which contributed to development of Latin alphabet.

Cursive. Type which resembles handwriting but with unconnected letters.

cut. Photoengraving.

cutoff rule. Hairline that marks the point where a story moves from one column to another. Also, all printing lines that create horizontal divisions between typographic elements in a newspaper.

cut without waste. Method of reducing large sheet of paper to smaller ones with minimum waste.

cyan. Blue-green filter used in color separations (*which see*).

cylinder press. Method of letterpress printing in which paper is impressed upon type by a cylinder.

Day-Glow. Trade name of ink with extremely high luminosity.

dead metal. That left around edges of photoengraving to protect plates during electrotyping or stereotyping. Also called bearers.

decal. Decalcomania, process for transferring pictures and designs onto glass and other materials from specially prepared paper.

deckle edge. Irregular, ragged edge of sheet of handmade paper, now produced mechanically.

delete. Proofreader's mark, to "take out."

descenders. Portion of a type character that drops below the baseline. Also those characters themselves, such as *g, j, p, q,* and *y.*

D-I, direct-image. Method of offset conversion where relief elements are printed to metal plate which is then debossed.

Diascan. Electronic scanning device for making color separations.

Diazo. Photocopying machine used to produce cold-type proofs.

Didot. Famous family of French printers for whom is named the system of printer's measurements used in that country.

die cut. Paper cut into shapes other than rectangular by means of thin steel blades bent into desired forms.

digitize. To give specifications for letterforms in binary code for CRT.

dingbats. Typographic decorations.

dirty proof. One with many typographic errors.

display. Type used in larger sizes and smaller quantity to attract attention, as opposed to body type (*which see*). Usually 12-point is smallest size classified as display.

distribution. Returning type and other printing material to receptacles for reuse.

Ditto. Transfer duplicator for office use.

doctor blade. Metal scraper that wipes ink off surface of intaglio plates.

dot etching. Method of correcting color separation negatives by dissolving the outer edges of halftone dots to make them smaller.

Doubletone. Drawing paper with two shading patterns made visible by application of developing fluid.

double truck. Two newspaper or magazine pages at the center of a section or signature that are made up as a single unit. Usually refers to advertising using this space, center spread referring to editorial use.

dragon's blood. Resin powder used to protect from acid those portions of a photoengraving that are to remain in relief as printing surfaces.

drawsheet. Top layer of paper on tympan of press.

driography. Offset printing process that does not use water as ink repellent.

drop-out. Highlight halftone (*which see*).

dry mat. Flong for making stereotype matrix.

dry offset. Method in which image is offset from rubber blanket where it has been placed by relief printing.

drypoint. Method of preparing an etching by incising lines with a cutting tool instead of with acid.

dummy. Detailed diagram instructing make-up man how to arrange elements of a printing job. (*See also* rough, comprehensive, mechanical.)

duotone. Printing produced by two plates, one in dark ink, the other in light, which produces a third color, usually the only one discernible.

duplex. Linecasting matrix that carries two character molds. Also, that character which occupies the secondary position on a matrix. Also, paper with different color, texture, or finish on each side of sheet.

duplicators. Devices for reproducing various forms of printing in small quantity and, sometimes, of low quality.

Dylux. Method for proofing platemaker's negatives without wet developing fluid.

dynamic. Layout pattern which balances elements in an asymmetrical form. (*See* informal balance.)

editorial. All matter in a publication which is not advertising.

eggshell antique. Soft, bulky paper with a finish that resembles the shell for which it is named.

Egyptian. Ethnic of Square Serifs whose serifs are same thickness as that of main strokes of letterform.

electro-mechanics. Devices used primarily in phototypesetting machines in which control and actuation functions are performed by combinations of mechanical devices such as gear trains, lever systems, cams, etc., and electrical devices such as small motors, solenoids, magnetic clutches, etc.

electronics. Devices applying controllable flow of free electrons through vacuum, gaseous atmosphere, or semiconducting solids, especially for counting and arithmetical functions in phototypesetting machines and computers.

electrotype. Duplicate relief printing plate made by electrolytic process depositing copper on a matrix of original form.

elliptical dot. Halftone screen pattern designed for greater fidelity of middle gray tones.

Elrod. Casting machine that produces rules, borders, and spacing material in a continuous strip.

em. The square of any type-body size. Unit of measurement for typesetting; a 9-point line 2 inches long, or 144 points, contains 16 ems; a 6-point line the same width has 24 ems. Commonly but inaccurately used as synonym for pica. Em quadrats are called "mutton quads" to avoid confusion with en quad.

embossing. Process for raising paper, by means of a die, in a relief pattern. This may be simultaneous with printing ink. Embossing without ink is blind embossing.

em-space. Spacing material less than a quad. A 3-em space is one third of the mutt quad of that face.

emulsion. Photosensitive material that reacts to light in photographic processes.

en. Half the width of an em of the same font. En quadrats are called "nut quads" to avoid confusion with em quad.

enameled. Book paper with highly polished coated surface.

encapsulate. To package liquid, usually perfume, in microscopic capsules which are emulsified in printing ink.

end papers. Sheets of sturdy paper that connect the cover to the pages of a book.

English finish. E.F., paper with a suedelike finish produced by a clay coating.

engravings. Relief printing plates created by photochemistry.

ephemera. Printing matter designed for short life: matchbook covers, handbills, memo pads, etc.

EPOI. Machine for electronic control of color separations.

etching. Removing nonprinting areas from a relief plate by acid. Also an intaglio process used to create fine art.

ethnic. First subdivision of type races.

eutectic. Descriptive of substance that expands upon freezing, e.g., typemetal.

expanded. Layout pattern in which an illustration projects in one or two directions from a basic rectangle.

eye fatigue. A factor that determines to a large extent the amount of type a person will read at one time.

face. Style or cut of type. Also that portion of a slug or type character which imprints upon the paper.

facsimile. Highlight halftone. Also system of transmitting visual images by wire or radio.

fake color. Simulation of the effect of four-color process plates by manual modification of black-and-white negatives.

family. First subdivision of type after race. It carries a trade name as identification.

Faxograph. Machine for transferring drawings and charts onto Mimeograph stencils or small offset plates or masters.

feed edge. That side of sheet of paper which is placed against guides in printing.

feet. Slight projections upon which a piece of type stands.

felt side. Right side, that surface of the paper which comes in contact with felt rollers during manufacture, as opposed to the wire side which rests upon the traveling screen.

filler. Coating of clay added to paper to give smooth finish.

filter. Sheets of colored gelatin used to make color separations (*which see*). Cyan, magenta, and yellow are those most commonly used.

fine arts. That use of the graphic arts to produce original works such as etchings, lithographs, serigraphs, etc.

fine papers. Bond, ledger, writing, and wedding papers.

finial. Curve that finishes a main stroke in some Italic faces, replacing the serif of the Roman.

finishing line. Thin black line surrounding a square halftone.

first revise. Proof pulled after errors discovered in a galley proof have been corrected.

flag. Nameplate of a newspaper. Commonly but erroneously called masthead.

flat. Group of engraver's negatives exposed and etched as a single unit before being sawed up into individual cuts. Also group of original pictures shot on one negative.

flat casting. Making relief plates by pouring molten metal onto a stereotype matrix.

flat color. Spot color, use of any color, other than black, which does not attempt to simulate the full spectrum of nature.

Flexowriter. Version of a typewriter used for cold-type composition.

flong. Sheet of papier-mâché used to produce a stereotype matrix. Also used to designate the matrix so made.

flop negative. Act of turning an engraver's negative face down before exposing it upon a metal plate in photoengraving, necessary to create mirror image required in a relief plate.

fluorographic. Process to produce highlight halftones photographically.

flush head. Short for flush-left head, a style in which each line begins near or at the left margin and aligns with that above and below it.

flyboy. Helper who works at delivery end of printing press.

folder. Leaf of paper folded once or twice.

folio. Sheet of paper 17 × 22 inches.

folio lines. Those which give the title and page number of a book. Also called running heads. In newspaper usage, lines which carry name of paper, date, and page number.

font. Subdivision of a series of type. It consists of all characters and spacing of one size of one series.

foreword. Introduction to a book written by a person other than the author.

form. Type and engravings, assembled within a chase, from which one page or signature is printed or stereotyped.

formal balance. Layout pattern that balances elements of equal size in exact mathematical relation to a vertical axis.

format. Shape, size, and general physical form of a publication.

former. Scorcher (*which see*).

Fotorex. Machine for producing cold type in display sizes.

Fotosetter. Phototypesetting machine utilizing the principles of the Intertype.

Fotoronic. Phototypesetting machine by Intertype.

foundry type. Individual characters of hard metal used for handsetting.

Franklin, Benjamin. Called the patron saint of American printers for his activity in the craft in early history of this country.

French fold. Single leaf, printed on one side and folded so blank is on inside of 4-page folder.

frisket. Protective paper to shield areas of printing paper from ink or photographic paper from light.

fullface. Normal design of a type face in regard to weight and width.

functionalism. Philosophy of typography that requires that every printing element contribute to conveying information.

furniture. Large spacing material placed around type area to lock it into a chase.

galley. Shallow, three-sided container of metal or wood in which composition is stored before being placed into forms. Also the container on a linecaster into which the slugs drop after casting. Also short for galley proof.

galley proof. First impression printed from composition in order to detect errors.

ganged. Several forms or plates combined for simultaneous printing on a single large sheet of paper.

gathering. Collecting printed pages in proper order for binding.

gelatin printing. Hectographing (*which see*).

geometric. Layout pattern which divides the total area into smaller shapes in pleasant relation to each other.

ghosted. Background which has been lightened by application of ink with an airbrush or of plastic shading sheets.

Giant Caster. Typecasting machine that produces display type.

Golden Rectangle. Approximately 3 × 5, considered by ancient artists as the most pleasant ratio for an area.

Gothic. Type of the Sans Serif race in which strokes are usually but not always monotonal. Also called Block Letter, Grotesk, or Antique.

grain. Predominant direction in which cylindrical cellulose fibers point in a sheet of paper.

graver. V-shaped steel cutting tool used by engravers.

gravure. Commercial application of intaglio printing. Sheetfed gravure prints upon individual sheets; rotogravure (*which see*) prints from an endless roll of paper.

Greeking. Simulation of head or body type in layouts.

green copy. One of first sheets to come off printing press.

gripper edge. Amount of paper left blank at edge of sheet to allow mechanical fingers to draw it into printing press and hold it during impression.

grippers. Mechanical fingers that hold paper onto impression cylinder of a printing press.

groove. Indention on bottom of a type character that separates the feet.

Grotesk. Gothic type.

ground. Protective coating placed on a sheet of metal through which an artist scratches lines to be incised by acid.

guideline system. Method of proofreading in which the error is circled and connected, by a line, to marginal instructions.

gum. Colloidal vegetable substance used to increase the repulsion of ink by water in lithography.

Gutenberg Bible. 42-Line Bible or Mazarin Bible, believed to be first book printed from movable type, about 1450.

Gutenberg, Johann. Inventor of moveable type and letterpress printing as we know it.

gutter. That blank space on two facing pages that meet at the binding edge. Also used to refer to the inner margin of a single page, although correctly that is the gutter margin and consists of only half the gutter.

Hadego. Machine for producing cold type in display sizes.

hairline. Thinnest rule used by printers.

hairspacing. Introduction of thinnest of spacing materials, usually between capitals, within a word, to improve legibility or to avoid excessive word spacing.

half-round. Curved stereotype plate.

half-title. The first page of a book after the end papers.

halftone. Printing plate which gives the illusion of gray tones by means of a dot pattern.

handlettering. That produced by artist in forms more regular than those of calligraphy.

hanging indention. Style for body and headline composition in which the first line is set full measure and all succeeding lines are indented an identical distance at the left.

hard copy. Typewritten copy produced simultaneously with perforated tape to actuate typesetting machines.

hardware. Computer machinery, as opposed to software (*which see*).

Harris Editing Terminal. Device for editing tape-stored copy using video screen as reader.

Headliner. Machine to produce display sizes of cold type.

hectograph. Gelatin process for reproducing limited quantities of copy written, drawn, or typed on paper master and from which it is transferred to gelatin surface for setting-off.

height-to-paper. Standardized measurement from feet to face of type and other printing elements.

hellbox. Receptacle into which is placed broken or discarded type.

high-etch. Dry offset, a combination of relief and planographic printing.

highlight halftone. Drop-out or facsimile, printing plate in which the dots in certain areas have been removed by mechanical or photographic means.

holography. Method of projecting three-dimensional image using laser beams.

horsing. Reading proof by one man without assistance of copyholder.

hot metal. Or hot type, linecaster slugs and foundry type as opposed to cold type (*which see*).

hue. That quality which makes colors as we recognize them. Also product of mixing two colors together.

ideogram. Early form of writing in which a symbol meant an entire word or idea. Still used in Japan, China, and Korea.

idiot tape. Raw tape, that for typesetting machine that carries no justification instructions.

illumination. Decorations applied by hand to early printing. Also that style of handlettering in which letters are decorated, often with miniature pictures. Also, in phototypesetting machine, that light which passes through photographic negative to create picture of type character.

imposition. Arrangement of several pages into a signature so they may be printed in one impression and, when folded, will follow in proper order.

impression. Printing of ink on paper, especially by letterpress, but commonly used for all printing methods. Also the printed copy produced by type or a plate. Also the pressure of type or plates upon paper, as a kiss impression (*which see*). Also the appearance of the printed piece, as "a clear impression." Also the number of times a press has completed a printing cycle.

imprinting. Printing additional material on otherwise finished sheet of printing, e.g., name of specific dealer added to leaflet, brochure, etc.

incunabula. Printing produced in the fifteenth century.

India paper. Bible paper.

informal. Layout pattern in which approximate balance is achieved by free distribution of elements around an imaginary pivot at the optical center.

initial. First letter of a word or sentence set in type larger than body size for decoration or emphasis. Its size is indicated by the number of lines of body type it occupies, as a 3-line initial. (*See* rising initial, inset initial.)

Inline. Form of Ornamented type in which a white line runs down the middle of the main stroke.

inset initial. Large letter, used for decorative effect, dropped into an area that would otherwise be occupied by body type.

instant negative. Offset conversion process which produces negative without darkroom or wet chemicals.

intaglio. Method of printing in which the image is carried in incised lines.

intensity. Strength and brilliance of a color.

intermediate color. That produced by mixing a primary color with a secondary one.

Intertype. Keyboarded linecaster.

inverted pyramid. Headline of two or three lines all centered, in which successive lines are shorter than the one above it. Usually abbreviated to pyramid.

Italic. Letterform in which characters slant to the right and are more decorative than their Roman (perpendicular) counterparts. Also, incorrectly, used to refer to all letters that slant to the right although these are correctly called Obliques. Abbreviated to Ital, Itlx, or X.

Itek. Line of photo processing machinery, especially that which produces offset plate without negative.

ivory. Finish of paper produced by coating it with beeswax and then calendering.

jazz. Connotative layout (*which see*).

jim-dash. Short, centered line used between elements of a headline or between headline and story. Often designated by its length, as, most commonly, 3-em dash.

job press. Printing press which takes paper up to 25 × 38 inches.

job shop. Commercial printing plant.

job ticket. Envelope which accompanies a printing job through all stages of production, carrying complete instructions and specifications and showing progress of work.

justify. To fill a line of composition so it aligns at both margins.

Justowriter. Typewriter that produces automatically justified lines of cold type.

Kalvar. Offset conversion system using heated typemetal to create negative image on film.

kerning. Also kern, that part of the face of a type character that projects beyond the body in Italic or Swash fonts.

key phrase. Groups of words repeated in each face and size of type in a specimen book.

key plate. Usually the black plate, which carries strong definition in color printing.

kicker. Short line in smaller, or accent, type above the main line of a head. Also called teaser, eyebrow, highline, and, erroneously, overline.

kiss impression. Ideal meeting of type and paper so that ink is deposited completely and evenly without indenting the paper.

kraft. German for "strong," a sturdy paper commonly used for wrapping.

Kromecote. Coated paper of extremely glossy finish.

Kromolite. Method of producing drop-out halftones photographically through the use of filters and combining line and halftone negatives.

L's, cropper's. Paper or plastic in the shape of a capital *L*, used to determine which portion of a photograph is most advantageous to use.

laid. Finish of paper simulating texture of old handmade paper.

laminated paper. That produced by pasting together two or more sheets. Also, sheet of paper protected by coating of transparent plastic.

lampblack. Intensely black pigment.

laser. Source of completely phased light.

layout. Arrangement of typographic units into a pattern. Also, in composing room, called make-up (*which see*). Also dummy (*which see*).

l.c. Lowercase, the small letters, or minuscules, of a font.

l.c.a. Lowercase-alphabet length, the factor which determines the number of characters of type per pica, used in copyfitting.

lead. (Pronounced leed) first or first few paragraphs in a newspaper or magazine story.

leader. (Pronounced leeder) line of dots or hyphens used to connect elements of tabulation.

leaf. Sheet of paper.

ledd. (Always pronounced ledd, although often spelled lead) thin strip of metal, up to 4 points thick, used to create interlineal spacing. As a verb, to insert such spacing material. When not instructed otherwise, the printer will insert 2-point ledds.

ledger. Paper with a smooth writing surface that withstands folding.

legibility. Or visibility, that quality of type that affects the quickness of perception of a single word, line, or compact group of lines. Often confused with readability (*which see*).

letterpress. Relief printing.

letterset. Printing method in which relief matter prints onto rubber blanket, then is offset.

letterspacing. Addition of extra spacing within a word, either to create more pleasing appearance or emphasis, or to fill out a line to proper measure.

library. All typographic resources available in a printing plant.

lift. Quantity of paper which can readily be placed on printing press or other machine. Also, to test type form for adequately tight lockup.

ligature. Type characters consisting of two or more letters united as fi, ffi, and æ.

Linasec. Simple computer without memory banks, for justifying raw tape.

linear definition. Line conversion, line plate made from continuous-tone art.

linecaster. Machine that casts an entire line of type as opposed to those that cast individual characters. (*See* Linotype.)

line cut. Photoengraving which prints only in lines and masses of black.

line gauge. Pica rule, ruler with pica increments.

linen. Writing paper whose texture closely resembles that of fine cloth.

lining system. Placement of letters upon the body so that all faces of the same point size will align on a common baseline. Most faces are designed in standard lining; those on art lining have a relatively high baseline to allow for longer descenders; those on title lining have low baselines because such fonts are made up of all capitals and no descenders must be provided for.

link. Element that joins the two circular portions of the *g*.

Linofilm. Phototypesetting system consisting of a keyboard, photographic unit, and composer.

linoleum block. Relief plate resembling a wood block but cut from linoleum.

Linotron. CRT phototypesetting machine by Mergenthaler.

Linotype. First keyboarded linecaster and used so widely today that, with a lowercase *l*, it is used as a generic term. Keyboarded linecasters assemble matrices automatically when actuated by keys. In others, matrices are assembled by hand.

lithography. Planographic printing process. (*See* offset.)

loading agent. Mineral substance added to give gloss to paper.

lockup. Process of fastening elements into a chase so they will remain firmly in place during printing or stereotyping.

logotype. Or logo, a single matrix or type body containing two or more letters commonly used together as *the* or *and*. Often confused with ligature (*which see*). Also often used to refer to small ornaments cast from linecaster matrices. Also signatures or trademarks used in advertising. Also flag or name plate of a newspaper.

loop. Semicircular portion of the *e*.

Ludlow. Linecaster usually used for display type. Its product is T-shaped slugs which are further supported by underpinning.

Lydel. Plastic material for wraparound plates.

machine finish. Calendered paper made very smooth by passing it between metal rollers during manufacture.

magenta. Filter used in making color separations.

Magnascan. Electronic device for making color separations.

magnetic ink. That containing small particles of magnetized metal to be read by electrical scanner.

Mainz Psalter. Early book printed by Gutenberg and considered by some to be the first printed from movable type.

marginator. Typewriter attachment to accomplish justification.

majuscules. Capital letters.

makeready. Process of adjusting contact between printing elements and paper to assure perfect impression.

make-up. Design of a newspaper or magazine page. Also, the physical process of assembling typographic units into pages or advertisements.

make-up man. Printer who assembles typographic elements into a form.

manifold. Onionskin, thin paper used especially for making carbon copies.

manuscript. Ms. (sing.), mss. (pl.), technically a handwritten copy, but commonly designating any original copy, especially for a book, for the compositor.

matrix. Mat, mold from which type, decorative materials, advertisements, or illustrations are cast. Linecaster matrices are brass; stereotype matrices are of cellulose fibers and adhesive. (*See* flong.)

matrix case. Carrier of matrices in a Monotype.

matrix disk. Carrier of negative images of characters in the Photon.

matte. Textured finish on photographic paper.

Mazarin Bible. Gutenberg Bible (*which see*).

mean line. X-line, the line that marks the top of lowercase letters that do not have ascenders.

measure. Length of a line of type.

mechanical. Detailed dummy used as copy by, or instructions for, a platemaker.

mechanical separations. Copy for the platemaker prepared by an artist with separate sections for each color to be used in printing.

memory. Means of storing information for later use, e.g., perforated tape or magnetic for composing machines, stored data in computers, etc.

mercury process. Printing process similar to lithography that uses mercury instead of water as ink repellent.

Mergenthaler Scanner. Electronic device for producing color separations mechanically.

metal paste-up. Method of preparing a printing form by pasting into position engravings of type and illustrative matter.

mezzotint. Form of fine-art etching in which the entire surface is burred to act as many intaglio wells.

minuscules. Lowercase, or small, letters.

Modern numbers. Those numerals which align at the baseline.

Modern Roman. That letterform distinguished by thin, straight serifs and marked variation between thick and thin strokes.

modified silhouette. Halftone engraving with one to three sides outlined.

modified vignette. Halftone cut in which one or more sides are straight, the others blending from the gray of the picture into the white of the paper.

monitor. Printer who services automatic typesetting machine.

monochromatic. Harmony achieved by using tints and shades of only one color.

Monophoto. Phototypesetting machine utilizing the principles of the Monotype.

Monotonal. Race of type with letterforms in strokes of equal weight and without serifs.

Monotype. Machine that casts individual pieces of type and assembles them into justified lines.

montage. Single photograph produced by using several negatives or parts thereof.

mordant. Any corroding substance used in etching printing plates.

morgue. Collection of reference material for a newspaper or an artist.

mortise. Opening cut in a printing plate for the insertion of type or other typographic material. An opening cut through lines of type for inserting other lines, illustrations, or ornaments. Formerly a mortise referred only to the area left open by cutting a rectangle out of a corner of an engraving. Today an internal mortise is one cut into the body of an engraving. Mortises may be, but rarely are, irregular in shape.

mosquitos. Nondecorative elements such as trademarks, pictures of plants or founders, etc., that must be used on a letterhead.

ms. or mss. Manuscript.

Munsell system. Method of designating colors by numerical gradation.

mutton. Mutt, an em quad.

negative. Photographic film on which tonal values are reversed so that areas appearing black on the original are white or transparent, and vice versa.

news line. Portion of a composing room devoted to setting editorial matter. Especially linecasters setting such material.

newsprint. Low-quality, weak paper commonly used to print newspapers.

nickeltype. Electrotype (*which see*) faced in nickel instead of copper.

nicks. Parallel grooves in the side of a piece of foundry type to identify it by font.

no-orphan. Orientation layout system (*which see*).

nondistribution. System of typesetting in which all used typographic matter is remelted instead of being distributed for reuse.

nonpareil. Former designation for 6-point type, now used to specify spacing material (a slug) of that thickness.

nonwoven fabric. Paper used for making clothing.

Novelty. Ethnic of Ornamented type race in which letterform is drastically altered.

nut. An en quad.

Oblique. Letters, other than Romans, which slant to the right.

oblique axis. Layout pattern in which type blocks are tilted off the perpendicular or set in a tilted parallelogram.

oblong. Rectangle of 2 × 3 dimensions.

occult balance. Dynamic layout (*which see*).

official envelope. Number 10, one which takes an 8½ × 11 letterhead folded twice.

offset. Offset lithography, printing process in which an image is lithographed or letterpressed onto a rubber blanket from where it is transferred to paper. Also, as off-set, the undesirable transfer of ink from one printed sheet to another.

Old English. Type family in race of Black Letter.

Old Style numbers. Those in which the 3, 4, 5, 7, and 9 project below the baseline.

Old Style Roman. Letterform distinguished by bracketed serifs, minimal difference between thick and thin strokes, and bowls that are on axes off the perpendicular.

one-up. Printing one impression of a form at one time. By using duplicate plates, jobs may be printed two-up or even in greater numbers in one impression.

onionskin. Manifold paper.

on-paper type. Cold-type copy pasted to surface of art.

opacity. That quality of paper that prevents printing on one side of sheet from showing through to the other.

opaque. To paint out unwanted shadows or other detail in the platemaker's negative.

open dot. Halftone screen pattern of perfectly round dots.

Optak. Photogelatin printing similar to Collotype except that it uses a halftone screen.

optical center. Point 10 per cent above the mathematical center of a page or layout.

optical character recognition. OCR, method of machine-reading type by recognizing visual form rather than code.

orientation layout. Buddy system or no-orphan system, whereby every element in a layout aligns with at least one other element.

Ornamented. Race of type in which the basic form is embellished or extremely altered.

Outline. Ornamented letter with only its outline defined.

overflap. Protective cover of tissue and/or kraft over a piece of platemaker's copy.

overlay. Transparent plastic flap over art work providing mechanical color separation.

overwire. Spiral binding concealed by the cover.

Oxford rule. Printing element that produces two parallel lines, one thick and one thin.

oxidation. Process whereby ink dries.

Ozalid. Photocopying machine used to produce cold-type proofs.

packing. Layers of paper between the impression cylinder and the tympan upon which paper rests during printing. Manipulation of packing to assure a perfect printing surface is called makeready.

padding. Simple method of binding paper by coating one edge of the sheets with flexible adhesive.

page printer. CRT phototypesetter that arranges letterforms in proper position on page.

page proofs. Sample impressions of a sheet of printing which are checked for errors. They may consist of one or several pages all on one sheet.

pagination. Arranging type so it will print pages in proper sequence.

painting-up. Method of preparing a one-color original to be used as copy for two-color plates.

panoramagrams. Printed image, seen through screen, for 3-dimensional effect.

Pantone. Mercury-process printing.

paragraph openers. Typographic elements to direct the reading eye to the start of a paragraph, usually without indenting.

parallax. Phenomenon of separate image seen by each eye being mentally combined into single 3-dimensional image.

paste-on. Cold-type characters that are pasted onto keyline copy.

paste-up. Process of affixing elements into position for engraver's copy. Also, the copy so produced.

patrix. Mold that casts right-reading, instead of mirror-image, type used for dry offset (*which see*).

pebble. Finish of paper with tiny surface dimples.

perfecting press. Rotary printing two sides of paper in one operation.

perfector press. Flatbed utilizing perfecting principle.

photocomposition. Typographic material produced and arranged photographically instead of by using metal type and engravings.

photoengraving. Printing plate produced by photochemistry for relief printing.

photogelatin. Collotype, a lithographic process using unscreened gelatin plates to make continuous-tone reproductions.

photography. Writing with light, utilization of the action of light upon sensitive emulsions that change color or density, in order to produce pictures or printing plates.

photogravure. Form of intaglio printing that does not use a screen but projects light between minute granules of resin.

photo matrix. Method whereby photo image is carried to offset plate without negative.

photomechanical. Machine that makes relief printing plates by removing unwanted areas by burning or cutting according to instructions from light-sensitive scanning device.

photopolymer. Plastic material for platemaking that is entirely photosensitive throughout its depth, not only on surface.

Photon. Phototypesetting machine.

Photostat. A photocopy.

phototypesetting. Photographic production of composition by a keyboard.

pi. As a verb, to mix up type. As a noun, type so disarranged.

pica. Lineal measurement of 12 points. Commonly but incorrectly called an em (*which see*). Also 12-point type.

piece fractions. Those produced by combining two linecaster matrices.

pig. Long bar of solid typemetal used to feed molten-metal pot on machines such as Linotype.

piggyback. Type set without any space between lines of characters.

pigment. Substance which provides the color in ink.

planer. Block of flat wood used to press type in a form into a perfectly flat printing surface.

planographic. Lithographic.

plastic binding. Method of loose-leaf binding.

platen. Flat surface upon which paper rests when it comes in contact with printing surfaces. Also short for platen press.

plates. Flat smooth pieces of metal which have been treated to create a printing surface. For offset, paper plates are often used.

ply. One of several pieces of paper pasted together to make Bristol board or similar stock which is then designated as three-ply, etc.

point. Unit of printer's measurement, .01384 inches, for practical purposes, 1⁄72 inch. Also any punctuation mark.

porcelain. Blotting paper to which a sheet of coated stock has been pasted.

posterization. Photographic manipulation that converts all intermediate grays into one or two tones.

pot. Receptacle on a casting machine which stores molten metal.

precipitation. Method of drying ink by causing certain of its components to solidify.

preface. Formal statement by the author that precedes the text of a book. As opposed to a foreword, written by another person.

preliminaries. Those portions of a book which precede the text itself.

primary colors. Red, blue, and yellow.

primary letters. Those lowercase characters which have no ascenders or descenders.

primary optical area. Focal point, that point in or near the upper left corner where the reading eye first looks at a page or advertisement.

printers. Men who prepare composition for, or actually perform, imprinting operations. Also machines which produce typewritten copy by electrical impulses, either independently or in conjunction with reperforating machines, as Teletype machines.

printer's devil. Apprentice or helper in a printing shop, so named because early printers were believed to owe their craft to a pact with Satan.

printmaking. That part of the fine arts concerned with producing original works by printing methods.

prints. Fine arts such as etchings, lithographs, etc., produced by various printing processes.

process color. A printing method that duplicates a full-color continuous-tone original copy by means of optically mixing primary colors.

ProFilm. Hand-cut plastic which forms stencil for silk-screen.

progressive proofs. Progs, proofs of each plate used for process color printing, singly and in combination with the others.

proofreader. Printer charged with responsibility of verifying that type perfectly reproduces the copy or manuscript.

proofs. Sample impressions of composition and engravings produced for inspection for errors. (*See* galley, repros, first revise, progs.) As a verb, to produce such an impression by "pulling."

ProType. Manually operated machine for setting cold type.

prove. To pull a proof.

pyramid. Placement of ads on a newspaper or magazine page.

pyramidal. Layout pattern that arranges elements in a regular or inverted V shape.

quadrant make-up. Layout pattern in which the page is divided in quarters, each designed independently of the others.

quadrat, or quad. Blank printing unit to create spacing. (*See* em and en.)

quoins. Toothed metal wedges used to hold printing elements tightly in chase.

rail, on the. Setting type in the duplex of linecaster matrices.

railroad. To hurry copy through a composing room by eliminating or scanting proofreading.

rattle. Stiffness of paper characteristic of bond.

raw tape. That for typesetting which carries no instructions for justification or lines.

readability. That quality which affords maximum ease and comfort in reading over a sustained period. (*See* legibility.)

reader. Device that feels holes in perforated tape and supplies corresponding electrical signals to control typesetting machines.

reading rhythm. Regular, comfortable motion of the reading eye.

ream. 500 sheets of paper.

rectangular. Layout pattern in which the total area is subdivided into smaller units which have harmonious relation to each other.

reducer. Solvent of the negative image on a photographic negative.

references. Material at the end of a book which expands upon, but is not a part of, the basic text.

reflex. Reflected, copy-making photo image by reflected rather than transmitted light.

register. Matching of impressions of color plates on a printed sheet. Loose register is that in which tight juxtaposition is not necessary. In hairline register two color areas meet precisely. In overlap register one color overprints the adjacent one by a small but definite margin.

register marks. Devices, often a cross imposed upon a circle, printed on color work to facilitate moving plates into perfect register.

reglet. Wood strips used for spacing. Sometimes, a 1-pica metal spacing strip.

reperforator. Machine, actuated by electrical impulses, that perforates tape used for automatic typesetting.

replate. To rearrange elements in a newspaper page and prepare a new stereotype mat and plate, often while an earlier plate is still being printed.

reproduction proof. Repro, that produced with great care, usually on glossy paper or acetate, then photographed to make printing plates.

reverse. Printing plate which gives the effect of white letters on a black background.

rhythm. Flowing movement of the reading eye through a layout.

right-reading. Film or photographic paper on which type characters appear in normal form, right-side up and from left to right, when viewed from emulsion side.

right side. Felt side of paper (*which see*).

ring binder. Most common form of loose-leaf binding in which sheets are fastened by two or more rings through pre-punched holes.

ripple. Finish of paper.

rising initial. One that aligns with smaller body type at the baseline. (*See* initial.)

roll a mat. To make a stereotype matrix by impressing a flong upon a printing form by means of a roller or by direct pressure.

Roman. Family of type with serifs and with an appreciable difference between thick and thin strokes. Subdivided into Old Style and Modern (*which see*). Also, incorrectly, upright type as opposed to slanting or Oblique.

ROP. Run of paper, color printed in a newspaper without the use of special presses. Also, ads not in preferred position.

rotary press. Letterpress in which paper, fed from a continuous roll, is printed as it passes between a cylindrical impression surface and a curved printing plate.

rotogravure. Commercial intaglio printing on endless rolls of paper.

rough. Dummy, in sketchy technique, which shows only masses, no detail.

routing. Removing nonprinting metal from a printing plate by grinding it away mechanically.

rule. Type-high typographic element that prints a line or lines.

runaround. Type set in narrowed lines to create opening into which is placed picture or other type.

running head. Name of a book and sometimes title of chapter at the head or foot of each page.

S-pattern. Classic layout which produces superior reading rhythm. The reverse-S is a frequently used variation.

saddle stitch. Saddle wire, method of binding by inserting staples or stitches along the fold of a page.

Sans Serif. Race of type without serifs and of monotonal strokes.

scaling. Determining dimensions of a picture which is enlarged or reduced from those of original art.

scanner. Device that inspects visual image and translates varying tonal values into electrical impulses.

schedule. All the headlines used by a newspaper.

scorcher. Equipment that forms a stereotype flong into a curve and drives out excess moisture prior to casting.

Scotchprint. Offset conversion method in which image from relief material is printed onto resilient transparent plastic.

scratchboard. White paper coated with black ink which is scratched away to show the paper in white lines. Also the picture so produced.

screen. Intersecting lines on a glass plate through which a projected continuous-tone original is broken into a dot pattern. The number of lines per lineal inch, as 55-line screen, indicates the fineness of the engraving. Also a tint block with a fine dot pattern.

screen printing. Silk-screen printing.

scribed lines. Those produced by scratching lines in the platemaker's negative instead of ruling them on original copy.

Script. Race of type resembling handwriting in which letters are connected, as opposed to Cursive in which letters do not join.

Second Coming type. Studhorse type, biggest and blackest headline, type reserved for use on epochal news stories.

secondary color. Violet, orange, green, produced by mixing two primary colors.

self-cover. Book in which the paper used for regular pages also makes the cover.

series. Subdivision of a family of type consisting of all sizes of a particular letterform.

serifs. Tiny finishing strokes at the end of main strokes of letters.

serigraphy. Silk-screen printing, method of reproduction using stencils.

set. Measurement, in points, of the width of *M* of a font. The collective set width of a font is measured as the lowercase alphabet length. Most commonly used to measure fonts used for automatic typesetting.

set-off. Off-set (hyphenated to avoid confusion with offset printing), smudging caused by transfer of ink from one printed sheet to another.

sewed-case cover. Binding process identical to a sewed soft cover (*which see*) except that its cover is stiffened with boards.

sewed soft cover. Binding process in which saddle-sewn signatures are fastened to each other and to a soft cover.

shade. Variation of a color by adding black.

Shaded. Ethnic of Ornamented race with modifications made to the face of the character.

Shadowed. Ethnic of Ornamented type race in which additions have been made to letterform outside its face.

sheet. Leaf of paper.

sheet-fed. Printing press which takes individual sheets of paper as compared to that which prints on a roll of paper.

sheetwise. Printing one sheet of paper at a time.

shell cast. Comparatively thin stereotype plate which is mounted on base to bring it to type-high, as opposed to type-high casting which is cast to the proper thickness.

shoulder. Space on the body of a slug or foundry type which provides for descenders and to separate successive lines. Also that nonprinting area surrounding the neck of type. Also a depressed ledge of metal that surrounds printing detail in an engraving.

show-through. Visibility, on one side of a sheet, of printing done on the other side or another sheet.

side wire. Side stitch, method of binding by inserting staples or stitches from the outside of folded sheets of paper, parallel to and near the fold.

signature. Group of pages printed on one sheet of paper so they will fold into proper sequence.

silhouette. Form of halftone in which the entire background is removed.

silk-screen. Stencil method of printing.

silverprint. Photocopy used as a proof of cold type.

sizing. Gluey substance added to paper to create a smooth writing surface and to make it resistant to moisture.

slant. Variation of the basic letterform to create Italic or Oblique characters, slanting to the right. Those which tilt to the left are called backslant.

sleeve. Flexographic plate made on cylinder of flexible material which is slipped onto printing cylinder.

slipsheet. Method of preventing set-off by inserting a blank sheet of paper between printed ones.

slug. Line of composition produced on a linecaster. Also a spacing unit, usually 6 points but sometimes thicker. (*See* ledding.)

small capitals. S.c., letters in the form of capitals but little if any larger than x-height.

smoke printing. Xerography (*which see*).

sock. Excessive pressure in imprinting.

software. Programming for computer.

solvent. Liquid in which is dissolved or suspended the pigment of ink.

spaceband. Steel device consisting of two sliding wedges which expand to equalize space between words on machine-composed slugs.

spacing. Separation between words or letters in type. Wordspacing is that between words; letterspacing, between letters. Optical letterspacing is arranging type characters so the apparent areas of white space are more equally distributed by mathematical means. Proportional spacing is the ability to assign, on a typewriter, varying space for thick and thin letters.

special screens. Halftone patterns created by tiny shapes other than conventional round dots.

spine. Backbone (*which see*).

spiral binding. Fastening of pages by threading a continuous spiral of wire through pre-punched holes.

split fountain. Technique for printing two colors at one time by dividing the ink fountain on a press.

spot color. Flat color (*which see*).

spots. Typographical decorative units.

spray. Method of preventing set-off by spraying freshly printed sheets with a liquid which crystallizes to keep the succeeding sheet from coming in contact with the ink.

spur. Serif-like projection from the short vertical stroke on some forms of the G.

Square Serif. Race of type in which serifs are the same weight, or heavier than, the main strokes.

stacked. Piggyback type (*which see*).

stage and re-etch. Method of correcting a photoengraving by protecting certain areas (staging) and subjecting others to further action of acid.

staggered type. That arranged on an irregular baseline and/or vertical axes.

stamping. Printing by impressing type through metal foil and into the surface of the printed substance. Blind stamping uses no ink or foil.

steel engraving. Printing plate made manually by cutting away nonprinting areas on a metal plate, leaving only thin lines in relief.

steel-engraving screen. Special halftone screen in which image is formed by varying thicknesses of random straight lines.

stem. Vertical stroke of a letter, especially those which also have a bowl or arms such as *b, d, p, q, k*, and *T*.

stereotype. Process of casting a printing plate from a papier-mâché mold. Also, the plate so produced.

stet. Let it stand, proofreader's direction to ignore a change made inadvertently on the proof.

stick. Composing stick (*which see*).

stock. The paper used for any printing job.

stock cover. Book in which heavier paper is used for the cover.

stone. Imposing stone, table, once of actual stone, now of metal, on which forms are assembled.

stoneman. Printer who assembles typographic elements into advertisements and pages.

stone proof. Beaten proof, rough impression of a printing form produced by placing paper over the inked form and impressing it with a flat block of wood which is pounded with a mallet.

straight matter. Body composition as opposed to display, set in rectangular columns and without typographic variations. Editorial matter as opposed to advertising.

strikeon. Composition by machines similar to typewriter.

strip test. Method of determining the direction of grain in paper.

stripping. Peeling the thin emulsion off an engraver's negative and positioning it onto a flat or combining it with another piece as in making combination cuts.

Striprinter. A machine for setting cold type in display sizes.

stroboscopic. Strobe, a bulb that produces an extremely brief but brilliant burst of light.

stylus. Needle-like instrument used to cut plastic shading film. Also, the pyramidal piece of metal that burns dot patterns into a Scan-a-graver plate.

substance. Weight of 1,000 sheets of paper in a basic size, that varies among categories of paper stock.

sulfate. Paper made of cellulose fibers of great strength produced by cooking wood chips in alkaline solution.

sulfite. Cheaper paper made from wood pulp cooked in acid solution and thus susceptible to self-destruction in estimated 30 years.

super-calendered. Super, paper which has been given a high gloss by repeated pressure between metal rollers during manufacture.

surprinting. Printing type over tint block or other area of color, or type characters apparently printed on a halftone by means of combination plate.

Swiss grid. Mondrian, or modular, layout in which area is divided into equal rectangles which are then arranged to create patterns.

syllabary. Method of writing in which a character represents an entire syllable.

symmetrical. Layout pattern consisting of two vertical halves which are mirror images of each other.

synthesis. Process of creating all colors of the spectrum by printing only three primary colors.

T-harmony. Complements and a third, harmony achieved by using two complementary colors plus one that is at right angles to a line drawn between the first pair on a color wheel.

tabloid. Newspaper format of approximately 11 × 15 inches.

tabular. Matter set in vertically aligned columns, i.e., market reports, box scores, etc.

tail. Lower portion of the g and the projection on Q.

tail piece. Small typographic ornament or illustration placed at end of copy, especially of a chapter.

take. Small portion of manuscript, often comprising only part of the whole, distributed among compositors so entire job may be set by several typesetters in minimum time.

tape. Perforated paper, in narrow rolls, which directs the action of automatic typesetters.

tearsheet. Single page of newspaper given to advertiser as proof of publication.

Telikon. High-speed printer using wire or radio.

tempera. Poster paint, opaque, water-soluble paint.

Tenaplate. Plastic molding substance used to make electrotypes.

terminal. End of a letter stroke that has no serifs or finials.

tertiary colors. Those produced by mixing two secondary colors.

Text. Black Letter, race of type based on the handwritten form of the Roman alphabet as developed in Germany. Also (not capitalized) editorial straight matter.

text type. Body type.

Thermo-fax. Copying machine which creates image by residue from burning process.

thermography. Process of applying resinous powder to fresh ink on a printed sheet, heating it to melting, then solidifying it in simulation of intaglio engraving.

thin space. Copper spacing material much smaller than spaces or quads.

30-dash. Mark that indicates the end of a story. Referring to the journalistic practice of ending a telegraphed story with -30-, probably a version of XXX.

Thompson Caster. Machine for casting individual pieces of type.

thumbnails. Small and very sketchy dummies. Also, half-column portraits used in newspapers, also called porkchops.

tied letters. Ligature (*which see*).

tint. Variation of a color produced by adding white.

tint block. Screen, printing plate used to produce a color area that carries no detail, usually to be overprinted by a darker ink. When the tone of a tint block is lightened by a dot pattern, it is called a screen.

title lining. System which assures a common baseline for all title fonts in the same point size. Title letters are all caps and thus no room need be provided on the body for descenders.

title page. First full page of a book, bearing its name and that of the author and publisher.

toenail. Quotation mark.

tone value. Intensity of a color or a mass of type, as compared to black, white, and gray.

tongue cover. Loose-leaf binding in which binding posts are concealed by a flap folding over from the cover.

tooth. Texture of paper particularly receptive to pencil or crayon.

totem pole. Vertical axis layout (*which see*).

transfer type. That which leaves plastic bearing sheet to adhere to art when pressure is applied.

Transitional Roman. That variation of the race of type which combines the characteristics, in varying degree, of Old Style and Modern.

transposition. Common typographic error in which letters or words are not correctly placed, as "hte" for "the," or "The Spangled Star Banner."

triad. Harmony achieved by using three colors, equidistant from each other on the color wheel.

trimetallic. Offset plate combining aluminum, copper, and steel or zinc.

TTS. Teletypesetter, device actuated by perforated tape, to operate keyboard of a linecaster.

tusche. Greasy liquid used for making lithographic plates and silk screens.

two-tone paper. Coated stock with different color on each of its two sides.

two-up. Two-on, printing a form in duplicate on a single sheet of paper to decrease number of impressions on press.

tympan. Sturdy paper that covers the packing (*which see*) on a letterpress.

type-high. .918 inches, the distance from the foot to the face of a type character, linecaster slug, or other printing material.

type metal. Alloy of lead, tin, and antimony.

Typesetter. (ATF), phototypesetting machine.

typographic errors. Typos, mistakes made by the compositor.

typography. Basic plan for the use of type, as contrasted to layout, which is the application of such a plan to a specific circumstance.

Typro. Machine for producing cold type in display sizes.

u. & l.c. Upper and lowercase, capitals and small letters.

undercutting. Action of acid as it cuts sideways, instead of only downward, in etching photoengravings.

underlay. Underprinting, printing in a light color over which other elements are printed in darker ink. An underlay varies from a tint block in that there need be no definite relationships between the area of the former and that of the overprinting.

underlines. Explanatory type matter that accompanies a picture.

underpinning. Low metal slugs that support the overhanging portion of a Ludlow slug.

universal fractions. Those designed to harmonize with all families in a type race.

upper case. Capitals.

Vandyke. Photocopy used as a proof of cold type.

Varityper. Typewriter which produces different type styles with only minor adjustment. It can produce justified composition semi-automatically.

vehicle. Liquid that carries the pigment in ink.

Velox. Screened photographic print.

vertex. Juncture of diagonal strokes in letters such as V and the lower ones in such letters as W and M.

vertical axis. Layout pattern in which elements align at left or right with a perpendicular line, real or imaginary.

Videocomp. CRT phototypesetter by RCA.

vignette. Form of a halftone in which the tone of the engraving blends almost imperceptibly into the white of the paper.

warm. Colors which seem to move forward in the reader's vision, usually reds, oranges, and some yellows.

watermark. Design pressed into paper while it is still wet during manufacture.

wave rule. Printing element that produces a regularly undulating line.

wavy line. Halftone pattern made of parallel wavy lines of varying thicknesses.

wayzgoose. Sentimental gathering of printers or other graphic arts people.

web-fed. Press that prints from a continuous roll of paper.

weddings. Smooth papers suitable for printing by intaglio and commonly used for invitations and other social stationery.

weight. Variation of a basic letterform such as Light, Bold, etc., created by varying the width of the strokes. Also, weight of 500 sheets of basic-size paper. (*See* substance.)

wet printing. Process of printing all process colors without waiting for any to dry.

white line. Wood engraving (*which see*).

widow. Short line of type at end of paragraph. Some typographers consider as widows only those lines less than a quarter full and/or those at the top or foot of page or column.

width. Variation of a letterform to create such forms as Condensed, Extended, etc.

wire loops. A method of loose-leaf binding.

wire side. Wrong side, that side of paper which has rested on the wire screen during manufacture. As opposed to felt, or right, side (*which see*).

woodcut. Printing plate made by carving relief masses into the grained side of a plank.

wood engraving. White line engraving, printing plate made by carving fine relief lines into the end grain of a plank.

wordspacing. That between words.

work-and-tumble. System similar to work-and-turn (*which see*) except that the sheet is turned so a new edge meets the grippers.

work-and-turn. W&t, a system of printing both sides of a printing piece on one side of a sheet, then turning it, so its gripper edge remains constant, and printing on the reverse side. Two sides are thus printed by one impression.

work-up. Unwanted deposit of ink caused when pressure forces quads and spacing material upward to meet ink rollers and the paper.

wove. A finish of paper which resembles that of tight cloth.

writing. Kind of paper with a smooth surface, sized to prevent ink from being absorbed into the fibers.

wrong font. Typographic error in which a letter of another face is used.

wrong-reading. Characters on film or photopaper which when viewed from emulsion side appear as mirror image of normal type.

X. Itlx, Ital, common abbreviation for Italics.

x-height. That of primary letters such as *a*, *o*, *m*, and *x*.

x-line. Mean line, that which marks the top of primary letters.

Xerography. Inkless printing method utilizing static electricity.

Xography. System of creating a printed three-dimensional image by affixing plastic as a viewing lens.

zinc. Metal most commonly used for photoengravings, also the engravings themselves.

Zip-a-Tone. Plastic sheets imprinted with regular patterns to achieve tones in line cuts.

Index

About the Author

EDMUND C. ARNOLD has been closely involved with the graphic arts since he edited his first weekly at the age of 17, some forty years ago. During World War II, he edited service magazines and newspapers, worked on *Stars & Stripes*, and was decorated for service as a combat correspondent.

An associate editor of *The Quill*, Dr. Arnold is contributing editor of *Editor & Publisher, Canadian Printer & Publisher, Quill & Scroll, Random House Dictionary*, and *Encyclopedia Americana*. He conducts workshops on typography throughout this hemisphere and has, as a consultant, participated in the restyling of many of America's most famous newspapers.

Since 1960, he has been professor and chairman of the graphic arts department of the School of Journalism of Syracuse University and only recently ended his active editing of *Linotype News* and left the weekly newspaper in Michigan of which he had been copublisher for more than twenty years.

He is also author of *Functional Newspaper Design*, the first book to win a George Polk Memorial Award, and *Modern Newspaper Design*, as well as other books, one in Spanish, another which was translated into Japanese.

73 74 75 10 9 8 7 6 5 4 3 2